THE AFTERLIFE OF AL-ANDALUS

SUNY series in Latin American and Iberian Thought and Culture

Jorge J. E. Gracia and Rosemary Geisdorfer Feal, editors

THE AFTERLIFE OF AL-ANDALUS

Muslim Iberia in Contemporary Arab and Hispanic Narratives

CHRISTINA CIVANTOS

SUNY PRESS

Published by State University of New York Press, Albany

© 2017 State University of New York

All rights reserved

Printed in the United States of America

No part of this book may be used or reproduced in any manner whatsoever without written permission. No part of this book may be stored in a retrieval system or transmitted in any form or by any means including electronic, electrostatic, magnetic tape, mechanical, photocopying, recording, or otherwise without the prior permission in writing of the publisher.

For information, contact State University of New York Press, Albany, NY
www.sunypress.edu

Production, Jenn Bennett
Marketing, Michael Campochiaro

Library of Congress Cataloging-in-Publication Data

Names: Civantos, Christina, author.
Title: The afterlife of al-Andalus : Muslim Iberia in contemporary Arab and Hispanic narratives / Christina Civantos.
Description: Albany : State University of New York Press, 2017. | Series: SUNY series in Latin American and Iberian thought and culture | Includes bibliographical references and index.
Identifiers: LCCN 2016049764 (print) | LCCN 2016051884 (ebook) | ISBN 9781438466699 (hardcover : alk. paper) | 9781438466705 (pbk : alk, paper) | ISBN 9781438466712 (e-book)
Subjects: LCSH: Spanish literature--20th century--History and criticism. | Arabic literature--20th century--History and criticism. | Andalusia (Spain)--In literature. | Spanish literature--Arab influences. | Spain--Civilization--Islamic influences. | Comparative literature--Spanish and Arabic. | Comparative literature--Arabic and Spanish.
Classification: LCC PQ6042.A4 C58 2017 (print) | LCC PQ6042.A4 (ebook) | DDC 860.9--dc23
LC record available at https://lccn.loc.gov/2016049764

10 9 8 7 6 5 4 3 2 1

Contents

Preface and Acknowledgments

During various research trips to Damascus in the late 1990s and early 2000s, for what became my first book and the seed for this second book, I often accompanied friends on excursions to beat the heat at Masbah al-Andalus, or al-Andalus Swimming Pool. Although this pool, with its modest entrance fee and equally modest gardens on the outskirts of the city, bore little resemblance to the lush splendor of the famous gardens and reflection pools that Spain has inherited from al-Andalus, for the people of the neighborhood it was a much enjoyed refuge for the senses and a place of relaxation and fun. This pool is just one small example of how al-Andalus is part of popular discourse and everyday life in the Arab as well as Hispanic worlds. As I worked on this book, every so often I remembered the entrance sign to that recreation area, proclaiming through its name the aspiration to offer a slice of al-Andalus, and I wondered what might have become of the adults and children who used to swim and play there since violent conflict erupted in Syria in 2011. While I carried out final corrections to the manuscript at the beginning of 2017, religious tensions were escalating in North America, the Middle East, and Europe. I hope this book can contribute in some way to resolving these conflicts that are tied to conceptions of ethnoreligious identity as played out in the discourses surrounding al-Andalus.

The earliest beginnings of this book can be traced far back. I grew up seeing a framed photograph of my parents decked out in faux Oriental garb in a real-life "Oriental" palace. The photo was taken in 1976 during one of my father's first trips back to Spain since leaving with his family during the civil war, he was accompanied by my Cuban mother, who was visiting for the first time the Andalusia from which some of her grandparents hailed. A stop in the portrait studio set up inside Granada's Alhambra palace was de rigueur. Seeing that photograph every day and the many questions that it raised in my mind certainly contributed to my pursuit of this project.

More specifically, this study grew out of my particular academic trajectory. I started my graduate training in comparative literature as a medievalist and then shifted to postcolonial studies. This book, then, is a melding of my first love—medieval Iberian studies—with my passion for understanding the world through the impact of colonialism. In particular, this project developed from the research I did for my first book, *Between Argentines and Arabs: Argentine Orientalism, Arab Immigrants, and the Writing of Identity*. A subset of texts by Euro- and Arab-Argentines invokes al-Andalus but did not completely fit within the parameters of that book. As I continued to work on those texts, I decided to place them within their broader thematic context and analyze them in relation to other works depicting or invoking al-Andalus.

As a result of this long process, there are many people and institutions to whom I am deeply grateful for many different types of support. Shawkat Toorawa has been a truly extraordinary mentor from my undergraduate days, when he first introduced me to the literature of al-Andalus, to his generous invitation to give the 2008 lecture that became the first tangible building block of this project, to his valuable comments on my first draft of this book. I am grateful to James Monroe for sharing his expert knowledge of the literature and culture of al-Andalus with me. More recently, Pedro Martínez Montávez generously shared texts from his personal library and put me in touch with Carmen Ruiz Bravo-Villasante, who also provided important texts and leads. I thank Daniel Rivera for facilitating my contact with Martínez Montávez. I also acknowledge Gonzalo Fernández Parrilla, who provided excellent suggestions for my nascent project. Dwight Reynolds, George Yúdice, Alex Elinson, and Gema Pérez-Sánchez provided important support, advice, and encouragement. While Gema provided detailed and astute comments on my first draft of the introduction, Ranen Omer-Sherman expertly pointed me to the key texts regarding the afterlife of Sepharad. I thank Mohsine Elhajjami, whom I met in Fez, for his helpful comments on the novel *Wallada bint al-Mustakfi fi Fas*. Randa Jarrar kindly provided me with a copy of the Arabic typescript version of Hussin's "Yawm Bwinus Ayris," long before I was able to obtain the print volume in which it appears. My thanks also go to Silvia Bermúdez, Ross Brann, Jane Connolly, miriam cooke, Aman De Sondy, Ehab Hafez, Nebil Husayn, Nada Naami, Rachida Salama Primov, Mazen Rabia, Khaled El-Rouayheb, Jonathan Shannon, and Mona El-Sherif for their valuable input on different pieces of this project.

I thank Alexandre Vigo, "Té y kriptonita," and an anonymous Wikipedia contributor for the use of their maps of Iberia and my sister Gloria for sharing her skills as a digital artist to remake these maps in a larger format and with standard spellings. I thank Riad Ismat for graciously giving me permission to quote from his unpublished play "Columbus."

Over the years I have presented sections of different chapters at various conferences. I thank Irene Oh for her thought-provoking comments at the 2009 American Council for the Study of Islamic Societies Conference. Similarly, Gema Perez-Sánchez and Hakim Abderrezak were excellent interlocutors at our 2010 WOCMES panel and beyond. I also thank my fellow panel members in the 2013 ACLA panel "Muslims, Jews, and Mediterranean and Middle Eastern Diaspora Literatures," the 2015 MESA panel "Authenticity, Memory, and Modernity in Contemporary Moroccan Literature," and the University of Seville 2016 liLETRAd Congress.

The University of Miami assisted with the development and completion of this project by granting me the 2013 Provost's Research Award, the 2013–14 Center for the Humanities Fellowship, and my 2014–15 sabbatical leave. Special thanks go to the Center for the Humanities fellows who made our colloquium such an enriching experience. I am also grateful to my department chair, Lillian Manzor, and the dean of the College of Arts and Sciences at the University of Miami, Leonidas Bachas, for their support.

As I developed and finalized this project, I had the good fortune to be able to teach four courses related to it. I taught two undergraduate courses on campus in Miami focused on this book's texts and issues: Arabic 310, "The Legacy of Muslim Spain" in fall 2011 and Spanish 501, "What to Do with the Past?" in spring 2016. In the summer of 2014 I led a study abroad program in Morocco and as part of that I taught Arabic 310, "Morocco: A Cultural Crossroads," which incorporated various elements of this study. As I finalized the manuscript, I taught a graduate course at the University of Miami on history and narrative that drew from this study and enriched it. I thank all of my students in these courses, particularly Sam DeFreze, Alfred Kilzi, and Ron Porcelli, for their inspiring comments, questions, and enthusiasm.

I thank my editor, Beth Bouloukos, her assistant, Rafael Chaiken, my production editor Jenn Bennett, and their colleagues at SUNY Press for their interest in my project as well as their professionalism and patience. I am especially grateful to SUNY's two anonymous evaluators of the manuscript who provided specific and fruitful suggestions for revision.

Other colleagues and friends, as well as my extended family, have provided valued support and encouragement during the book-writing process. I thank *los primos,* Mari and José, for generously providing a home away from home in Spain while I worked on different stages of this project. I thank my wonderful sisters, Gloria and Marlene, for contributing child care that enabled me to work and opportunities to relax that allowed me to recharge, on both sides of the Atlantic. I am grateful to my mother not only for help with child care but also for sharing her love of Washington Irving's *Tales of the Alhambra*, flamenco, and all things *andaluz*. I thank my father for connecting me to the Alpujarra and for insisting that I study French. Ironically, as I worked on this project related to historical memory, he lost his once prodigious storehouse of historical knowledge to Alzheimer's disease. His situation is a stark testament to the significance and fragility of the past. I thank my parents-in-law for child care and for the many conversations in which they bore witness to religious violence as well as tolerance. Sadly, my mother-in-law did not live to see the completion of this book, but hopefully she knows how much I thought of her life story as I wrote. My greatest debt of gratitude is to Sameet, Javier, and Miguel for their patience, their inadvertently pushing me to be more efficient when their patience ran out, their inspiring imaginations, and the many reminders that they offer of how joyful life can be. May we continue to collaborate on creatively translating our various cultures, and their stories about the past, for many years to come!

Notes on Translations, Transliterations, and Terminology

Note on Translations

In the interest of space, almost all cited texts are presented only in English translation, with original-language phrases inserted, usually in brackets, where deemed significant. Unless otherwise noted, all translations are my own. Where I quote a published English version, pagination is given with the translation page first and the original-language page following in brackets. When citing a passage without including a direct quotation, if only one page number is provided it is the page number of the text in the original.

Note on Transliterations

I transliterate Arabic into Latin script using the International Journal of Middle East Studies (IJMES) transliteration system. However, for the sake of clarity and ease of reading, I modify the IJMES usage guidelines in the following ways. All terms that are familiar to English-language readers are presented with the spellings commonly used in English (e.g., Quran) and technical terms do not carry full diacritical markings. Regarding authors' names, if a particular transliteration has become common, I use that transliteration and present the IJMES transliteration in brackets. Similarly, if using the IJMES transliteration, I present any known alternate transliteration in brackets. Therefore, unless there is a need to distinguish between words, the only diacritical markings that appear are ʿ for the letter ʿayn and ʾ for hamza. However, to facilitate further research, all diacritical marks are provided in the bibliography and for names of authors and artists and titles of works in the endnotes. Last, in the notes, for Arabic text of more than a few words I retain the Arabic script.

Note on Terminology

In English it is common to use Andalusian as an adjective for people and things from eighth to fifteenth-century al-Andalus. However, this creates an overlap with the adjective for people and things from the southern Spanish region of Andalusia [Andalucía] and, as will become apparent, the distinction between al-Andalus and Andalusia is significant. For this reason, although some texts that I cite use Andalusian as an adjective for al-Andalus, throughout this study when referring to the medieval entity, I use the Arabic adjective Andalusi [Andalusī], which is also in common usage in Spanish (Andalusí). To avoid confusion and/or to emphasize the distinction, I occasionally use the Spanish adjective andaluz instead of Andalusian to refer to people and things from the region of modern Spain. Aside from some surnames that are also place names, I use English spellings for place names.

The common term in English for the indigenous peoples that the Arabs encountered in North Africa is Berber. However, as I explain in the introduction, this term carries a negative connotation of barbarism or primitive savagery. Berber is rejected by many of those to whom it refers and is usually replaced with the autochthonous term that was revived in the 1940s: Amazigh. The plural form of Amazigh in the Tamazight languages is Imazighen; given how different this plural formation is from that of English, as is often done I have opted to use the English-based plural Amazighs. Hence, I use Amazigh(s) as much as possible, but do use Berber when quoting sources that use it.

Given the presence of the Amazigh peoples in North Africa, when referring to the broader cultural region in which Arabic is a strong presence (if not a native or primary language), I try to use as much as possible terminology that in some way includes the Amazigh cultural element. For this reason, I use terms such as MENA (Middle East and North Africa), Arabo-Muslim, and Arabo-Maghrebian.

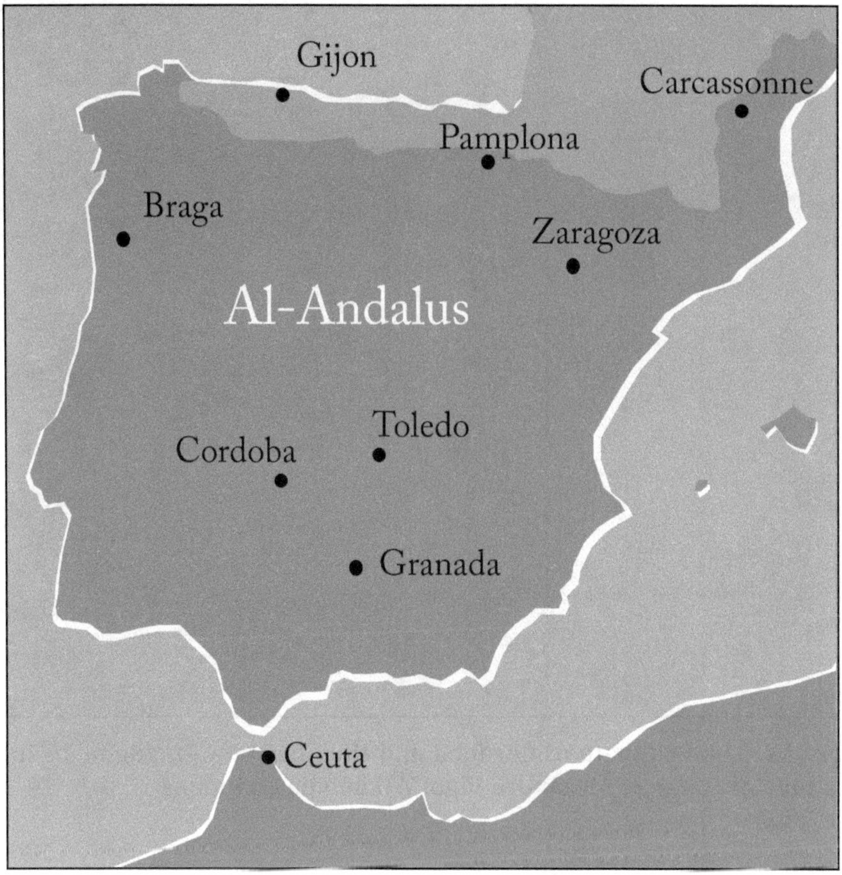

Figure I.1. al-Andalus under the Umayyad Caliphate in 732 AD. Source: Wikimedia Commons.

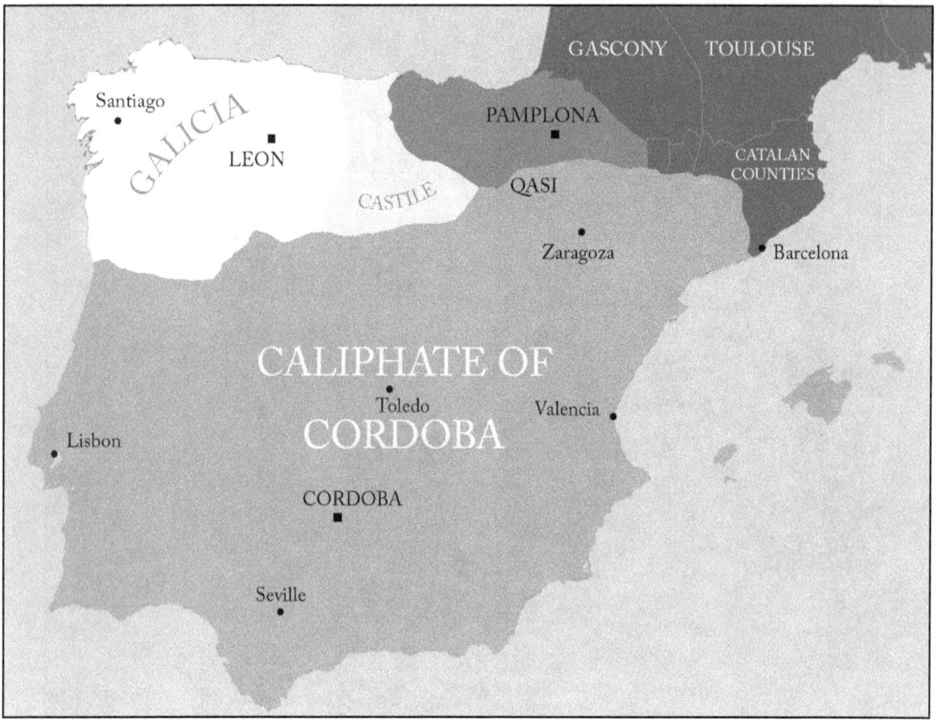

Figure I.2. The Caliphate of Cordoba and the Christian Kingdoms of Iberia, circa 1000 AD. Source: Alexandre Vigo, Wikimedia Commons.

Figure I.3. The Christian Kingdoms and part of the Almohad Caliphate in the twelfth to thirteenth centuries AD. Source: Alexandre Vigo, Wikimedia Commons.

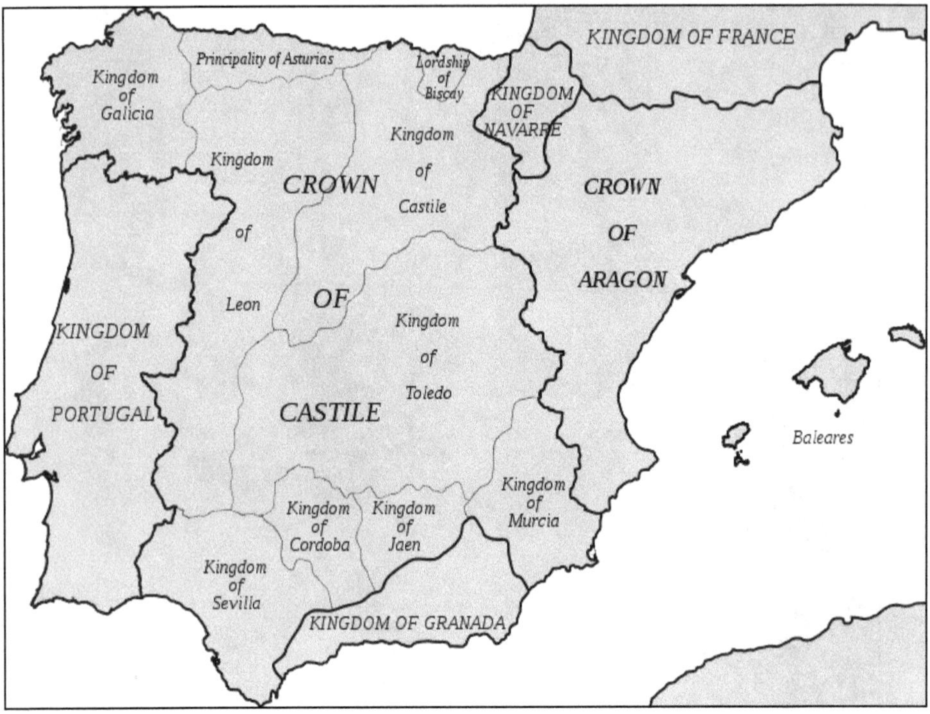

Figure I.4. The Kingdoms of the Crown of Castile and the Emirate (or Kingdom) of Granada in 1400 AD. Source: Té y kriptonita, Wikimedia Commons.

Introduction

Shared Legacies and Connected Histories

More than any other period in Islamic history, the "Moorish" Iberian civilization of al-Andalus has often demonstrated an extraordinary ability to make itself relevant to different historical periods and agendas, and the contrasting historical perspectives on the expulsion invariably touch on wider debates concerning the Islamic presence in Spain, the meaning of Spanish national identity, the relative values of "Oriental" versus "Western" civilization, and the relationship between Islam and Christianity. [. . .] Today, at the beginning of the twenty-first century, Moorish Spain continues to insinuate itself into contemporary political agendas, at a time when the Islamic and Western worlds are locked in a complex and multifaceted confrontation with religious, cultural, and political dimensions.

—Matthew Carr

With regard to the relationship between Arabs and Spaniards, it is not exactly a simple task. [. . .] But it's probably prudent not to completely abandon hope, or reason, or feeling. I am increasingly convinced, sensibly and clearly convinced, that a good start for tackling it would be precisely to see al-Andalus as a shared object, as a common heritage. As something that *was* and that *existed*, but that *has not ceased to be* nor *to exist*. As something past, but not extinguished. Like a finale that has its peculiar continuity. To see it, evaluate it, and explain it in that way, also jointly, is above all an intellectual exigency.

—Pedro Martínez Montávez (*Significado y símbolo de al-Andalus*)

Like the Cordoba Mosque [as redesigned and virtually rebuilt to be a sacred space for all by Canadian Pakistani architect Gulzar Haider and his student Zara Amjad], al-Andalus too can be reimagined and relocated, liberated "from the wounds of history," and infused, as Amjad and Haider assert, with "the essence of life" so that pluralism and humane futures flourish.

—Ziauddin Sardar

Just as thinkers in medieval Iberia dedicated a great deal of their scholarly efforts to translations and commentaries of earlier writings, many people today "translate" medieval Iberia to (re)weave narratives about the past and the present and suggest particular futures. These contemporary translators of medieval Iberia attempt to bridge temporal and cultural distances, often grappling with the accessibility of the past and other linguistic communities and cultures and struggling against the authoritative versions of the past. Their linguistic, cultural, and temporal translations are all the more significant when we consider the prominence of conflicts centered on cultural, religious, and ethnoracial difference in the early twenty-first century and how often Muslim Iberia, or al-Andalus, is cited in relation to these.

Figures as divergent as Osama bin Laden's deputy Ayman al-Zawahiri and US President Barack Obama have invoked al-Andalus, each pointing to a different vision of Muslim Iberia. Al-Zawahiri, in infamous video statements circulated soon after the terrorist attacks of September 11, 2001, vowed that the tragedy of the fall of al-Andalus would not be repeated. In his celebrated 2009 Cairo speech, Obama cited al-Andalus, and specifically Cordoba, as an example of religious tolerance in the Muslim tradition.[1] This is but one pair of a host of instances that could be cited from just the past few decades in which public figures from diametrically opposed ideological positions have invoked well-established cultural narratives about al-Andalus. Beyond the statements captured by the media, what are other voices, especially those that can be seen as the direct inheritors of the legacy of al-Andalus, doing with traditional versions of the story of al-Andalus? How are they translating and retelling the past?

The December 1992 issue of a monthly literary magazine published in Cairo, *Adab wa-Naqd* (*Literature and Critique*), offers a glimpse at alternative responses to customary narratives about Islamic Iberia. The essay by Farida al-Naqqash that introduces this issue's special dossier on the 500-year anniversary of the end of Muslim rule in Iberia is tellingly titled "Nahnu La Nabki ʿala al-Atlal" ("We Do Not Cry over the Abandoned Encampment"). Here, through the allusion to the archetypal poetic trope of mourning for the departed beloved, al-Naqqash rejects the Arabo-Muslim discourse of mourning over the loss of al-Andalus.[2] In addition to this refusal to cry over the past, flying in the face of traditional Arabo-Muslim historiography, al-Naqqash declares that "in spite of all that the Arabs and Muslims accomplished in Spain, they were colonizers [*mustaʿmirin*]" (9). The rest of this quincentenary dossier includes poetry produced in al-Andalus, articles on the literature and history of al-Andalus, and a translation into Arabic of a screenplay about

Averroes by the contemporary Spanish writer Antonio Gala.[3] This issue of *Adab wa-Naqd* points to the existence of alternate discourses about the legacy of al-Andalus that take into account its imperial dimensions and seek intercultural contact through literal and figurative translation. In this way, it encapsulates the core concerns of my investigation of the "afterlife" of medieval Muslim Iberia in Arab and Hispanic cultures from the twentieth century on. This book centers on the crucial role of coloniality and the linked issues of migration and gender in contemporary narratives about al-Andalus, including the counternarratives that constitute a translation of the standard stories about the foundations of self and other.

The history of al-Andalus, of what it was actually like, is a complex, ideologically charged, and much debated topic. This work is not interested in rating the historical accuracy of portrayals of Muslim Iberia. Instead of searching for accurate or "true" depictions of al-Andalus, or trying to determine which version of the story we should believe (tolerant or intolerant, paradise on Earth or romanticized idealization), this book is an inquiry into how al-Andalus, as a site of cultural contact, is presented and used today. What are the stories that al-Andalus continues to tell? What do writers and filmmakers in the "Hispano-Arab world" do with historical and legendary figures: how do they embellish or depart from historical record; how do they build on or tweak received historical narratives and legend? What does this process and the choices of which it is made reveal? This book answers these questions by studying al-Andalus in modern Arab and Hispanic visual and literary narrative and drama with particular attention to the sociopolitical dimensions of these texts. The following statement made by anthropologist Michael Taussig applies: "my subject is not the truth of being but the social being of truth, not whether facts are real but what the politics of their interpretation and representation are" (xiii). Thus, this is not a search for al-Andalus per se but for what people make of it a millennium later. This project looks at a particular phenomenon within medievalism, that is, within conceptions of "the medieval" that shape core ideological elements of modernity such as nationalism and the colonial civilizing mission.[4] It is a study of "al-Andalusism" or the history of al-Andalus as a cultural sign—an icon or symbol of identity—in twentieth- and twenty-first-century cultural products from the Arab world and its diaspora, Spain, and Argentina.

What are these Hispanic and Arabo-Maghrebian texts referring to when they invoke al-Andalus? The simplest answer is that they are referring to a "chronotope," Mikhail Bakhtin's term for the literary representation of a time-space intersection. William Granara and José

Antonio González Alcantud make use of this term to point to al-Andalus as a time period (711 to 1492, and more broadly until 1609) in a geographic territory.[5] At its height this territory included nearly the entirety of the Iberian Peninsula, the Balearic Islands, Sicily, and a strip of present-day southern France, but over time it shrank down to the emirate of Granada, which itself shrank successively from roughly half of today's Spanish region of Andalusia and part of the region of Murcia down to about a third of today's Andalusia or roughly 28,500 square kilometers (something between the size of the US states of Maryland and West Virginia) (see Figures I.1 to I.4). The time period referenced is the period of Muslim rule, initially under a single empire, the Umayyad Caliphate, and subsequently under a variety of often rival dynasties and emirates, some headed by Arabs and some by Amazigh (Berber) leaders. As Muslim-ruled areas shrank and then disappeared in 1492, more Jews and Muslims lived under Christian rule in the peninsula, and although many had accepted conversion to Christianity, they were eventually ordered to leave through a series of expulsion decrees.

During the European Middle Ages, the cities of al-Andalus, ruled by Muslims but also inhabited by Christians and Jews, flourished as centers of intellectual inquiry and artistic production. Toledo, Cordoba, and other cities were multilingual cultural centers that facilitated exchange by producing translations and commentaries between Arabic, Hebrew, and Latin works.[6] The height of this cultural burgeoning is considered to be the Caliphate of Cordoba (929–1031), founded by Abd al-Rahman III. This caliphate crumbled due to a civil war (the Fitna of al-Andalus) that revolved around disputed succession and resulted in several independent Muslim emirates known as the *taifa* kingdoms. That first taifa period was followed by the Amazigh Almoravid [al-Murabitun] Dynasty, a second taifa period, the Amazigh Almohad [al-Muwahhidun] Dynasty, a third taifa period, and finally, given the simultaneous gains of the Christian kingdoms, the final holdout in the Emirate of Granada. Muslim rule in Iberia ended in 1492 with the fall of Granada.

Soon after the surrender of Granada, the Catholic Monarchs expelled all Jews who were not willing to convert, with those *conversos* who remained subject to persecution by the Inquisition. However, during the Reconquista process and after the fall of Granada, most of the Muslims continued to live in the peninsula under Christian rule and became known as the *mudéjares*. This changed in 1499 when the Christian authorities of Granada carried out forced conversions and public burnings of Arabic manuscripts. In response to these events, which broke the treaty of the surrender of Granada, Muslims rebelled against the Spanish authorities in what is known as the First Rebellion of the Alpujarra (1499–1500), in reference to the mountainous region (south of the city of Granada) where the uprising took place. The Castilians quashed the rebellion and gave the Muslims the choice of baptism or exile. Most accepted baptism, although an indeterminate number remained crypto-Muslims and continued to live in Iberia. This was followed by the Second Rebellion of the Alpujarra (1568–71) and increasing socioeconomic tensions that led in 1609 to the first decree mandating the expulsion of the *moriscos*, or Muslim converts to Christianity. Between 1609 and 1614 the moriscos were officially expelled from all of the peninsula's kingdoms.[7] Thus, there was nearly a millennium of Muslim and morisco presence in Iberia; long after this period al-Andalus continues to be invested with symbolic value.

Although a great deal of scholarly research has been done on the temporospatial formation known as al-Andalus and its immediate aftermath, much of it has been limited by specific ideological agendas that focus on different periods (e.g., the splendor of Cordoba, the splintering of the taifas, or the fall of Granada) and interpret them according to their interests. This has led Gema Martín Muñoz to comment, "It is quite probable that no other period in history has been as interpreted, manipulated and struggled against as al-Andalus" and that "it remains subject to ideological manipulation" (67). She goes on to specify that "the irrelevant but noxious theory of the clash of civilisations, the 9/11 attacks and the growing Islamophobia that has been unleashed since, have ensured that al-Andalus remains an object for barter at the service of ultra-Catholic, nationalist, and Islamophobic ideologies" (67). More than five centuries after the fall of the Emirate of Granada, al-Andalus still functions as a popular symbol for paradise lost and religious conflict, depending on whether it is viewed as a time of interfaith tolerance and cultivation of knowledge and the arts or as a time of intolerance under threatening Muslim power (Islamic Empire, Islam in Europe, etc.) or threatening Catholic consolidation of power (oppression and expulsion of Jews and moriscos, the Inquisition, etc.).

The Formation and "Translation" of Identities

Why has Muslim Iberia been such an enduring and contested symbolic reference point? In addition to current global concerns about interfaith relations, which have led to efforts to find earlier models, for certain communities al-Andalus is central to what Paul Ricoeur refers to as "the mobilization of memory in the service of the quest, the appeal, the demand for identity" (81). Specifically, for people from the Arabo-Muslim and Hispanic Catholic worlds, al-Andalus is a key element in narratives of religious, national, and ethnolinguistic identity. Ricoeur notes the fragility of identity and points to "the heritage of founding violence" as one of the sources of this fragility: communities arise from "founding events [that] are, essentially, violent acts legitimated after the fact" (82). The tensions generated by founding violence are particularly significant here because, similar to the situation of Jerusalem and the Holy Land, al-Andalus is claimed as part of the heritage of distinct cultural groups that today are often in conflict and seen as incompatible. Al-Andalus is a heritage—*turath/legado cultural*—shared across cultures with conflicting legitimating narratives. Attentive to the ways the same motifs and patterns of representation are seen across these cultures, I examine this case of shared heritage by looking at the main actors in the construction and rewriting of the foundational myths tied to al-Andalus.[8]

Given the role of religion in the establishment and dissolution of al-Andalus, and the role of religion (or political acts carried out in the name of religion) in the conflicts of our day, a better understanding of the creation and dismantling of the guiding narratives linked to al-Andalus is vital to people the world over. Many writers and filmmakers have participated in cementing rigid identities through cultural narratives linked to al-Andalus. Lebanese author Amin Maalouf eloquently explains the dangers of unyielding understandings of identity:

> But in the age of globalization and of the ever-accelerating intermingling of elements in which we are all caught up, a new concept of identity is needed, and needed urgently. We cannot be satisfied with forcing billions of bewildered human beings to choose between excessive assertion of their identity and the loss of their identity altogether, between fundamentalism and disintegration. But that is the logical consequence of the prevailing attitude on the subject. If our contemporaries are not encouraged to accept their multiple affiliations and allegiances; if they cannot reconcile their need for identity with an open and unprejudiced tolerance of other cultures; if they feel they have to choose between denial of the self and denial of the other—then we shall be bringing into being legions of the lost and hordes of bloodthirsty madmen. (*In the Name of Identity* 35)

With the intensification of intercultural contact that we know as globalization, which produces increased commonalities and increased inequalities, comes an intensification of the need or desire to assert specific identities.[9] Claude Lévi-Strauss refers to this dynamic as the tensions between the forces that seek homogenization and those that seek ways of creating distinct identities (*Myth and Meaning* 7). Concern for authenticity, and within this the construction and maintenance of traditions such as the established narratives about al-Andalus, are central to the ideologies that support the homogenizing dominance of certain cultures and also to the drive to create distinction. At the same time (as I discuss further in the conclusion), the contestation of the standard narratives, their cultural translation, is central to emerging conceptions of tolerance.

Lévi-Strauss, in his earlier work *Race et histoire*, asserted that civilization implies the interaction and collaboration of cultures of great diversity and even depends on this coexistence. In a similar vein, Cathleen Kaveny, addressing religious pluralism in the US context, points to thoughtful engagement as a third option that is an alternative to both assimilation and defiant (even violent) rejection of the dominant culture. The need for such a third option makes translatability a crucial issue within the transnational and migrant identities created and fought against in a globalized world. The rewriting or translation of narratives about al-Andalus is part of the response to the forces of globalization that affect Spain, Argentina, and the countries of the Middle East and North Africa (MENA). Whether identity formation is rooted in (peripheral) European or settler culture nationalisms, as in the cases of Spain and Argentina, or in postcolonial nationalisms that are trying to protect against the consequences of imperial projects and ongoing neocolonial relations, it leads to invocations of al-Andalus by diverse social actors and producers of culture. In opposition to the dangers of rigid, exclusive identities that make no allowance for tolerance pointed to by Maalouf, my research on al-Andalus in contemporary culture points to a pronounced trend that can be understood as an act of cultural and temporal translation: the transformation of mythologies about the past into new narratives.

L. P. Hartley famously began one of his novels with the line "The past is a foreign country: they do things differently there." In this sense, just as al-Andalus is known for its translators and interpreters between cultures and is used to comment on intercultural contact, today's producers of culture translate the narratives inherited from the past to comment on and reshape the present. In reference to Arabic novels that employ the past, Wen-chin Ouyang notes that there is "a dear price to be paid for always resorting to the past, to the language of the past, to express the desire for the future" (vi), but happily, some works are able to engage with the past "without resorting to the language of the past" (225). To build on James Wertsch's usable past, productively using the past requires a separation from the language—or structures of thought—of the past and this in turn entails a translation of sorts.

Translation—understood not as a "faithful" transfer but as adaptation and transformation—serves as an apt model for the process of maintaining a sense of identity through elements of tradition without maintaining the conceptions of identity that lead to violent or otherwise problematic assertions of self. In the late twentieth and early twenty-first centuries, translation studies has moved toward a recognition of the role of the translator not so much as an instrument of transmission as an active interpreter who can assert his or her own power. This understanding of translation highlights the hermeneutic, creative, and political aspects of the translation process (Venuti 4, 8, Gentzler). In keeping with this, I use translation understood both as linguistic transmission and adaptation of meaning and as a broader cultural reworking of legendary figures and mythic narratives about the past. In this way, I add to debates on translatability by connecting them to broader issues of East–West and North–South conflict and contact. In chapter 1, in addition to analyzing works that depict translators and/or the act of translation, I engage with the work of Emily Apter regarding translatability and global networks of power and assert the importance of attending to the metalevel of translatability: what underlying assumptions shape understandings of translatability? Throughout this book, I also use translation as a trope for a specific type of cultural translation: the transformative transfer of past into present.

Some recent texts invoking al-Andalus reiterate narrow conceptions of knowledge and identity, but others use al-Andalus to comment on twentieth- and twenty-first-century sociopolitical issues—lack of freedom of expression, dictatorial rule, gender and sexual oppression, labor migration and economic disparities, restrictive religious and nationalist ideologies, and postcolonial identity politics. These are many of the same issues that have led to heightened misunderstanding and violence between "East" and "West" in the last few decades. While some cultural actors reinscribe hierarchical and exclusionary relationships, others try to use the past to envision new ways of being, including understanding al-Andalus as a narrative and taking on the role of storyteller. Through these transformed or translated narratives about al-Andalus, we can arrive at a deeper understanding of the rhetoric and ideological assumptions that are used to package the past. Narratives about the past—passed down as hallowed heritage—establish truths and identities that often limit the degree to which (cultural) translation is deemed possible in the present. For some, though, the stories of al-Andalus are taken as highly translatable in the sense that they become malleable artifacts to be recodified. The ability to retell the story of al-Andalus and of religious, national, and ethnolinguistic identities is tied to issues of authority, which in turn are part of coloniality, migration, and gender. Postcolonial, migrant, and gendered subjects must negotiate the authority to create meaning. Many of those who invoke al-Andalus must work to claim the authority to translate the story of the past and rewrite the present.

Although al-Andalus is often brought up in discussions of intercultural contact to cite what is referred to as the Cordoba paradigm, this use of Cordoba as an example of interfaith harmony is typically based on an idealized, utopic vision. I believe that a Toledo paradigm would be more beneficial because it points to not only intercultural contact but also the arduous work that is part of such exchanges: the painstaking labor, traversed by politics and power, of the translator and commentator. Modern-day "translators" of al-Andalus must also struggle, against censorship and grand narratives that have been sanctified, to produce new knowledge, new works of art, and new understandings of identity.

Many have gestured toward al-Andalus in general and Cordoba in particular as a model for peaceful coexistence that offers the present a fruitful paradigm. The Cordoba paradigm focuses on that locale because of its role as the zenith of Andalusi culture, in spite of the relatively short time span of that high point and the strife that followed it.[10] A Toledo paradigm could be deemed equally problematic in that various scholars have pointed to the mythical or at least overstated nature of the so-called Escuela de Traductores de Toledo or Toledo School of Translators. Traditional historiography understands this school as a somewhat coherent group of scholars located in Toledo who were involved in translation, primarily from Arabic to Latin but also from/to (and through as intermediary versions) Hebrew, colloquial Arabic dialects, and Romance (early Castilian), during the twelfth and thirteenth centuries, after the eleventh-century Castilian conquest. However, current scholarship questions that there was a school as such, whether interpreted as a pedagogical institution or as an explicit translation methodology developed in Toledo.[11] Nonetheless, Charles Burnett characterizes the scholarly work in Toledo as a "translation program" (*Arabic into Latin* VII: 249) and the translators of Toledo as a "scholarly community" that was "multifaceted" in nature ("Communities of Learning" 17) and Alexander Fidora demonstrates that through their translation work, scholars carried out philosophical dialogues across religious divides. In addition, the twelfth- and thirteenth-century translation work that took place under Christian rule and patronage built on the previous scholarly and translation activities under Muslim rule (Burnett, *Arabic into Latin* VII: 249, Vegas González 12). Furthermore, it is indisputable that in Toledo and throughout medieval Iberia, whether under Muslim or Christian rule, there was a great deal of translation activity that attests to a belief in the plausibility and importance of translation. Yet as Pym emphasizes, as is often the case in other contexts, the power of institutions and patronage was deeply implicated in Toledan translation.

For all of these reasons, while not wishing to uphold the mythical status of Toledo as a (Christian-ruled) space of interlingual and intercultural translation, and in fact to reject idealizations of such exchanges, I propose viewing al-Andalus through the lens of translation. On one hand, when we understand al-Andalus as a space of translation we acknowledge that the coexistence that took place was not the result of an effortless devotion to learning and the arts. Rather, it was the result of great efforts, difficult linguistic and cultural decisions, charged negotiations, and often imperfect but nonetheless praiseworthy results. On the other hand, when we view the invocations of al-Andalus in today's cultural products through the lens of translation, we are encouraged to attend to the mediation of language and the construction of knowledge, specifically narratives of identity, while recognizing that the translation of the past into new narratives is a process that involves struggles, risks, and gains that are linguistic, cultural, and political.

The body of literary and visual texts examined here demonstrates the assumptions underlying identity constructions and in many cases also dismantles those assumptions through a process of translating received narratives into new stories. These texts undo essentialist conceptions of the Arab world by pointing to the diversity within it, and of oppositional East/West identities by revealing not only shared history but cross-identifications and shared challenges. This body of works contains cases of textual dialogue and thematic convergence across the supposed East/West divide that debunk the clash of civilizations thesis and point to creative dialogue around shared cultural heritage as a path to critical awareness of identity construction and greater intercultural understanding.

Coloniality and European Peripherality

The many links between al-Andalus and coloniality have informed my delineation of the corpus of works to be treated here and my approach to these works. Al-Andalus is a nexus between Arabo-Muslim conquest of Amazigh North Africa, Muslim and then Christian (re)conquest of Iberia, and men's sexual conquest of women and also served as the point of departure for the Castilian conquest of the Americas. In addition, the North Africans and Arabs who identify as Andalusis or experience al-Andalus as part of their cultural heritage have undergone Ottoman Turkish and European colonization, and Spain, in part due to perceptions of its Andalusi past, sits at the edge of Europe. To acknowledge and investigate this interconnectedness, this study sets out to examine the interaction between cultural products invoking al-Andalus from the MENA region, Spain, and Argentina. My framing of these works seeks to bring together the concept of historical or collective memory and the interdisciplinary field of empire studies, which identifies and critiques the workings of power in contiguous land empires, overseas colonial empires, and unofficial forms of hegemony, with their many means of establishing and maintaining power, as well as many varieties of resistance to domination. This type of approach is necessitated by the fact that in each of the cultural contexts I address, there are layers of complexity that belie neat binary oppositions of colonizer/colonized. While recognizing the writers' and filmmakers' location in (or identification with) the Global South and Europe, I am attentive to the nuances and paradoxes in their positioning vis-à-vis coloniality.

Most of the MENA region was ruled by the Ottoman Empire from the early sixteenth century to the early twentieth century, and subsequently it was colonized by European nations in the nineteenth and twentieth centuries. Also, historical Palestine is understood by many as still existing in a form of colonization. Yet prior to these years of being the colonized, there was a powerful Arab-led Muslim empire that emerged in the seventh century AD and conquered lands from East Asia, across North Africa, and into Europe and had its Golden Age of cultural and technological advancement while Europe was still in its "Dark Ages."

Traditional and still dominant narratives of Arab and Muslim history from the MENA region and the Muslim world do not present the expansion of the Muslim empire as "imperial" or "colonizing" but solely as faith-driven conquests [*futuh*, from the singular *fath*, or opening]. In some accounts the territorial expansion of Islam is even understood as the spread of religion with little to no resistance from the territories' inhabitants. Fred Donner's *Narratives of Islamic Origins* demonstrates that a central theme in early Islamic historical writing is the legitimation of Muslim hegemony over non-Muslims through narratives regarding divine will and Muslim military victories (174–82). As Donner elucidates, in early Islamic communities there were certain means of legitimating special status within the community: degree of piety (98–103), "genealogical legitimation" or ties of kinship and ethnicity (104–11), "theocratic legitimation" or the appeal to God's will/the divine plan (111–12), and "historicizing legitimation" or validation via narratives about the past (112–22). These methods were sometimes intertwined (119), and over time there was a shift from the primacy of piety to the primacy of historicization (118). The means of legitimating special status within the community of believers was part and parcel with the legitimation of Arab Muslim leaders vis-à-vis their non-Arab and/or non-Muslim subjects. Hence one of the main purposes of early Islamic historical narratives was to affirm that the Islamic conquests were part of God's plan by pointing to previous conquests as proof of Muslim power and legitimacy. This historiography notwithstanding, even today indigenous minority groups in the MENA region maintain their own languages, customs, and religious beliefs and practices and, to varying degrees, regard Arabs and/or Muslims as foreign invaders.

Of particular importance to this project is the interaction between conquering Arab Muslims and the indigenous inhabitants of North Africa, the Amazigh people who are commonly known as Berber, and, in Algeria, are traditionally known by a name that refers to their primary region: *Kabyle*. Arab Muslim attitudes toward the Amazigh, who were Christian, Jewish, and animist at the time of the Muslim conquest, are reflected in the Arabic name for them: *Barbar*. Though of unclear etymology, *Barbar* shares with cognate words in Latin and Greek (as well as the English *barbarian*) a connotation of primitive savagery and literally means "to speak gibberish." The Amazighs are a racially diverse ethnic group sharing a family of related languages and dialects, known by the name of the main dialect among them, Tamazight.[12] The Amazighs put up strong resistance to the Arabo-Islamic conquest of Egypt and North Africa that began in the middle of the seventh century. As a result, it was not until the early eighth century that the Arabs had conquered most of North Africa from the Byzantines and converted the Amazighs to Islam. The Amazigh tribes retained their customary laws, but, in tandem with the process of Islamization, they were subjected to a process of Arabization, or forced linguistic and cultural assimilation. While some collaborated with the new invaders, embraced Islam, and took important administrative and military positions, others, particularly those of what is today western Morocco, strongly rebelled against Muslim Arab rule. Given this situation, from the mid-eleventh through the mid-sixteenth century a series of powerful Muslim Amazigh dynasties arose. Most notably, the Almoravid [al-Murabitun] and the Almohad [al-Muwahhidun] Dynasties dominated the Maghreb and al-Andalus, that is, much of present-day Spain and Portugal.

In the nineteenth and twentieth centuries, in order to use existing Amazigh feelings of disenfranchisement vis-à-vis Arabs to benefit the French colonial agenda, the French had a policy of promoting French–Amazigh ties and privileging Francophone Amazighs within the colonial hierarchy. After the end of European colonial rule, the Amazighs resisted Arabization through a mix of nationalism (in opposition to pan-Arabism), pro-French attitudes, and violent protest.[13] For instance, the 1980 protests and civil activism in Algeria known as the Berber Spring, the violent clashes of the Black Spring in Algeria in 2001, and the resurgence in Amazigh activism in Morocco and Libya in the wake of the 2011 Tunisian revolution of the Arab Spring are all part of the ongoing transnational political-cultural rights movement sometimes known as Berberism or Amazighism.[14]

In addition to the Amazigh, another minority group in the MENA region that has a noteworthy relationship to al-Andalus is that of the various denominations of Christian Arabs (or Arabic-speaking Christians, depending on their ethnic identification). Although their Christianity usually predates the advent of Islam, they are often associated with European encroachment or are viewed as having uncertain allegiances. Given the emphasis on differences of faith in traditional narratives about al-Andalus, Christian Arabs are in a unique and ambiguous, if not precarious, position vis-à-vis al-Andalus. For these reasons, the Christian Arab authors and filmmaker addressed in this study have stances that are markedly pluralist, secularist, and in some cases Arab nationalist. They claim al-Andalus as part of their heritage by dint of the Arab role in that historical and cultural phenomenon, and they use al-Andalus to further their pluralist and secularist aims.

Turning to the northern Mediterranean, though geographically part of Europe, Spain has struggled to define its identity at the edge of Europe and as a former part of the Muslim empire. With the rise of the Christian kingdoms of Iberia in the fifteenth century, not only did Castile and Aragon take over the remaining Muslim kingdom of Granada, but they began to build an empire that would stretch from the Philippines, across the Americas, and into neighboring North Africa—thus reversing Iberia's subjugation under Arab and Amazigh Muslim rule. Nonetheless, the Spanish empire began to crumble in the early nineteenth century with the Spanish-American independence wars, and by 1898 Spain was down to its North African and West African colonies, which it surrendered by the mid-twentieth century. At the same time, in the second half of the nineteenth century, the ideas of "scientific racism" served to support the European image of a barbaric Spain, one whose primitiveness or passionate sensuality could be traced back to North Africa and the Arab world. The rest of Europe's questioning of Spain's racial-cultural identity gave rise to the famous sayings "Europe ends at the Pyrenees" and "Africa begins at the Pyrenees." The loss of Spain's status as a great empire alongside perceptions of the country in the rest of Europe made the establishment of a clearly European identity and entry into the nascent European Union seem more pressing to the Spanish state and created divergent negotiations of identity among the Spanish regional nationalisms (e.g., Catalan, Galician, and Andalusian nationalisms).

Spain has a long tradition of strong cultural and/or linguistic regions, many of which espouse forms of nationalism known as *nacionalismos periféricos*. From the perspective of these peripheral or noncentral nationalisms, Castilian centralism is a colonizing force. Toward the end of the nineteenth century many of these regions, among them Andalusia, witnessed Romanticism-inspired regionalist movements that promoted political autonomy on the basis of cultural difference from the other regions of the peninsula. While the *andalucista* (Andalusianist) movement saw different, mostly cultural manifestations during the following decades, it burgeoned in the postdictatorship period. The various regionalist and nationalist movements, which had been suppressed by the Franco regime, experienced a resurgence with the transition to democracy and with the preparation of the 1978 constitution that reorganized the country politically on the basis of Autonomous Communities. In 1976 the Partido Socialista Andaluz (Andalusian Socialist Party), which later became the Partido Andalucista (Andalusianist Party), was established with the aim of demanding autonomy for Andalusia; it achieved this goal in 1981.

Among the regional nationalisms, that of Andalusia is particularly positioned as both subordinated to centralist Spain and linked to al-Andalus. As a historically economically depressed region, Andalusia has sent laborers to other regions of Spain, where they often experienced the oppression of class and cultural hierarchies. The twentieth-century emigration experience intensified Andalusian awareness of cultural differences from other Spaniards. Although within Europe Spain's "Europeanness" is questioned, within a national framework, that element of "Africanness" (backwardness, barbarity, etc.) attributed to Spain is ascribed specifically to Andalusia. Hence the Spanish saying that defends against "Africa begins at the Pyrenees": *Andalucía es África* ("Andalusia is Africa").[15]

Later I discuss the role of al-Andalus in the *andalucismo* (Andalusianism) movement, but for now, suffice it to say that andalucismo has included an identification with those most famously disenfranchised by powerful Castilians: the Moors.[16] Whether by tracing a Moorish genealogy, using the Moor as a figure for the disenfranchised, or only carrying out a class analysis, key andalucista writers have pointed to Castilians and the central Spanish government as colonizers of Andalusia. This perspective on Andalusian history was first put forward by Blas Infante (1885–1936), a musicologist and writer who is seen as the father of Andalusian nationalism.[17] It is also manifest in later works such as Antonio Burgos's

Andalucía, ¿Tercer Mundo? (Andalusia, Third World?, 1971) and José Acosta Sánchez's *Andalucía: reconstrucción de una identidad y la lucha contra el centralismo (Andalusia: Reconstruction of an Identity and Struggle Against Centralism*, 1978).[18] As these titles indicate, Andalusia is not only on the periphery of Spain, a country already on the periphery of Europe but, due to its socioeconomic state, is structurally similar to the "Third World."

Nonetheless, Spain once had a vast empire with most of its holdings in the Americas. In the period of the exploration and colonization of Spanish America, Iberians frequently interpreted the cultures that they encountered, and interacted with them, through the lens of Christian–Muslim contact in al-Andalus and the Reconquista.[19] After the wars of independence, the new nations went through a process of settler culture identity construction. The hierarchies of the colonial era—based on race and place of birth (i.e., Spain versus the Americas)—transformed into the hierarchies of the newly formed states with *criollos* (of Spanish descent but born in the Americas) taking the place of Peninsular Spaniards in the national elites. The process of criollo identity construction consisted of negotiations between differentiation from the mother country (a Spain that was seen as backward and not European) and celebration of criollo, European, and to some extent and in a subjugated position, indigenous ways. In the later nineteenth century, another element was added to this mix when Latin American governments attracted European immigrants to simultaneously boost the labor supply and "whiten" the population. Argentina (like Brazil and the United States) experienced a nineteenth- and twentieth-century immigrant influx that was massive in comparison with that of most other Spanish American nations. This led to differences in demography and the dominant conceptualizations of national culture. Early twentieth-century Argentina (and other parts of Spanish America) saw strong *criollismo* movements that posited the criollo as the authentic national subject. In urban Argentina in particular, given the magnitude of the largely European immigrant influx and the nineteenth-century decimation of the indigenous population, criollismo gave way to a more cosmopolitan, Europe-focused cultural discourse. In this way, Argentines are also somehow at the edge of Europe, balancing on the threshold as former Spanish subjects who may be seen as culturally, if not biologically, "mixed" by contact with indigenous America. But they often enjoy greater white privilege (including ties to other parts of Europe through family immigration histories) and economic power than other Latin Americans and certainly than most others from the postcolonial world at large.

To attend to the complex dynamics that are part of these connected histories of conquest, subjugation, and identity formation, I use and rework the concepts of "postcoloniality" and the broader "coloniality" in specific ways. I use the term *postcolonial* to refer to the time period and socioeconomic conditions after formal independence and the official end of colonial rule, though this period is in fact characterized by various forms of external political, economic, and cultural domination that continue to exist. Ella Shohat, Anne McClintock (in "The Angel of Progress"), and others have discussed the ambiguities and pitfalls of the term *postcolonial*.[20] These include an indeterminate temporality that can mask continuing forms of hegemony, a lack of distinction between different types of hybridity (that of the colonizing settler and that of the colonized), and unchecked antiessentialism that leaves little opportunity for agency and resistance. Yet the field of postcolonial studies yields valuable theorizations and analyses of the discourses of power and constructions of hybrid, often contestatory identities in cultures directly affected by colonialism—all the more so when care is taken to attend to particularities such as issues of persistent hegemony, differentiated hybridity, and agency, and the material reality of socio-economic environments and political circumstances. Although my object of study is cultural production, I attend to both the discursive and the material because, to borrow the phrasing of Hosam Aboul-Ela, "Power is economic and political as much as it is discursive and cultural" (16). My aim is to take heed of not only textual specificities and the challenges of the creation of meaning through the mediation of language and across languages and cultures, but also the conditions of material reality in which the works were produced and the ways the works take an active stance against these conditions.

By comparing works from the Arab world and the Maghreb, Spain (and within that Andalusia), and Argentina, I hope to shed light on the various centers and peripheries and the various forms of postcoloniality in the world and how they interact. In the past couple of decades, scholars have critiqued the pattern in postcolonial studies, comparative literature, and translation studies of focusing solely on center–periphery relations along a single axis where the center is typically the heart of Europe. A prime example of the shift away from this problematic pattern is Françoise Lionnet and Shu-mei Shih's *Minor Transnationalism*, which, in an effort to disrupt the Eurocentric tendency and provide a framework for inquiry into South–South relations, proposes the concepts of "minor transnationalism" and "transcolonialism." With a particular interest in attending to the lateral networks between minoritized cultures, they explain "transcolonialism" as a term that "denotes the shared, though differentiated, experience of colonialism and neocolonialism (by the same colonizer or by different colonizers), as a site of trauma, constituting the shadowy side of the transnational" (11). In their formulation, the transcolonial serves as a means to recognize minority identity constructions that develop through North–South and South–South dialogue and identification, rather than solely center–periphery opposition.[21] My project follows this South–South paradigm to consider cultural expression from the Maghreb, the Arab world, Argentina, Andalusia, and even Spain vis-à-vis the rest of Europe, in its transversal dimensions. Yet the present study also seeks to recognize the fluidity in the roles of colonizer and colonized and the points of convergence between different empires across geographic, cultural, and temporal markers.

The literary and visual narratives from the MENA region and Argentina that I examine were produced under ongoing twentieth-century colonialism or under its aftereffects, though in the Argentine case the authors are part of the settler culture of European origin. The elements of a form of settler culture are also apparent in some of the works from the MENA region that directly and indirectly address Arab Muslim imperial domination in Iberia and, to this day, in the Maghreb, with some Maghrebian writers identifying as the indigenous colonized vis-à-vis the Arabs. The works I look at from Spain were written under the effects/aftereffects of Spanish imperialism and colonialism, as well as the aftereffects of medieval and early modern Muslim conquests—in which Spain is traditionally positioned as a defending colonized nation that reconquered what had been "theirs." However, according to revisions of the Reconquista, Spain is revealed to have been the product of the alliances and expansion (i.e., conquests) of Iberian Christian kingdoms over a period of nearly 800 years.[22] In this way, in works from and about the Maghreb and Iberia, I aim to highlight the deep layers of imperial domination that interact with more temporally recent layers.

Can al-Andalus be "postcolonial"? The twentieth- and twenty-first-century depictions and invocations of al-Andalus that are the core focus of this project are clearly part of postcoloniality (for the reasons already surveyed and as I demonstrate in detail in the chapters to come). But can the earlier layers of the Muslim conquest of North Africa and Iberia and the Christian "reconquest" of Iberia be understood in such terms? In my view, the much-debated question of whether the Middle Ages can be postcolonial requires a separation of postcolonial theory and the historical period of modern (post)colonialism.[23] Postcolonial theory can, and indeed has been, used fruitfully to examine medieval phenomena and the connections between the medieval and the modern, given that modernity is often defined in contrast to a period characterized as uniformly "dark" and primitive. Moreover, many of the same general paradigms of power dynamics and negotiations of identity were part of pre-1492 and post-1492 empires, and for this reason earlier conquests are linked through collective memory (legends, songs, icons, etc.) to modern colonial and postcolonial situations. However, at the same time, it is important to recognize the particularities of modern state imperialisms and their practice of colonialism (which began in the fifteenth century) as well as the various periods of decolonization (from the late eighteenth century and on) and their relationships with larger global economic systems, versus the imperial ideologies and strategies of previous centuries. To maintain the particularities of communities that achieved political independence in the modern period (or are still struggling to do so), I reserve the use of *postcolonial* for those late eighteenth- to twenty-first-century contexts.

Yet the hinge moment of the fall of Granada and the possession of the first New World colonies in 1492, in addition to the temporal overlap between New World colonization and the final routing of morisco rebels in southern Iberia (the 1568–1571 Second Rebellion of the Alpujarras) followed by the staggered expulsion decrees (1609–1614), point to the many connections and continuities between the different periods and forms of empire-building before and after that (in)famous year.[24] To point to these continuities in imperial relations of power, as well as the interactions between various empires and world systems and between various colonized communities, across the globe and across historical periods, I propose the broader term *transcoloniality.* While drawing from the emphasis on lateral relations elaborated by Lionnet and Shih, transcoloniality is also based on the concept of "coloniality" that was developed by Latin American cultural critics and members of the Latin American subaltern studies group. In the late 1980s and early 1990s, Peruvian sociologist Aníbal Quijano introduced the concept of "the coloniality of power," which has since been glossed and further developed by Walter Mignolo and others. Coloniality of power points to the European domination of the Americas starting in the fifteenth century as having established a racial, economic, and cultural hierarchy that, in spite of the end of the age of formalized empires, continues to operate today as the foundation of globalized capitalism. Indeed, Quijano points to coloniality as constitutive of modernity, and Mignolo characterizes it as the darker side of modernity. Mignolo explains it concisely as follows: "Globalization has two sides: that of the narrative of modernity and that of the logic of coloniality" (*The Darker Side of Western Modernity* 5). However, asymmetries of power and conceptions and demarcations of center/periphery are more evident when the long historical panorama—one that stretches from the earliest encounters of conquest between Iberia and North Africa in al-Andalus—is considered.

Coloniality of power points to the racial hierarchies and privileging of European reason within knowledge production that were part of the justification for colonization of the Americas and persist today. Thus the concept is effective at highlighting the role of European domination of the "New World" as a key moment that has established lasting hegemonic systems. But by virtue of the focus on European (and US) hegemony, the historical presence of other empires is eclipsed. In my view, this limits our understanding of not only the workings of the world system that was inaugurated in the fifteenth century, but of the definitions of self and conceptions of power that exist in contexts where earlier empires are still part of cultural memory. This is the case of the Arab, Maghrebi, and Hispanic contexts that are the direct inheritors of the legacy of al-Andalus, which started as part of the Islamic empire, that at its height reached as far east as China and as far west as North Africa and Iberia. By viewing the works at hand through the lens of transcoloniality, I consider power relations across time periods, cultures, and empires and thus gain greater insight into today's uses of al-Andalus by Maghrebis who identify as Amazigh, those from the Mashriq or Arab East (Egypt and the Levant) who critique dominant narratives of the Muslim empire, Argentines negotiating their relationships to Europe and the indigenous, and Andalusians and other Spaniards who are navigating between identifications with Europe and a Moorish past.

The concept of transcoloniality brings to the fore the nature of coloniality as temporally layered and having multiple origins and axes. Through transcoloniality, I aim to cross the divide that marks the start of modernity and consider nodes of power outside of Europe and thus understand how earlier imperial expansions and exercises of power relate to the power dynamics that persist today. In other words, I conceive of the cultural products that I study here within the framework of transcoloniality to capture the colonizer/colonized power dynamics that were part of earlier and non-European colonizations and imperial expansions and impinge on later hegemonic relations. My larger intention is to promote a broader view that takes into account the interactions and overlaps between different empires, as well as the current dominance of Euro-American political and economic empire-like formations and the enduring patterns of colonial power relations.

Given this focus, the present study responds to Waïl Hassan's call for greater interaction between postcolonial critique and Arabic literary and cultural studies. In "Postcolonial Theory and Modern Arabic Literature: Horizons of Application," Hassan points to a lack of intersection between postcolonial analysis and Arab cultural production, with the only exception being Arab literature of French expression—an exception that itself reproduces colonial hierarchies. Luckily, in the decade following Hassan's essay, a great deal of innovative work has been done bringing to bear postcolonial theories and practices of analysis on Arabic literature and culture. One of the issues that Hassan addresses is how "the anti-essentialist zeal of the discourse on hybridity obscures the pivotal role of cultural memory both in colonial and anti-colonial discourses" (53). He goes on to comment that "the Marxist privileging of class struggle, poststructuralist anti-essentialism, the universalism of psychoanalysis, and feminism's critique of patriarchy all effectively foreclose any consideration of the kind of cultural memory that marks colonial history in the Arab world with a unique character, which should neither be theorized in terms of a universal postcolonial condition, nor elided in a unitary conception of 'the postcolonial world'" (54). Although Hassan refers specifically to the role of cultural memory about the Crusades in Euro-American and Arab contexts (53–54), I would like to point to al-Andalus as a significant element of Arab and Hispanic, and indirectly Euro-American, cultural memory.

Historical Memory

Earlier imperial relations and those initiated outside of Europe, such as those that are part of al-Andalus, retain relevance and power because they are passed down through cultural memory as familiar paradigms of relations with others. Memory relates past and present and is part of the definition of individual and group identities. What has been referred to as "collective memory," "historical memory," and "sites of memory" includes personal memories, family lore, monuments, cultural traditions, and ceremonies, as well as myths, legends, folk tales, and symbols. The past is not fully translatable in the present, but how it is translated is significant. Jan Assmann coined the term *mnemohistory* to refer to a field of study that, in contrast with "history proper," "is concerned not with the past as such, but only with the past as it is remembered. It surveys the story-lines of tradition, the webs of intertextuality, the diachronic continuities and discontinuities of reading the past" (9). The present study is part of this field; rather than ascertaining truth, my interest lies in analyzing the phenomena of historical memory as registered in narratives about specific figures. My central concerns here are what kinds of importance cultural agents in the present ascribe to the past and, intertwined with this, how dominant accounts of this importance are contested.

Al-Andalus is a constellation of sites of memory. Some early twenty-first-century commentators refer to a "memory boom" that began in the late 1970s and has spawned a memory industry—the commodification of nostalgia as well as the interdisciplinary academic field of memory studies (Olick, Vinitsky-Seroussi, and Levy 3, 4, 37). However, the late twentieth-century scholarship on cultural memory by the French *Annales* school of history and specifically Pierre Nora's work on *lieux de memoire* (sites of memory) draws from earlier work by French sociologists and philosophers Émile Durkheim and Maurice Halbwachs (*Lieux de mémoire* 22–25). In 1915 Durkheim developed the concept of "collective representations" to refer to symbols, beliefs, and values that are accumulated over time and have a common meaning among the members of a group. Building on Durkheim's work, Halbwachs developed his concept of "historical memory," or the traces of events that no one still has firsthand (autobiographical) memory of but that serve to constitute a group identity understood as continuous over time. For Nora, a *lieu de mémoire* (plural: *lieux de mémoire*) is a place, object, or act that is invested with a symbolic aura integral to group identity.

What interests me most about lieux de mémoire and other elements of historical memory is the processes of reconstruction and production out of which they arise. Although Nora suggests a conception of naturally occurring premodern cultural memory that I find suspect because its essentialism obscures the process of social production of cultural memory, he does indicate that modern sites of memory are constructed: "*Lieux de mémoire* originate with the sense that there is no spontaneous memory, that we must deliberately create archives, maintain anniversaries, organize celebrations, pronounce eulogies, and notarize bills because such activities no longer occur naturally" ("Between Memory and History" 12).[25] Assmann further emphasizes the crafting of cultural memory when he states: "The past is not simply 'received' by the present. The present is 'haunted' by the past and the past is modeled, invented, reinvented, and reconstructed by the present" (9). In Alon Confino's call for a more nuanced and contextualized examination of memory and its political dimensions, he asserts that one of the problems that arises in writing the history of memory is the separation of the construction of narratives about the past from their contestation. Instead, Confino urges scholars to "write the history of memory as the commingling of reception, representation, and contestation" (1399). Olick, Vinitsky-Seroussi, and Levy mention that along these lines, various scholars point to "counter-memories" to highlight the difference and dynamics between official and contestatory memory (249).

Discourses and acts that are focused on the past are often seen as nostalgic—with a negative connotation to the term that suggests a malady, an inability to be oriented toward the present and the future.

Svetlana Boym, recognizing this bias against nostalgia, distinguishes between two broad types of nostalgia: one that is "retrospective" and "restorative" and another that is "prospective" and "reflective." Boym explains her typology as follows: "Restorative nostalgia does not think of itself as nostalgia, but rather as truth and tradition. Reflective nostalgia dwells on the ambivalences of human longing and belonging and does not shy away from the contradictions of modernity. Restorative nostalgia protects the absolute truth, while reflective nostalgia calls it into doubt" (xviii). The dangers of restorative nostalgia that Boym points to underlie many versions of al-Andalus: both the nostalgia for the Islamic Golden Age that is deployed by terrorists in the name of Islam and the nostalgia for an epoch of Celtiberian, Roman, and Visigoth Christian "purity" or ascendance that is mobilized by Spanish nationalist anti-immigrant groups, as well as nostalgia for an era of heterogeneity revered for its cultural achievements that has been invoked by Andalusian nationalists, Arab immigrants in Argentina, and US Latinos as they negotiate different aspects of minority identities. Boym states: "It is the promise to rebuild the ideal home that lies at the core of many powerful ideologies of today, tempting us to relinquish critical thinking for emotional bonding. [. . .] In extreme cases it can create a phantom homeland, for the sake of which one is ready to die or kill" (xvi). In contrast, prospective nostalgia includes a "consideration of the future" that "makes us take responsibility for our nostalgic tales" (xvi). For this reason, "reflective nostalgia cherishes shattered fragments of memory and temporalizes space. [It] can be ironic and humorous. It reveals that longing and critical thinking are not opposed to one another, as affective memories do not absolve one from compassion, judgment, or critical reflection" (49–50). Thus, reflective nostalgia can produce countermemory that contests dominant modes of viewing the past that insist on unquestionable truth. Together with Granara, I propose that "the nostalgia for Al-Andalus is at once *restorative* and *reflective* [. . . .] Here, writing history is less literal and may even venture into ironic and even humorous modes to open up Al-Andalus to new temporal and spatial significations" (Granara, "Andalusian Chronotope" 62). Moreover, the reflective approach to al-Andalus is part of a translation of the past that, as I demonstrate in the chapters that follow, produces new meaning.

Whether presented in the form of literary, film, or television narrative, or drama, stories are a prime site for rehearsals of official memory and restorative nostalgias, as well as creative contestations against them and the production of new narratives. Cultural memory is made up of a wide array of texts, images, and rituals, but the oral and performative elements of these can be difficult to capture and only tell part of the story.[26] In this study I examine the traces of cultural memory in written and visual narratives. Some display retrospective textual rituals and others break with nostalgia altogether, rejecting official discourses and questioning, in large and small ways, how the past is constructed and how that construction is used and can be used in the present and future. Before addressing key issues in the relationship between history and narrative, I present a survey of the dominant narratives about al-Andalus and how they are employed in Arabo-Maghrebian and Hispanic cultures.

al-Andalus in the Arabo-Maghrebian World

In postcolonial contexts, restorative nostalgia and the reflective critique of countermemory are part of the delicate interplay between the need to affirm identity in the face of the delegitimation of local language, culture, and religion and the need to exercise critique of concepts of authenticity as well as modernity and progress. Elizabeth Kassab details this issue by noting that in the postcolonial context, the "quest for an affirmative sense of self" has led to various questions, among them:

> How is one to regain dignity and pride without falling into self-glorification? [...] What are the pitfalls and temptations of cultural authenticity and cultural essentialism? How does one reappropriate one's own history after it has been told and made by others? [...] How can one re-create a living relationship with one's history and heritage after one has been estranged from them by colonial alienation? Which history? Which heritage? Who is to decide and on what basis? (7)

The issue of what to do with one's past is encapsulated in the Arabic term *turath*, which means heritage, legacy, or traditional culture. The work of defining, resuscitating, and curating turath, as well as advocating for what its role should be vis-à-vis Ottoman and European influences and especially European modernity, was one of the primary missions of the Arab intellectuals of the late nineteenth to early twentieth centuries. This period of Arab cultural revival known as the *Nahda* attempted to both critique the past (turath) and strategically use it to face the challenges of European colonialism and improve the present. After the collapse of the Ottoman Empire in 1919, the Nahda became intertwined with nationalist movements as well as with pan-Arab nationalism. Key early twentieth-century Nahda figures, such as Jurji Zaydan, laid the intellectual foundation for pan-Arabism, the ideological project that sought to promote the idea that all Arabic speakers have a shared history and culture and the emerging political project, built on this ideology, of dissolving the boundaries imposed by colonialism and forming an independent, unified Arab nation. A key element of this movement was the conception of a shared heritage, carefully crafted by works such as Zaydan's historical novels (one of which I analyze in chapters 3 and 5).[27]

Colonialism, the Nahda, and independence movements were followed by postindependence states and the defeat in the 1967 Arab-Israeli War. That defeat revealed those states to be problem-ridden and intensified awareness of the need for self-examination. The post-1967 period, referred to by some intellectuals as the second Nahda, was characterized by an increased desire for totalizing and/or compensatory ideologies—such as pan-Arabism, alongside the radicalization of critique (Kassab 2, 20). Pan-Arabism was mainly promoted politically by the Baʿath Party, which had been founded in Syria in 1947. Although the party only held power in Syria (1963 to the present) and Iraq (1963 and 1968–2003), it soon established branches in other Arab countries. The Baʿathist leaders—anti-imperialist, secular, often socialist, Arab nationalist autocrats—attempted to implement the ideological aim of establishing a union between Syria, Iraq, and/or Egypt. The shared high points of Arab history, al-Andalus among them, supported unification through a common Arab past of civilizational glory. Thus, conceptions and mobilizations of turath continued to be part of these ideologies and eventually also of critiques. Kassab indicates that in the major pan-Arab conferences of the 1970s and 1980s, "tradition and the past occupied a major place" (13–14), and culturalist concerns regarding heritage, authenticity, and identity took precedence over critique (65, 115). But by the 1990s there was growing concern with the political questions of justice, secularism, democracy, agency, and critical thinking (65, 344–46). For instance, the work of Moroccan historian and novelist Abdalla Laroui [ʿAbd Allah al-ʿArawi] points to the need to replace ahistorical thinking with a demystification of absolute, essentialist conceptions of identity and tradition and to critically historicize reality (Kassab 82–91).[28]

Yet the same period of the 1970s to 1990s also witnessed the rise of Islamism. After the failure of the official secular projects of the 1950s and 1960s, such as pan-Arabism and socialism, fundamentalist movements arose as an alternative for the disenfranchised and an ideological tool for political purposes. The 1990–1991 Gulf War (also known as Operation Desert Storm or the First Gulf War) brought Saddam Hussein's brand of secular Baʿathist Arabism head to head with Islamism, with the issue of US intervention becoming tinder for radical Islamists. The initial Iraqi invasion of Kuwait pitted the secularist ideology against that of the neighboring Muslim kingdom of Saudi Arabia and the subsequent entry of US and other non-Muslim military personnel in Saudi Arabia to end the occupation of Kuwait led to a shift in the role played by Saudi Arabia vis-à-vis Islamist groups. Saudia Arabia, in the face of Islamists' condemnation of Saudi cooperation with the United States, could no longer function as an authoritative restraining force, and the Saudi response (repressing domestic Islamists who criticized the Saudi regime while increasing support to other Islamic groups) fueled the rise of radical Islamism. Like other fundamentalist movements, the discourse of Islamists is marked by restorative nostalgia, including invocations of al-Andalus as a place and time of Muslim ascendance that should be regained. Islam, whether embraced, questioned, or rejected, is central to issues of heritage. As noted by Kassab, "the dominating religious understanding of heritage has given to tradition a sacral character and turned any break from it into an act of blasphemy" (342). This makes the revision of heritage narratives a daunting, if not risky undertaking.

As Nelly Lahoud argues, the concept of turath is ideologically complex because many political, religious, and intellectual stances are built on a process of using the turath selectively to create a particular image of the past that is used to interpret the present—all with the aura of authenticity endowed by the turath. Ouyang, in her study of the Arabic novel as simultaneously negotiating Western form and the Arab past, interprets Arabic literature as demonstrating both restorative and reflective forms of nostalgia (52) but, like Lahoud, recognizes the complexities of this use of tradition. Ouyang asserts that "Heritage (*turāth*) [. . .] has come to serve as the hallmark of post-colonial Arab identity. The Arab novel revives, incorporates and interrogates this heritage, simultaneously manifesting a new understanding of its own past. This 'new' understanding is paradoxical. Even though its legitimacy may be questionable, it can nevertheless serve as the first step towards linking the past with the present and harmonising between them" (225). Although Ouyang refers to the use of turath in the Arabic novel as a step in the right direction, Lahoud maintains that intellectuals who respond to the cultural and political situation in the Arabo-Islamic world, specifically the rise of Islamism, by interpreting the philosophical dimensions of the turath end up in a bind. On one hand, they are further cementing the authority of the turath. On the other hand, they draw on the work of postcolonial and postmodernist thinkers to identify the turath as an indigenous heritage that has been marginalized by Western imperialism; however, they do not acknowledge that the turath itself has its roots in imperialism (47–49). Although Lahoud seems to be pointing to the formation of the turath via the curatorial process that began in the nineteenth century through contact with Western imperialism, the archive of the turath that modern Arab intellectuals have worked with is itself a product of the Muslim empires, from the earliest caliphates of the seventh century to the Ottomans. Thus, the process of taking up or transforming the turath is one with transcolonial dimensions and implications. Works, like some of the ones I address here, that recognize and critique the transcolonial resonances and narrative character of Arab heritage stand to minimize the problematic aspects of reworking the turath.

Further layers of transcoloniality emerge when we consider the migrations between West Asia, Iberia, North Africa, and the Americas that began as far back as a millennium ago. In addition to the Damascus-based Umayyad dynasty's role in the founding of al-Andalus, the figure of Umayyad prince ʿAbd al-Rahman—also known as al-Dakhil ("the Enterer"), who escaped the Abbassid Revolution, went into exile in al-Andalus in 755, and soon became its leader (ʿAbd al-Rahman I)—is the cornerstone of a perceived connection between modern-day Syria and al-Andalus.[29] With the late nineteenth- and early twentieth-century migration that led inhabitants of the Ottoman province of Greater Syria to settle in the Americas, migrants took these cultural narratives about al-Andalus with them, using them to address their situation as part of a minority group and participate in Syrian nation-building discourses.

The exilic and migratory connections are even more pronounced in the Maghreb and especially Morocco. Due to internal political conflicts under early Muslim rule, the successive advances of the Christian kingdoms in the Reconquista, and the expulsion edicts that began in 1609, Andalusi exile communities formed throughout North Africa. As explained by Bahrami, González Alcantud, Shannon, and others, in Morocco there is a particular mythology surrounding the Andalusi past and a distinct role for the Andalusi exile communities that has socioeconomic and political implications. The country's political and cultural elite proudly traces its origins to al-Andalus, and thus it has a unique role as a key element in Moroccan elite identity formations. Many of the elite families in cities such as Fez, Tetuan, and Rabat identify as Andalusi and take pride in those origins. The Andalusi cultural capital enjoyed by these families gives them a privileged place in Moroccan power hierarchies, in which they often serve as advisers to the king, ambassadors, and other government positions, while, as González Alcantud notes, it simultaneously excludes Amazigh communities ("El canon andaluz" 374). For this reason, as Shannon remarks, rhetorical references to al-Andalus have had a central place in the shaping of Moroccan national identity (90).[30]

Moreover, in an inversion of the Iberia-to-North Africa migration flow, in the twentieth and early twenty-first centuries Morocco has sent a steady flow of migrants to Spain. A 2005 UNESCO report states that

European sources place the total number of North Africans in Europe at just over two million, but the estimates from the countries of emigration are nearly double that. More than half of these émigrés are Moroccan, and currently Spain is the country that receives the second highest number (after France) of Moroccan immigrants (Baldwin-Edwards, Zohry). These numbers are not surprising given that since the 1960s the Moroccan government has had an official policy of stimulating emigration as a means of dealing with economic problems and internal political opposition. The regime encouraged emigration to relieve unemployment and specifically targeted marginalized Tamazight-speaking areas known for their rebellion against the central government. The hope was that remittances would increase prosperity and also diminish political resistance. Thus, the phenomenon of emigration to Spain in search of work, with the high risk of drowning while trying to cross the Straits of Gibraltar or being deported on arrival, is a result of Moroccan mismanagement as well as neocolonial economic power structures.[31] For all of these reasons, in North Africa the archive of texts and traditions linked to al-Andalus carries a special weight.

Given the ideological charge of the turath—the establishment of the canonical archive as well as its deployment as a voice of authority, Fadia Suyoufie has pointed to the ambivalence of Arab intellectuals, particularly women writers, between rejecting tradition and embracing it, even with the purpose of reworking it (219). This ambivalence notwithstanding, many writers continue to work with the material of turath, and in fact there has been a rise in interest in doing so. Muhsin al-Musawi refers to this trend that began in the late twentieth century as a turn toward exploring the historical record as a collection of imaginative narratives:

> Although strongly committed to social realism, Arab novelists have recently developed a new outlook that leans heavily on historical accounts and popular lore. Reconstruction of past turmoil and conflict is so close at times to contemporary realities that it calls attention to itself, provoking the reader to question that very past as well as its identical present. History itself is read as narrative, with its gaps and omissions that invite some active imagination to recreate. [. . .] Through intertextuality, enchassement and reenactment of the past, some Arab novelists have been able to shake the complacent view of history as too sacred to be questioned. (259)

Al-Andalus is a key component within the transcolonial web of (re) interpretations of the past in that its leading figures and texts are used to evoke a period of Arabo-Muslim glory and might and/or to question that narrative of the past.

The Arabo-Muslim discourses about al-Andalus that carry the imprimatur of having been categorized as part of the turath emphasize the valor and divine guidance that led Tariq ibn Ziyad, other leaders, and their troops to victory in their conquests. They portray the Visigoths as corrupt, oppressive leaders and the arrival of the Muslim armies as a liberation that was welcomed by the populace, which was treated justly by the new Muslim regime. The other common theme is that of the literary, artistic, architectural, and scientific achievements of the Muslim societies that developed in al-Andalus. These narratives have generally remained stable, but there is divergence in the explanation of how al-Andalus fell. More Islamist accounts blame the corruption of Islam in the peninsula due to Christian influences and the military and religious zeal of the Christian kingdoms for al-Andalus's downfall. Other accounts point to the rivalries and corruption among Muslim leaders or the Almoravid and Almohad dynasties' strict interpretation of Islam. As a result, in contemporary Arabic poetry twentieth- and twenty-first-century Arab rulers are often referred to as *muluk al-tawa'if* (sectarian or party kings) or *muluk al-nihaya* (kings of the end) in reference to the in-fighting and petty interests that divide and weaken modern day rulers, just like the "party kings" (taifa rulers) of the decline of al-Andalus.[32]

As the chapters that follow make evident, since the mid-twentieth century, alongside the continued reiteration of traditional accounts of the genesis and decline of al-Andalus, a strain of literary and cultural products from the MENA region has questioned and contested these prevailing narratives. This contestation of traditional histories about al-Andalus is part of a shift away from retrospective nostalgia and toward reflective and prospective nostalgia and even some anti-sentimental, satirical attitudes regarding al-Andalus.

This attitudinal shift, and the concomitant opening to new stories about al-Andalus, is layered on top of centuries of nostalgia expressed even before 1492, followed by centuries of perhaps more limited engagement with al-Andalus, and then a resurgence of interest in al-Andalus that began in the late nineteenth century as part of the response to the fall of the Ottoman Empire and the rise of European empires. As elucidated by Alexander Elinson in *Looking Back at al-Andalus*, since at least the eleventh century poets have been composing Arabic verse lamenting the fall of specific cities to Muslim rivalries or the Reconquista, in the process investing al-Andalus with symbolic value. In addition to ʿAbd al-Rahman I in the eighth century, famously longing for his native Syria through verses about a palm tree in al-Andalus, after the eleventh-century disintegration of the Umayyad Caliphate of Cordoba due to factionalism, poets began to look back nostalgically at the grandeur of Cordoba. When according to legend Boabdil, the last Muslim ruler of al-Andalus, lamented the loss of Granada, Arab poets had already been looking back nostalgically and linking al-Andalus to loss for centuries. These layers of nostalgia laid the foundation for the subgenre of *Andalusiyyat*, that is, nostalgic or elegiac writing on al-Andalus.

Traditionally, Arabic literary history considered that starting in the mid-twelfth century, while al-Andalus was still flourishing, the rest of the Arabic-speaking world entered a period in which the collapse of central caliphal authority had dampened literary production. For this reason, the entire period from 1150 to 1850 is conventionally referred to as "the Decadence." In the latter part of this period, starting in the sixteenth century, al-Andalus, as a political and cultural entity, had already become a thing of the past. Although renewed scholarly interest in this understudied early modern period may yield further insights, thus far the Arabic poetry of the period seems to have been focused elsewhere.[33] Nonetheless, al-Andalus continued to have a distinct role in the rich *Adab* literature (*belles-lettres*) of the time.[34] The degree to which the nostalgic element of the Andalusi theme was central (rather than secondary) in Arabic letters of this period has emerged as a topic of debate. Nizar Hermes, in his work on a seventeenth-century travelogue written by a Moroccan diplomat who visited Spain, argues that this text is one of the foundational pieces in post-Reconquista nostalgic Andalusiyyat, though he asserts that "the nostalgia for al-Andalus in the text is largely more reflective than restorative" (4). In contrast, other scholars indicate that seventeenth- and eighteenth-century nostalgia for al-Andalus was rather muted. Ralf Elger's work on seventeenth-century scholars and litterateurs demonstrates that al-Andalus continued to be a frequent theme and point of reference in early modern prose. However, he notes that in these works elegiac nostalgia is tempered and arises as a concern with "the problem of fate" in the work of several seventeenth-century authors from the Mashriq (290). Similarly, Justin Stearns, working with historical writings about al-Andalus from North Africa and elsewhere, contends that through the eighteenth century these texts were not imbued with nostalgia. He finds that in the historical texts written during and soon after Muslim rule in Iberia, what predominates is a vision of al-Andalus as a land of wonders, jihad, and eschatological events. Along these lines, Stearns, Nieves Paradela Alonso, and Pedro Martínez Montávez maintain that even in the writings of seventeenth- and eighteenth-century Moroccan diplomats to Spain, the nostalgic conception of al-Andalus as a "paradise lost" did not regain prominence until the writings of late nineteenth-century Arab travelers to Spain. Regardless of the unclear antecedents, these travelers from the Mashriq employed al-Andalus in the negotiation of their stances toward the crumbling Ottoman Empire and the rise of the British Empire.[35] Foremost among these is the Egyptian philologist, translator, and pan-Arabist Ahmad Zaki Pasha (1867–1934), who visited Spain in 1892 and wrote about his experiences there. This was followed by the writings of Ahmad Shawqi (1868–1932), the prominent Egyptian neoclassical poet whom the British forced into exile in Spain from 1914 to 1919. Before his exile Shawqi had already begun to invoke al-Andalus and during and after his stay in Spain he wrote various al-Andalus-infused works.[36] As Yaseen Noorani deftly demonstrates, the longing-filled "Siniyya" poem that Shawqi wrote after visiting the Alhambra and the mosque of Cordoba is the product not only of the grandeur of Muslim Iberia but of the author's colonial context and serves to construct a new national political subject.

Soon after Shawqi, early twentieth-century Levantine Arab writers who had emigrated to the Americas (known as the *mahjar* or émigré writers) turned to al-Andalus in various ways. Some, such as Syrian immigrant to New York Nasib ʿArida (1887–1946), experimented with the strophic form and refrain of the *muwashshah*, a popular poetic form developed in tenth-century al-Andalus. In this way, al-Andalus, while still connected to displacement and longing, was the source of innovation and part of the transformation of Arabic letters propelled by the North American mahjar school. In a different type of gesture, in 1933 the mahjar writers of Brazil established the literary society al-ʿUsba al-Andalusiyya (the Andalusi League) in reference to their sense of connection to Ibero-America via al-Andalus.

As the twentieth century progressed, pan-Arabists, particularly the Baʿthist Syrian regime (building on the Umayyad connection), and Islamists turned to the theme of al-Andalus to foment group identity and pride. For secularist thinkers, al-Andalus is the site of Arabo-Muslim scientific and literary advancement, whereas for those of an Islamist tendency, in addition to being a source of cultural capital, it is a site of Muslim hegemony. For some social actors from all currents, al-Andalus has been used to compensate for the dire circumstances of the present. For others, whether invoked nostalgically or otherwise, it is a conduit for critique with a view to change. To date this has been noted most frequently in invocations of al-Andalus that serve to comment on the situation of Palestine. However, there is a broader interest in using al-Andalus to critique the present. For this reason, William Granara has stated regarding the role of al-Andalus in literature:

> Far more complex than the prevalent view that writing Al-Andalus expresses a nostalgia for a paradise lost, the Andalusian [Andalusi] chronotope in modern Arabic literature signifies the heightened focus of the "now" as well as the hopes and aspirations of what is to come. It is less a dialectic of "what was" vs. "what is" than a dialectic of "what is" and "what should or shall be" that compels Al-Andalus to be remembered and re-created over and over again. (Granara, "Nostalgia" 72)

It is important to make clear that this present- and future-oriented engagement with al-Andalus is not limited to the reiteration of the established mythology. As the chapters that follow elucidate, certain works support and further entrench problematic cultural myths, but others rewrite the established stories about al-Andalus.

Elsewhere Granara concludes that "the story of al-Andalus remains a transhistorical structure for modern Arabic literature, and its retelling over and over again never ceases to fascinate as long as the forces of good and evil continue in battle" ("*Extensio Animae*" 70). However, rather than retell a single story to rehash centuries-old oppositions, many in the MENA region create new versions of the myths surrounding al-Andalus to question the boundaries of the inherited positions of good guy/bad guy, colonizer/colonized, Christian/Muslim, and self/other. María Rosa Menocal stated in *The Ornament of the World* (2002) that "within the Muslim world [. . .] al-Andalus is reckoned more a nostalgic curiosity than anything else—and mostly, in the end, a failure, because Islam did not survive as one of the religions of Europe" (10). Similarly, Reuven Snir states, "Inspired by nostalgia, the picture that most frequently appears in modern Arabic literary writings is that of al-Andalus as the lost paradise, '*al-firdaws al-mafqud*'" (264–65). Atef Louayene notes a shift away from retrospective nostalgia regarding al-Andalus, but he places it in the twenty-first century. He uses the phrase "pathology of Moorishness" to refer to the deployment of the memory of al-Andalus in "major political conflicts with the West" and states that "In most twentieth-century Arab writing [. . .] al-Andalus is constantly evoked with elegiac nostalgia as the site of an ideal past against which the violent failures of modern Arab politics are measured" (35–36). He identifies a break with this mythification of al-Andalus in post–September 11 literature (36). Yet the corpus of works I present in the chapters that follow challenges these assessments of the role of al-Andalus in contemporary Arab-Maghrebian cultures. Many of the works that I examine, published as early as the 1960s and with several from the 1980s and 1990s, create new versions of al-Andalus to carry out ideological critiques. They use Muslim Iberia to undercut pervasive narratives such as the incommensurability of East and West, Arab superiority over the Amazigh peoples, al-Andalus as an objectified woman, and the promises of national liberation struggles, pan-Arabism, and globalization.

al-Andalus in Spain, Andalusia, and Argentina

Traditional Spanish discourses on al-Andalus have been dominated by nationalist ideology and the rhetoric of the Christian Reconquista of Iberia: an eternal Spain recovered by a Christian populace of largely Visigoth origins who recuperated their usurped lands from the bloodthirsty, lascivious Muslims and reestablished homogeneity.[37] Nonetheless, recent scholarship has pointed to the ambiguities at play in medieval and early modern Spain's mix of maurophobia and maurophilia and modern Spain demonstrates a variety of paradoxical official and popular discourses regarding al-Andalus.[38] This mix of ideological positions and cultural practices is explained by Spain's unique situation, which Susan Martin-Márquez aptly summarizes as follows: "Spain is a nation that is at once Orientalized and Orientalizing" (9). She explains that this "dynamic resembles a Möbius strip, calling into question the possibility of any location 'outside' Orientalist discourse." She asserts that this simultaneous insider/outsider status can lead to a strong sense of "disorientation" that complicates understandings of subjectivity. Twentieth- and twenty-first-century Spanish literary and cultural narratives on al-Andalus reflect these disorientations, at times in efforts to assert Spain's power and Europeanness and at times in efforts to question the traditional premises of Spanish identity—those constructed both within the peninsula and outside of it.

Barbara Fuchs explains Spain's position, which complicates the very concept of Orientalism, by stating that, on one hand, Spain manifests a hybrid culture that includes elements of Moorishness—practices and objects that, whether or not they can be traced to the Arabo-Muslim world, are understood to be linked to it. Yet on the other hand, historically Spain's European rivals represented it as "Oriental" to counter its imperial triumphs (Fuchs, *Exotic Nation* 3). While Spain has produced both demonizing and romanticizing forms of Orientalism, it has also been the object of Orientalist essentializations through what is known as the Black Legend (*la leyenda negra*). The term refers to anti-Spanish rhetoric that arose primarily in Britain and France first during the Reformation, as part of Protestant–Catholic conflicts, and then in the late eighteenth century and after as part of the Napoleonic occupation and its aftermath. These discourses pointed to the Spanish Inquisition and Spain's treatment of the indigenous inhabitants in its overseas colonies as proof of Spanish cruelty and barbarity. These representations gained greater momentum in the latter half of the nineteenth century with scientific racism's justification of the connection between Spanish barbarity and Moorish influence.[39] The discourses that were subsequently labeled "la leyenda negra," in reference to the Spanish perception that these were unwarranted negative stereotypes, led to various Spanish responses across these periods, ranging from the rejection of Moorishness to an embracing of it. The result, as the work of Yiacoup, Fuchs, Martin-Márquez, and others indicates, is a deep Spanish ambivalence regarding all things (perceived as) *moro.*

Within Spain, in intellectual circles and the press, the question of what to make of the almost 800 years of Arab-Amazigh Muslim rule in the Iberian Peninsula, as well as the process of the Reconquista and the eventual expulsion of Jews and moriscos, has been heatedly debated from the eighteenth century on. The fact that Spain had not followed the same trajectory of political and economic modernization as most of the rest of Europe led to attempts to explain the country's so-called decadence. This created two broad tendencies among Spanish intellectuals throughout the next centuries: those who saw the expulsion of Jews and Muslims and the Inquisition as the cause of this decline, and those who saw the Jews and Muslims as a negative influence on Spain that needed to be eliminated. Intertwined with this was the question of whether Spaniards were primarily a Celtiberian, Roman, Visigoth people, or whether the centuries of Jewish and Muslim presence had had a profound impact on the Spanish ethos. This debate went on to produce, in the eighteenth century, positions as diverse as the assertion of Spanish nationhood by reevaluating Spanish history and pointing to the glories of the period of Muslim rule; the idea that al-Andalus was part of the progression toward modernity, based on Enlightenment archaeological research; the notion that the Moors were barbarians; and a renewed desire to conquer North Africa (after earlier interest in doing so had been redirected into the conquest of the Americas).[40] In the first decades of the nineteenth century, Spanish Romantics looked back at Muslim Iberia as part of the process of defining a postabsolutist, liberal Spain; then in the 1840s, growing interest in the exotic and the medieval took over and al-Andalus was seen through an Orientalist lens. Late nineteenth-century racialist discourses made attributions of "Moorish blood" part of regional and national identity formations.[41] At the end of the nineteenth century the Spanish-American War and the loss of Spain's last New World colonies led the Generation of 1898 to intensify the inquiry into the *ser español*—the Spanish way of being. The Generation of 1898 was a group of writers driven to soul-searching by the apparent decline in Spanish culture and the questions of how this decline had come about and how Spanish culture could be understood in a positive light. The Generation of 1898 can be seen as having posed the questions about Spanish cultural identity that the next generation of intellectuals, that of 1914, tried to answer.[42] The debate regarding the place of al-Andalus in Spanish culture is typified by the dispute between two intellectuals of the Generation of 1914, both of whom were living in exile in Hispano-America as a result of the Spanish Civil War.

Américo Castro (1885–1972), a philologist and historian who hailed from Granada, is famous for having developed the concept of *convivencia*, while Claudio Sánchez Albornoz (1893–1984), a historian from Madrid, is known for championing the opposing idea of Spanish Senequism. Castro developed the term *convivencia* (literally, *cohabitation*) as part of his interpretation of medieval Iberia as having enjoyed a Muslim-led tolerance between Christians, Jews, and Muslims. According to this interpretation, tolerance was one of various significant Muslim contributions to Spain's unique cultural history.[43] Drawing from Castro's work, the term *convivencia* has taken on a life of its own and is often used to refer to a utopian vision of interfaith harmony. The idea of "the Spain of the three religions" (anachronistic, since it was not yet "Spain") grew out of this and has become a catchphrase that is featured in a certain vein of Spanish historiography and in the promotion of tourism in Spain.[44] Sánchez Albornoz's contribution to the polemic on the ser español was Spanish Senequism, which posits a Roman (Seneca-based) stoicism as the root of Spanish identity. Through the focus on the Roman philosopher and statesman Seneca, who was from what is now Cordoba, Sánchez Albornoz posited that Spaniards have a stoic character based on Gothic, Germanic, and Roman—that is, purely European—elements.

Radically different conceptions of Spanish identity and the role of al-Andalus in it have continued to have a strong political role in the twentieth century and beyond. A concept akin to convivencia was part of Spain's colonial project in North Africa. In a contradictory stance, during the first half of the twentieth-century the Spanish military and colonial authorities espoused the idea of Spanish–Moroccan *hermandad* (brotherhood) rooted in al-Andalus as a way to justify their presence in North Africa.[45] Nonetheless, the official nationalist ideology of the Franco dictatorship (1939–1975) was based on a rhetoric that explicitly invoked the spirit of the Reconquista and its mission to restore the unity of Spain through Catholicism.[46] After Franco's death and during the transition to democracy (1975 until as late as the mid-1980s), al-Andalus continued to be debated in academic circles and the media and was employed in centralist and regional nationalisms (*nacionalismos periféricos*) as well as discourses around immigration.[47] These issues, in turn, are linked to Spain's ongoing negotiation of its role on the periphery of Europe.

Before turning to European integration and immigration, it is important to understand the complex role al-Andalus has played in the regional nationalism of Andalusia. The region of Andalusia had been considering its relationship to al-Andalus since long before the transition to democracy and integration into Europe. But with the postdictatorship period's rise in cultural and political movements centered on regionalisms and nationalisms, the invocation of al-Andalus as part of the andalucismo movement also intensified. Although the historical narratives used by andalucistas to explain the hierarchical relationship between Castile and their region as the vestiges of Castile's relationship with al-Andalus (as discussed above) have been difficult to prove or disprove, geographic location, place names, and famous monuments forge a strong link between Andalusia and al-Andalus. The fact that, aside from Toledo, the cities most associated with the height of Andalusi civilization—Cordoba, Granada, and Seville—are part of the present-day region of Andalusia facilitates the identification between that region and al-Andalus. Additionally, although geographically al-Andalus and Andalusia are not identical, the etymological connection between the place names has served to heighten the perceived connection between the contemporary Spanish region and the former Muslim political and cultural entity.[48] Unlike the Catalan, Galician, and Basque nationalist movements, Andalusia does not have a language to call its own, so andalucistas have turned to the language of historical memory to leverage a more advantageous position within the Spanish state.

The cultural aspects of andalucismo include highlighting and celebrating the characteristics of Andalusian culture that are understood to be a part of its Andalusi heritage. It would be difficult to ascertain the degree to which such a cultural continuity exists since the official historical record indicates that almost all moriscos were expelled and any remaining morisco cultural or religious practices were aggressively quashed. The prevailing nationalist view of Spanish history, and within it Spanish demography, is that all Jews and Muslims were expelled and the areas they had inhabited were repopulated through a policy of bringing in Christians from elsewhere in the peninsula and distributing the Muslims' confiscated property among them. A contestatory account posits that sizable Muslim and Jewish populations assimilated enough to escape the notice of the Inquisition and stayed in Iberia. According to some of these narratives, the remaining Muslims and Jews were relegated to working the lands of the Christian knights who had colonized the region.[49]

Regardless of whether andalucista identification with al-Andalus is largely a construction or the reemergence of a long suppressed culture, the identification between the region and the medieval Muslim entity is also related to Andalusia's underdog status within Spain. As an economically depressed region that has been viewed from the outside as an extension of North Africa, the ideologues of andalucismo as well as certain veins of popular sentiment have embraced a moro connection. This connection consists of promoting the positive side of the presumed Andalusi legacy—the cultural achievements and splendor of al-Andalus, as well as its perceived heterogeneity—as part of Andalusian identity. Although the bedrock of narratives of Spanish identity that emphasize Celtiberian, Roman, and Visigoth origins (as well as those of the regional nationalisms other than andalucismo) is the concept of "pure" bloodlines, Andalusia has been associated with ethnic and religious mixture, Moorish impurity, and primitiveness, if not barbarity. Andalucistas, in turn, have often embraced not only the accomplishments of al-Andalus but the heterogeneity associated with it.[50] Although Steven Gardner in his essay on andalucismo and the Spanish writer Antonio Gala (whose works I discuss in chapters 2 and 4), emphasizes that the concept of an Andalusi identity for Andalusians is one imposed by politicians, during the 1970s and 1980s it was also espoused in Andalusian popular culture precisely because it expressed both the feelings of alienation created by labor migration and the compensatory fantasy of a glorious and powerful past, as well as a fighting spirit.

González Alcantud's work on Andalusi/Andalusian identities is key to understanding the dynamics at hand, in which the Andalusians of today can identify with both the colonizers and the colonized. This Spanish anthropologist defines the term "intermediate lands [*tierras intermedias*]," borrowed from González Ferrín, as "places that bear [*soportan*] the status of the colonized at the same time as they are a support [*son soportes*] for external colonization. This is the case of Andalusia, an intermediate, or meridional, land par excellence" ("El canon andaluz" 368). Andalusians, in the position of colonized, have long been the object of the imposition of stereotyped identities from the outside. At the same time, in this intermediate, southern zone, the malleable and fixed remnants of Andalusi culture—legends, place names, and architecture—are encountered by the (colonizing) inhabitants every day, thereby creating the phantom presence of the Moor. Thus, in Andalusia, meaning is created "upon the base of the merging of the external stereotype and authoctonous collaboration (González Troyano). From there a human and social type arises that simultaneously takes part in the irredentist image of the tragic, of which it must redeem itself, and of the colonizer that it in and of itself embodies" ("El canon andaluz" 369). Thus, the concept of *lo andaluz*—that which is Andalusian—is a myth that has been accepted as true, but one which González Alcantud proposes can be useful in developing strategic social pacts ("El canon andaluz" 378).

Through this reference to social pacts, González Alcantud suggests that, mythical though it may be, the Andalusi base of andalucismo is a type of strategic essentialism. This concept, introduced by Gayatri Spivak in the 1980s, refers to the political expediency of minority groups temporarily essentializing themselves. By glossing over differences and pointing to a simplified group identity, the group can achieve worthy political goals. In the case of the andalucistas, however, the group can also be said to be appropriating and essentializing the identity of another group—actual Muslims, who during the post-Franco period began to arrive to work in Andalusian agriculture. Just how the essentialism is put to use is of utmost importance. As Diana Fuss asserts in *Essentially Speaking*, essentialism is not "essentially" good or bad and "the radicality or conservatism of essentialism depends, to a significant degree, on *who* is utilizing it, *how* it is deployed, and *where* its effects are concentrated" (21; emphasis in original). The context surrounding a given instance of essentialism can allow the essentialism to operate in an interventionary fashion.[51] For this reason, in the chapters that follow I attend closely to the specific dynamics of the various iterations of andalucista uses of al-Andalus that arise in Spanish cultural production. Some of the decisive issues will be socioeconomic class (identification with migrant labor versus deposed royalty) and problematic links with Spanish colonialism in North Africa.

As Andalusia and other regions of Spain were reconfiguring their relationship to the previously highly centralized state, Spain was renegotiating its relationship to Europe. In 1982, amid heated debate within Spain, the country joined the North Atlantic Treaty Organization (NATO) decades after its founding. Similarly, Spain was a relative latecomer to European integration. It was not part of "the inner six" who established the European Communities in 1951, nor "the outer seven" who formed the European Free Trade Association. Rather, it joined the European Communities (which later developed into the European Union) in 1986. Simultaneously, in the 1980s there was a rise in North African immigration to Spain that added to the questioning of Spain's relationship to Europe and the legacy of al-Andalus.

Since at least the 1990s, right-wing Spanish populists have evinced and fomented fears of a Muslim reconquest of Spain, primarily in the form of Moroccan immigrants. Leonard Harvey notes that although the Catholic Monarchs' victory at Granada was not followed by any significant counterattack from the Muslim world, given the Mediterranean coast's vulnerability to pirate raids, "at times there was almost a Spanish psychosis related to the cry '*Moros en la costa*' (the Moors have landed)" (325). This fear of the Moors that Daniela Flesler describes as the effects of an experience of trauma, has been stirred up by the rise in North African immigrants and manipulated by Spanish political interests. Before 1985 Moroccans did not need visas to enter Spain, and many young Moroccan men went to Spain temporarily to work in agriculture and industry. In the 1990s the number of migrants from Morocco to Spain began to rise significantly. For this reason, until 2002 Moroccans were the largest immigrant group in Spain. Since then, in yearly statistics they have typically been the second largest group, closely following Romanians or Ecuadoreans, and occasionally still the largest group (*España en cifras*). Relative to France, there have only been a limited number of issues regarding Muslim immigrants being prohibited from wearing a hijab or headscarf to school. However, there have been violent manifestations of anti-immigrant sentiment, namely, in 2002 in southwestern Almeria province, most famously in the town of El Ejido. As Flesler indicates, Spanish rejection of North African immigrants in particular is rooted in the historical relationship with North African Muslims.

In addition to cultural and economic frictions at the local level, the rise in immigrants has had broader implications. Paradoxically Spain's integration into the European Union led to a dramatic rise in North African immigration to the country. The European Schengen Convention, a 1990 supplement to the earlier Schengen Agreement, dissolved internal European borders, thereby making entry through Spain even more desirable for migrants who could then use the country as a stepping stone to other points in Europe. These changes led the European Union to pressure Spain to intensify its policing of the borders of "Fortress Europe"—a term referring to the network of border patrols and detention centers meant to reduce illegal immigration into the European Union, as well as to the anti-immigrant attitudes associated with the implementation of this system.

The 1990s also saw the celebrations and counterprotests of the Columbus quincentenary. Spain invested years of planning and large sums of money in various elaborate events marking the 1992 anniversary of Columbus's arrival in the New World. In addition to various commemorative events that included a re-creation of the voyage using replicas of the ships, there were tie-in events at the summer Olympic Games in Barcelona and the Universal Exposition (Expo '92) in Seville. The events met with mounting scholarly revision that questioned the common rubric of discovery and the outcome of that intercultural encounter, as well as protests by indigenous groups in the Americas and their allies. In some sectors, the quincentennial was viewed as a public relations coup for Spain, but the resulting debate regarding Columbus's legacy revived the Black Legend, that is, discourses about Spanish religious intolerance and cruelty. On one hand, this brought increased financial and cultural ties between Spain and Latin America, yet on the other hand, it brought international attention to Spain's imperial role in the end of al-Andalus, the near-end of indigenous America, and the country's cultural location between East and West, North and South.[52]

The arrival of Iberians in the Americas led to al-Andalus becoming part of the intellectual and cultural idiom of Latin America. Arguably, most (if not all) of the canonical texts of the Spanish medieval and early modern periods grapple in some way with the centuries of Jewish and Arab-Amazigh Muslim presence on the Iberian Peninsula and what it means regarding Spanish identity. Many of these works are canonical pieces in Spanish Americans' education in Hispanic letters. As the relationship between the newly independent states and Spain changed over the nineteenth and twentieth centuries and Latin American statesmen and writers sought to define national identities while aligning Latin America with the Occident as an extension of Europe, various texts demonstrate an interest in using al-Andalus as part of that negotiation of cultural identity.[53] This situation has led Hernán Taboada to state,

> an even cursory examination of Latin American literature shows a variegated ideological use of the Reconquista and the "three religion Spain," from the moment of Iberian arrival in the American continent up to contemporary debates. The variety and the frequency of these uses indicate that we are dealing with a moment of European medieval history that has been especially important in Latin American thought. (124)

In particular, the early twentieth-century movement known as Hispanism [*hispanismo*], a spirit of reconciliation with Spain that entailed a revalorization of Hispano-America's Spanish heritage, led Spanish American writers to look to the intercultural contact of medieval Iberia as an interpretive lens for their national situations. In their efforts to delineate national traditions, these thinkers were influenced by Spanish intellectuals' search for the essence of the Spanish "being." As Carlos Altamirano and Beatriz Sarlo indicate, Latin American intellectuals who were swept up in the hispanismo movement read the work of Ángel Ganivet (1865–1898) and that of members of the Spanish Generation of 1898 (74). The Granadan writer Ganivet, considered a precursor to the Generation of 1898, first introduced the issue of the role of Arabo-Islamic influence on Spain to the modern period's deliberations on the ser español (and also influenced the andalucismo movement I discussed previously). In Argentina, writers and the reading public were especially attuned to the medieval and early modern history of Iberia due to the number of immigrants from Spain that settled in Argentina at the turn of the twentieth century and during the Spanish Civil War, as well as the presence of one of the key figures in the debates about Spanish identity. Spanish intellectual Sánchez Albornoz, because of differences with the Franco regime, spent decades living in Argentina and teaching at universities there. For these reasons, al-Andalus is also a living part of Latin American, and especially Argentine, culture, with the first half of the twentieth century being its period of greatest vitality.

In Spain the academic debates surrounding the legacy of al-Andalus continue to the present day and are often visible in the media and in politics. Martin-Márquez notes that in the late twentieth and early twenty-first centuries there has been a backlash against convivencia in the form of a resurgence of rhetoric about a homogeneous Spain that has always been European (316–17). This has led to Spanish academics, such as Serafín Fanjul and Rosa María Rodríguez Magda, railing against the mythification of al-Andalus to the point of demonstrating an anti-Muslim bias. As a counterpoint, academics such as Mercedes García Arenal, Luis Molina, and Eduardo Manzano Moreno seek a more research-based approach that questions the rosy picture of convivencia while recognizing the achievements of the period of Muslim rule in Iberia. Spaniards who oppose North African immigration to Spain take up the work of Fanjul and others as scholarly support for their stance.[54]

In modern Spanish literature, film, and television, the complex relationship with al-Andalus has led to texts that invoke it in romanticizing and/or Orientalist historical fiction, in attempts at radical revision of dominant discourses, in the rhetoric of immigrant invasion, or in sympathetic depictions of immigrant plight. As discussed by Flesler, some Spanish writers portray North African immigrants conquering à la Tariq ibn Ziyad (the general who initiated the Muslim conquest of Iberia in 711 AD) or nostalgic for a glorious past as the rulers of Iberia. Other contemporary Spanish texts display a fear of North African immigrants as Moors seeking to regain what was once theirs with a reconquest.[55] Flesler has astutely analyzed this phenomenon through Jacques Derrida's concept of the ghost. Flesler argues that Spaniards have received North African immigrants not as migrants but as invaders because of the ghostly traces of the medieval conquest perceived as trauma (Flesler 55–57).

González Alcantud has also used the ghost, which is a frequent trope in Spanish and Moroccan literature on Moroccan migration to Spain, to analyze the phenomenon of al-Andalus more broadly.[56] He states:

> The category of the phantasm or ghost, taken from Lacanian psychoanalysis, is completely pertinent in this regard [. . .]. The Granadan Moors, by leaving the territory progressively and under Castilian

> pressure, between 1492 and 1609, left a myth behind them: that of being a civilization that was more brilliant, tolerant, and harmonious than that of the Christian conquerors. This complex, made explicit in the compulsive desire, in and of itself, to conquer the Nasrid metropolis, created a phantasmagoria of impossible uprootedness. The ghost is the emptiness that presence leaves behind, and it is more persistent than presence itself. To combat the ghost, the activation of a new mythology, and its success, is necessary. ("El canon andaluz" 369)

This psychic need to drive away the ghosts of the past by establishing a new narrative of al-Andalus no doubt underlies the subgenre of historical novels on al-Andalus. In Spain since the last decades of the twentieth century, there has been a boom in the publication and consumption of historical novels. Within this widely distributed and popular genre, there is a sizable subset of works that are set in Islamic Iberia.[57] A common characteristic of these novels is the inclusion of texts from the Andalusi turath. The allusions to these Arabic works and citation of them within the novels, as well as the frequent use of source citations, bibliographies, and words transliterated from Arabic, give the novels an air of authenticity and authority.[58] Nonetheless, the works focus on the theme of an idealized convivencia and rarely reflect on the cultural appropriation and construction of truth in which they are involved. As Flesler indicates in reference to two of these novels, "[the] texts avoid and engage with the present of Moroccan immigration through the construction of an exoticized, imaginary past. We can thus explain the success of these types of narratives as a displacement of the anxiety—cultural, racial, religious—produced by 'the return of the Moor'" (Flesler 115). Through my focus on specific key figures in the history of Iberian-Arabo-Amazigh contact, I elucidate the ways the historical narratives about al-Andalus attempt to dispel or embrace ghostly figures and anxieties about the future.

History and Narration

This study is built on a belief in the centrality of story in which, on one hand, fictional narrative is part of the same continuum as history and, on the other hand, stories (whether they function as expressive culture and entertainment or as documented truth about the past) shape, support, and also transform dominant cultural constructs.[59] According to Geoffrey Roberts, from the 1960s to the present the core debate in the field of history has revolved around the narrative character of history (1). One branch of this debate that emerged in the 1980s, referred to as the linguistic turn in history, promotes the viewpoint that historical narratives are to a large extent literary and fictional accounts about the past. Hayden White has been a key figure in arguing that history is a textual phenomenon built on events that can be said to be objective reality but that are selected, organized, and framed within a narrative and thereby shaped by interpretation. In response to the "scientific history" of groups such as the Annales School, White foregrounded the aesthetic elements and interpretive framework that characterize historical writing. Drawing from White and others, Celia Fernández Prieto notes that "the past always arrives to us semioticized, codified, and interpreted" (179). Thus, packaging the past in a particular way reflects the realities of the present and the hopes held for the future.

Another main branch of the debate surrounding the narrative character of history draws attention to the narrative quality of human consciousness. One of the ideas that underlies White's *The Content of the Form*, which had been put forth by theorists before him, is that narrative orders and structures reality, creating meaning out of disparate experiences. In this way, narrative is the mechanism through which we shape (and reshape) our sense of individual and group identity and our conception of reality.[60] The broader postmodern turn also affected the debates among historians, giving rise to the realization that historians participate in the process of the narrative construction of the ideologies that shape lived experience. This awareness has entered literary production in the emergence of the postmodern historical novel in which alternative or counterfactual histories are presented and metafiction and anachronisms are used to invite reflection on the constructed nature of history.[61] Metafiction is a literary device that, through a variety of self-referential techniques, draws attention to a work's status as fiction, as an artifact. By self-consciously highlighting the narrative process, this device raises questions about the truth claims of history and the ways metanarratives function. Metanarratives, also known as master or grand narratives, are comprehensive accounts of historical and social meaning that serve to propagate and legitimate social and political ideals and actions. The term was developed by Jean-François Lyotard to refer to a totalizing narrative that is built on a notion of universal truth, a type of schema that is presented as universal.

Building on White, Lyotard, and others, Linda Hutcheon asserts that all postmodern fiction is historical metafiction. What Hutcheon refers to as "historiographic metafiction" questions the nature of history, narrative media's ability to represent it, and how readers interpret textual history (47–61). Echoing the concerns of many critics,

Alan Robinson points to the paradoxes and dangers of postmodernist pronouncements regarding the inaccessibility of the past. He points out that "influential claims about the ineluctable absence of the past, which are unquestioningly accepted in the context of historiographic metafiction, coexist incompatibly with discourses of spectrality, the uncanny, trauma, photographic postmemory and cultural memory, which all stress the persistent afterlife of the past" (Robinson xiii). Moreover, "the denial of historical 'truth' undermines efforts to document and contest racist, class, and gender oppression" (Robinson 27). As historians increasingly focus on the practice of writing history while maintaining an awareness of its narrative qualities and attending to the roles of social actors, scholars in literary and cultural studies need to maintain an awareness of the broader societal implications of assumptions about the (in)accessibility of the past and of other cultures.

Many works in the corpus of contemporary cultural production invoking al-Andalus respond to traditional forms of historiography, sometimes by representing in a new way a specific figure from the past who has taken on symbolic functions and other times by bringing that past into the present or into a transtemporal space. In so doing, they highlight the narrative nature of history and the power of the present over the past: the power to be found in rewriting the past. Although most of the works studied here are clearly fictional retellings, one belongs to the genre of the memoir. Rashid Nini's *Yawmiyat Muhajir Sirri* (*Diary of an Illegal Immigrant*) is a memoir in that it chronicles the portion of the author's life in which he participated in the historical (and ongoing) phenomenon of clandestine Maghrebi migration to Spain. In the continuum between fictional narrative and history, memoir is an intermediate form that displays the particularities and commonalities found along the continuum. Although memoir carries the aim or pretense of exact truth, it contains the potential for fictive elements and certainly the presence of rhetorical moves that package events, ideas, and sentiments in a particular way. That is, it displays the aesthetic features and interpretative framework of historical writing and the narrative character of human experience in general. Thus, memoir is not necessarily a factual record, but a crafted account based on lived experience. Nonetheless, the announcement of the text as a memoir lends it greater truth value and a more authoritative voice, and this aura of truth has an impact on the work's production of meaning.

Another genre whose inclusion here may be questioned is that of drama. Plays—as dramatic text and especially as theatrical performance—convey meaning in ways that are distinct from novel, short story, and memoir. They are centered on mimesis (showing) rather than diegesis (telling or narrative description), yet they still present stories. Drawing from various literary scholars, I view narration as "a communicative act in which a chain of happenings is meaningfully structured and transmitted in a particular medium and from a particular point of view" (Hühn and Sommer) and hold that narration is an integral part of dramatic works.[62] These works convey stories through genre-specific techniques and constraints. While my analyses of the plays in this corpus will concentrate on the dramatic text, I am attentive to the impact of stage directions on the production of meaning. In the case of the visual narratives offered by film and television, I address the elements of staging that create the visual image, as well as the camera work, editing, and sound elements that are part of the storytelling at hand.[63]

Irrespective of genre, in more than half of the works treated here that demonstrate a turn toward exploring the historical record as a collection of imaginative narratives, this exploration takes the form of metafiction. When used to address central figures from the hallowed past, metafictional techniques further highlight the narrativity of what is understood as historical truth or venerable legend. Rewriting the past, especially with metafictional gestures, can disrupt dominant cultural assumptions and suggest ways of reconceptualizing self and other and with these the cultural history of a given community. Whether through metafiction or other narrative strategies, the recognition of the textual nature of history enables these authors to undo received notions of individual and community identity. By presenting history as part of storytelling, these works destabilize cultural narratives—narrative constructions of identity and truth—that are the basis for the conceptions of (un)translatability that in turn hamper or encourage intercultural communication. For this reason, I conceive of these writers and filmmakers as translators of the Andalusi past, active interpreters who rewrite received tales across cultural and temporal distances.

The State of the Field and the Parameters of This Study

This study contributes to existing scholarship on contemporary Arab and Hispanic cultural production and on the legacy of Islamic Iberia more globally. Critical studies of modern literary representations of al-Andalus focus primarily on Arabic poetry or the work of Spanish Romantics. In contrast, my study focuses on narratives ranging from mass-market visual media to highbrow literary works within a comparative framework. Various scholarly works have looked at contemporary Arabic poetry that invokes al-Andalus. Many of these studies examine the poetics of loss or the mystical elements (i.e., invocations of Ibn

ʿArabi) in these works and focus on the Levant or Palestine specifically.[64] A particularly innovative approach to invocations of al-Andalus in Arabic poetry is found in Najat Rahman's *Literary Disinheritance: The Writing of Home in the Work of Mahmoud Darwish and Assia Djebar*, which advances the argument that Darwish is not engaged in a poetics of nostalgia but is using al-Andalus to reflect on new beginnings and future possibilities.[65] In Hispanic studies there are examinations of the Moor in nineteenth-century Spanish Romantic literature, especially the *novela morisca*, or novel on morisco themes, which was first developed in the sixteenth century, and Romantic poems on heroicized Arab figures.[66] In the present study, I focus exclusively on the twentieth and twenty-first centuries to appreciate the most recent manifestations—the outer limits—of the legacy of al-Andalus and consider intersections with postcoloniality. I primarily examine narrative works—whether literary fiction, feature films, or television series—and dramas for two reasons: to address works that have not received much (if any) critical attention and to investigate the relationship between received historical narratives and recent creative works with special attention to the legitimation of storytellers and the construction of truth.

There are a handful of book-length studies devoted to the topic of contemporary Arab representations of al-Andalus across genres. Most notably, Martínez Montávez's *Al-Andalus, España, en la literatura árabe contemporánea* (*al-Andalus, Spain, in Contemporary Arab Literature*, 1992) has been a crucial resource for me. I hope to build on Martínez Montávez's work by distinguishing between representations of medieval Iberia and those centered on modern Spain (and concentrating exclusively on the former), considering the postcolonial and/or gender dynamics in the texts, and juxtaposing the Arab works with relevant Hispanic texts. Ibrahim Khalil's *Zilal wa-Asda Andalusiyya fi al-Adab al-Muʿasir* (*Andalusi Shadows and Echoes in Contemporary Literature*, 2000), which has also been a valuable resource, examines various genres and also carries out comparisons with other literatures ranging from Hispanophone to Anglophone works. In the present study I aim to delve deeper into the Hispanic/Arab nexus by focusing exclusively on those corpora and treating a wider range of texts within them. The topic of al-Andalus begs for a comparative study across the languages of the cultures most closely involved. To this end, this project is trans-Mediterranean and trans-Atlantic in scope. Through this framing I seek to overcome the disciplinary barriers that have imposed a separation between the Arabophone and Francophone literatures of the Maghreb, which replicates the logic of colonialism, as well as between the different inheritors of the legacy of al-Andalus around the Mediterranean and beyond, which replicates the logic of nationalism and East/West binaries. In the spirit of the type of historiography known as connected history, I aspire to elaborate here a connected literary and cultural history of the more recent afterlife of al-Andalus.[67]

I readily acknowledge that one piece of this trans-Mediterranean and trans-Atlantic puzzle will not be addressed in this book: the perspective of contemporary Jewish writers and filmmakers on Muslim-ruled Iberia. In addition to the facts that my disciplinary training and space limitations preclude the consideration of contemporary representations of Sepharad (the Hebrew name for al-Andalus), the focus on empire and coloniality of the present study also have a role in the delimitation of my corpus. Jews were certainly a vital part of the cultural life of al-Andalus/Sepharad, and as such they too are direct inheritors of the legacy of Muslim Iberia. For this reason, Sepharad continues to operate symbolically in modern Jewish literature in more than one language.[68] However, in medieval Iberia, Jews were not primary stakeholders in empire building. Although they certainly were involved in the political maneuvers of the period, they did not participate in the establishment and maintenance of an empire defined by Jewishness in Iberia, as was the case with the Muslim and Catholic empires. Thus, the symbolic function of Sepharad in contemporary culture is not linked directly to empire building and associated nationalisms but is connected indirectly to these issues through concern with the rights of ethnoreligious minorities, the condition of diaspora, and/or Zionism. The situation of the Jews of Iberia as culturally active yet politically disenfranchised and ultimately expelled, rather than as powerbrokers, is what shapes today's uses of Sepharad in the delineation of Jewish and Israeli identities.

In order to examine a manageable corpus of Arabo-Muslim and Hispanic texts, and one that carries a high degree of cultural significance, I focus on the possibility of linguistic and cultural translation and on the translation of the past in texts that refer to specific cultural icons. Within memory studies, scholarly works on "the celebration of heroes have called attention to the importance of the representation of individuals as icons for and screens on which to project collective identity" (Olick, Vinitsky-Seroussi, and Levy 250). For this reason, I organized my study of the vast array of narratives and dramas about al-Andalus according to the figures that are most prominent and recur most frequently in the broader corpus of modern creative works on al-Andalus. Part I, "Cultural (Un)translatability and Narratives of Identity in Representations of Ibn Rushd/Averroes," centers on the medieval Cordoban polymath Ibn Rushd, known in European languages as Averroes, and foregrounds issues of translatability. Part II, "To and from al-Andalus: Migration and

Coloniality," examines figures who are known for their movement in and out of al-Andalus—the initial Muslim conqueror Tariq ibn Ziyad, the exiled last Muslim ruler Abu ʿAbd Allah or Boabdil, and modern-day immigrants—and emphasizes transcoloniality. Part III, "Florinda, Wallada, and Scheherazade, or the Women of al-Andalus and the Stories They Tell," treats representations of the two most famous women of al-Andalus and focuses on women as storytellers and al-Andalus as narrative. Each part consists of two interrelated chapters.

Chapter 1, "Borges and His Arab Interlocutors: Orientalism, Translation, and Epistemology," is a comparative analysis centered on Jorge Luis Borges's short story "La busca de Averroes" ("Averroes's Search," 1947). In it I assert that Borges's "La busca" demonstrates a problematic relationship to Orientalism and cross-cultural relations and that the responses of two early twenty-first-century short stories, Moroccan Abdelfattah Kilito's "Du balcon d'Averroès" ("Concerning Averroes's Balcony") and Iraqi Jabbar Yassin Hussin's "Yawm Bwinus Ayris" ("The Buenos Aires Day"), make Borges's search more complex and more successful. In modern Hispanic and Arab-Maghrebian literature, Ibn Rushd functions as an icon of cultural (un)translatability. I argue that what matters most is not determining whether ideas are in the abstract translatable but how and why translatability is deemed to be hampered or enabled. What are the assumptions and attitudes that underpin understandings of translatability? In Borges's story, underlying conceptualizations of reason and the radical Otherness of "the East" are what create a barrier to translatability.

My analysis of Kilito's text shows that his story, in contrast with Borges's foreclosed cultural contact, actually promotes a deromanticized openness to cultural contact. Kilito's form of cultural contact is aware of postcolonial sociopolitical hierarchies, but avoids anchoring identity in a single language. I argue that although Kilito's dream-based story presents a case of the Untranslatable—of the ironies, paradoxes, and mediations of language and the multiplicity of interpretations which spring from these—it simultaneously brings language politics into the Borges story and brings those lessons to bear on the modern Maghreb by calling for more fluid concepts of identity. Like reason, linguistic and cultural translation have epistemological limits and are intertwined with power; that doesn't mean that reasoning or translation should be eschewed but that they should be carried out with careful awareness.

Hussin's story responds to Borges's ambiguously Orientalist depiction of Ibn Rushd with a fantastic tale in which Ibn Rushd travels through time and space to meet Borges in Buenos Aires. Hussin's treatment of Ibn Rushd points to an inclusive conception of epistemology, one that embraces nonrational elements. By focusing on Ibn Rushd's imagined sensorial experience and desires, rather than only the life of a closed mind presented by Borges, Hussin responds to Borges's portrayal of Ibn Rushd as a symbol of cultural separation and inability to create meaning with an Ibn Rushd that symbolizes cultural connection and the endless possibilities of signification. The two literary responses to Borges bring in issues of postcolonial identity and assert the possibility of intercultural dialogue through other forms of signification and identity construction.

Chapter 2, "Ibn Rushd and Freedom of Expression: The Construction and Fragmentation of Identity Narratives," examines a more indirect textual dialogue between three works that portray Ibn Rushd: Egyptian Yousef Chahine's 1997 film *al-Masir* (*Destiny*), Spaniard Antonio Gala's 1985 television screenplay "Averroes," and Tunisian ʿIzz al-Din al-Madani's 2000 play *Shadharat min al-Sira al-Rushdiyya* (*Fragments from the Averroan Biography*). The three works share a concern with constraints on freedom of expression and the fashioning of narratives of identity and truth. In addition to presenting Ibn Rushd as a champion of rationalism who supports the compatibility of secularism and Islam—as a bridge-building figure to be emulated, the three works employ Ibn Rushd in different types of self-definition and help reveal the limits of narratives of cultural identity.

Chahine's *al-Masir* uses Ibn Rushd to address threats to freedom of expression in the late twentieth-century conflict between Islamists and secularists in Egypt, whereas Gala's screenplay inserts Ibn Rushd in the regional nationalism of andalucismo and decries limits on freedom of expression in the post-Franco period. Chahine's and Gala's versions of Ibn Rushd are highly translatable, in contrast with that of Borges. In fact, they are translatable to a fault because they do not problematize the identities they construct via Ibn Rushd. Chahine's unproblematized fusion of past and present in Ibn Rushd leads to the film's superficial treatment of Islamists. Similarly, Gala unequivocally accepts cultural translatabilty, positioning Averroes as manifestly Andalusian to construct a regional identity in the face of centralist Spanish nationalism and oppose the censorship of that nationalism.

Al-Madani's play, like the works of Gala and Chahine, uses Ibn Rushd to contest religious dogmatism. However, al-Madani primarily opposes dogmatism through a deconstruction of religious authority that rests on narrative-based concepts of truth. The play posits that meaning is not transparent, not easily translated, but filtered textually, and thus points to the need for critical inquiry. Whereas Chahine and Gala put censorship on trial without interrogating the representation of Islamists or al-Andalus-based andalucismo, al-Madani puts the very concepts of narrative and identity on trial. This comparison elucidates that narrative assembles truths and identities that then impinge on cultural translatability. That is, narrative constructions of identity and truth are the foundation for the conceptions of (un)translatability that hamper or encourage intercultural communication.

The Ibn Rushd–focused texts provide a framework through which to understand the discourses on al-Andalus, including the works treated in the following chapters, and intercultural contact in general. The belief in a greater degree of translatability relies on a metaphysics of presence, or a belief in the immediate access to meaning. Inversely, belief in a greater degree of untranslatability rests on the conviction that all humans can attain is limited knowledge mediated by language and cultural positioning. The challenge, which is played out in the narrative, dramatic, and filmic representations of Ibn Rushd, is how to acknowledge mediation without adopting a narrative of antagonism—a belief in an inevitable clash of cultures, how to build tolerance and equity within mediated, partial knowledge. The existence of this textual dialogue in and of itself supports the possibility of meaningful cultural contact: not a facile, idealized vision of convivencia or Muslim supremacy but a careful negotiation that considers how knowledge is constructed.

In Part II, chapters 3 and 4 and a coda delve into the core narratives of identity and truth that are part of the legacy of al-Andalus by examining three pivotal historical figures in the physical movement and power dynamics between Iberia, North Africa, and the Americas and by revealing that Arab and Hispanic cultural production links them to various migration flows from the nineteenth through twenty-first centuries. Chapter 3, "The Migration of a Hero: The Construction and Deconstruction of Tariq ibn Ziyad," centers on representations of the general of Amazigh origin who started the Muslim conquest of Iberia. Traditional representations of Tariq from the MENA region emphasize the military leader's identity as a Muslim and the glory of the Muslim empire. In the process, Tariq's probable non-Arab identity and the subjugation of the Amazigh peoples are erased. Since the mid-twentieth century, Tariq has been the topic of several dramas and narratives from the MENA region and its diaspora, including Egyptian Mahmud Taymur's *Tariq al-Andalus* (*Tariq of al-Andalus*), Syrian-Argentine Zaki Qunsul's *Tahta Sama' al-Andalus* (*Under the Skies of al-Andalus*), and Moroccan Driss Chraïbi's *Naissance à l'aube* (*Birth at Dawn*). Through my analysis of these works, I identify significant temporal and regional differences.

First, those from the middle of the twentieth century as well as the most recent one (the 2004 Egyptian miniseries *al-Tariq*) present a glorified, manly Tariq who frees the Iberians from Visigoth oppression and spreads justice. These romanticizing narratives are part of compensatory discourses about the grandeur of the Muslim empire that seek to offset the current state of the MENA region with regard to geopolitics and human security. Interestingly, though, the works written by Maghrebian writers in the 1970s and 1980s dismantle Tariq's mythic status by connecting him to other conquests in the region (the Muslim conquest of the Amazigh peoples and the French conquest of the Maghreb), deconstructing the process of the construction of historical narrative, or linking him to contemporary North African migration to Spain. By pointing to the forces that drive desperate labor migration, these works highlight the disjuncture between triumphalist narratives of the past and present social, political, and economic conditions.

While Hispanic cultural production has shown little interest in Tariq, it demonstrates a veritable obsession with Boabdil. Chapter 4, "Abu ʿAbd Allah Muhammad XII (Boabdil) and Other Migrants," examines works ranging from the 1926 novel *Zogoibi* (a nickname for Boabdil, from the Arabic for "unfortunate one") by Argentine Enrique Larreta, to the 1990 Spanish miniseries *Réquiem por Granada* (*Requiem for Granada*), to the best-selling 1990 novel *El manuscrito carmesí* (*The Crimson Manuscript*) by Gala and later historical novels. My analysis of these works finds a temporal shift from experimentation in the 1970s and 1980s to traditionalism in the 1990s and beyond parallel to that of the works on Tariq from the MENA region. The twentieth- and twenty-first-century Spanish representations of Boabdil mostly take their cue from the Romantic writers and craft the last Moorish king of Granada as a melancholic figure. Boabdil repeatedly appears as the king of sadness: a romanticized, destiny-bound figure that typically embodies the weakness of the Other and thus affirms Spanish power. Although works from the 1970s and 1980s identify with Boabdil—however problematically—as part of the cultural nationalism of Andalusia, from the 1990s and on he is once again the tragic Moor, with no questioning of the process of constructing historical narrative or of the symbolic value of Boabdil.

I clarify that the temporal differences in the works on Tariq and Boabdil are linked to specific cultural shifts related to Islamism on one hand and Spanish national identity vis-à-vis Europe and North African immigration on the other hand. Furthermore, I argue that the regional difference in attitudes toward Tariq is the result of the Maghreb's own experience of conquest by Muslim Arabs from the Arabian Peninsula and the Levant. Drawing from the enduring friction between Arab and Amazigh cultures and their modes of religious practice, Maghrebian writers disrupt the image of the idealized Tariq and thus the narrative of Muslim unity in the Golden Age of the caliphate on which the image of Tariq is based. Just as many of those contestatory works link Tariq to labor migration, the only contemporary prose works from the MENA region that represent Boabdil (*Léon l'Africain* [*Leo Africanus*] by Lebanese Amin Maalouf and *Yawmiyat Muhajir Sirri* [*Diary of an Illegal Immigrant*] by Moroccan Rashid Nini) link him to issues of migration and exile. Interestingly, while the upsurge in Maghrebi migrants is often depicted in Spain as a new Moorish conquest, one Spanish novel uses Boabdil to offer an opposite message. Boabdil (like Tariq in the Arabo-Muslim world) is also part of Spanish children's literature and one of these works, the 2010 novel *Las lágrimas de Boabdil* (*The Tears of Boabdil*) by Mercé Viana, while reiterating the pathos, uses him to normalize migration and point to the shared history of Spaniards and Maghrebi migrants via al-Andalus.[69] Thus, I argue that migration reveals the falsehoods of triumphalist narratives (whether Christian or Muslim) but can open the way to shared narratives of al-Andalus.

The coda to part II considers another border-crosser who often appears in tandem with Boabdil, was the catalyst for large-scale European conquest, and connects al-Andalus to the Americas: Christopher Columbus. I compare the representations of Columbus in late twentieth- and early twenty-first-century works from Spain, North Africa, and Syria and consider the early twenty-first-century phenomenon of US Hispanic converts to Islam and their invocations of al-Andalus. In works from the MENA region, Columbus is a lightning rod for thinking about alternatives to the trajectories of Muslim and Spanish-Catholic empire. Issues of empire are closely related to the positioning of US Hispanic converts to Islam, who refer to their conversion as a return to the religion of their forebears in al-Andalus and identify with the moriscos. The texts that address Columbus, together with the Latino "reverts," point to the connected histories that shape the present and are rewritten to attempt to transform the present and the future. By adopting a broad view of history that takes into account cross-cultural and imperial encounters, they highlight shifts between religious identifications and between the positions of colonizer and colonized—dominant power and subaltern, as well as enduring patterns of subjugation. These discourses emphasize not only the destructive capacity and ephemeralness of empire and the persistence of the disenfranchisement of immigrants from the Global South but also the possibilities for imagining and establishing new patterns and realities.

In part III, the final chapters reflect on women as an integral part of the conquest narrative by looking at issues of gender, sexuality, and narrativity. Chapter 5, "Florinda and Wallada: Subjugation, Seduction, and Textual Transformation," considers the two women most frequently associated with al-Andalus: Florinda, the legendary figure whose rape/seduction is said to have led to the Muslim conquest of Iberia, and Wallada, an eleventh-century poet who was the daughter of the penultimate Umayyid ruler of Cordoba. Within Spanish and Arab discourses, Florinda and Wallada are still portrayed in twentieth- and twenty-first-century narrative and dramatic texts. Through my analysis of works ranging from the 1903 historical novel *Fath al-Andalus* (translated as *The Conquest of Andalusia*) by Lebanese-Egyptian Jurji Zaydan to the 1970 postmodern narrative *Reivindicación del Conde don Julián* (*Count Julian*) by Spanish writer Juan Goytisolo, I find that representations of Florinda oscillate between that of a passive victim and that of a dangerous seductress. Either way, the figure of Florinda remains objectified or subjugated as the foil of a male hero.

With regard to Wallada, in Arabic-language works from the twentieth century and the early twenty-first century, she is relegated to a muted, ornamental, secondary role as the beloved of the famous poet Ibn Zaydun. In Spanish texts from the same period, she is presented as an outspoken woman, a proto-feminist, and even a butch lesbian, but even these representations that purport to present a strong (sexual) renegade silence her by imposing an Orientalist conception of sexual freedom. Nonetheless, there are two significant exceptions to this in the form of two novels that question the process of the textual construction of historical figures: Spaniard Miriam Palma Ceballos's *La huella de las ausencias: un relato sobre Walada* (*The Trace of Absences: A Tale about Walada*, 2009) and Syrian 'Abd al-Rahman Muhammad Yunus's *Wallada bint al-Mustakfi fi Fas* (*Wallada, Daughter of al-Mustakfi, in Fez*, 1997). Yunus's novel in particular offers a radical departure by creating a Wallada who time-travels to twentieth-century Fez to comment on sexual and political oppression as well as how historical figures are heroicized. These works use the mythology of al-Andalus to reflect on the mythification process itself and offer alternate narratives about al-Andalus and its women. While many of the works on Florinda and Wallada reinscribe the paradigm of al-Andalus as a subjugated or seducing woman, others critique those power dynamics, bringing to the fore the process of the discursive construction of cultural icons and the connections between sexuality and power. In this way, the works draw attention to al-Andalus as a narrative of seduction.

Chapter 6, "Scheherazade: al-Andalus as Seduction *and* as Story," further explores issues of narrativity in works that address al-Andalus more broadly: Iraqi Daisy al-Amir's 1964 short story "Qissa Andalusiyya" ("An Andalusi Tale") and Egyptian Radwa Ashour's 1995 Granada Trilogy.

While the story questions the construction of history/story and its seductive capacity, the novel trilogy gives women a creative role in the very construction of al-Andalus and Arab tradition. I assert that by focusing on the transformative power of storytelling, including storytelling as survival and al-Andalus as a narrative, these texts suggest a Scheherazade [Shahrazad] figure who recasts conceptions of gender and al-Andalus. I conclude that in Ashour's trilogy, stories—including the stories about al-Andalus—are malleable artifacts that women, as storytellers and not just the objects of narrative, can use to create equity and cultural resilience. The innovative works on the women of al-Andalus constitute an imaginative departure from both discourses of restorative nostalgia and forced exile and the versions of al-Andalus that replay East–West conquest through romantic and/or sexual relationships.

Traditionally the invocation of al-Andalus has been understood as a purely nostalgic gesture, and more recently it has been seen as a reenactment of medieval conflict. I argue that on one hand, al-Andalus is a key element in narratives of identity, and paying attention to the rhetoric and symbolism employed reveals how various types of oppression are reiterated. On the other hand, my inquiry reveals that various writers and filmmakers depart from traditional invocations of al-Andalus and creatively reinterpret the past. These reworkings of iconic figures critique various sociopolitical issues (lack of freedom of expression, dictatorial rule, gender and sexual oppression, labor migration and economic disparities, restrictive religious and nationalist ideologies, and postcolonial identity politics), imagine new migrant and gendered identities and different types of cultural integration, and point to the richness of al-Andalus as a story that can be retold. In short, these works reveal and transform the concepts of cultural, religious, and gender identity that are the foundation of traditional discourses about al-Andalus, Arabness, Maghrebi and Spanish identities, and East–West relations at large. Al-Andalus is not a fixed history of conquest and reconquest but a site of creativity, a story that can be re-created to imagine better, more tolerant futures.

PART I

Cultural (Un)translatability and Narratives of Identity in Representations of Ibn Rushd/Averroes

Al-Andalus is also Averroes.

—Jabbar Yassin Hussin (*Memorias olvidadas*)

Nothing is translatable.

[. . .]

Everything is translatable.

—Emily Apter (*The Translation Zone*)

We have not finished burying Averroes.

—Abdelfattah Kilito (*La langue d'Adam*)

In a 2006 invited lecture at the University of Guadalajara (Mexico), the Iraqi author Jabbar Yassin Hussin spoke about East–West relations through a focus on al-Andalus. After mentioning the poets Ibn Zaydun and Wallada and the musician Ziryab, Yassin Hussin declared: "al-Andalus is also Averroes" (Memorias olvidadas 38). Known in European languages as Averroes, Ibn Rushd truly has a central role in both the cultural history of al-Andalus and twentieth- and twenty-first-century discourses about Islam and East–West relations. The twelfth-century Cordoban physician, judge, and philosopher is arguably the Muslim thinker who is equally well known in Europe and the Middle East and North Africa (MENA) region. Although many readers are familiar with his appearance in the Afterlife as depicted by Dante in The Divine Comedy, Ibn Rushd also enjoys a representational afterlife in twentieth- and early twenty-first-century

Spanish, Latin American, Arab, and Maghrebi cultures. Famous for having written a commentary on Aristotle that reintroduced the latter's ideas in Europe, Averroes/Ibn Rushd is the site of discussions about the plausibility of cultural translation and the material used in various negotiations of identity.

In part I, I analyze the representations of Ibn Rushd in twentieth- and twenty-first-century narrative and dramatic works from the Hispanic and Arab worlds, understood in the broadest sense. This corpus consists of the following six works, the first three of which are the subject of chapter 1 and the remaining three the topic of chapter 2: Jorge Luis Borges's "La busca de Averroes" ("Averroes's Search," 1947), Abdelfattah Kilito's short story "Du balcon d'Averroès" ("Concerning Averroes's Balcony," 2007), Jabbar Yassin Hussin's short story "Yawm Bwinus Ayris" ("The Buenos Aires Day," 2000), Antonio Gala's television screenplay "Averroes" (1985), Yousef Chahine's film al-Masir (Destiny, 1997), and ʿIzz al-Din al-Madani's play Shadharat min al-Sira al-Rushdiyya (Fragments from the Averroan Biography, 2000). I was motivated to find and bring together this group of texts by reading Borges's "La Busca de Averroes"—meaning either, and both, "Averroes's Search" and "The Search for Averroes."[1] Borges's story and its failed search left me feeling uneasy because of its complex relationship to Orientalism, and thus I began to dig deeper into the story and look for other depictions of Ibn Rushd. Ultimately, Borges's search led me to seek the implications that this group of Averroes-centered cultural productions has for cross-cultural representation in general. I found that representations of Ibn Rushd vary greatly in terms of whether they emphasize limitations (versus potential) for meaningful contact between the realms of East versus West and religious versus secular. Similarly, they vary greatly in terms of whether they take Ibn Rushd as the stuff of narratives of identity and truth or as an impetus for deconstructing the concept of truth. My comparative analysis elucidates how questions of translatability are intertwined with Orientalism and narrative constructions of self. Ultimately I argue that narrative constructions of identity and truth are the foundation for the conceptions of (un)translatability that hamper or encourage intercultural communication. To introduce the cultural context and the broader issues at hand, I begin by addressing the place of Ibn Rushd in historical and contemporary discourses.

Ibn Rushd (1126–1198) was born in Cordoba into a family of Muslim legal scholars. He also became a *faqih*, or expert in Islamic law, but his scholarly work covered a range of topics from philosophy and theology to music theory to medicine and astronomy. Ibn Rushd's reception has also been greatly varied. In the medieval period, his work influenced thinkers from Jewish scholar and fellow Cordoban Maimonides to Christian theologian and Scholastic philosopher St. Thomas Aquinas. In Europe Ibn Rushd became most known for his commentaries on the works of Aristotle, which he read in Arabic translations produced by others. Although in the 1200s Aristotelian and Averroist teachings were banned as heretical at the University of Paris, Latin translations of Ibn Rushd's *Commentaries* reintroduced the Greek thinker to Europe and led to the creation of Scholasticism, in which Christian doctrines were analyzed through reason. Thus, Ibn Rushd is often credited with having introduced secularism into Western Europe and paving the way for the European Renaissance.

To this day, in Europe the Andalusi thinker is held up as a symbol of cross-cultural intellectual inquiry. For instance, the Rencontres d'Averroès (Averroes Encounters; also known as Encuentros Averroes and Multaqa Ibn Rushd) is an annual event inaugurated in 1994 that takes place in Marseille, with occasional coordinated events in cities such as Rabat, Beirut, Montreal, and Cordoba. The event features debates, film screenings, musical performances, and book displays meant to foment interchange between academics, journalists, writers, and artists from around the Mediterranean. The political dimensions of such invocations of Ibn Rushd are quite evident in the case of Spain's Comité Averroes (Averroes Committee). With the transition to democracy, the Spanish government sought to improve relations with Morocco. But when tensions between the countries intensified, in 1996 the Spanish government responded by convening a group of Spanish and Moroccan leaders from civil society to meet periodically and discuss barriers to mutual understanding and how they could be overcome. This group was named Comité Averroes, using the twelfth-century thinker as an icon of tolerance and shared heritage for promoting cross-cultural dialogue.[2]

In Arab and Muslim cultural spheres, although Ibn Rushd still has many detractors and positive allusions to him are not as visible on an official level, in the modern period he has come to be similarly invoked as a sign of secular reform. Ibn Rushd is held in high esteem today as a legal scholar of the Maliki school of Islamic law; however, certain strains of Islam have rejected his ideas.[3] Ibn Rushd opposed the Ashʿari theology championed by al-Ghazali by arguing that humans do have a degree of agency and that rational deduction should be part of all inquiry, including religious inquiry. The polymath promoted a reconciliation of Islamic theology with Aristotelian philosophy, arguing that religion and philosophy are not at odds but are different ways of arriving at the truth. The supporters of al-Ghazali and other Muslim thinkers of Ibn Rushd's day, as well as some Islamists of today, reject Ibn Rushd's work because of his position in support of both faith and reason.[4]

For centuries Ibn Rushd was largely marginalized in the Muslim theological and philosophical tradition, but starting in the mid-nineteenth century he was taken up again by intellectuals of the *Nahda*, or

Arab cultural revival. As thinkers such as Farah Antun (1874–1922) and Muhammad Rashid Rida (1865–1935) considered how to reconcile understandings of modernity (linked to Europe) and authenticity (linked to Arab and Islamic institutions and practices), they turned to Ibn Rushd as a model who had successfully negotiated different cultural traditions through rationalism. In this way, Ibn Rushd emerged as an icon of sought-after secularism.

Moreover, as Malek Khouri notes in his analysis of Chahine's film on the philosopher, in the Nahda movement that embraced Ibn Rushd, "discussions around the interpretation of the religious text soon expanded to include wider and even more vigorous debates around breaking away from the sanctification of language and written texts in general" (18). These trends have continued in the late twentieth and early twenty-first centuries, as Ibn Rushd has remained central to the work of Arabs and Muslims who invoke him and espouse his ideas to promote secularism and rationalism. For instance, the Ibn Rushd Fund for Freedom of Thought was founded in 1998 to support rationalism and tolerance in the Arab world, and Fawzi al-Najjar reports that in 1992 a group of Egyptian intellectuals founded the Enlightenment Society (Jamʿiyyat al-Tanwir) and used Ibn Rushd as the basis for a counterattack on Islamists.[5] Similarly, Ibn Rushd has been taken up by prominent contemporary philosophers such as Moroccan Muhammad ʿAbid al-Jabiri (1935–2010) and Egyptians Hasan Hanafi (b. 1935) and Muhammad ʿAtif al-ʿIraqi (b. 1935), who have been controversial among conservative Muslims.[6] The effort to use Ibn Rushd to promote a progressive Islam that is seen as compatible with secularism continues in the work of younger Muslim scholars.[7] Thus, as Nezar Andary puts it, "Ibn Rushd has come to represent much more than his intellectual contributions to philosophy, history, and the social sciences. Ibn Rushd, like al-Andalus itself, becomes synonymous in [. . .] contemporary Arab identity with Islamic pride, secularism, and past Arab glories in science, philosophy, and jurisprudence" (108).

All of the Arab and Maghrebi works on Ibn Rushd are connected to this phenomenon in which the scholar, although marginalized within Islamic tradition, is today invoked as a model of bridge building between the Muslim world and other cultures or of progressive Islam.[8] As a bridge figure, Ibn Rushd is a cultural translator; as a champion of progressive Islam, he embodies a spirit of critical inquiry applied to religion, one that often includes the deconstruction of textual authority. In what follows I discuss the intertwined issues of translatability, epistemology (the study of knowledge), and the construction of meaning as pertains to representations of Ibn Rushd.

CHAPTER 1

Borges and His Arab Interlocutors

Orientalism, Translation, and Epistemology

In modern Hispanic and Arab-Maghrebian literature, Ibn Rushd functions as an icon of cultural (un)translatability. The critical work of Emily Apter is helpful for delving deeper into this issue. In *The Translation Zone: A New Comparative Literature*, Apter notes that "As this book unfolded, it became clear that two opposing principles—'Nothing is translatable' and 'Everything is Translatable'—consistently emerge as poles of translation theory" (8). The goal of The Translation Zone is to study the role of translation studies in the development of the discipline of comparative literature and consider how, in an age of war and translation technologies, translation studies can be used to redefine comparative literature. In the process, Apter suggests that there is nothing fully translatable or fully untranslatable, but rather there are challenges to the definitions of language and the human subject.[1]

However, in her next book, *Against World Literature: On the Politics of Untranslatability*, Apter promotes the concept of "the untranslatable" as a means to create an alternative history of ideas that foregrounds mistranslation as a sort of creative spark in the face of dominant configurations of world literature. She notes that in the enthusiasm for promoting world literature, broad projects of anthologizing or literary criticism "fall prey inevitably to the tendency to zoom over the speed bumps of untranslatability in the rush to cover ground" (3). Against this tendency, in which world literature functions as the literary analogue to the dominant model of globalization in which Euro-American products (or Euro-American packaged products) have the greatest prestige and Euro-American financial interests have the greatest power, Apter foregrounds untranslatability. Her argument is directed at literary critics and the publishing industry and their packaging of "world literature." Although critics and avid readers of world literature may gloss over the filter and barriers of translation and assume legibility, the discourse of a "clash of civilizations" has created a general assumption of verbal translatability but *cultural* untranslatability.

In the context of enduring discourses of a clash of cultures, and specifically religion understood as culture, the opposite danger to that of a hierarchical (literary) globalization (in which meaning is assumed to be transparent across languages and cultures) is the danger of accepting culture clash as inevitable because of the assumption of incommensurability, incongruity, and untranslatability. Furthermore, this sense of incommensurability is largely one-sided: Euro-Americans (i.e., the West) tend to assume that all things "Third World" or Asian, Middle Eastern, African, and Latin American are difficult and in some cases impossible to grasp; although they question whether Euro-American ways are translatable to other parts of the world, they assume that a wholesale transference is desirable. Thus, a topic often discussed in the media is whether Western secularism, democracy, and even rationalism can be translated to Muslim cultures. I would like to assert that translatability, understood both as linguistic translation and in the broader sense of cultural commensurability, is, as Apter suggests in *The Translation Zone*, neither possible nor impossible, neither fully porous nor fully foreclosed, but an issue of degrees and emphasis. Furthermore, I argue that what matters most is not determining whether or not ideas are, in the abstract, translatable but how and why translatability is deemed to be hampered or enabled. What are the assumptions and attitudes that underpin understandings of translatability?

As I discuss further on, in Borges's Averroes story, underlying conceptualizations of reason and radical difference are what create a barrier to translatability. To varying degrees, the texts I examine here all portray a translator and the process of translation, with the works by Borges and Kilito doing so directly and that of Hussin more obliquely. Thus, they are examples of transmesis. The term *transmesis* was coined by Thomas Beebee, by fusing *translation* and *mimesis*, to refer to the representation in fiction of translators and the translation process. As explained by Beebee, who draws from the work of Susan Bassnett, the final product of the translation process usually conceals the power dynamics involved in translation's production of meaning. Beebee refers to the typically obscured zone that lies between the source text and its target language version as "the black box," the hidden space of transformation. Texts that contain transmesis offer a window onto the process and context of translation because the representation of translation "restores context, positionality, and process to translation and interrogates communication, 'national language,' and the principle of equivalence between linguistic utterances" (Beebee 10). Indeed, the three texts discussed in this chapter offer insight into both linguistic and cultural translatability.

Borges and the Orient: Searching Averroes

Although the interest of Argentine literary giant Jorge Luis Borges (1899–1986) in various facets of the Orient—from South Asia to the Arab world to Islamic mysticism and the Kabbalah—is well known, relatively little scholarly work on his writings has considered it within the context of the critical concept of Orientalism brought to the fore by Edward Said. Throughout Borges's oeuvre, his keen insights into the workings of identity construction and his deft irony dismantle many essentialisms, but as I detailed in *Between Argentines and Arabs*, certain ambiguities remain in his representations of the Arab world and Islam, and especially of Arab, Muslim, and Druze immigrants in Argentina.[2]

Compared to some of Borges's other works, the story "La busca de Averroes" can seem like a clear indictment of Orientalism *avant la lettre*. This 1947 story features a surprise twist epilogue that uses metafiction to point specifically to the construction of the Orient as a process that reveals more about the identity of the constructor than it does about the Orient. Although this story faces head-on the constructedness of the Orient and presents a meditation on the possibility of representing a historical figure from the medieval Islamic world, problematic essentialisms remain. On one hand, an Orientalist conception of Islam lingers; on the other hand, the abandonment of any hope of knowing the other—that is, of any possibility of cross-cultural contact—creates a representational and existential impasse.

Borges's story ambiguously positions Averroes as both commentator and translator of Aristotle, although the historical Ibn Rushd wrote a commentary based on another scholar's translation of Aristotle.[3] The positioning of Averroes as Aristotle's translator and not just "interpreter" (in the broader sense), allows Borges to present the issues of cultural contact through the concrete example of a troubled linguistic translation and allows for revealing transmesis. The story portrays the supposed scholar-translator as he works on a philosophical treatise and is disturbed by an unresolved question in another work in progress: his *Commentaries* on Aristotle. Ironically, as Ibn Rushd engages in the first work in a debate about whether divinity discerns only the general, species-wide laws of the universe or also those that have to do with the individual, in the second work his intellect is restricted by the principles of his specific cultural sphere. Averroes is perturbed by a philological problem in his commentary on Aristotle: the meaning of the words *tragedy* and *comedy*. As the narrator puts it: "no one in the sphere of Islam could conjecture what they meant [. . . .] These two arcane words pullulated throughout the text of the *Poetics*; it was impossible to elude them."[4] No doubt following the lead of French Orientalist Ernest Renan, whose study of Averroes Borges quotes in his epigraph, Borges bases his story on the now debunked idea that medieval Arab culture had no live, nonreligious theater.[5] Moreover, he foregrounds "the sphere of Islam," portrayed as an impermeable and isolated civilization, not taking into account the reality of Muslim societies' contact with various cultural traditions, especially in medieval Iberia.

Within this closed sphere, Averroes spends the time of the afternoon siesta writing. As he writes, he is still able to feel, as a sensation of well-being, the house that surrounds him. The uninvolved, third-person narrator, trusting in biological determinism, states that Averroes enjoys the sound of the murmuring fountain because "something in the flesh of Averroes, whose ancestors came from the Arabian deserts, was thankful for the constancy of the water."[6] Averroes has taken upon himself the project of interpreting Aristotle, and this goal arouses in the narrator both admiration and pity. The narrator describes Averroes's work in the following way: "Few things more beautiful and more pathetic are recorded in history than this Arab physician's dedication to the thoughts of a man separated from him by fourteen centuries; to the intrinsic difficulties we should add that Averroes, ignorant of Syriac and of Greek, was working with a translation of a translation" (149 [94–95]). This one sentence conveys, on one hand, the narrator's attitude of superiority toward Averroes, whom he considers equally admirable and pitiable, and, on the other hand, hints at the links between the medieval writer and the narrating writer who, centuries later and through other linguistic filters, attempts to represent his predecessor.

Dramatic irony intensifies the pathos surrounding Averroes as well as the tone of superiority. Twice he is offered the key to understanding Aristotle's puzzling terms, but he is unable to take hold of it. First, looking out from his enclosed balcony, he sees three children playing: they are acting out the roles of muezzin, minaret, and congregation. But Averroes does not take note of the small-scale theatrical performance before him. Later, he goes to dinner at the house of a Quranic scholar, Farach, and is part of a conversation in which the traveler, Abulcásim, recounts having seen a play in a theater in China. At first Farach thinks these people—the actors—that Abulcásim is describing were insane, and Abulcásim attempts to explain, to no avail, that these people were telling a story through actions and words. Farach responds: "'In that case, [. . .] twenty persons are unnecessary. One single speaker can tell anything, no matter how complicated it might be.' Everyone approved this dictum" (153 [99–100]). Among those who agree is Averroes, who does not so much as suspect that what this traveler saw is the key to those enigmatic terms *tragedy* and *comedy*.

The topic of conversation between Farach, Abulcásim, and Averroes immediately shifts to high praise for the Arabic language and differing opinions about Arabic poetry. Only at this point does Averroes take an active interest in the discussion. He defends traditional Arabic poetry against innovation using the reasoning that "'Time broadens the scope of verses and I know some which, like music, *are everything for all men*. Thus, when I was tormented years ago in Marrakesh by memories of Cordova, I took pleasure in repeating the apostrophe Abdurrahman addressed in the gardens of Ruzafa to an African palm'" (154, emphasis added [102–3]). In arguing for the universalism of classical texts, Averroes adds that the writings of the ancients and the Quran contain all poetry, and he diminishes the worth of attempts to innovate. The others listen with pleasure to this vindication of tradition. Ironically placing too much faith in the core texts of his religious and cultural tradition, as well as in the notion of universalism, later that night Averroes erroneously thinks that he has arrived at the meaning of those two troubling words: "With firm and careful calligraphy he added these lines to the manuscript: 'Aristu (Aristotle) gives the name of tragedy to panegyrics and that of comedy to satires and anathemas. Admirable tragedies and comedies abound in the pages of the Koran and in the *mohalacas* of the sanctuary" (155 [103]).[7]

In the next paragraph, the narrator, speaking from the first person for the first time and thus inserting himself in the narrative, describes Averroes looking into a mirror before going to bed. Pointing to the mediated nature of all of his knowledge about the Cordoban philosopher, the narrator states: "I do not know what his eyes saw, because no historian has ever described the forms of his face" (155 [103]). The narrator immediately continues with something about which he is certain: "I do know that he disappeared suddenly" (155 [103]). Averroes and all those people and things surrounding him in this story abruptly disappear, and it is not until the next paragraph that the reader understands why.

In the final paragraph, separated by a few spaces, the narrator explains how he decided to write about Averroes and what his objective was in doing so: "In the foregoing story, I tried to narrate the process of a defeat" (155 [103]). The narrator recounts how various historical figures that experienced failure came to his mind and how he decided that the case of someone who chose to take on a challenge that was impossible for him, but would not have been for others, was "more poetic" (155 [104]). It was then that he "remembered Averroes who, closed within the orb of Islam, could never know the meaning of the terms *tragedy* and *comedy*" (155 [104]). Then the narrator, with great situational irony, goes on to reflect on the process of narrating this story about Averroes:

> as I went along [. . .] I felt that the work was mocking me. I felt that Averroes, wanting to imagine what a drama is without ever having suspected what a theater is, was no more absurd than I, wanting to imagine Averroes with no other sources than a few fragments from Renan, Lane and Asín Palacios. I felt, on the last page, that my narration was a symbol of the man I was as I wrote it and that, in order to compose that narration, I had to be that man and, in order to be that man, I had to compose that narration, and so on to infinity. (The moment I cease to believe in him, "Averroes" disappears). (155 [104])

In one sense, we have here a poignant realization that one can never fully "know" the Other, and that in trying to do so one is likely to produce a testament to who one is at that moment. Long before the critiques of Abdel-Malek and Tibawi in the 1960s and that of Said in 1978,[8] here Borges points out that often when the Other is "represented" what is really re-presented is the self.

The narrator no longer believes in his ability to know and therefore represent the Other. However, his evaluation of what limits Averroes's insight remains unchanged, as demonstrated by the recurrence in the first-person epilogue of the phrase "encerrado en el ámbito del Islam"—enclosed or locked within the sphere of Islam. In addition, Borges's response to his realization—to stop writing about Ibn Rushd—establishes attempts at knowing the other not only as complex and slippery but as futile. By pointing to the textual mediation that is the author's only channel of access to Averroes, the story rejects the Enlightenment paradigm centered on seeing and knowledge that rests on the assumption that knowing is a transparent, unmediated process. However, it is a limited rejection. First, comprehension through vision is still crucial: the inability to see Averroes's face through reliance on the existing archive causes the tale to come to a halt. Second, the Borges figure who speaks in the final paragraph maintains his position as knowing subject because he is aware of this mediation and does not duplicate Averroes's error. Even with the limited rejection of a traditional rational-empirical epistemology, the story offers no alternative way of knowing. Borges's Averroes simply ceases to exist. Thus, in "La busca de Averroes" cross-cultural representation, rather than stereotypical or objective, is simply impossible, and any attempt at it only mocks the author. In this way, meaning about the Other emerges as not only infinitely contingent and subjective but simply unachievable.

The narrator's acknowledgment of the unknowability of self and Other posits an infinitely other Other—different cultures that are mutually unintelligible. The two poles create a hall of mirrors that reflect each other "to infinity."[9] Such a conceptualization makes any cultural translation impossible. Although it is one thing to say that our knowledge of ourselves and of others is built on mistranslated images and translations of translations and is circumscribed by our cultural environments, it is quite another to say that there is absolutely no way to craft even tentative translations and decentered representations.

Many scholarly works have examined Borges's "La busca de Averroes," with most of them arriving at a version of one of the following conclusions: language and culture are untranslatable (e.g., Daniel Balderston and John Stewart), or (mis)translation is a source of innovation (e.g., Dominique Jullien and Sergio Waisman).[10] However, none of these critical assessments notes the underlying Orientalist bias in the story. In a nutshell, the Borges figure in the story becomes enlightened regarding his limitations, but Averroes never does. The narrator and the Borges figure who speaks in the epilogue try to pick apart the process of the construction of knowledge about the Other, but ironically they remain within the unquestioned position of Western knowing subject, while the "Averroes" that they realize is only a fiction disappears before any moment of insight.

Stewart and Balderston see the story as a commentary on particularity or cultural difference. Stewart in particular latches on to the principle of linguistic relativity popularly known as the Sapir–Whorf hypothesis. This principle maintains that the structure of a language influences or even determines how its speakers conceive of the world. Stewart takes it to its furthest extent, one with a nihilistic outlook: "The short story presents us with a thesis about the intimate connection between culture and language and the ultimate futility of translation and crosscultural knowledge and comprehension" (321). As Stewart notes, "Borges anticipates many of the most celebrated epistemological and hermeneutical theories of our day" (321), but those theories do not necessarily lead to the conclusion that efforts at cross-cultural communication are pointless, and interpretations of them as such have met with a great deal of debate regarding the ethical and pragmatic implications of such a stance. Though language certainly mediates and circumscribes thought, efforts at intercultural communication need not halt; rather, they should proceed with an awareness of the complexities at hand. These complexities include essentialisms and hierarchies inherited from imperial mind-sets, that is, Orientalism. Yet Stewart accepts without question the narrative of radical difference in "La busca": "There Borges reconstructs for us a culture and an age radically different and temporally distant from our own" (320).

Concerned with the relationship between Borges and theory, Balderston argues that "La busca" tells of the impossibility of theory, of generalizing principles. As part of this, he notes that "Averroes's disappearance before the mirror signal[s] the failure of the narrator's imagination" (205). Indeed, in a sense the story demonstrates the limitations of rationalism. Borges's "La busca de Averroes" presents Ibn Rushd as the consummate rationalist whose rationalism fails him. Logical deduction does not serve this Averroes. Furthermore, the Borges figure who speaks in the epilogue is restricted to rational means of constructing meaning, but the rational approach also fails him in his quest toward an understanding of Averroes. As I explain shortly, the works by Kilito and Hussin suggest that the irrationality of dreams and the sense perceptions created by imagination are needed to complete what rational methods alone cannot attain.

In her essay on the idea of the conceptual framework in "La busca de Averroes," Dapía argues that rather than posit an unsurmountable difference between cultures, in this story Borges is commenting on the difference between Platonic and Aristotelian paradigms. That is, in Borges's view, the difference between a belief in abstract concepts and general categories as realities that order the universe versus a schema in which particular phenomena are the basis for knowledge. Although some elements of Dapía's argument have merits, overall I find it unconvincing because it downplays the Orientalism of the first part of the story and the impact of the second part, in which the narrator makes his presence—and his failure—known. Dapía is right to point to the fact that Abulcásim's description of the theatrical performance he saw in China proves that the cultures at hand are not sealed off from one another. Yet only one of the group, the one who saw it firsthand with the help of a local merchant's explanation, is able to grasp the concept of theater. Moreover, some of those assembled at this gathering consider Abulcásim to be a disbeliever. This suggests that only someone who has left Islam behind can comprehend unfamiliar cultural forms.

Jullien and Waisman consider Borges's Averroes story within the framework of translation as a creative process. Jullien observes that "La busca" exhibits an attitude toward translation that is different than that of Borges's other writings. She notes the difference between the stance Borges takes toward translation in essays such as "Las versiones homéricas" (1932) and "Los traductores de las *1001 noches*" (1936) and that which he presents in "La busca." The two essays celebrate translation and even mistranslation as a creative act that produces multiple versions, each of which is a worthy innovation. Jullien argues that, in contrast, the story about Averroes "conveys a far more paradoxical, ambiguous, and melancholy view than the triumphant cosmopolitanism prevalent in those essays" (210). In sharp contrast with his attitude toward translation in his other writings, in "La busca," instead of considering Averroes's commentary on Aristotle as an inventive version of *Poetics* that paradoxically had greater impact in Europe than correct translations of the same Greek text,[11] Borges portrays Iberian Muslim culture as a closed, dogmatic sphere and focuses on the lacunae in Averroes's scholarly work, which he describes as a case of "defeat" ("una derrota" [103]). Within Jullien's reading of the somber attitude toward cultural difference in the story, she comments on the narrator's reference to a red-haired slave who is harassed by the other slave women: "In this story of cultural miscommunication, the slave takes on a symbolic function, as her obvious physical difference (red hair) and probably cultural difference leads to rejection and persecution by the other women" (212). The story's reference to the slave is left as a loose end, an unresolved difference parallel to those between Averroes and Aristotle and between the writer figure and Averroes.

Jullien points to the fact that Borges wrote the piece on Averroes soon after World War II and suggests that the historical moment accounts for the much bleaker attitude found in this story (213–214). I would add that in Argentina, where Borges was earning his living as a cataloger in a branch of the Buenos Aires Municipal Library, Juan Perón came to power a little more than a year before the Averroes story was published. Borges had already made a public statement against fascism within Argentina when Perón was elected president in February 1946. That same year, Perón essentially fired Borges by "promoting" him from his post in the library to that of poultry inspector for the Municipal Market, a position Borges declined. Thus, the year preceding the publication of "La busca de Averroes" was one in which Borges noted the mounting fascism of his country and began to experience political harassment.

Although the historical moment may well be a key factor in the story's negative outlook, I propose that another question remains: why, at that moment and with that defeated attitude toward cross-cultural communication, did Borges choose to present his ideas via a figure from the Arab Islamic world? Given the way the Orient functions in many of his other works, I interpret the recourse to Averroes as a utilization and reinscription of the Orient as the locus of ultimate difference. In "La busca de Averroes," the Orient is not only nearly beyond the rational and the real (as is the case in "Abenjacán" as well) but it is actually outside of the limits of the knowable, of that which can be known empirically and rationally. In this text, the Oriental subject and his Other are unable to understand each other—they are each locked in their own cultural logic. Thus, as occurs in other Orient-themed texts by Borges, the Orient functions as a figure for absolute difference. Even within the setting of al-Andalus, famed for its East-West cultural contact or *convivencia*, the impermeability or untranslatability of Muslim cultures prevails.

In *Borges and Translation: The Irreverence of the Periphery*, Sergio Waisman examines various works in Borges's oeuvre—including fiction, essay, and translation—and argues that for Borges translation was a creative act in which the cultural distance of his location in the periphery (vis-à-vis Europe) allowed for irreverence and insight.[12] Here the term *periphery* requires further explanation. Among Latin American countries, Argentina in particular has a complex relationship with Europe. Argentina was a site of settler colonialism in which the indigenous population was nearly annihilated and, from the vantage point of the urban center of Buenos Aires, is often conceived of as nonexistent, other, or inferior. In addition, large-scale European immigration occurred in the late nineteenth and early twentieth centuries. For these reasons, Argentine and especially urban Buenos Aires–based identities have been built on the notion of a transplantation of European culture. The crafting of Argentine identity is a matter of negotiation between identification with the center (Europe) and promotion of a specifically Argentine culture through attention to the elements of indigenous and especially colonial-based (*criollo*) ways. Furthermore, as Waisman notes, though Borges was certainly involved in the exploration of Argentine identity and expression, his upbringing, with a British grandmother and nanny and a decade of his youth spent in Geneva and other Continental cities, was highly European (28–29). Waisman proposes, then, that the periphery "is not only geopolitical, but also—and especially for Borges—a theoretical space delineated to challenge many of our basic suppositions about translation and literature" (13). Building on this conceptualization of the periphery, Waisman contends that "Borges narrates a story of defeat, while paradoxically demonstrating the value of otherness itself. Articulated from Borges's periphery, the text seeks to account for the distances between Aristotle, Averroes, and Borges *not* by correcting or denying difference, but by engaging in highly productive processes of rereading/rewriting/mistranslating" (125).

However, Waisman's argument regarding the insights afforded by peripheral status does not hold for the specific case of "La busca de Averroes." Beatriz Sarlo's assessment of Borges's cultural position between cosmopolitanism and Argentineness is apropos here. Sarlo notes, regarding Borges's oeuvre: "there is a tension in it caused by mixing with, and feeling a nostalgia for, a European culture which can never wholly offer an alternative cultural base. At the heart of Borges' work, there lies a conflict" (3–4). In this particular story, although the tensions that Sarlo identifies and Waisman names as "Borges' periphery" lead to the contesting of some suppositions regarding translation, culture, and knowledge, those same tensions create a stumbling block for the challenging of other suppositions. If difference allows for irreverence and insight, in "La busca" that only works when the subject is positioned in an Occidental Argentina, like the narrator who reaches insight into identity construction at the end of "La busca." The narrator knows that he can only approach Averroes through the writings of other scholars, but in contrast, Averroes is convinced that he has understood Aristotle's text. For this reason, in the Borges story, Averroes—though acknowledged to be fictional—remains pathetic, and his illumination cannot even be imagined. Averroes remains culturally constrained because the authorial voice, by knowing more than Averroes, attains knowledge and thus power. The emphasis on the authority (in both meanings of the word) of the speaking subject in the final sentence of the story—"(The moment I cease to believe in him, 'Averroes' disappears.)"—makes it clear that the fictional Averroes, precisely because he is imagined as having culturally conditioned ignorance, serves as a means to attain whatever modicum of knowing power is left to the author figure.

In Ian Almond's essay on the representation of Islam in Borges's writings, he contends, with contradictory arguments, that "La busca de Averroes" represents a departure from the Orientalism of Borges's oeuvre. Almond argues that in all of Borges's texts that treat Islam, Islam is linked to failure and restriction and that in some of his works, there is also an underlying fear of Islam. He then presents "La busca de Averroes" as the final result of Borges's evolution away from Orientalist conceptions of Islam and the "East." Almond contends that "The various tones with which Borges addresses his Islamic content differs from story to story; observed and interpreted in the correct order, the dozen stories concerning Islam that Borges wrote between 1933 and 1956 show an increasing awareness of the complexities involved in writing about a collection of metaphors such as 'Islam'" (436). In this passage, Almond clearly espouses the idea that there is a "correct" (and by extension an "incorrect") order in which to read Borges's works. Here and elsewhere in his essay he uses the "correct" reading to try to establish a narrative in which this story is an end point, an arrival in a process of linear development: "It is a key moment in the evolution of Borges's relationship to the Islamic Orient, a final realization of the fictitious foundations and illusory claims of the Orientalist project" (Almond 451); "Borges's abrupt breaking-off of the tale in 'Averroes' Search' would, in this sense, be the culmination of an increasing discomfort with Orientalism in general, a 'coming clean' as it were with the impossibility of writing about that which we are not" (Almond 453). I disagree with this assessment of the story for two main reasons. First, there is not much of a coming clean because a view of the Muslim world as radically Other persists in the story's epilogue. Second, the Borges figure that appears in the epilogue is not in fact in the same position as Averroes; rather, he has enough insight to know that he cannot fully know the subject of his inquiry. This very insight, to which Averroes does not have access, allows the speaker to attain a sense of control over the radical alterity that he perceives.

Referring to the various layers of translation and textual mediation in the story (Aristotle-Averroes-Renan-Borges–the reader), Waisman asserts that "the process of translation between each of these simultaneously fails *and* succeeds; it succeeds to the extent that it is undertaken knowing that it will fail" (143). Nonetheless, at least one of the figures in the story's sequence of mediations—Averroes, marked as he is by extreme difference—does not know that he will fail. Waisman explains that the process of the search—that is, the attempt at translation—constitutes each figure's identity and refers to "the disappearance of the narrator once he ceases to think about Averroes" (144); however, it is not the narrator who disappears at the end of the story but rather Averroes because he is only a construct in the narrator's mind and is ultimately inaccessible. Waisman concludes his analysis of "La busca" by describing the hermeneutic process of the story as one characterized by "failure" but also by "opening, through rereading and mistranslation, which resists closure" (146). Yet given Averroes's exclusion from the process of insight and the awareness of failure, he is limited to closure.

As seen, since his own era Ibn Rushd has been known as a champion of rationalism, and today he is held as a model of Muslim secularism and/or progressive Islam among many Arabs and Muslims. Ironically, Borges took Ibn Rushd, or Averroes, as an example of a person tragically limited by his religious worldview and as a site for the realization that we are all circumscribed by our cultural sphere and our pursuit of self-definition. To whatever extent Borges's reflection on Ibn Rushd undoes conventional conceptions of the formation of identity and knowledge of the Orient, ultimately it also re-creates some fixed ideas about the Orient and Otherness. "La busca de Averroes" leaves the reader with a conception of the Muslim world as a nearly hermetically closed sphere—that is, as the site of ultimate difference—and without any hope of being able to connect with the Other. In sum, rather than point to the difficulties and complexities involved in contact between all cultures, the story closes any possibility of making meaning across the specific cultures and languages of "East" and "West." It posits a void in the realm of signification and particularly signification between the Arabo-Islamic and the Christian Euro-American worlds. Moreover, it places the Euro-Argentine writer (the Borges who speaks in the epilogue) in the position of the knowing subject: he becomes aware of the limits to his knowledge and cuts off his story, but retains the position of mastery in that he knows more than Averroes. The perceived radical Otherness of "the East" leads to radical untranslatability. In Borges's story, the champion of reason is not able to harness reason but lies just outside of "Western" reason. The ultimate irony of "La busca" is that while the author figure in the story is aware of the mediation of language and cultural difference, he is unaware or uncritical of Orientalist assumptions and the narratives of identity it thrives on and supports.

Ibn Rushd on His Balcony: Owning Language and Translating Identity

A short story by well-known Moroccan writer and literary critic Abdelfattah Kilito [ʿAbd al-Fattah Kilitu] (b. 1945) brings fragmented, self-conscious narrative, postcolonial language and identity politics, and the construction of meaning together with the balcony that Borges imagined for Averroes. In his 2007 story "Du balcon d'Averroès" ("Concerning Averroes's Balcony"), Kilito engages in a subtle yet clear literary dialogue with Borges's "La busca de Averroes." To begin with, the title of Kilito's story is a direct reference to the scene in Borges's story in which Averroes goes out on his balcony overlooking the street, a scene that Kilito references in the body of his story. In addition, the crafting of the narrator in Kilito's story is very Borgesian: the narrator is an unnamed "I" that speaks with the persona of Kilito and muses about an epistemological conundrum. In the case of Kilito's text, the conundrum centers on a semantically rich yet oxymoronic phrase about language that Kilito-the-narrator heard in a dream, uttered by none other than Averroes. Through various digressions and references to the retelling of dreams as a tedious story genre, the essay-like text presents the narrator's search for the meaning of the enigmatic phrase that came to him in a dream. Given that the phrase challenges concepts of ownership and belonging as related to language and that the other person who appears in the dream is Kilito's translator into Arabic, who engages in various forms of language-based identity politics, I propose that the story uses Averroes, as a representative of classical Arab philosophy and al-Andalus, to meditate on the absurdities of language and identity politics specifically in modern-day North Africa.

Since the late 1980s, there has been growing scholarly interest in the intersection between translation studies and postcolonial studies. One of the works to come out of this type of inquiry is Douglas Robinson's *Translation and Empire* (1997). Robinson points to three roles translation has had in the colonial context: instrument of conquest, notable site for cultural inequalities, and conduit for decolonization and postcolonial writing. Beebee explains the centrality of translation in colonization as follows:

> Colonization [. . .] is the largest and most visible cultural and historical surround for translation practices, and one that impels some of its subjects toward conversion through translation. Conversion is a word that—like translation—in English originally referred to a physical or somatic change (and which still does so in the case of inanimate objects, such as a house or car engine), but which also invokes a mental one, such as beliefs about the divine world and the afterlife, or indicates the exchange of one cultural mazeway for another. Translation becomes a hermeneutic exploration of the truth of conversion. (16)

Though mental conversion, or transculturation, gives way to a variety of strategies of expression, such as code switching and polyglossia, the strategy of transmesis (the representation of translation) is of particular significance. In multilingual postcolonial contexts the use of one language versus another and the ways languages are brought together are part of political and cultural power dynamics. Within such contexts, through transmesis "one can report on the subaltern language via the dominant one through translational backformation, the appearance of translators as characters, and other devices" (3–4). The "translational backformation" includes items otherwise hidden in the black box of translation such as socioeconomic power differentials.

Beebee argues that authors from postcolonial contexts have a tendency to use transmesis because it is a vehicle for postcolonial reason (16). In a process that is analogous to that of the textual translator, the postcolonial writer transfers his or her culture to other linguistic, cultural, and aesthetic norms. Thus, when representing translation in postcolonial contexts, postcolonial writers are representing not only the act of translation but also the act of cultural translation that is tantamount to postcolonial reasoning. Here Beebee draws from Gayatri Spivak's *Critique of Postcolonial Reason* (1999), in which she demonstrates that the concept of pure reason is actually built on

Eurocentrism and the historical moment of European global supremacy (Beebee 18). Kant's chief work, the *Critique of Pure Reason* (1781), sought to elucidate the relationship between reason and human experience, thus resolving conflicts between rationalist and empirical approaches. Spivak aims to show that reason is implicated in socioeconomic inequities, and yet this complicity should not lead to a rejection of reason but to constant self-critique.

Kilito's "Du balcon d'Averroès" exemplifies the roles of translation and transmesis in postcolonial contexts and in the process demonstrates both the limits of reason and the need to continue pursuing it in tandem with other forms of knowing. From the outset of the story, the narrator, a Kilito figure, indicates that he is puzzling over a phrase he heard in a dream, but he delays revealing the phrase until the fourth page. There the phrase is presented in transliterated Arabic, "loughatouna-l-a'jamiyya," along with an approximated French translation, "notre langue étrangère" (158). The phrase can be transferred into English as "our foreign language," although both of these translations lose the connotations of the Arabic *ʿajami*, which, as the narrator explains, is an archaic term that means "a stranger, one who does not speak Arabic" (158–59). In the dream, the narrator is looking out of a window onto a courtyard. Barely visible in the window to his right he senses the presence of Averroes, and in the window to the narrator's left, leaning on the ledge, he sees his translator "A. K.," whom the narrator refers to tongue-in-cheek as the person who "claims" to translate his French-language works into Arabic (160). Across from the narrator there is a closed fourth window that he says serves to add an element of mystery and perhaps menace (160).

Much of "Du balcon d'Averroès" consists of the narrator thinking through various possible interpretations of the phrase—how can a language be both foreign and part of one's own culture?—and wondering about its historical authenticity, that is, whether it was ever actually produced by Averroes. In the process of considering these issues, the narrator presents various moments in Arab history in which the phrase could have been interpreted in a certain way or a particular scholar could have written it. Ultimately the narrator points to Ibn Mansur (d. 1311), author of the foundational Arabic dictionary *Lisan al-ʿArab*, who wrote when Turkish and Persian represented a cultural threat to the Arabic language, as the more likely source of the phrase. This historical reference as well as others serve to highlight that the "threat" of other languages encroaching on Arabic has been felt since long before the French colonization of North Africa and that the judgment of others based on whether they use Arabic versus French is small-minded.

The translator figure, A. K., is a key component in Kilito's story because he embodies the type of linguistic pettiness and cultural chauvinism that the narrator critiques. With a playful, irreverent tone, the narrator describes his distaste for A. K. which stems from A. K.'s attitudes toward language and toward Kilito as a Moroccan who teaches French and writes some of his work in French. For instance, in describing the dream scene of the four windows overlooking the courtyard, the narrator states that although Averroes's phrase shakes him, Averroes's presence nearby barely perturbs him. In contrast, the narrator feels displeasure at the presence of his translator, who from now on will be "a neighbor that he must put up with all the time" (160). The translator annoys the narrator not only because he insists that Kilito himself has cited this phrase from Averroes in one of his books but because of his underlying attitudes: A. K. insists on only speaking to the narrator in Arabic, never in French, and thinks that Kilito looks down on Arabic (162). The narrator links these attitudes to Arabo-centrism when he taunts the translator for supporting the ludicrous ideas that Adam spoke Arabic and that the Arabs invented poetry (163). In short, A. K. stands for the most restrictive and even destructive aspects of identity politics, and specifically of postcolonial identity politics. Ironically, the reasoning the translator uses is actually a version of European nationalist ideology in which allegiance to a single nation is tied to allegiance to a single language. In other words, the concept of nationhood that operates in Arabist Moroccan nationalism is informed by or at least analogous to ideas from the European Enlightenment.

Language politics is a complex, if not thorny topic in Morocco.[13] As Gonzalo Fernández Parrilla explains, it is no coincidence that soon after the start of the nationalist movement in the 1930s, Moroccan intellectual ʿAbd Allah Kannun wrote the first history of Arabic literature in Morocco: *al-Nubugh al-Maghribi fil-Adab al-ʿArabi* (*Moroccan Genius in Arabic Literature*, 1938). This work, which sought to highlight the deep-rootedness of the Arabic literary tradition of Morocco and the contributions of that tradition to Arabic letters and Islam, was a key step in the establishment of a national literary canon for Morocco. For these reasons, Kannun's book, which was published under the Spanish protectorate, was deemed seditious and banned by the French colonial authorities (González Parrilla, "Breaking the Canon" 4–5). In 1956, after decades of being under French and Spanish rule, Morocco gained political independence, and an Arabization program was taken up as a reaction to the Francophone policies of the colonial regime. Questions about the place of the Amazigh languages in Morocco are on the rise and a few writers still use Spanish as their language of literary production; however since Amazigh does not have a strong literate tradition and the use of Spanish in writing has become relatively limited, the main tension in the realm of cultural production has been the choice between

French and Arabic.[14] The period of national (re)definition that followed independence was marked by an effort to establish a language-based nationalism built around Arabic and emphasizing Arab identity. For instance, during the 1960s and 1970s the Rabat-based literary magazine *Afaq* (*Horizons*, 1963–present) promoted Arabic as the language of Moroccan culture that would return the nation to its true Arab identity. This began to change through the mission of another Rabat-based literary journal: *Souffles/Anfas* (*Breaths*, 1966–1972), which sought to challenge the traditional Francophone versus Arabophone literary divide by encouraging experimentation, translations, and collaborations. The efforts to move away from the language polarization of the decolonization movement continued in the 1980s, with a change in the editorial outlook of *Afaq* and the works of writer Abdelkhebir Khatibi (1938–2009), who focused on the linguistic diversity and hybridity of Morocco. Nonetheless, certain individuals and entities maintain a more hardline approach to the relationship between language and identity in postcolonial Morocco. Kilito's oeuvre in general is concerned with these issues; in a practice that is unusual in Morocco, he writes and publishes in both Arabic and French, rather than choosing one language.

"Du balcon d'Averroès" in particular addresses the rationale and sentiments associated with the Arabization project using the space of the balcony to stage an ideological encounter. In the narrator's dream he is at a window, that is, a threshold of contact and potential change, between his conspicuously positioned, outspoken translator on one side and a shadowy Averroes on the other. In Kilito's story, more than a portrayal of Averroes, we find an invocation of him. Nonetheless, certain details are evocative and lead to the question: why place the oxymoronic phrase on Averroes's tongue? To begin with, this Averroes, like that of Borges, is faceless. But here, lack of knowledge about Averroes's face is not the catalyst for a breakdown in accessibility, as occurs in the Borges story. Instead, in a parenthetical rhetorical question Kilito lightheartedly explains this facelessness as the condition of all figures from ancient times (160). At the same time, this ambiguous figure is connected to a contemporary philosopher, one with similar Andalusi-Mediterranean cultural origins. At one point, as the narrator muses about the meaning of the phrase "our foreign language," he discusses Jacques Derrida's statements on the ownership of language and wonders if perhaps the philosopher concealed by the window isn't Averroes, but Derrida (173). By linking Averroes to a thinker associated with France in spite of his Jewish Algerian upbringing and Sephardic origins, this text uses an ambiguous Averroes to suggest an alternate map of intellectual networks that centers on a heterogeneous Mediterranean.[15] Furthermore, this presentation of Averroes as mistakable for an iconoclastic contemporary thinker contributes to the text's dismantling of the aura surrounding Averroes.

Kilito's story uses this ambiguous Averroes to critique the consecration of figures in Arab tradition and the narrative crafting of al-Andalus. The narrator jokes about his brazenness in attributing a phrase to one of the venerable ancients and says that readers must think that in his crafting of fiction, he presents the supposedly Averroan phrase as arising in a dream to diminish their anger at his insolence (166–67). In this way, Averroes is positioned as a voice of authority, but one to which Kilito cheekily attributes an "absurd" phrase (167). The narrator continues with his irreverent metafictional discussion of his inclusion of Averroes by confessing that he has not read Averroes's works and noting that neither has his indignant reader (169). He says that instead of being read, Averroes is cited as an emblem and standardbearer of al-Andalus; people mention him as part of the repertoire of figures pulled out as a "topo"—a sketch or quick review—of al-Andalus as a place of tolerance and harmony (169). Those who present these sketches seem to believe in them and to be happy and confident in their belief (169). These comments on Averroes and the *topo* of al-Andalus, offered in the context of a text that calls attention to the narrative process, point to the narrative construction of al-Andalus by those who invoke it. In Kilito's story, the constructed nature of the Andalus mythology and the characteristics with which it has been imbued are also exposed by the contrast with various historical locales, referred to through figures such as Ibn Mansur and Derrida, in which there were also a plurality of cultures and languages but which have not been fashioned by cultural myth as spaces of openness and exchange.

Kilito's text, through the narrator's comments on Borges's "La busca de Averroes," further emphasizes the connection between Averroes and language, and in the process points to the transcolonial dimensions of language. In doing so, "Du balcon d'Averroès" signals the complexities, akin to the oxymoronic phrase "our foreign language," that are often brushed aside in the crafting of a particular image of al-Andalus. Kilito-the-narrator indicates that Averroes's linguistic landscape is of great interest to him. The narrator then cites the balcony scene in Borges's text, noting the similarity between the space of the window in his dream and the space of the balcony in Borges's depiction of Averroes (174–75). Without delving into the purported limits of Averroes's capacity for insight that emerge in Borges's story, the narrator refers to Averroes's contact with nascent Spanish as he watches the children playing on the street below while speaking in a dialect of Latin. The narrator cites (in

French translation) Borges's text—"[Averroes] heard them dispute in the *vulgar* dialect, that is, in the incipient dialect of the peninsula's Moslem populace"—and wonders whether this street language might be that to which Averroes refers with the phrase "our foreign language."[16] Apparently questioning his own hypothesis, the narrator indicates that according to Borges's story, Averroes turns from the children to read a classical Arabic text (thereby missing the clue to his interpretative impasse regarding drama). This passage in Borges to which Kilito draws our attention is striking because, contrary to the expectation that proto-Spanish will be associated with the Christian community, Borges attributes it to the Muslim lower classes. Since Borges makes no further direct commentary on the language, one wonders if he is pointing to an unexpected form of transculturation whereby lower-class Muslims take on the language of the Christian subjects of al-Andalus, who are their peers in terms of socioeconomic status. Alternately, this passage may demonstrate that in Borges's vision of al-Andalus, or specifically of Averroes's perspective, Christians are not present in any form. Either way, as Kilito indicates, by immediately turning his attention to a classical Arabic text, the Borgesian Averroes rejects the language of the street in favor of the written language of power (74). Steeped in the linguistic hierarchies of al-Andalus, Borges's Averroes rejects linguistic plurality and especially the plebian Romance language that has passed from Christians to Muslims, in favor of the language that conveys Arabo-Muslim power.

Kilito subtly connects the imperial hierarchies of language present in Borges's depiction of the Andalusi scholar to his own twenty-first-century present by turning in the next paragraph to the tense relationship between Kilito-the-narrator and his translator, A. K. In what the narrator refers to as a parenthetical remark, he notes that he can see A. K. on his left, "A. K. who speaks and teaches Arabic (how to translate his initials?), while me, I am a professor of French and am supposed to write in that language" (175). This staged digression serves to suggest that the dynamics of language and power that were at play in twelfth-century Cordoba are akin to those that, through the translator A. K., trouble the Kilito persona who is navigating his position in postcolonial Morocco.

In sum, Kilito's story presents Averroes as a philosopher linked to a diverse Mediterranean intellectual sphere, as a venerated figure used to construct al-Andalus, and also as a linguistic purist (similar to A. K.) who sought the language of authority and high culture. In this way, the story does not use Averroes to give classical weight to the oxymoronic phrase but rather to question the construction of authority and of narrative, and the politics of language and identity that strive to fix origins and the relationships between self and other through language. After another hypothesis about the meaning of the enigmatic phrase and interruptions by A. K. in which he makes fun of the narrator for his disquisition, similar to the narrator in Borges's story, Kilito's narrator realizes that it is impossible to pinpoint the origin and meaning of the troubling phrase. The closing line of the story reflects this by stating that the fourth window, facing him, "dark and mysterious, remains closed" (179). On one hand, A. K. uses faulty reasoning to impose the exclusivity of Arabic. On the other hand, the Kilito figure, who retells the dream and comments on it echoing the disjointed structure of a dream, is not able to use logical deduction or empiricism to identify with certainty the source and meaning of the ambiguous phrase. Instead, via the digressive and associative logic of the dream-space Kilito's narrator is able to approximate the phrase's meaning. Through this process, near the end of the text A. K., unlike Borges's Averroes, rather than remain oblivious to the insights regarding language and identity politics, undergoes a transformation himself: letting go of his judgments regarding language use, for the first time A. K. speaks to the narrator in French.

Apter argues that in his oeuvre Kilito "formulates something like the divine right of untranslatability," and she discusses "Du balcon d'Averroès" in this vein (*Against World Literature* 254). She states that in his Averroes story Kilito "gives us a parable of the Untranslatable" and she draws parallels between the Kilito story and that of Borges (254–55). Although untranslatability certainly is an important element in Kilito's story, I argue that a more holistic reading reveals that it uses untranslatability to point to a plethora of possible translations and, in the process, to critique postcolonial identity politics. In this way, while meditating on a possibly untranslatable phrase, Kilito, in contrast with Borges's foreclosed cultural contact, actually promotes a deromanticized openness to cultural contact. Kilito's form of cultural contact is aware of sociopolitical hierarchies but avoids anchoring identity in a single language. Although the phrase on which the story centers cannot be translated exactly into French (or English), I contend that the story is not primarily about barriers to translation, but about how humans construct narratives that turn into formulations of identity that are based on attachment to a single language, and these identity narratives, in turn, are what give rise to a phrase such as "our foreign language."

Unlike in the Borges story, in Kilito's text there is no correct translation that is being missed; rather, the phrase requires a gloss when transferred to other languages, and it actually lends itself to multiple interpretations. There is no cultural barrier to meaning, simply the need for further explanation and a phrase that is oxymoronic in any language or culture. The narrator receives the phrase (or produces it in his sleep) in a language in which he is highly proficient, his "native" language, though the phrase problematizes this concept of nativeness. Kilito presents the phrase as mysterious and having a range of possible meanings (158); there is no significatory void or transcendental signified but a plethora of meaning. The phrase (initially) attributed to Averroes is not comprehensible only within a Muslim or Arabic-language sphere; it is always somewhat nonsensical, just as language and identity politics are always somewhat absurd.

In keeping with the focus on language and power that characterizes Kilito's oeuvre, this story meditates on what makes a language "ours" versus "foreign," or somehow both at once. Thus, it considers what makes French a permissible and even legitimate language for Kilito and his translator. Kilito, who has also written a substantial number of works in Arabic, chose to write this piece in French. By doing so, Kilito is able to perform many of the issues at hand and thereby foreground the power struggle between Kilito-the-narrator and his Arabic translator. Thus, while Kilito's story presents a case of the Untranslatable—of the ironies and paradoxes and mediations of language and the multiplicity of interpretations that spring from these, it simultaneously brings language politics into the Borges story and brings those lessons to bear on the modern Maghreb by calling for more fluid concepts of identity. Linguistic and cultural translation, like reason, have epistemological limits and are intertwined with power, yet that doesn't mean that reasoning or translation should be eschewed, but that they should be carried out with careful awareness.

Ibn Rushd in Buenos Aires: In Pursuit of Fluid, Multifaceted Knowledge

In the version of Ibn Rushd created by prominent Iraqi exile writer Jabbar Yassin Hussin [Jabbar Yasin/Jabbar Yasin Husayn] (b. 1954), the terms and outcome of Borges's search are inverted and Ibn Rushd carries out a more successful search for Borges. In the story "Yawm Bwinus Ayris" ("The Buenos Aires Day"), published in 2000, Hussin, who has lived in exile in France since 1976, takes the twelfth-century scholar directly to Borges.[17] Hussin uses an intertextual rewriting to respond cleverly and poetically to the issues raised by Borges's representation of Ibn Rushd, specifically to what I have described as lingering Orientalism and the foreclosure of any meaningful contact with the Other, of any translatability. Hussin creates an Ibn Rushd who champions both rationality and irrationality over religious dogma, makes contact with Borges in spite of the vast geographic and temporal distances between them, and plays with imaginative and irrational forms of knowledge as a complement to rationalism and as an incitement to try to know more.

In Nancy Berg's essay on Borges's and Hussin's paired short stories, she uses Haun Saussy's concept of the membrane text to explain their intertextual relationship. Membrane texts are classic works within a given culture that "serve as membranes through which foreign texts can be imported. By refracting new texts, the indigenous text opens new worlds and infinite possibilities" (Berg 149). Berg concludes that "Borges reveals Averroes's writing as the membrane through which Aristotle is brought into Arabic letters, and Hussin, in turn, identifies Borges's story as the membrane through which Ibn Rushd is introduced to Spanish readers, as well as to al-Andalus. Hussin's story is a riff on Aristotle, an homage to Borges, and a reclamation of Ibn Rushd" (159). In what follows I delve into the specific ways Hussin reclaims Ibn Rushd and the broader implications of his response to Borges.

There are various differences in setting and action, such as it is, between Borges's story and that of Hussin. The main differences are that Hussin's Ibn Rushd takes his afternoon nap and afterward joins Abu al-Qasim al-Ashʿari and Farah (Abulcásim Al-Asharí and Farach in "La busca") who have arrived as guests at his home. There is a preexisting conflict between al-Ashʿari and Farah, and when the conversation about al-Ashʿari's travels threatens to lead to Farah tricking al-Ashʿari into showing that he is a *kafir* (a disbeliever), Ibn Rushd refuses to be complicit. Sensing where the tense interaction is headed, Ibn Rushd wants to cite from one of his works: "We must examine everything in existence with syllogistic reasoning" (my trans. [113]).[18] However, realizing that the conflict has not yet erupted, instead of turning to rationalism, he turns to irrationality and changes the subject by recounting the dream he had while napping. Finally, annoyed by Farah's response to the dream, he stops describing it, and he and al-Ashʿari resign themselves to listening to Farah. After the two guests have left, the story closes with Ibn Rushd wishing he could recount his dream to al-Ashʿari alone and deciding to ask him the next day about a fruit he had been offered in the dream.

Before entering into the true meat of the story—that is, the dream itself and its relationship to the framework of the story—it is worth noting the difference in dynamics between al-Ashʿari, Farah, and Ibn Rushd in this story versus that of Borges. Borges presents an Ibn Rushd who is a spokesman for maintaining cultural and religious tradition. Whereas in Hussin's narrative Ibn Rushd's role in the conversation is to be a voice for rationalism to protect al-Ashʿari from accusations of being a disbeliever and ultimately to tacitly form an alliance with al-Ashʿari, the traveler accused of straying from Islam, against Farah, the rigid Quranic scholar. The most telling relationship in Hussin's text, however, is that between Ibn Rushd and Borges, but to discuss this we must turn from the physical to the mental action of the narrative.

The storyline I have outlined is actually secondary to the "action," if you will, that goes on in Ibn Rushd's head. This primarily consists of the dream itself and Ibn Rushd's recurring memory of a woman he once saw in Marrakesh. The story opens and closes with his memory of a face he often enjoys recalling: that of a woman he saw years ago when he was on his way to see the sultan in Marrakesh, who at that meeting would ask Ibn Rushd for a commentary on Aristotle. As the unveiled woman walked across the alleyway, Ibn Rushd stopped to watch her pass. The narrator notes, "the image of her face remained embedded in his memory to this very day" (113 [111]). Then the narrator asks, "What radiant face did he see?" (my trans. [111]). Here Hussin's narrator responds: "He never told us—nor did Abd al-Wahed al-Marrakeshi, who wrote a lot of stories about [Ibn Rushd]—about the image of that face" (113 [111]). This passage clearly echoes the moment in "La busca" in which the Borgesian narrator states that he does not know what Averroes saw when he stood in front of the mirror. In the case of Borges's story, the lack of information about the face—that is, the identity—of the subject of the story leads to the abrupt end of the story and the bankruptcy of attempts at representing or finding Averroes. In contrast, in Hussin's text the features of the woman's face are unknown to the "we" that includes the otherwise uninvolved narrator and the reader, but this does not impede the main character's relationship to the Marrakeshi woman. In fact, "the features of the woman's face had been imprinted in his mind for years," so much so, that when she comes to mind at the end of the story, he brushes her image aside in order to think more about a new object of desire: the exotic red fruit (my trans. [117]).

With regard to the dream, the way it begins is very suggestive. While lying in bed contemplating his mental image of the Marrakeshi woman's face, with heavy eyelids Ibn Rushd hears seagulls, then sees multicolored ocean birds that are unfamiliar to him, and after this falls asleep. The sequencing of sounds, new sights, and sleep strongly suggests that the dream is actually a vision. Although throughout the story the narrator and main character refer to the experience as a dream, this passage hints to the reader that perhaps it was something else and produces uncertainty regarding the border between wakefulness and sleep, reality and dream. Thus, from its very start, the dream implies that not only is the space between cultures traversable, but the space between sleep and wakefulness, dream and reality, and imagination and reason is also porous. Imagined sensorial experiences intermingle with reason.

After waking and joining his guests, Ibn Rushd recalls the entire dream/vision bit by bit, but he does not recount it in its entirety. Instead, much of the narrative consists of his thought process as he recalls the dream and past events and considers saying these thoughts out loud. In the dream, he travels to a new land, without getting dusty from the journey, and there, in a city called Buenos Aires, a blind man named Borges welcomes him into his home. Unlike the Averroes imagined in "La busca de Averroes" and cited by Kilito, this one does not reject the incipient Spanish of al-Andalus and has a conversation with Borges in Spanish, or *castellano* ("*bi-lahja qashtaliyya*," 115), to be precise. Borges talks with him about the classical tradition, quotes Averroes's own texts, asks him about the cause of Averroes's exile, and offers him a type of fruit he had never seen before: tomatoes. Ibn Rushd smells the strange scent of the fruit, but at that moment he is drawn away from it to Borges's question about his misfortune—his loss of the caliph's favor and exile from Cordoba.

The element that ties together Ibn Rushd's gathering with al-Ashʿari and Farah, the memory of the Marrakeshi woman, and the Buenos Aires dream, is the leitmotif of the face. Although in "La busca" the face represents a lack, an absence of markers of identity that is the catalyst for the end of that representation of Ibn Rushd; here, as witnessed by the visage of the Marrakeshi woman, faces are accessible and enduring, in spite of the vagaries of time. Yet at the same time they are not accessible to all. The narrator and reader have no access to the details of this face, and the narrator simply accepts this lack of information. Hussin's Ibn Rushd is not characterized by ignorance and enclosure in a faith-based cultural realm vis-à-vis a knowing narrator, instead he has access to knowledge that the narrator and reader do not hold.

Furthermore, in Hussin's story faces are mutable: the characters' faces fluctuate in appearance at different points. In contrast with the case of the Marrakeshi woman's face, with regard to Borges the character, not only does the text make it clear that Ibn Rushd saw Borges's face, the narrative also includes a description of what he saw. Moreover, in a melding of different personalities and then disparate times, places, and realities, Borges's face and that of the two guests in Cordoba come to resemble each other. As the guests are enjoying hearing about the dream, Ibn Rushd notices that "the contours of their faces appeared similar in spite of their difference in appearance" (my trans. [115]). The dream-vision has such a transformative effect that even these adversaries come to look alike. Furthermore, as Ibn Rushd looks at their faces, he notices that "Abu al-Qasim al-Ashʿari's clean-shaven face reminded him of the features of his companion in the city of the dream. So he continued" (my trans. [115]). The resemblance encourages him to go on to recount more details about his Buenos Aires interlocutor. Earlier the narrator describes al-Ashʿari's face only partially, but he tells us that it shines in the light of the lantern, and thus, through him, the reader is given a sense of the appearance of all three of Ibn Rushd's interlocutors while also teased with the message that there are details that Ibn Rushd knows but we do not. In this way, in Hussin's reworking of "La busca," faces and the identities that they represent are partially accessible and open to transformation; that is, partial knowledge and fluid identities are part of reality—such as it is.

In a related intertextual reference, the redheaded servant who appears in Borges's story as the victim of the dark-haired servants in a conflict about which the master of the house, Averroes, does not (yet) know, appears transformed in Hussin's story. In "La busca" the redhead has two symbolic functions. On one hand, given her strife with those of different appearance, she represents difference as a source of discord. On the other hand, she symbolizes that which, like the concept of theater, the Cordoban scholar does not know, that which he fails to perceive in his surroundings. In contrast, in Hussin's text she is an untroubled, undifferentiated source of inspiration. She is an "offstage voice" only glimpsed by Ibn Rushd once, but heard or mentioned by him four times. Unlike her initial version in Borges's story, she is not a victim but is linked to beauty and inspiration. She sings the same song as Wallada, the famous eleventh-century Cordoban poetess, and her singing and calls are interwoven with Ibn Rushd's dreams and thoughts. Far from symbolizing oppressed difference and hidden strife, here she represents a constant that carries variation within it. Her voice always reappears, but each time in a new way. This movement and vigor inspire Ibn Rushd to pursue his desires. After leaving aside the image of the Marrakeshi woman to think about the tomato, Ibn Rushd's mind wanders again to other details of the dream. But in the last lines of the story, the redheaded servant's call for dinner is an impetus for Ibn Rushd to make up his mind. Upon hearing her voice, he smiles and resolves to ask al-Ashʿari about the tomato the very next day.

Berg points out that the recurring references to the woman from Marrakech that Ibn Rushd remembers creates or intensifies "an undercurrent of eroticism" in Hussin's story; similarly, tomatoes are associated with eros (157–58). The repeated moments in which Hussin's Ibn Rushd recalls the sight of the woman from Marrakech and the smell of the tomato create a dynamic tension with rationalism. In Hussin's version, the Cordoban philosopher uses not only reason but also remembered and imagined sensory experience to know about the world. This melding of rational and nonrational epistemologies is analogous to another feature of Hussin's text: the mixture of written (supposedly rational) and oral (supposedly nonrational) modes. Berg astutely notes that "Borges's piece highlights textuality." In contrast,

> The textual and the oral are further entwined in Hussin's story. The epigraph taken from Borges's story establishes the textuality of the piece as much as its intertextuality. But the protagonist here is not depicted in the act of writing, nor are the physical texts present in concrete form. His manuscript is referred to only in its absence, when Ibn Rushd wants to tell his friends about it, to recite from it. The books that are mentioned are in his dream, in Borges's home. Even the written stories of the historian ʿAbd al-Wāḥid al-Marrākishī are referred to as absence, the narrator reporting what they do not say. [. . .] These images suggest a written text, but in each case, the use of text is metaphorical or fantastical.
>
> Orality—and especially the oral roots of the Arabic literary tradition—seems to dominate Hussin's story, in which characters recite ancient poetry, quote Ibn Rushd's work, sing songs of the eleventh-century poet Wallādah, and recite from the Qurʾān. Again, the Qurʾān—bolstered by many of the above examples—destabilizes the oral-written binary by the paradox of it being the written document of an oral recitation. (Berg 153–54)

In addition to demonstrating the porous boundaries between dream and reality, and imagination and reason, Hussin's story highlights the confluence of orality and literacy. Moreover, Berg's comments have led me to note that in Hussin's story, not only is the protagonist never depicted in the act of writing, he is never depicted in the act of translating.

Perhaps in an effort to rectify Borges's ahistorical presentation of Ibn Rushd as both commentator and translator of Aristotle, or to shift attention to broader, figurative conceptions of translation, in Hussin's text there is no mention of Ibn Rushd as a translator. In fact, the only reference to the two terms that are the central axis of Borges's story of mistranslation—tragedy and comedy—and possible oblique reference to Ibn Rushd as a translator occurs in the epigraph to the story (109). Interestingly, this epigraph, in which Ibn Rushd's interpretation of the two troublesome terms appears more as a commentary than a translation, is itself a case of mistranslation or miscitation. Hussin uses as his epigraph a short passage that is attributed to a text by Borges and evokes the moment near the end of "La busca" in which Averroes writes down what he deems to be the meanings of *tragedy* and *comedy*. The epigraph certainly does not re-create the meaning of that passage in "La busca." First, as Jarrar indicates in her notes to the English translation, this epigraph adds a term of negation and changes a phrase found in the Borges story, such that Averroes, after (mis)identifying tragedy as panegyric and comedy as invective (rather than indicate that panegyrics and invectives abound in the Quran and the pre-Islamic poems known as Muʿallaqat), states that in the Quran and in "the sacred texts" there is no place for the sorcery of panegyric/tragedy or invective/comedy. In addition, in Hussin's pseudo-citation from Borges, the text in which Ibn Rushd glosses these terms is identified as his refutation of the ideas of al-Ghazali (Tahafut al-Tahafut), not his commentary on Aristotle, as occurs in Borges's story and in Ibn Rushd's manuscripts. As Berg points out: "From the literary standpoint, which version is accurate [i.e., which the historical Ibn Rushd wrote] is inconsequential [. . .] Within the reading of [Hussin's] story as such, it is less important to know whether Ibn Rushd finds tragedy and comedy in the Qur'ān and other sacred literature or not, than it is to see the slippage between the two versions and to see it as part of the conversation" (155). Within the context of the Borges-Hussin conversation, the discrepancy between the Spanish original and the Arabic translation seems to confirm Borges's stance regarding East–West translation. Or does it?

One can conjecture that the Arabic translator either misread the passage because it did not fit within his cultural schema, or he purposely changed the meaning to dissimulate (what he perceived as) Borges's misconception and/or to make the story more acceptable and accessible to Arabic readers. However, this mistranslation is not present in the one Arabic translation of Borges's "La busca de Averroes" that I have found, which is titled "Bahth Ibn Rushd" ("The Search of Ibn Rushd"). In that published translation, the Spanish original is followed closely. Furthermore, the title cited as the source of Hussin's epigraph is not "Bahth Ibn Rushd."[19] Instead Hussin's epigraph is labeled as coming from "Mihnat Ibn Rushd" ("The Ordeal/Misfortune of Ibn Rushd"), from the volume *El Aleph*, with Borges as author. Why does the epigraph cite this apocryphal source that presents a version/mistranslation of a passage from Borges's story? Did Hussin misremember the title and passage, or did he purposely create a new version of the story or a new text altogether? To what end? Given Hussin's statements elsewhere about the importance of cultural contact through translation, it does not seem likely that he intends to make a point about the impossibility of translation that would echo Borges's message.[20] Rather I submit that the miscitation is a testament to the fluidity of ideas, if not due to the vagaries of memory. What is important for Hussin's story is not the exact reproduction of the details of Borges's text but the idea that Borges wrote about Ibn Rushd writing about Aristotle. Borges tried, unsuccessfully, to access Ibn Rushd through the logic of writing, whereas Hussin's Ibn Rushd was successful in making contact with

Borges through the interstices of literacy and orality and the conjoining of reason and a sensory experience that exceeds the limits of reason.

This leads us to another point related to the particular fusion of the oral and the written that Berg traces in Hussin's story. This fusion is also a merging of the episteme of logic and that of sensory experience. Derrida's critique of the unwarranted logocentrism of the European metaphysical tradition notwithstanding, there is a long-held assumption that the ability to reason is linked to the ability to write. The history of imperial encounters between literate societies and those that were illiterate, or literate in different ways, bears testimony to this pairing of the ability to reason and writing.[21] During the Renaissance and Enlightenment, the codification of writing in grammars was understood as the disciplining or civilizing of oral language. Writing was established as a way to impose and display reason and cultures without (alphabetic) writing were deemed to have a lack of rationality. Since at least the 1960s many linguists and anthropologists have used the indeterminate concept of abstraction (or a culturally specific definition of logic) to point to differences in cognitive capacity between oral and literate societies. To avoid this radical distinction and claims of cognitive superiority, J. Peter Denny has emphasized that there are no differences in cognitive capabilities across cultures, only differences in cognitive habits, patterns of thought that become automatic. Furthermore, he establishes that current research does not support the common belief that literate cultures are more abstract, complex, or logical than oral cultures. By interweaving oral and written forms in the way that he does, Hussin calls into question the separation between orality and literacy on which conceptions of primitiveness and civilization are built.

In addition, Hussin's melding of the oral and the literate brings to the fore the mediation of language in the construction of meaning. In Derrida's critique of the privileging of speech in the European philosophical tradition, he glosses over the differences between written and oral discourse as part of his aim of deconstructing European philosophy's fixation on the "presence" of the spoken word. Derrida is not concerned with modes of discourse, but with linguistic signification in general, with the constant mediation of language. His critical project centers on the idea that the Western philosophical tradition's definition of "thought" relies on the repression of writing, because writing puts on display thought's dependence on signification. Rather than acknowledge dependence on signification, this tradition has focused on "presence"—essence or thought existing outside of language and outside of the mediation of signs. Hussin's story, through its at times fantastic merging of orality and literacy, highlights the mediation of experience through signs, while maintaining a desire to attempt to construct meaning. One example of the melding of orality and literacy is the culmination of Ibn Rushd's conversation with Borges in which Borges, immediately after offering him a red fruit the Cordoban had never seen before, asks Ibn Rushd about the cause of his exile. Ibn Rushd responds by recounting a dangerous miscommunication that occurred due to the transference of a scribe's stutter to the written page.[22]

Ibn Rushd's recounting of the unfortunate episode with the scribe is yet another instance of storytelling, and stories within stories—or metafiction, in "Yawm Bwinus Ayris." Berg observes that it is "as much a story about memory—of what happened, and of what did not, or could not, happen—as about narration (e.g. rāwiyah, yaqūlu, ḥakā), and sensation (e.g. samiʿa, shaʿara, naẓara, shamma)" (158). Indeed, the narration reflects Ibn Rushd's consciousness and the senses steer much of the narration. Hussin's Ibn Rushd is constituted by mind as well as by body, and the senses are what fuel his interest in learning about the tomato. In Hussin's story, Ibn Rushd takes on a role similar to that of the narrator in Borges's story in that Ibn Rushd has an illusory experience (in Hussin's text, a dream). However, in Hussin's text, though Ibn Rushd's retelling of the dream is interrupted by Farah's impertinent questions and Ibn Rushd cuts his retelling short, later he decides to continue exploring the alternate reality of his dream. Moreover, Hussin's Ibn Rushd is driven to learn about and comprehend his new object of desire, the tomato, because of its aroma and his curiosity about its taste. Where reason would lead to a significatory aporia, openness to the sensorial knowledge offered by the dream, and the hope of an explicative story from his friend al-Ashʿari, who has traveled to distant lands, promise to satisfy his desire for knowledge.

"Yawm Bwinus Ayris" closes with this shift from the face and voice that Ibn Rushd knows so well to the unknown fruit (the tomato) and his desire to know about its taste. The Marrakeshi woman, the redheaded servant, and the tomato are all beautiful, enticing, and not fully known to the reader in the first two cases and to the character in the third. But in all instances, there are points of contact even when the object of desire is not fully knowable. In and of itself, the not implausible idea that Borges and Ibn Rushd (time travel permitting) could dialogue through a common language (Spanish/proto-Spanish Romance) is in stark contrast to the barriers to contact that Borges posits. In contrast with "La busca," which ends with a hall of mirrors that reflects unknowability and defeat into infinity, Hussin's narrative is built on the idea of the possibility of cultural translatability and ends with the enticing possibility of knowing, even outside of the rationality of space and time, even if only partially and subject to transformation.

When we consider that Hussin is a political exile, and when he wrote the story had not been to his native Iraq for almost three decades, we can appreciate that, like Borges, Hussin also uses the figure of Ibn Rushd to reflect on his own identity.[23] In "Yawm Bwinus Ayris," the identification between Ibn Rushd and Hussin is based on the common situation of exile.[24] This mirroring of author and main character reveals that this story is not only a response to Borges's treatment of Averroes but also a meditation on exile. This reflection produces a conception of exile that includes both a sense of estrangement and the opportunity for new discovery. Overall, Hussin's story points to the space in between dream and reality, lost home and current exile, past and present, fiction and truth, what is thought and what is uttered, and what is seen and smelled but not tasted in order to tell us that the borders between the two can be porous and permeable. Often, we cannot grasp with certainty even concrete reality, but we can know the pursuit of reality, the desire to know—the desire to taste the tomato.

Al-Musawi's comments on intertextuality, within his work on the postcolonial Arabic novel, can help clarify the effect of Hussin's story. Building on the work of Sabry Hafez, who in turn draws from Barthes and Kristeva, al-Musawi argues that

> Intertextuality is a contested space mapped in terms of transgressive or initiative strategies of identity, difference, and transculturation. Hence is the pertinence of the premise to literary postcoloniality. While it remains a tenable marker of patterns of assimilation, acculturation, or transculturation, intertextuality, insofar as it involves recollection, classification, and choice, is never innocent. As long as there is an agent, there is a choice, which is overtly or implicitly informed by some site or other. (175–76)

While Borges writes from a periphery (albeit one strongly identified with Europe), this leads to the opportunity to playfully contest the center and also the possibility of echoing the controlling discourses of the center, as seen in his relationship to Orientalism. The choices that Hussin makes in rewriting Borges's Averroes have the effect of stripping off the Orientalist filters and thereby removing Ibn Rushd from the sphere of radical alterity and consummate unknown. This allows Hussin to use Ibn Rushd to open up the conception of representation as a closed, barren circuit and offer the desire to know more, the desire to taste new fruit, via multiple forms of knowledge. Hussin responds to Borges's ambiguously Orientalist depiction of Ibn Rushd with a fantastic story in which Ibn Rushd travels through time and space to meet Borges in Buenos Aires. By focusing on Ibn Rushd's imagined sensorial experience and desires, rather than only the life of a closed mind presented by

Borges, Hussin's story responds to Borges's portrayal of Ibn Rushd as a symbol of cultural separation and inability to create meaning with an Ibn Rushd that symbolizes cultural connection and the endless possibilities of signification.

* * *

For Borges, Ibn Rushd is a symbol of cultural separation and significatory void, whereas for Kilito he is associated with endless possibilities of signification. For Hussin, the same figure is a symbol of cultural connection and a broad conception of epistemology (one that includes nonrational elements). Kilito and Hussin, in works that directly address that of Borges, take up issues of postcolonial identity and assert the possibility of intercultural dialogue through other forms of signification and identity construction. Hussin in particular creates an Ibn Rushd who is able to make contact with Borges in spite of the vast geographic and temporal distances between them. Hussin's Ibn Rushd not only champions rationality over dogmatism but carries out a fantastic journey to meet Borges in Buenos Aires and thus demonstrates how creativity and inquisitiveness can build cultural bridges.

Significantly, both Hussin and Kilito's texts center on dreams—the space of the irrational par excellence—and the effort to convey them to others beyond the dream state. Thus, in terms of the specific details mentioned above as well as their overall narrative thrust, these works interweave different epistemologies. In this way, they counter the entrenched belief that there is only one valid system of knowledge—that which is based on the rationalism of Euro-American science and technology.[25] At the same time, these works do not fall into a rejection of rationalism, which itself leads to a host of problems. Kassab (233–35, 337) and Hassan (49–52), among others, point to the pitfalls of the trend toward anti-Enlightenment theories that promote nonrationalism and nonuniversalism. Poststructuralism, by emphasizing the mediation of language and anti-essentialism, and certain strands of postcolonial theory rely on an assumption that transcultural communication is impossible because meaning is ultimately inaccessible. The result of this has been "that the 'non-Western' Other remains inaccessible and unknowable" (Hassan 51). Instead, in the texts by Hussin and Kilito, Euro-American reason is no longer the privileged producer of knowledge but is interwoven with nonrational ways of knowing. Thus, Hussin and Kilito respond to Borges by establishing epistemological plurality and the possibility of knowing beyond cultural boundaries.

The disjuncture between Borges and his Arab interlocutors—that is, their radically different assessments and responses regarding the same scholar—in and of itself could support Borges's stance in "La busca" regarding intercultural communication. However, hope springs eternal. After the moment of critical insight into Orientalism and despondent concession of defeat in the face of cross-cultural representation that "La busca de Averroes" represents, Borges went on to represent the Other many times. Although Ian Almond positions "La busca de Averroes" as a point of culmination with regard to the treatment of Islam in Borges's oeuvre, this body of work does not form a linear evolution. Rather, the many versions of Borges and Borgesian writing that follow the story on Averroes spiral out to display a multitude of attitudes toward the Arab or Muslim Other, some of them even more Orientalist than the piece on Averroes. My point is not to call attention to the recurrence of Orientalism even after the limited critical epiphany found in "La busca de Averroes." Instead, I seek to highlight the fact that Borges did recover from the despondence regarding representation that the figure of Averroes inspired in him. Even if he did fall into the same representational traps again, he endeavored to make more direct contact. In fact, his desire to better understand the culture that had so often sparked his creativity led him to spend his last days studying Arabic.

In 1986, Borges, at the age of eighty-seven, already blind for a few decades and dying of lung cancer in Switzerland, spent the last weeks of his life taking Arabic lessons from an Egyptian tutor (Tornielli, D'Amico). With his physical condition making the odds of him attaining any proficiency extremely low, it must have been the playful dynamism that Borges found in the act of translation, and in writing in general, that motivated him to try to connect across cultural and linguistic distances, distances as far as those successfully traveled by Ibn Rushd himself in Hussin's text. Moreover, D'Amico reports that the Egyptian tutor was overcome with emotion when he saw who would be his student. The tutor, who immediately recognized Borges, had read all of his works in French translation. Clearly, for the tutor translation had been successful in creating some form of connection. Certainly without translation Kilito and Hussin would not have had access to Borges. Indeed, the textual dialogue that these translations facilitated and inspired (starting from Ibn Rushd's translation/commentary of Aristotle) supports the possibility of meaningful intercultural contact. Although Borges's text reveals the underlying assumptions that create notions of untranslatability, together with those by Kilito and Hussin it offers hope that attention to how knowledge is created and transferred can lead to fruitful dialogue.

CHAPTER 2

Ibn Rushd and Freedom of Expression

The Construction and Fragmentation of Identity Narratives

The type of dialogue that occurs between the works by Borges, Kilito, and Hussin occurs in a more indirect fashion between three works from Egypt, Spain, and Tunisia. In chapter 2, I examine these three versions of Ibn Rushd that, though quite heterogeneous, have in common a concern with restrictions on freedom of expression and the crafting of narratives of identity and truth. The three works—a feature film, a television screenplay, and an avant-garde play—hold up Ibn Rushd as a champion of rationalism who supports the compatibility of secularism and Islam, that is, as a bridge-building figure to be emulated. Moreover, the works employ Ibn Rushd in different types of self-definition and help reveal the limits of narratives of cultural identity.

Egyptian Yousef Chahine's 1997 film *al-Masir* (*Destiny*) uses Ibn Rushd to address threats to freedom of expression in the late twentieth-century conflict between Islamists and secularists in Egypt. Spaniard Antonio Gala's 1985 TV screenplay "Averroes," while bearing many similarities to Chahine's work, takes us into issues of Spain's regional nationalisms and limits on freedom of expression in the post-Franco period. Chahine's and Gala's versions of Ibn Rushd, in contrast with that of Borges, are highly translatable. In fact, they are translatable to a fault. Tunisian ʿIzz al-Din al-Madani's 2000 play *Shadharat min al-Sira al-Rushdiyya*, like the works of Gala and Chahine, uses Ibn Rushd to contest religious dogmatism. However, al-Madani does this primarily through a deconstruction of religious authority that rests on narrative-based concepts of truth. Although Gala and Chahine do not problematize the identities that they construct via Ibn Rushd, al-Madani posits that meaning is not transparent, not easily translated, but filtered textually, and thus points to the need for critical inquiry.

Ibn Rushd at the Movies: Freedom of Expression and a Mythical, Manichean al-Andalus

Although various critical works have analyzed the representation of Ibn Rushd and Islamists and extremism in *al-Masir*, none have considered it within the context of other representations of Ibn Rushd.[1] This film by renowned director Youssef Chahine (1926–2008), who was born in Egypt to a Melkite Catholic family of Lebanese origin, uses the figure of Ibn Rushd to transmit a different message from that of Borges.[2] Whereas Borges at worst depicts Averroes as a dogmatic, even chauvinistic Muslim (given his conception of the Quran as a text that contains all literary forms, including tragedy and comedy), and at best considers the Andalusi scholar an unknowable entity, Chahine takes a completely different approach. Chahine's Ibn Rushd is not a pathetic or culturally/religiously constricted figure who is part of an East–West impasse but a highly accessible figure who faces an impasse between liberal "lovers of life" and dogmatic despots—and comes out victorious. Nonetheless, the construction of this version of Ibn Rushd, which mirrors Chahine's position as a liberal intellectual, in contrast with demonized Islamists, creates a Manichean view of both al-Andalus and contemporary Egypt.

Participating partially in the romanticizing, celebratory visions of al-Andalus as the pinnacle of Arab civilization, Chahine creates a figure who is in close contact with people from a variety of cultures and religions, is accused by the dogmatic dominant powers of the time of being heretical or anti-Islamic, and is freely rounded out and humanized by various fictional secondary elements that demonstrate his joie de vivre. *Al-Masir*, using elements of the musical, Hollywood camp, and adventure movies, portrays Ibn Rushd and his personal and political situation in twelfth-century al-Andalus to make a statement against late twentieth-century religious fundamentalism and a statement in favor of freedom of interpretation and expression, as well as intercultural contact. Although the film does not present al-Andalus as a utopian space, it does present a romanticized vision of Muslims, Christians, Gypsies, commoners, and intellectuals living in harmony and uniting against their common enemy, the Islamists. With abundant music, dance, and laughter in a street café, and Ibn Rushd's participation in these gatherings, as Nezar Andary points out, the film turns al-Andalus into a site of carnival (130–31).[3]

Moreover, the film presents Ibn Rushd as an ideal intellectual. Andary notes that it depicts how the "public intellectual mediates between the people, the state, and conservative religious forces" (118). In this way, in the context of the rising influence of Islamist groups that started in the mid-1980s, the film responds to the situation of Chahine and other intellectuals in Egypt and beyond by presenting Ibn Rushd as a model of the triumphant liberal intellectual.

Chahine's film begins in southern France with the Christian Inquisition burning a man at the stake for translating Ibn Rushd's works into Latin and closes with a mirrored scene in which Muslim leaders burn Ibn Rushd's texts in Cordoba. The narrative link between the pyres is the French translator's son, Joseph, who escapes to go to Cordoba and study under Ibn Rushd. There he finds a climate in which Caliph al-Mansur (the third Almohad caliph, Sultan Abu Yusuf Ya'qub al-Mansur, c. 1160–1199) is turning on Ibn Rushd because of the caliph's political reliance on a Muslim fundamentalist sect that is against individual interpretation (*ijtihad*). The caliph ultimately orders the exile of Ibn Rushd and the burning of his books. However, Ibn Rushd is able to leave Cordoba joyfully, even throwing the last book into the fire himself, because he knows that copies of his writings have reached safe haven abroad. The film ends with the following message appearing on screen: "Ideas have wings, no one can stop their flight." The mirroring effect of the two pyres reflects violent religious dogmatism in both Christianity and Islam and moreover demonstrates the ways ideas can fly far from their point of origin—whether in the form of a son (Joseph) who continues his father's cross-cultural scholarly pursuit or in the form of manuscripts reaching scholars abroad. That which escapes the fires—Joseph and the manuscripts—embodies ideas as a source of hope, not futility.

In addition to the fires that create a neat opening and closing structure for the film, there is another mirroring element that resembles that used by Borges in "La busca," but with a significant difference. Similar to the way in which Borges (or at least the narratorial and authorial persona that speaks at the end of the story) establishes himself as a double, a mirror image, of Averroes, *al-Masir* subtly suggests parallels between the Christian Egyptian filmmaker and the Muslim Andalusi scholar. Chahine and Ibn Rushd arise as reflections of each other through the similarity of their circumstances and a few anachronistic details within the film. The situation in which Ibn Rushd finds himself in the film is akin to the situation in which Chahine had found himself a few years before *al-Masir*'s release in the wake of his previous film *al-Muhajir* (*The Emigrant*, 1994). *Al-Muhajir* depicts the story of Joseph, an important figure in the biblical Book of Genesis who also appears in the Quran and is revered as a prophet in Islam. The film met with strong protest from Islamic groups objecting to the visual representation of a prophet; several weeks after its release the movie was banned and Chahine was sued for producing this representation. It took a year for

Chahine to successfully defend his film and have it return to theaters, where, as Malek Khouri indicates (15), it became a huge success as the highest-grossing film by Chahine up to that point.

Unfortunately, Chahine's trial was not an isolated incident. Islamist groups in Egypt and elsewhere were targeting other intellectuals during that same period. In 1992 Egyptian writer and activist Farag Foda was assassinated by Muslim extremists. In 1994, one week before the trial on *al-Muhajir* was going to begin, extremists attempted to assassinate Nobel Prize–winning Egyptian author Naguib Mahfouz and ended up seriously wounding him in the neck. These events are reflected in *al-Masir* in the Islamists' two attacks on the Gypsy singer Marwan, who is first stabbed in the neck to keep him from singing and then is killed. Thus Chahine's trial and these related events led to his interest in the figure of Ibn Rushd. Indeed, Chahine began the production of *al-Masir* about a year and a half after his trial, and he used the name of the main character of the contested film, Joseph, as the name of a key character in *al-Masir*—the son of the French translator who is instrumental in taking Averroes's work abroad. In addition, the film, through its portrayal of al-Mansur cynically using the Islamists only to have this backfire, can be understood to offer a commentary on parallel relationships between the state and fundamentalist movements in modern-day Egypt, namely, that of President Anwar Sadat fomenting Islamist attacks on leftist university students during the 1970s. Thus, *al-Masir* not only criticizes religious fundamentalisms in general and governments that attempt to exploit them, it also comments on cases of censorship or assault of Egyptian intellectuals in particular and, among these cases, reflects the director's own experience with challenges to freedom of expression.

In addition to the film's anti-Islamist storyline, there are two anachronistic elements of Chahine's film version of Ibn Rushd that function to tie the story, set entirely in the twelfth century, to contemporary life. First, the film presents twelfth-century Andalusi Arabs speaking in present-day Egyptian colloquial Arabic. Although since the late 1980s many historical films have been made in the Middle East and North Africa (MENA) region, they are typically produced in the standardized, formal register of Arabic (*fusha*) and not in a regional, colloquial dialect. In the case of *al-Masir*, almost the entire film is in Egyptian colloquial Arabic. This is done at least partly because of market considerations, but the strong aural element also serves to make the message easily applicable to contemporary Egyptian life. (I return to other dimensions of the use of the colloquial below.) Second, in the final scene, when Ibn Rushd himself throws the last book into the pyre, he throws a volume that looks much more like a twentieth-century printed tome than like a twelfth-century hand-bound manuscript. This closing visual key works to bring home the allegory to the late twentieth-century cultural and political climate. In addition, Andary notes that "the cinematic space divides and conquers the Islamists by long shots, penetrating zooms, and telescopic pans" (Andary 124). The anachronistic details and the camera work, together with the situation presented in the narrative, reflect the victory of two figures at once—Ibn Rushd and Chahine. Both are able to triumph over those who sought to shut down their production of meaning, including their narratives about figures from the past: Aristotle and the prophet Joseph. Thus, through *al-Masir* Chahine defines himself as a liberal Arab intellectual and announces his triumph over censorship. His personal victory became quite salient when Chahine was acknowledged at the 1997 Cannes Film Festival with the Palme d'Or fiftieth anniversary Lifetime Achievement Award.

On one hand, Chahine's film highlights the heterogeneity and secularism within the Arabic-speaking world; on the other hand, it creates a caricature-like image of the Islamist. Outside of the MENA region in particular, the film serves to undo Orientalist attitudes. Khouri explains this anti-Orientalist effect convincingly: "For an audience that is unfamiliar with Arab culture and history the film brings to light references that have been long absented by 'Orientalist' discourse on Arabs and the Arab world. As such Chahine's film counteracts perceptions that allege a long-standing historical clash between, on the one hand, a Western civilization that is [a] beacon of secular and rational discourse and, on the other, an Arab/Muslim culture that is inherently irrational, fanatical, violent and anti-progress" (12). Many of these moments in which expectations are overturned send a message to viewers outside and inside Egypt. For instance, Garay Menicucci points out the symbolic value of the film depicting Ibn Rushd's threatened manuscripts finding refuge in Egypt (34). This not only disrupts views of Egypt from the outside as a place of intolerance since time immemorial, but reminds Egyptians, both Islamists and secularists, that Egypt was once a safe haven for intellectual inquiry. For audiences inside and outside the Arab and Muslim world, this focus on diversity and secularism presents "the struggle against religious fundamentalism also as a struggle for reviving a heterogeneous Arab identity and unity" (Khouri 17).

Khouri links this plural Arab identity to the use of colloquial Arabic in the film and the nineteenth- and early twentieth-century *Nahda* movement's attention to the modernization of the Arabic language. In reference to the film's use of colloquial language, Khouri asserts that "on the ideological level this also represents a break from the monopoly of presenting history through the mediation of high and inadvertently sanctified text (i.e., through classical Arabic)" (22). Writers of the Nahda movement helped separate Arabic from its religious associations as the language of the Quran and thus promoted nonsectarian, nationalist identities. In this way, "Chahine's use of more popular and popularized tools to address his subject denotes continuity in the endeavor initiated in mid-19th and early 20th centuries by Arab modernists. [*Al-Masir*] juxtaposes contemporary colloquial Arabic 'against' the official history of the period" (Khouri 22). Although the rest of Khouri's argument becomes opaque, this assertion is sound: the use of the colloquial to treat a high-culture, historical topic distances Arabic from religious connotations and emphasizes secular conceptions of Arab and Egyptian identity.

Nevertheless, as more than one critic has indicated, the representation of Islamists that *al-Masir* offers is quite schematic and flat. Andary describes this representation as creating an image of "the Sufi, homoerotic, alien, cultish world of the Islamist" (124). "Al-Andalus allows Chahine to remove the Islamists from their present spaces and recreate them as a separate ethnicity. Al-Andalus allows the Islamist to become an Other to a superior liberal and secular Arabo-Islamic world. The Islamist is mystical, primitive, and simple-minded, and yet the most worldly accomplished liar and manipulator" (Andary 125). J. Gugler comments on the resulting binary as follows: "Chahine adopts a Manichean perspective of good liberals against evil fundamentalists. [. . .] The simplistic characterization of fundamentalists is matched by a refusal to consider their appeal"—that is, the issues that lead young people to join different types of Islamist groups (257). Andary astutely explains that "al-Andalus allows for this binary because Chahine can erase references to state economic policies, immigration, and other conflicts" (Andary 124). Thus, ironically, in the process of using Ibn Rushd and al-Andalus to address late twentieth-century conflicts between competing constructions of Muslim, secular, Arab, and Egyptian identities, the recourse to an earlier period facilitates a simplistic depiction of Islamists.

The essentializing depiction of Islamists, by erasing the social issues of postcoloniality and late modernity that are part of the Islamist phenomenon, enables Ibn Rushd to serve as a conduit for modern-day secularism. But his translatability—the ways he carries twentieth-century characteristics and thus is accessible to audiences—erases the nuances that can serve to find common ground and reach solutions to the Islamism/secularism conflict. For this reason, although Khouri argues that in *al-Masir* "Chahine forges an inter-textuality which links the past, the present and the possibilities for future change: a sort of cultural memory" (22), I contend that *al-Masir*'s depiction of Islamists greatly hampers the film's potential for motivating change. In this film and elsewhere, Chahine has made his belief in the possibility of contact across culture and time periods clear. In an interview after the release of *al-Masir*, he stated: "Knowledge knows no boundaries. It travels from one country to another via sharing. [. . .] Without memory, we are doomed to repeat the mistakes of the past, which have sometimes led humanity to its worst excesses" (Fargeon 48). However, the unproblematized transfer between twentieth-century Egypt and twelfth-century Cordoba leads to blind spots in the film that limit its potential.

In sum, on one hand, despite a similarity with regard to mirroring techniques, Chahine's depiction of Ibn Rushd is a far cry from the representation of Ibn Rushd found in Borges's "La busca." While Borges's Ibn Rushd is a traditionalist Muslim, isolated in a cultural bubble, who is nonetheless known to be an enigma by the Western narrator, Chahine's Ibn Rushd is an unorthodox thinker whose ideas were contested by literalist Islam, who was friends with Iberian Gypsies and Christians, and whose life history can elucidate contemporary lives. On the other hand, Chahine's Ibn Rushd narrative is quite different from those of Kilito and Hussin. In its treatment of Islamists, it does not account for layers of complexity and generally does not recognize the need for careful negotiation between that which is translatable and that which is not. Chahine's Ibn Rushd is able to transcend the limitations of language (translation into French and across registers of Arabic), space, and time and is used to defend freedom of expression. Yet this Ibn Rushd is so translatable precisely because he is created through contrast with a narrative of identity that is essentialist.

Ibn Rushd on the Small Screen: Seeking Intellectual Freedom through a Mythical Andalus/cía

The last two texts about Ibn Rushd that I discuss are striking because they converge on the scene of his trial, yet display a sharp divergence with regard to their underlying concepts of narrative and identity.[4] The first of the pair is "Averroes," an episode of the TV series *Paisaje con figuras* (*Landscape with Figures*) that was produced and aired by the Spanish public broadcasting company RTVE (Corporación de Radio y Televisión Española) during two periods between 1976 and 1985, the first of which was interrupted by censorship.[5] The scripts for both periods of the series were written by best-selling Spanish author Antonio Gala (b. 1930) and were published in book form immediately after the end of the series.[6] Gala is a somewhat controversial figure due to his bisexuality, his anti-Jewish sentiment, and the sometimes negative reception of his work by literary critics.[7] Nonetheless, his essays, poems, novels, plays, and screenplays have proven very popular among a broad Spanish audience. A key part of Gala's theatrical persona and his abundant oeuvre is his strong identification as Andalusian.[8] Gala's promotion of his Andalusian identity has led one critic to quip that "Gala acts as a professional Andalusian [*Gala oficia de andaluz de profesión*]" (Fanjul, "Divulgación" 305). Certainly, his projection of *andalucismo*, the cultural and political movement I detailed in the introduction, is central to his portrait of Ibn Rushd/Averroes.

The series *Paisaje con figuras* consists of thirty-minute episodes presented by Gala that portray a Spanish historical figure at a key moment in his or her life. The fact that Averroes is included among the dramatized biographies of "relevant figures from Spanish history" (as stated by RTVE) reflects the Spanish attitude toward al-Andalus when the show was made.[9] This conception of Spanish history embraces, or rather uncritically appropriates, al-Andalus as a culture of Hispano-Arab fusion—with an emphasis on the Hispanic element—that was part of Spain's national history. Gala's introduction to "Averroes" reflects this understanding of al-Andalus by stating: "Averroes is the culmination of the Arabo-Spanish philosophical movement and, the beginning, on the one hand, of the definitive death of Arab philosophy, and, on the other hand, of the advent of Latin Scholasticism. Averroes opens the way for the European science that arises from the continuous contact of the Christian kingdoms with Spanish Islam" (*Paisaje andaluz con figuras* 133). Given that here Averroes arises from what Gala anachronistically names an "Arabo-Spanish" philosophy movement and "Spanish Islam," as the historical figure marks the close of Arab philosophy and the burgeoning of European knowledge, with this introduction Gala clearly claims Averroes as more Spanish than Arab or Muslim.

Gala wrote his "Averroes" script when Spain, as a result of the restoration of democracy, was sorting out its relationship to the rest of Europe and global powers. A latecomer to NATO and the European Union, Spain hesitantly integrated into the EU and simultaneously experienced a rise in North African immigration that stirred up the issue of its "Arab past" and its relationship to Europe. At the same time, in the postdictatorship period andalucismo was burgeoning along with the other regional nationalisms of Spain. In the case of andalucismo, though, the movement largely consisted of a celebratory identification of the characteristics of Andalusian culture that were deemed to come from its Andalusi heritage. Gala's Averroes text presents one iteration of the strategic use of al-Andalus within andalucismo. In this TV screenplay, al-Andalus is used to create an Andalusian regional identity in order to oppose the imposition of centralized Spanish unity and to critique related postdictatorship government censorship. Alberto Egea Fernández-Montesinos argues that Gala's works create a horizontal, rather than centralized and hierarchical, nationalism (59) that is an alternative to exclusionary nationalism (66–67). However, Egea Fernández-Montesinos does not recognize the problematic aspects of Gala's andalucismo. In the process of crafting an Andalusian character whose enduring essence is its heterogeneity, Gala ignores the power dynamics inherent in cultural hybridity and the narrative dynamics that underlie representations of Averroes and representations of Andalusia. In "Averroes," Gala presents the philosopher on the day of his trial, occasionally looking back at key moments in his life, and then saying good-bye to his beloved Cordoba before going into exile. The introduction states: "[Averroes] personalizes the forever present Andalusian attitude [*actitud andaluza*]: the reception, imitation, and emanation of cultures. [. . .] Averroes, here, is the man of reason, the eternal questioner and the eternally unsatisfied; he is the constant figure of the lucid intellectual oppressed by a society that maintains a distance from anything that is not part of its own petty ambitions" (133–34). Thus from the outset it is clear that this Averroes embodies two main messages: (1) Cordoba and Andalusia are intrinsically tolerant spaces of cultural convergence, and (2) then and now, intellectuals are embattled with the oppression of those who aspire to power. Note that here al-Andalus and Andalusia are conflated under the name of the modern autonomous region of Spain and the same occurs, in the voice of Averroes, throughout the dramatic text. The slippage between al-Andalus/Andalusia is what makes the messages possible by making Averroes Andalusian, rather than Andalusi, and thus creating not only historical continuity but a complete identification between eras and cultural formations separated by about 500 years.The drama supports this fusion of time periods visually by having Averroes walk though Cordoba "crossing paths with common people from today," as indicated by the stage directions (135). The script begins with Averroes walking though Cordoba and speaking to his city about its wonderful characteristics, including people of balanced temperament (135). In this way, Cordoba is personified as his interlocutor and thus given greater weight as the legendary site of civilization and tolerance. Averroes explains that this equilibrium is reflected in the skin color and hair of the "Andalusians," which is a sort of middle ground between those of Arabia, Africa, and the Nordic countries (136). The text suggests a racial fusion without going into how this might have come about—what power dynamics might have been at play—and creates a myth of ethnic homogeneity in the region that is reflected in a supposedly uniform physiognomy.

After stating that he wants to become part of the Andalusian soil when he dies (136) and making a reference to his compassion toward "the exiled Andalusians [*los andaluces desterrados*—literarily: deterritorialized]" (137), which could be interpreted as a reference to those exiled by the civil war and Francoism and/or the Andalusian economic migrants, Averroes enters the mosque where he will be tried. The religious leaders who support the ruling Almohad caliphate accuse Averroes of impiety, heterodoxy, and putting philosophy before theology. As Averroes tries to explain his position that religion and science are not at odds (146), a central interchange takes place that reveals the ties between the text and Andalusian nationalism:

> 9TH VOICE: You declared that there is no tyranny worse that that of the ulama or theologians.
>
> 2ND VOICE: And that the army is the protector of the people, not its owner.
>
> AVERROES: Those statements must be understood in the midst of the context that surrounded them. I am a philosopher. It seems to me that religious intransigence is a mistake. I am an Andalusian [*Soy un andaluz*] . . .
>
> 2ND VOICE: (Interrupting) He is proclaiming Andalusian nationality [*la nacionalidad andaluza*] before the Almohad Empire.
>
> AVERROES: I'm not proclaiming anything. I'm saying that Andalusia [*Andalucía*] has a vast tradition of civilization and wisdom. It cannot be governed like other countries with a less distinctive character. Andalusia [*Andalucía*] has always conquered its conquerors.
>
> VARIOUS VOICES: What more do you want to hear. Let's go to the Sultan. (147)

As part of his argumentation, Averroes states that he is "Andalusian," and this phrase incites the ire of one of the accusers, who sees it as a proclamation of "Andalusian nationality" that challenges the Almohad regime. Averroes's response side steps the idea of a proclamation of nationality while insisting that Andalusia has a unique tradition and marked character. He sums this up with the rich yet enigmatic phrase, "Andalusia has always conquered its conquerors." Given the generality of the phrase and the fusion of time periods in the text, it could refer to various specific conquerors, from the Romans to Tariq ibn Ziyad to the Almohads to the Catholic Monarchs to Franco's Nationalist troops. Moreover, through this phrase that evokes the multiple layers of transcoloniality, Averroes asserts that in any and all of these cases Andalusia has maintained its particular character and imposed it on its would-be conquerors. This sentiment lends strong support to the *andalucista* cause. By equating Averroes with Cordoba, Cordoba with al-Andalus, and al-Andalus with Andalusia and insisting on its enduring essential character as a space of tolerance and cultural blending, Gala uses Averroes to craft a regional Andalusian identity, separate from the nationalist Spanish identity. Yet he does so without questioning the workings of this identity politics.

The interchange regarding Andalusian nationalism is immediately followed by one of the accusing voices making a reference to intellectuals:

> 6TH VOICE: Intellectuals are individualists and opposed to the State
> AVERROES: That's not so [. . .]
> 7TH VOICE: What is it that legitimates power?
> AVERROES: Honesty, wisdom, and prudence. (147–48)

The discussion continues with Averroes's accusers interpreting his comments as a challenge to the Almohad authorities. At this moment of heightened tension, Averroes recalls a day when he was working on his translation of Aristotle during the time of the afternoon siesta, a setting that is reminiscent of Borges's Averroes story. In Gala's work, instead of Averroes not understanding the terms Aristotle uses, he doesn't understand the implications of the poem that he hears Aben Guzmán [Ibn Quzman] recite through the window.[10] When he looks back from the moment of the trial, though, Averroes understands that the poem was a reference to his impending banishment. Indeed, he is brought back to the present of the trial by the declaration that he has been convicted (150). Gala's "Averroes" ends with the momentary loss of Cordoban tolerance: Averroes's books are burned as he bids farewell to Cordoba, lamenting that he must leave and be buried elsewhere but certain that the city's tolerance will return (151–52). The closing, then, frames Averroes as an exiled intellectual and Cordoba, as well as Andalusia at large, as the site that must carry on the legacy of tolerance (152).

Through its concern with freedom of expression and the scriptwriter's own experience of censorship, Gala's portrayal of Averroes is similar to the portrayal by Chahine. In 1976, during the initial period of the transition to democracy, the airing of the TV series *Paisaje con figuras* was halted for several months by order of the Spanish government. The order was a reaction to the third episode of the series, which had incited furor among certain sectors in Spain. That episode, which was devoted to the fifteenth- to sixteenth-century Spanish Basque explorer Juan Sebastián Elcano, included a scene in which Elcano recites the "Our Father" in Basque (or Euskera). The prayer in Basque was deemed supportive of the Basque national liberation movement, which had intensified its violent struggle during the transition to democracy, and an affront to Spanish national unity, which is largely based on promoting Castilian as the national language ("Antonio Gala publica"). As author, Gala was indicted and the issue escalated to the point where he received death threats. This incident no doubt led him to present Averroes, in the second period of the series, as a symbol of the oppressed intellectual struggling against the censorship of the state. Although the closing scene of Chahine's film is more uplifting with its message about the enduring power of ideas, the works of both Gala and Chahine focus on Ibn Rushd as an intellectual embattled with censorship. They use Ibn Rushd/Averroes and al-Andalus to promote freedom of expression and tolerance.

Whereas Chahine's film draws clear parallels between al-Andalus and twentieth-century Egypt, Gala's piece goes so far as to erase the historical specificities of al-Andalus versus Andalusia and casts the merged entity as the source of a blended culture that is identical with that of today's Andalusia. As a result, in strong contrast with Borges's Averroes, but similar to Chahine's, Gala's Averroes is completely knowable, to a fault. Kilito and Hussin connect Ibn Rushd to the many possibilities of translation and signification, yet they maintain an awareness of the challenges inherent in capturing and conveying meaning through language and story. Unlike these works, Gala's script assumes the transparency of language and meaning as well as the unproblematic identification with Averroes as an Andalusian. For Gala, there is nothing about Averroes that is inaccessible because he is not a Muslim Other, but rather, unquestionably *andaluz*.

Ibn Rushd on Stage: Putting Narratives of Identity on Trial

The last text I examine in part I, and the second text to focus on the moment of Ibn Rushd's trial, is the drama *Shadharat min al-Sira al-Rushdiyya* by the Tunisian ʿIzz al-Din al-Madani (b. 1938), author of novels, short stories, and most notably plays and a leading figure of the Tunisian avant-garde.[11] In spite of the common focus on the trial's process of questioning and debate, the works by Gala and al-Madani are paradigmatically different in their approach to language and the construction of meaning. Al-Madani uses Ibn Rushd to question the construction of truth in religious tradition and in narrative, which are tied together through the hadith, the corpus of accounts of the words, deeds, and teachings of the Prophet Muhammad. Other techniques employed in the theater piece are strategic anachronisms and a fragmentation of the narrative and scenes that reflects the fragmentation of seamless truth.

This iconoclastic, absurdist play can be understood as a response to the sociopolitical context in which it was written: the Zine El Abidine Ben Ali regime (1987–2011) in Tunisia. Ben Ali succeeded Habib Bourguiba, who was revered as a symbol of anticolonial resistance (given his role as a leader in the independence movement and as the country's first president) and a modernizer, but who was also an authoritarian who stamped out pan-Arabism and any form of opposition. Although Ben Ali initially seemed to seek a more democratic political process and greater freedom of the press, his regime soon came to be known for its corruption and repression. Al-Madani's theater piece emerges, then, as a commentary on the monopoly on truth exerted by authoritarianism—whether religious or secular. But unlike Gala's work, which decries authoritarianism by asserting another narrative of identity presented as indisputable truth, al-Madani uses Ibn Rushd to question all such narratives.

Al-Madani's play is largely made up of alternating and at times intersecting scenes featuring the discussions among a group of narrators and the discussions between Sultan al-Mansur, the sultan's vizier, and Ibn Rushd.[12] The piece's humorous, absurdist quality is created through sarcasm and wit (often used by Ibn Rushd to debate his opponents), word play, and scenes featuring talking donkeys and a conversation among the gates of Cordoba. In this work, al-Madani plays with the overlap in meaning between hadith understood as "prophetic traditions" and hadith meaning narrative in general or a rambling tale in particular. Throughout, the work makes use of metafictional techniques to draw attention to the process of narrative construction.

Al-Madani's play is divided into parts (*abwab*) and, rather than scenes, these parts are divided into "narrations" (*riwayat*). This nomenclature together with the troupe of narrators creates a multiplicity of contested narratives. Like Gala and Chahine, al-Madani presents a critique of unjust rulers, but rather than have Ibn Rushd defend himself against Voices that represent Islamic jurists, as seen in Gala's piece, al-Madani highlights the relationship between narrativity and power by having a group of narrators challenge Ibn Rushd and accounts about him. The dramatis personae include a head narrator, Shaykh al-Ruwa, and a group of five other narrators. The name used for the head narrator—a shaykh or man of (religious) authority—brings to the fore the double meaning of "narrator" in the work. Here *narrator* refers to someone who relates a story and someone who relates a saying or deed of the prophet, and thus becomes part of the transmission and legitimation of the saying or deed.

The hadith of the prophet were first passed down orally and hence the chain of transmission, that is, the *isnad* (chain of narrators who reported the specific hadith) is important in determining legitimacy. In the eighth and ninth centuries the hadith were written down and evaluated for authenticity. Some of the various classifications are *sahih* (sound, correct) for those deemed authentic and *mawduʿ* (fabricated) for those deemed inauthentic. The hadith categorized at the highest levels of authenticity are used as sources in the interpretation of the Quran and in Islamic law. The narrators in al-Madani's *Shadharat* provide comic relief but also raise questions about the narrative process as they point to the legitimation of narrative and thus the intertwined construction of narrative and truth.

The play opens with the narrators and Shaykh al-Ruwa utters the opening line: "bi-smi Allah al-rahman al-rahim" ("In the name of God, the Most Gracious, the Most Merciful"). This phrase (known as the *bismillah*) is the opening of the Quran recited by Muslims before almost all *suras* (chapters) of the Quran and in other contexts to consecrate what follows. In *Shadharat*, the bismillah leads into a recitation of isnad for hadith of the prophet (9). Nonetheless, the titles of the two opening scenes prepare the way for the questioning of narrative-based religious authority that follows. The first scene is titled "Opening [*Istiftah*]" but it ends abruptly and is followed by a scene titled "Correction to the Opening [*Istidrak ʿala al-Istiftah*]." The titles of the scenes themselves point to the instability of meaning: rather than a final, fixed authoritative decision, there is an ongoing process of challenging and refining meaning.

In the first scene the Shaykh of the Narrators and four narrators discuss verified or legitimated hadith, but at the start of the "correction" scene, the Fifth Narrator arrives and claims to have a hadith that is not in either of the two most definitive compendiums (10).[13] The Fourth Narrator asks the Fifth Narrator to explain this hadith's isnad and the Shaykh of the Narrators encourages him to speak by saying that he is before "experts in narrative successions [*salasil al-ruwa*]" (10–11). Other narrators chime in that they are experts on the circulation of texts, on their conditions, and their context (11). However, the Fifth Narrator proposes postponing his presentation of the chain of transmission until after they have eaten (12). During the scene of "The Narrators' Banquet," they discuss the problem of apostate philosophers (16–17) and divide up the choicest pieces of meat according to the hierarchy of the group, with the Fifth Narrator receiving the hooves (18). Their interactions point to hierarchies and petty conflicts within sites of power. This dismantling of traditional sites of power is underscored by the Fifth Narrator's recitation of the aforementioned hadith. After the meal, when the Fifth Narrator finally presents his hadith, it is a rejected hadith that ends with the phrase "He who dies in love will have a reward equal to martyrdom" (19).[14] This is a profane version of traditional formulas regarding how religious merit tantamount to that of martyrdom can be earned through other deeds or suffering. Although the statement could be understood to refer to love for God, the cited source of the hadith precludes this. The compendium in which the hadith appears indicates that it was narrated by the Abbasid poet Abu Nuwas, famous for writing verse about all things forbidden, thereby linking this hadith to blasphemy and irreverence.[15] In al-Madani's play, upon uttering this dubious (if not sacrilegious) phrase the Fifth Narrator flees to escape the reaction of the other narrators. The Fifth Narrator represents rebellion against a system of knowledge and truth that is based on narrative, which by definition is carried out by humans, with all of their desires—both lofty and base—and all of their foibles.

The next scenes consist of discussions between Ibn Rushd, the sultan, and his vizier in which the philosopher opposes the sultan's policies (in particular his new decrees that oppress Jews), defends Christians' right to carry out a religious procession, and criticizes unjust regimes. This leads to a debate on the concept of tolerance (35). Later the work includes anachronistic references to extremism (66) and democracy and secularism (68). Thus, like Chahine's and Gala's works, al-Madani's criticizes unjust rulers in a way that brings the criticism from the twelfth century into the present of the creation and reception of the work. In al-Madani's case, however, this is done with humorous touches that make the sultan a ridiculous figure.

Although the titles and content of the first two scenes create a sense of doubt and equivocation, these opening scenes are followed by part 1 (al-Bab al-Awal), whose title promises much certainty: "The Undoubted News [*al-Khabr al-Yaqin*] about the Caliph" (21). This turns out to be only apparent or momentary certainty. For in the second "narration," or scene, of part 1, the head narrator returns and addresses the audience telling them that the preceding scene was created by lying narrators (31). During that scene and the next (part 1, narrations 2 and 3) Shaykh al-Ruwa turns everything upside down, pointing out the inaccuracies and historical inconsistencies in the previous scene between Ibn Rushd and the sultan. His comments destabilize the narrative by pushing the viewer/reader to question the narrative, to be an active viewer/reader and thus a participant in the building of the narrative. The head narrator disrupts the narrative further when, in the midst of the ongoing political discussions between the sultan, his vizier, and Ibn Rushd, the head narrator addresses the sultan, offering to find support for the sultan's positions in religious texts (37). Although the sultan responds by telling him to shut up, the head narrator speaks anyway, wondering how to silence Ibn Rushd and declaring that he will do so through the Quran and the hadith (38). Ultimately Ibn Rushd is accused of immorality and apostasy (48), and these scenes reveal that Shaykh al-Ruwa himself is an unreliable narrator. Although he accuses others of narrating falsehoods, he manipulates the body of prophetic narratives to silence Ibn Rushd and his quest for justice and tolerance.

The group of narrators in *Shadharat* is further ridiculed and discredited in subsequent scenes. The first scene in part 3 features four speaking donkeys that represent the four traditional narrators. As the donkeys transport Ibn Rushd, they talk about the fate of the "judge of judges," and the scene ends with the fourth donkey giving a mock isnad (78). Later the narrators question Ibn Rushd's neighbors and associates as character witnesses, but these witnesses all say great things about him (79). In spite of this, the narrators find a way to accuse Ibn Rushd of wrongdoing (80). These scenes are part of the message that those who decide on legitimacy and correctness—and thus truth—are often incorrect themselves. This idea is presented again in the last scene of part 3: the *faqih* who questions Ibn Rushd's readiness (*tahara* and *wudu'* or ritual purity and ablution) for prayer turns out to be corrupt (99). Ibn Rushd wants to teach the people in the mosque, but they follow the faqih's lead and reject him as an apostate and a nonbeliever, even going so far as to deny that he is Cordoban or Arab (99–103). Thus, corrupt and unreliable narrators question the accounts about Ibn Rushd's identity and reject his right to narrate or construct his own identity.

The sense of fragmentation is emphasized by the last act of the play, part 4, which starts with various short scenes performed simultaneously and depicting a post-Averroan Cordoba in which Ibn Rushd is rejected, creativity is challenged, and the only interest in learning and inquiry comes from Christians. In the first "narration" of part 4, the conversation among the gates of Cordoba reveals more about the image of Ibn Rushd that was created among the people of the city. The talking gates use rhyming word play to complain about the woes of the common people under the sultan and demonstrate that the merchants blame their problems on Ibn Rushd and all philosophers, though they were caused by the sultan (108). Thus, Ibn Rushd becomes a scapegoat. In one of the parallel scenes, the profligate Cordoban poet Ibn Quzman has a run-in with an official and defends his importance as a creative power (114–20) and "the Sultan of letters and words" (119).[16] Meanwhile, in another parallel scene, there is a lack of interest in books and thus in the realm of knowledge, demonstrated by a man who wants to buy books by weight not to read them but to decorate his palace and by the contraband status of Ibn Rushd's works (125–31).

After the set of simultaneous scenes, the drama presents the state of philosophy through a conversation between Ibn Rushd and his former student. Even the student doesn't appreciate Ibn Rushd: he complains that he didn't teach him anything useful, that he only taught him about Aristotle (141). Ibn Rushd replies that Aristotle is the one who taught him how to search for the truth (142); nonetheless the student says he'll leave philosophy and join the jurists [*fuqaha'*] to avoid problems with the sultan (143). The former student declares that philosophy has ended and so has al-Andalus, but Ibn Rushd responds that philosophy won't die as long as people seek the truth (144). After this hopeful call to inquiry, the play closes by circling back to where it started: the trial of Ibn Rushd. Here the narrators create word play out of the litany of accusations against the philosopher (145). But the Fifth Narrator, the renegade , intervenes, telling them to do away with their recitation of the transmission of hadith because he is going to present them with another hadith. He recounts a story in which the sultan questioned Ibn Rushd, stripped him of his positions (as physician of the sultan, head judge of Cordoba, and teacher at the Great Mosque), and exiled him to a village, but this was met with an uproar of protest from the people of al-Andalus and the Maghreb. Were it not for God's benevolence, Ibn Rushd would not have had high standing among the communities of al-Andalus, the Maghreb, and the Mashriq and within the thought of the elite. This alternate version of the legacy of Ibn Rushd is interrupted by the head narrator, who tells the Fifth Narrator to shut up and says that his story is an impure fabrication ("hadithak mawduʿ mudannas") and that only he, the head narrator or Shaykh al-Ruwa, has the true story ("al-sahih") (152–53). He begins to narrate the story with the invocation "bi-smi Allah" and cites the account of a historian in which the atheist Ibn Rushd was exiled, his books were burned, and his students were punished, but there was no reaction from the people of al-Andalus, the Maghreb, or the Mashriq. He closes this account by citing invective verses against Ibn

Rushd that the vizier had ordered poets to write and stating that in this way the sultan cut the lineage of philosophy and exposed its evils, and by the grace of God, all rational intellectual sciences came to an end in al-Andalus and the Maghreb (153–56).

Throughout al-Madani's *Shadharat*, the multiplicity of narrators and question of isnad points to difficulty with establishing authenticity and singular truth. In the last scene depicting the trial, this dismantling of singular truth is taken further by presenting two opposing versions of Ibn Rushd's legacy and labeling them with terms used for the hadith of the prophet: mawduʿ or sahih. Pointing to religious texts as narratives that have been authorized by an elaborate system that is nonetheless carried out by humans, with all their flaws and idiosyncrasies, *Shadharat* not only questions the validity of the hadith as sacred and legal texts but also points to the power dynamics of narrativity and its role in the creation of meaning, including group identities (as Cordoban, Andalusi, Arab, Muslim, Jewish, philosopher, atheist, etc.) and the individual identity of Ibn Rushd as understood by subsequent generations.

The final scenes of the play serve to show that Ibn Rushd is appreciated more in Christian and European spheres than in Arab and Muslims spheres but is important to both. In the final segment, a merchant from Cordoba tells the story of an old Christian monk who asks the merchant if he has any books by Ibn Rushd. The merchant says no and asks why the monk searches for them so urgently, to which the monk replies that these books are important because they offer humanity hope. When the merchant returns to Cordoba, he finds no trace of the philosopher's books nor of the philosopher, whom no one seems to have heard of. It is as if he was the character in a legend (157–62).

By pointing to the degree to which Ibn Rushd has been subject to the erasure of competing narratives about him while highlighting his importance to humanity, al-Madani's play carries two main messages: (1) given that narrative and truth are subject to power and our access to them is fragmentary, meaning is not transparent; (2) but books (ideas) offer hope and there is a need to return to intellectual inquiry to question and search for the truth. Whereas Chahine and Gala put censorship on trial without interrogating the representation of Islamists or al-Andalus-based andalucismo, al-Madani puts the very concepts of narrative and identity on trial.

All three works examined in this chapter comment on a lack of tolerance and freedom of expression, whether in Egypt and Tunisia, and by extension the Arab world at large, or in Spain. However, Chahine's unproblematized fusion of past and present in Ibn Rushd leads to the film's superficial treatment of Islamists. Similarly, Gala unequivocally accepts cultural translatability, positioning Averroes as manifestly Andalusian to construct a regional identity in the face of centralist Spanish nationalism and its censorship. Al-Madani alone gets to the crux of the matter: narrative constructs truth and identity stories that impinge on cultural translatability and tolerance of opposing viewpoints.

* * *

As I have demonstrated, issues of cultural translation and the construction of meaning are central to the Ibn Rushd–focused texts. For this reason, these works provide a framework through which to understand the broader discourses on al-Andalus, including the works on Tariq, Boabdil, Florinda, and Wallada. Here I present a set of analogies that I believe illuminates the representations of Ibn Rushd and al-Andalus at large and their far-reaching ramifications. Translatability is to untranslatability as the *convivencia* (idealized site of tolerance) version of al-Andalus is to the clash of cultures version of al-Andalus. That is, a belief in a greater degree of linguistic and cultural translatability—what might be called an idealist reading of the period—pairs commensurability and tolerance to understand the period as a time when harmonious interaction prevailed. Inversely, a belief in a lesser degree of linguistic and cultural translatability produces a view of the period in which one group oppressed another (or others) and strife prevailed. The Muslim paradise version of al-Andalus, the version espoused by Islamists, appears from a secularist perspective to support the clash of cultures; however, from the perspective of a supporter of political Islam, it is an ideal space in which Islamic law rules. In this way, it is analogous to translatability in that this version of al-Andalus is built on the premise that Islamic law is completely transferable and commensurate with other times and spaces.

What underlies these analogous relationships is the positioning vis-à-vis another contrasting pair. Translatability is to untranslatability as transparent ideas and accessible knowledge are to mediated and partial knowledge. In other words, a belief in a greater degree of translatability relies on a metaphysics of presence, or a belief in the immediate access to meaning. Unwavering confidence in our ability to attain knowledge underpins faith in complete translatability. Inversely, belief in a greater degree of untranslatability rests on the other end of the continuum in the conviction that all humans can attain is compromised knowledge that is mediated by language and cultural positioning. The challenge, which is played out in the narrative, dramatic, and filmic representations of Ibn Rushd, is how to acknowledge mediation without adopting a narrative of antagonism—a belief in an inevitable clash of cultures, how to build tolerance and equity within mediated, partial knowledge.

Borges's representation of Averroes created an opportunity for direct textual dialogue among Borges, Kilito, and Hussin and all of the Averroes-centered creative works offer an ongoing opportunity for readers/speakers of Spanish, French, Arabic, and translations into other languages to consider and question the limits and possibilities of cross-cultural contact and the construction of meaning. The various versions of Ibn Rushd highlight the desire for intercultural dialogue and the role of al-Andalus in helping work though contemporary issues of tolerance and difference. The existence of this textual dialogue in and of itself supports the possibility of meaningful cultural contact: not a facile, idealized vision of convivencia or Muslim supremacy but a careful negotiation that considers how knowledge is constructed.

In a literary essay titled "Le transfert d'Averroès" ("The Transfer of Averroes"), Kilito comments on the 1199 funeral cortege that took Ibn Rushd's corpse from Marrakech to Cordoba to be buried for a second time and its figurative relationship to Ibn Rushd's place in Arab and European cultural history.[17] Kilito notes that Ibd Rushd's death signaled for Arabs the end of an era or its displacement to Europe. Kilito puts forth the idea that the translation error on which Ibn Rushd based his much circulated, highly influential *Commentaries* should not be understood as a mistake but as "the gateways to discovery" (63). This leads him to conclude: "We have not finished burying Averroes" ("Le transfert" 63). Ibn Rushd, through his ongoing representational afterlife, not only champions secularism and freedom of expression, he also illuminates the process of the construction of meaning and the possibility of enriching intercultural contact.

PART II

To and from al-Andalus: Migration and Coloniality

> The story of al-Andalus is eminently one of exile, conquest, and movement: if not rise and decline, then ebbing and flowing, like the sea that partially forms its boundaries, defines its points of access, and sets its limits.
>
> —Jonathan Shannon

> Nowadays, the Mediterranean represents one of the most active friction-planes when considering North-South imbalances in the globalized world; it is the setting both for sharp socio-economic contrasts and for various kinds of migratory phenomena which derive from global inequality and instability. The origins of trans-Mediterranean disequilibrium lie in the history of past economic and political contact and power asymmetries between the two sides of the Mediterranean.
>
> —Natalia Ribas-Mateos

In the previous chapters, we saw that Ibn Rushd has been imagined as a scholar enclosed in a static Muslim sphere, enmeshed in the politics of language, embattled with oppressive authorities, or even capable of journeying across time and space to have an intellectual encounter. There are certain figures that have gone down in history and remained in the cultural imaginary precisely because of their travels to or from Iberia. How are these figures presented and used in twentieth- and twenty-first-century texts? Part II looks at a group of key figures in the physical movement and power dynamics between Iberia, North Africa, and the Americas: Tariq ibn Ziyad, the Muslim general who initiated the conquest of Iberia in 711; Abu ʿAbd Allah Muhammad XII (better known outside the Arabic-speaking world as Boabdil, the Hispanized version of the Andalusi pronunciation of his name), the last Muslim leader of al-Andalus whose exile took him to the mountains south of Granada and then to Fez, Morocco; Christopher Columbus, whose famous journey marks a shift in imperial and cultural supremacy; and the modern-day migrants linked to these historical figures through narratives in which the migrants are authors and/or objects of representation. I propose that the Arab and Hispanic representations of the historical figures connect them to various modern migration flows: that of Andalusians and other Spaniards to more prosperous regions in the mid-twentieth century and again in the early twenty-first century, that of North Africans to Spain and points beyond in the late twentieth century, that of southern Europeans and Levantine Arabs to South America in the late nineteenth century, and that of the ongoing movement of Latin Americans to the United States. In what follows I identify and analyze the connections between al-Andalus, imperial structures of power, and migration.

A wide-angle view of the body of cultural production that depicts the two Muslim figures, Tariq and Boabdil, reveals intriguing contrasts. In the modern period Arab and North African writers and producers have created several works that depict Tariq ibn Ziyad, but only a few with somewhat secondary references to Boabdil. In modern Hispanic cultural production, the opposite is true: there are only a few works that give a secondary role to Tariq, but several that focus on Boabdil. Although one might conclude that Arabs and North Africans are more comfortable with or find more comfort in the figure of the triumphant conqueror, while Spaniards and Spanish Americans are more interested in contemplating the end of Muslim rule in Iberia, when we look more closely at the works, the situation is more complex.

As I demonstrate here, the Spanish texts and those of the Mashriq, or Arab East, reaffirm in different ways and for different reasons Tariq's status as mythical conqueror; in contrast, the North African texts, including some that depict migration, clearly problematize the traditional vision of Tariq as a figure of Muslim power to be revered. In the case of Boabdil, the initially divided depictions—with Spaniards focusing on the tragic, melancholic Boabdil—end up converging through the issue of migration. Thus, for both Tariq and Boabdil, modern immigration is often the key issue at play in the story of medieval times. As Lara Dotson-Renta notes, in the hands of migrants Muslim Iberia "is being recast as living history," given that al-Andalus and Moorishness are understood as "points of departure," movement rather than stasis, that the writers relate to their contemporary situation (149–50). Arab-Maghrebian representations of Columbus, who had his fateful meeting with the Catholic Monarchs, Isabella and Ferdinand, in Granada soon after Boabdil had surrendered the city to them, add further nuances to the intersections between imperial power and migration.

CHAPTER 3

The Migration of a Hero

The Construction and Deconstruction of Tariq ibn Ziyad

Oh my warriors, whither would you flee [ayna al-mafarr]? Behind you is the sea, before you, the enemy. You have left now only the hope of your courage and your constancy. Remember that in this country you are more unfortunate than the orphan seated at the table of the avaricious master. Your enemy is before you, protected by an innumerable army; he has men in abundance, but you, as your only aid, have your own swords, and, as your only chance for life, such chance as you can snatch from the hands of your enemy. [. . .] Put far from you the disgrace from which you flee in dreams, and attack this monarch who has left his strongly fortified city to meet you. Here is a splendid opportunity to defeat him, if you will consent to expose yourselves freely to death. Do not believe that I desire to incite you to face dangers which I shall refuse to share with you. In the attack I myself will be in the fore, where the chance of life is always least. Remember that if you suffer a few moments in patience, you will afterward enjoy supreme delight. Do not imagine that your fate can be separated from mine, and rest assured that if you fall, I shall perish with you, or avenge you. You have heard that in this country there are a large number of ravishingly beautiful Greek maidens, their graceful forms are draped in sumptuous gowns on which gleam pearls, coral, and purest gold, in the palaces of crowned kings. The Commander of True Believers, al-Walid, son of Abd al-Malik, has chosen you for this attack from among all his Arab warriors; and he promises that you shall become his comrades and shall hold the rank of kings in this country. Such is his confidence in your intrepidity. The one fruit which he desires to obtain from your bravery is that the word of God shall be exalted in this country, and that the true religion shall be established here. The spoils will belong to yourselves. Remember that I place myself in the front of

> this glorious charge which I exhort you to make. At the moment when the two armies meet hand to hand, you will see me, never doubt it, seeking out this Roderick, tyrant of his people, challenging him to combat, if God is willing.
>
> —Tariq ibn Ziyad, addressing his troops at the beginning of the Islamic conquest of Hispania[1]

> And consequently, almost everywhere, the anticolonial utopias have gradually withered into postcolonial nightmares.
>
> —David Scott

Tariq ibn Ziyad (670–720) is known for crossing the Strait of Gibraltar, impeding his troops' retreat to North Africa, and succeeding in subjugating most of the Iberian Peninsula. For these feats he got a rocky cliff named after him, Jabal Tariq, Latinized as Gibraltar, and by extension the strait itself, which is named after the promontory. His name also became synonymous with Muslim military might. Reflection on Tariq [*Ṭāriq*] and naming leads to another observation. Whether by destiny or chance, Tariq's name points to his role as the inaugural figure in the movement between North Africa and Iberia: the one who started many crossings to come. The Arabic verb *ṭaraqa* means to knock on a door or to arrive somewhere, especially at night. The noun *ṭāriq* means "knocking" or "nocturnal visitor." Another form of the same root, *ṭarīq*, means path or road. In this way, Tariq ibn Ziyad is not only the historical conqueror of Iberia but a consummate figure for the traveler, the border-crosser, and even the clandestine immigrant or night traveler. Centuries after his famous crossing, other North Africans traverse the strait—or die trying to—without military might, obstruct their own possibility of return, and hope for success in Iberia. The convergences and divergences between these two kinds of travelers are in fact part of at least a few narrative depictions of Tariq.

Depictions of Tariq have positioned him as an epic hero of Islam; for this reason, Nizar Hermes refers to the many verse and prose texts about him as "hagiographical stories and legends which turn Tariq ibn Ziyad into one of the most celebrated characters in Islamic culture and the most epically quoted in modern *Andalusiyyāt*" (6–7).[2] Portrayals of Tariq's life have a great deal of creative leeway because the historical record on him is fairly limited and sometimes contradictory.[3] Few medieval historians offer any information about Tariq's ethnic origins, and the Arabic sources that do address origins were written 400 or more years after Tariq's lifetime and present three different versions: that he was a Persian from Hamadan, that he was part of the Yemeni Kindah tribe of Bedouin, or that he was Amazigh from one of various North African tribes. The earliest known reference to his origins, found in the work of twelfth-century geographer al-Idrisi, identifies him as a member of the Zanata Amazigh tribe.[4] Whether or not this is accurate, in the Arabic-speaking world Tariq is generally assumed to be of Amazigh origin.

Tariq's relationship to his Arab superior, Musa ibn Nusayr (640–716), the emir of the Muslim province of Ifriqiya (North Africa), is also unclear. Although many sources indicate that Tariq was Musa's slave, centuries later Tariq's descendants denied this. Some accounts point to Musa's feelings of jealousy toward Tariq for his military successes in al-Andalus and subsequent popularity. Musa, who served under the Umayyad caliph al-Walid I, had appointed Tariq governor of Tangier after the city's conquest. When the opportunity to continue the conquest toward the north arose, Musa appointed Tariq head of that campaign. Adjacent to Tangier, the Visigoth outpost Ceuta was governed by a Christian named Julian [Julián in Spanish/Yuliyan in Arabic] who served the Visigoth king Roderick [Rodrigo/Ludhariq]. Legend has it that Julian sent his daughter Florinda to Roderick's court in Toledo to be educated, and Roderick raped her. In search of vengeance, Julian then helped the Muslims invade the Visigoth kingdom of Hispania. In the earlier Spanish versions of the legend, Roderick is a sinner whose act led to the fall of the Visigoths, whereas starting in the fifteenth century, Florinda, known as la Cava Rumía, is a seductress who tempted the Visigoth king. In Muslim versions of the legend, Florinda is an innocent virgin who is taken advantage of by the Christian king. I discuss the figure of Florinda and the roles of seduction and subjugation in discourses about al-Andalus in chapter 5, to focus the present chapter on constructions of masculinity in representations of Tariq.

The sexualized nature of accounts of the Muslim conquest is a core element in the only major work from within modern Hispanic literature that gives Tariq a substantial role. The novel *Reivindicación del Conde don Julián* (*Count Julian*, 1970) by renowned Spanish writer Juan Goytisolo (b. 1931) is an iconoclastic work that uses the sexually charged legends and historical accounts about the conquest to present a hypermasculine Tariq for the purpose of attacking Orientalist and conservative constructions of Spanish identity. In his 1981 collection of essays, *Crónicas sarracinas*, Goytisolo explains that while Spanish chronicles, legends, and ballads blamed the so-called destruction of Spain on the illicit sex between King Roderick and Florinda, in Spanish discourses this was transformed into a fear of the lascivious, raping Moor (27–46). José Antonio González Alcantud points out that Goytisolo goes beyond "las dos Españas"—the Republican and Nationalist camps that confronted each other in the civil war—by laying bare the fear wielded by both groups via the image of the sexually violent Moor (*Lo moro*, 205). Nonetheless, given that the myth of *La España sagrada* (Sacred Spain) was a key component of Franco's Nationalist Catholicism, Goytisolo's critique of this Orientalist Moorish figure goes to the heart of Nationalist discourses. As Jo Labanyi points out, Goytisolo targets the Falangist nationalist ideology that grew out of the Generation of 1898's belief that Spain had deviated from its origins and sacred destiny due to the Muslim conquest and subsequent events.[5] In medieval and early modern discourses, the Muslim conquest, with Muslims cast as sexual predators, was understood as punishment for Roderick's sexual misconduct; building on this and the Generation of 1898's ideas about Spanish national character, in Falangist rhetoric it was virtuous Christian knights who were called upon to protect Sacred Spain. Given Goytisolo's strong opposition to the Franco dictatorship, in *Reivindicación* he parodies the vision of Spanish identity propagated by Francoist fascism, and the ideal of the chaste, noble Christian knight on which it is built, to attack that ideology.

In the 1960s Goytisolo began using experimental narrative techniques to criticize Spanish identity in a trilogy of novels of which *Reivindicación* is the second work. The stream-of-consciousness novel presents a narrator-protagonist (recognizable as the trilogy's Álvaro Mendiola) who is a Spaniard living in Tangier who identifies with the historical Count Julian, governor of Ceuta and ultimate symbol of betrayal against Spain. The syphilitic narrator envisions himself as Julian and meets up with Tariq, his lover, to smoke *kif* (cannabis) and plan Tariq's invasion of Spain.[6] The text's iconoclastic stance not only establishes an identification with Julian, the traitor par excellence, but glorifies Tariq as a hirsute, manly man of action who is superior to delicate Spanish men who are concerned with book learning.[7] Throughout the novel, Tariq is marked by his thick moustache and tiger-like appearance—markers of animalistic machismo. By sympathizing with Julian and Tariq and having Julian enable the destruction of Spain via the sexual aggression of Tariq and his Muslim troops, *Reivindicación* tears down the pillars of traditional Spanish Catholic nationalism and shifts the perspective on the Muslim invasion of Iberia, which is a cornerstone of the nationalist, Reconquista-based Spanish ethos. Thus, the symbolic, satirical representation of Tariq found in *Reivindicación* is meant to dismantle the traditional discourses about conquest as rape. Although Goytisolo attacks oppressive Spanish traditionalism, he does so via a glorification of violence, particularly sexual violence, and an eroticized conception of North Africa. As Labanyi puts it, given the ambiguities inherent in parody, "the novel perpetuates the mythical vision it sets out to subvert" (*Myth and History* 196), and in the process it criticizes an essentialized Spanish identity through an essentialized Moor (*Myth and History* 206).

By opposing the denial of the body found in official Spanish discourses with a focus on the body, Goytisolo constructs an Orient that is a zone of erotic liberation. In particular, Muslim North African men are represented as violent, animalistic, and oversexed. Thus, while lampooning the fear of the vile Muslim invader, by presenting, for instance, Spanish women looking forward to an orgy with the well-endowed Arab invaders (219, 241–42, and 295–96), Goytisolo maintains a particular type of essentialist view of the Maghreb and the Muslim world. Though Tariq is the narrator's idealized male, he is idealized as a primitive figure that violently penetrates the effeminate Spain. Brad Epps has analyzed in detail the hypermasculine identity and homophobic and misogynistic attitudes manifest in this author's works. Epps summarizes the problems in Goytisolo's oeuvre as follows: "a fairly constant subject/object divide (reciprocity and reversibility are typically excluded), a reification of marginality (the pride of the pariah as opposed to gay pride); a tendency to totalization (of the West, Islam, homosexuality, and so on); and a persistent dismissal, if not denigration, of women (the specter of homosexual misogyny)" ("Goytisolo, Juan" 91). Regarding this novel in particular, Epps states: "*Conde Julián*'s much-touted subversiveness is constrained by the aggressiveness of its discourse, constrained to repeat and even to serve the ideological structures it purportedly rejects. More importantly, Julián, despite his persistent denunciation of oppression, brandishes the phallus with such rapturous ferocity that he ultimately seems to be in collusion with a phallocentric order that strives to suppress manifestations of otherness and difference" (*Significant Violence* 99). Epps notes that by celebrating machismo and conflating it with active homosexuality, Goytisolo's *Reivindicación* denigrates those seen as sexually passive.

Although in the novel Tariq is not a revered, righteous figure, he is admired as a virile man of action. As Epps puts it, "the one thing that *Conde Julián* preserves from attack, and that serves as its essential core of energy, is *masculine* identity" (Epps, *Significant Violence* 100; emphasis in original). In this way, *Reivindicación* has commonalities with a strand of the Arabo-Muslim depiction of Tariq that, as I shall demonstrate, is apparent in the work of Taymur and especially that of Chraïbi: the conception of Tariq as hypermasculine.[8] This convergence between a Spanish depiction of Tariq and that of some writers from the Middle East and North Africa is not an indication of a shared Spanish and Arabo-Muslim outlook on Tariq but reflects the degree to which Goytisolo is at odds with mainstream Spanish perspectives. Goytisolo's opposition to Franco led him to go into exile in Paris in 1956, and all of the author's works were banned in Spain until after Franco's death in 1975. The Spanish transition to democracy did not necessarily bring Goytisolo back into the fold as he moved to Marrakech in the mid-1990s and has lived there since. Perhaps, then, Goytisolo, who is famous for rejecting nationalist identities and viewing himself as a noncitizen wherever he is, can be considered if not within the category of Moroccan writers then somehow outside of the category of Spanish writers.[9] Regardless of how we understand Goytisolo's affiliations, he is certainly an exception within Hispanic letters.

To my knowledge, the only other Hispanic narrative that focuses on Tariq is *Tariq y Musa: conquistadores de Al-Andalus* (*Tariq and Musa: Conquerors of Al-Andalus*, 2011) by Spanish historian Antonio Torremocha (b. 1950). Given its weak character development, this work is closer to a novelized history than a historical novel. Like Goytisolo's novel, this work reinscribes certain Orientalist images; however, unlike the earlier novel, the Tariq in Torremocha's text is vanquished and feminized. Whereas Goytisolo's text is an oneiric, parodic tale of hypermasculinity and hypersexuality, Torremocha's narrative is a straightforward account of the political and military aspects of the Muslim conquest of Iberia. Nonetheless, *Tariq y Musa* feminizes Tariq as part of its portrayal of the figure as a fallen warrior rather than a hero.

Torremocha's account uses a few Orientalist clichés, but in direct opposition to Goytisolo's novel, it does so as it presents a pro-Christian interpretation of events. Some examples of essentialist tropes in the work are that it repeatedly presents the Amazighs as vicious and brutal, and it describes Tariq as having an enigmatic smile that inspires distrust (129, 200). The pro-Christian perspective is evident in various elements of the narrative. For instance, the one time the omniscient narrator dwells on a character's inner turmoil is in a single paragraph about Julian's feelings of self-doubt, and this is used to absolve him of the label of traitor (104) and later establish the Muslims as the double-crossers (134, 162–61). Also, though Torremocha refers to some of the same legends referenced by Arab and Maghrebi narratives, unlike some of those works, he downplays the role of religion in the Muslim conquest, highlighting instead Tariq's military and political ambition and the "Berber" soldiers' interest in booty.

Torremocha's text is very masculine given its emphasis on the external world of public action (versus intimate relationships) and its vision of a male universe with no female characters. Moreover, within this male narrative landscape, Tariq is relatively feminized. The story begins with a young Tariq crying, then passes through his many military triumphs and humiliation at the hands of Musa, and ultimately ends with both conquerors crying. The novel opens with an adolescent Tariq who is hunting a gazelle and cries out of impotence and anger when his hunt is unsuccessful (9). After his many military successes, in which he demonstrates only anger or ambition, he must deal with Musa's jealousy, which results in Musa humiliating him by whipping his face (254) and requiring that he hand over all the booty he had gained in Iberia (256–57). Eventually, both men are reprimanded by the caliph, and after he has ordered that they present themselves before him in Damascus, Tariq and Musa cry as they leave al-Andalus (281). Tariq dies young, disillusioned and forgotten, with his cause of death unknown (305). Through this retelling of Tariq's story, Torremocha is able to place Tariq in the position of the vanquished. Here Tariq is overpowered by emotion, by Musa and the caliph, as well as by history itself—the one that Torremocha says has forgotten Tariq and the one that Torremocha himself crafts. Yet Tariq is far from forgotten, and in Spanish discourses he remains a ghostly threat that hovers outside at the periphery—the coastline that is the national border—as a potential danger.

In addition to the sexualized and gendered elements of the narratives of Tariq's conquest, two other key features of the legends surrounding him are what he did with the boats used to cross the strait and what he said to his troops after that. Both components of the Tariq myth are implicated in contemporary migration from North Africa to Spain. Al-Idrisi, writing four centuries after the conquest, was the first to state that upon landing on Iberian shores Tariq burned his ships to impede the retreat of his troops.[10] This incident, apocryphal or not, is well known in the Muslim world and functions as a symbol of forcing a project forward to motivate success.

Even more well known in the Arabo-Muslim world is a prebattle oration that Tariq is said to have delivered to his troops before the decisive Battle of Guadalete. In this famous speech Tariq declared to his men that they had nowhere to flee and much to gain if they battled valiantly. The version of this speech that is most well known is that presented by North African historian al-Maqqari (c. 1578–1632). But since al-Maqqari wrote even a few centuries later than al-Idrisi (about 900 years after the fact), there is impassioned debate surrounding the speech's authenticity. Nizar Hermes, correcting the misconception that the speech is only reported by al-Maqqari points out that other versions of the oration are found in earlier sources, from the ninth century and on

(17–18).[11] Despite the doubts regarding authenticity, in 1938 a Moroccan nationalist identified Tariq's speech as the first prose work of Moroccan literature, and it continues to be memorized by millions of students across the Arab world (Fernández Parrilla, "Breaking the Canon" 4).[12] Indeed, the two accounts about Tariq's initiation of the conquest have become fused in a legend in which Tariq, just after burning the boats, tells his troops that they have no means by which to return, but the opportunity to make great gains lies ahead.

The theme of taking the risk to cut ties with the past in pursuit of financial gain and status is echoed by the hundreds of thousands of North Africans who, since the 1970s and especially from the 1990s to 2011, risked their lives to emigrate to Spain in search of economic opportunity.[13] In *The Return of the Moor*, Daniela Flesler establishes that twentieth-century Spanish discourses represent contemporary North African migration to Spain as a reenactment of the eighth-century invasion and the subsequent conflict between Christians and Moors; thus, they display the ghostly fear of North African immigrants as Moors seeking to regain what was once theirs. Flesler indicates that some migration narratives written by Spaniards directly or indirectly invoke Tariq ibn Ziyad as part of their use of the trope of invasion. One example of this is the testimonial work *Dormir al raso* (*Sleeping Unsheltered*, 1994), created through a collaboration between a Spaniard and a Moroccan immigrant in Spain and classified by Flesler as one of various "less-than-successful efforts to 'give voice' to the immigrants by using the testimonial genre" (Flesler 14).[14] Through a passing reference to Tariq and other figures of the medieval past, the text participates in a rhetoric of invasion that equates immigrants with unwelcome conquerors (Flesler 85–89).

Flesler includes within this phenomenon of invasion-inflected migration discourse one text written independently (without collaboration with a Spanish writer) by a Moroccan, that of Rashid Nini (93–94). Yet my analysis of this text by Nini, together with other Arabic- and French-language texts from North Africa, indicates that while the North African authors refer to Tariq in relation to migration, any triumphant invasion is either questioned or left far in the past. Among these writers, Rachid Nini is the only one who was himself a clandestine immigrant or night traveler [*ṭāriq*]. Nini's 1999 *Yawmiyat Muhajir Sirri* (Diary of an Illegal Immigrant) is the memoir of the author's trip from Morocco to Spain as a professional turned illegal day laborer.[15] Nini (b. 1970) is a Moroccan journalist who has been active in promoting Amazigh culture. In 1997, when he was able to obtain a visa to enter Spain to cover an Amazigh conference, he used the visa as an opportunity to enter

Spain, never attended the conference, and overstayed his visa. During a period of about three years, living as an illegal immigrant, he published a memoir of his experiences by installments in the Arabic-language Moroccan newspaper *al-ʿAlam*. The entries were published as a book in 1999 and appeared in Spanish translation a few years later.

As Ruth Rodríguez López states in reference to Nini, "the author recuperates that which is Andalusi [*lo andalusí*] as a literary and symbolic bridge that allows him to interpret his migratory experience in Spain" (1). This is evident in the course of the memoir when Nini refers to physical and performative remnants of al-Andalus as well as two historical figures: Tariq ibn Ziyad and Boabdil.[16] At one point early in the memoir, Nini is in the countryside with a Spanish friend and they see ancient fortifications. When his friend wonders why the Arabs built their fortresses on hills, Nini answers that is was to keep watch on the Christians below (Nini 7). Flesler rightly points to this episode as an example of "the rhetoric of medieval confrontations in which Christians were humiliated and defeated" that the narrator uses "to establish a contrast to the present situation" (93). Flesler sees this discourse as contributing to the troubled reception of Moroccan migrants in Spain: "it creates the belief that those who migrate do so, following [Spanish priest and political figure José] Chamizo's words, 'to claim what is theirs,' to re-reconquer lost al-Andalus" (94). Although the desire to reinstate past hierarchies, or at least remind others that previously the tables were turned, is a response to the living conditions and status of immigrants, it feeds anti Moroccan sentiment in Spain. This desire arises again in a later passage but is short-lived.

Roughly halfway through Nini's diary of a North African immigrant experience in Spain, he invokes Tariq ibn Ziyad in what seems to be a response to his Spanish's co-worker's reference to Boabdil. Having left back-breaking agricultural work, Nini has found a job at a pizzeria. While working there, his Spanish co-worker Alfonso refers to Boabdil as a figure humiliated by Ferdinand and Isabella and says that the Arabs' days in Spain had come to an end then. Nini tells him jokingly that the Arabs are returning: "Sure, we aren't soldiers in an army and we don't have a leader like Tariq ibn Ziyad, but we are invading al Andalus again" (Nini 89). Alfonso laughs and points out the differences between arriving as a conqueror and as an immigrant. "It's true, conquerors don't make pizza; they don't climb trees to pick fruit," Nini adds, and they both laugh (89). This vignette ends with Nini thinking to himself, as he kneads the pizza dough, that "our ancestors did not knead the dough in al-Andalus. They spent many centuries creating a grandeur that doesn't deserve now to only be immortalized by the Spaniards in a naïve celebration that is a reminder for new generations of the ancient defeat that befell the Arabs" (Nini 89). The celebration to which Nini refers is the Spanish tradition of Moros y Cristianos festivals—carnival-like reenactments of the battles between Moors and Christians—one of which Nini attends in the town of Benidorm.[17] The ostensibly playful verbal sparring that takes place between Nini and Alfonso displays Nini's use of Tariq ibn Ziyad as a deflective shield against the triumphant Christian commentary and pathos surrounding Boabdil. Tariq serves as an entry point into a discourse of past greatness, but it is a short-lived indulgence. The co-worker immediately points to the differences between Tariq and the typical immigrant, and as Nini kneads the pizza dough while Alfonso tends to customers, Nini is painfully aware of this difference. No measure of retrospective nostalgia can change the present-day status of North African immigrants in Spain.

Denise Filios considers Nini as an intellectual exile or an "economic refugee" (101) in Spain and notes that for Nini, "while al-Andalus was a magnificent Arab civilization, it primarily serves today as a measure of the depths to which the Maghreb has sunk on both sides of the Strait" (101). Similarly, Rodríguez López indicates that Nini's references to al-Andalus highlight the difficulties of late twentieth-century life in the Arabic-speaking world (9). Specifically, Rodríguez López notes the difference between the invocations of al-Andalus by early twentieth-century Arab immigrants to Brazil, who used an idealized al-Andalus as a source of refuge and solace, and Nini's use of al-Andalus in which it becomes a tool to expose the difficulties of immigrant life in Spain and thus shatter idealized African visions of Europe (11 and 13). As Parvati Nair explains, globalization spreads Euro-American neoliberal values and creates stark juxtapositions between the affluence of the North and the poverty of the South. Through advertising, mass media, and tourism, the gap in standards of living becomes particularly palpable to residents of North Africa. In this way, globalization fuels migration from the Maghreb to Europe and other areas seen as offering not only personal freedom but also opportunities for economic stability and material acquisitions (Nair 24–27). Nini's references to Tariq ibn Ziyad at first may seem like a nostalgic or compensatory gesture, but ultimately he uses Tariq to highlight the transnational class hierarchies exacerbated by neocolonial globalization. This becomes particularly salient in the final pages of his memoir, where he invokes al-Andalus, and specifically Tariq, in a markedly different way.

In these final pages Nini abruptly moves from the news of the discovery of Algerian immigrants' corpses in a car in Milan to memories of his primary school history lesson about the conquest of al-Andalus. He notes that in school he was surprised that Tariq could have burned his boats and delivered that famous speech. Yet for Nini what is truly strange about that history class is that it only mentioned Tariq at the moment of the conquest—and no one knows what happened to him after that. Nini comments on this by stating: "History is funny sometimes" (176). This reflection leads him to see similarities between Tariq, who burned his boats, and the immigrant who burns his travel documents so there is no turning back. A practice of contemporary clandestine immigrants and refugees is to burn their identity documents or otherwise dispose of them before arrival, because they believe (and often it is the case) that authorities in the receiving country are more likely to deport persons who carry a valid travel document or who can be proven to be above a certain age. This strategy of burning passports is common among those crossing the Strait of Gibraltar, and thus Nini comments:

> Now I also understand why immigrants, when the lights of al-Andalus glimmer before them, burn their passports and throw them into the open sea. They do that so that no one returns alive to the other shore. It's either death or plunder. The burning of one's passport does not differ greatly from the burning of the ship of return. It appears that that history lesson will continue to repeat itself throughout the centuries in a tragic way. But the truly funny part of the whole story is that there is no booty at all to be plundered there. (176–77)

In this passage, it is noteworthy that Nini refers to "the lights of al-Andalus," rather than those of "Spain" or "Andalusia"—the contemporary name for the southern region or autonomous community of Spain which is commonly used in transliterated form in Arabic-language references to the region. By referring to al-Andalus in this context, Nini implies that, just as al-Andalus no longer exists, those glimmering lights announce nonexistent or inaccessible wealth and well-being. Just like Tariq's troops, contemporary migrants are pushed to risk everything for material and social improvement, but the lights of al-Andalus symbolize the illusion of migration to Europe as a direct path to prosperity. The reality is that "there is no booty" to plunder. Indeed, Nini goes on to describe the physically demanding work that immigrants must undertake to earn a living in Spain.

Nini concludes his diary noting that for the immigrant who works the fields in Spain, his hands serve as his true identity card. When the immigrant shows his worn hands to the police, the officer sees that the immigrant is doing work that no one else wants to do and lets him continue on his way. The laborer's hands are more meaningful than the hard-to-obtain temporary residency card with writing in cheap ink (Nini 177). Here legal documents become irrelevant to the authorities;

documentation is trumped by the local need for desperate laborers. This passage seems to contradict the idea of cutting ties with the past by burning boats and identity papers, but in fact it reveals a significant paradox: the immigrant who does physical labor is not able to fully rid himself of identity credentials, is not able to completely cut ties with the past. His identity as someone toiling amid poverty remains unchanged and in fact is inscribed on his body. By burning his travel documents and working the Spanish fields, the North African immigrant loses his personal identity and takes on (or is left with) one based largely on class. The identity of someone who does the harshest physical labor—whether Moroccan, Argentine, or Gypsy, to mention Nini's co-workers in the fields—is documented by his hands.

In Nini's *Yawmiyat*, initially, lost greatness—Tariq's conquest of European territory and his role in founding a renowned center of civilization—is invoked to defend against immigrants' low status, but this only highlights the differences between conqueror and immigrant. Later in the text commonalities are found between conqueror and immigrant: burning boats is akin to burning passports. Nonetheless, the diary closes with the immigrant whose identity as a laborer is embodied in his rough hands. Paper substantiations of identity are ultimately irrelevant in the face of global economic hierarchies. This realization only makes the disjuncture between Tariq and immigrants even more profound. Overall in Nini's memoir, and even more overtly in other North African texts, al-Andalus and in particular Tariq ibn Ziyad are used to erase and/or redefine boundaries of identity quite distinct from those of *moros y cristianos*. While Nini suggests a questioning of history when he says, "History is funny sometimes," all of the Maghrebian narratives about Tariq that my research has yielded engage in different ways in a deep revision of the history of Tariq and the Muslim conquest of Iberia. Significantly, this dismantling of the truth claims of history and even the heroic status of Tariq is only present in works from the Maghreb. In stark contrast, the works from the Mashriq uphold to varying degrees the traditional mythic status of Tariq and the discourse of the glory of the Muslim conquests of which it is a part. In the conclusion to this chapter I discuss the historical and cultural factors behind this split in Maghreb/Mashriq visions of Tariq.

As noted earlier, in his diary Nini is struck by the fact that his school history lessons never said what happened to Tariq after the conquest. Various authors from the Mashriq and the Maghreb, perhaps also noting such a gap in their history lessons, have taken it upon themselves to fill in history's holes with their versions of the Tariq story. In doing so, they allow us to understand his legacy far beyond not only the conquest but his lifetime and that of the Muslim kingdoms of Iberia. As mentioned, traditional images of Tariq, akin to Nini's first invocation of him as a powerful, conquering leader, abound in the Mashriq region. Next I examine certain signal works from different time periods, different genres, and different national and religious affiliations that demonstrate the shared characteristics of traditional conceptions of the figure of Tariq ibn Ziyad.

Tariq in the Mashriq: The Mythic Hero

Traditional representations of Tariq ibn Ziyad from the Arabic-speaking world emphasize the military leader's identity as a Muslim and the glory of the Muslim empire. In the process, Tariq's probable non-Arab identity and the subjugation of the Amazigh peoples are erased. The earliest such texts in the modern period are the play *Fath al-Andalus* (*The Conquest of al-Andalus*, 1893) by Mustafa Kamil (1874–1908) and the novel *Fath al-Andalus* (*The Conquest of al-Andalus*, 1903) by Jurji Zaydan (1861–1914).[18] These works were later followed by other texts that began to problematize the mythic status of Tariq, albeit in limited fashion.

Kamil, a prominent Egyptian nationalist, wrote his only play as a young man, and in it he promotes a pan-Arab Muslim identity that predates the specifically Egyptian territorial nationalism he later championed. Overall, the play presents an account of Tariq as the honorable hero who ends Visigoth oppression and to whom Muslims owe a debt of gratitude.[19] Leaving out the commonly accepted identification of Tariq as Amazigh as well as the legendary struggles between Tariq and Musa, the play narrates a conflict between, on one hand, Tariq and Musa and, on the other, a group of Byzantines who are trying to stop the Muslim conquest of Spain. Dennis Walker interprets this plot as a reflection of the tensions that were rising at the time of the writing of the play between the Arabo-Muslim elite and the Armenian and Syrian Christians who were supporting the British colonization of Egypt (59–60). Kamil's play, perhaps offering a lesson to his contemporaries, attributes the conquest of Iberia to Christian disunity and the might of Muslim unity. In the process, intra-Muslim differences are swept under the rug.

Zaydan's historical novel *Fath al-Andalus* is probably the most well known and widely read of the works on Tariq, and even on al-Andalus in general, in the Arabic-speaking world. Zaydan, a Lebanese Greek Orthodox immigrant to Egypt, was a prominent figure in the late nineteenth and early twentieth-century Arab cultural revival known as *al-Nahda*. A prolific author of historical novels, Zaydan's works were integral to the establishment of a pan-Arab secular identity. As William

Granara puts it, in reference to another novel by Zaydan that focuses on a later period of al-Andalus, "Jurji Zaydan exploited the textual resources of the classical literary heritage to assert an ethnically based and historically uninterrupted Arab identity against the onslaught of western modernity and political and cultural imperialism" (Granara, "Nostalgia" 63). Zaydan's novel on the earliest period of the conquest of Iberia was first published serially under the title *Fath al-Andalus aw Tariq ibn Ziyad* (*The Conquest of al-Andalus or Tariq ibn Ziyad*). Tariq appears in the novel as a strong, honorable Muslim warrior, but the bulk of the text is dedicated to other figures, among them Florinda and her beloved. As I elucidate in chapter 5, it is through Florinda and the gender dynamics of the text that Tariq emerges as a central figure. In this text, while Tariq's Amazigh origins are mentioned, what is highlighted is his role as a manly hero who saves damsels in distress and rights wrongs—among them the wrongs of corrupt Visigoth rule in Iberia.

A few decades later, another Egyptian author, Mahmud Taymur (1894–1973), crafted another account of the conquest, *Tariq al-Andalus* (*Tariq of al-Andalus*, circa 1940), in which the depiction of Tariq is more complex, but this only serves to cement his mythic status. Taymur became famous during the 1920s to 1940s when he published prolifically across every genre of prose. He is noted as one of the pioneers of the modern Arabic short story but also garnered attention for his work as a playwright, although *Tariq al-Andalus* is one of his lesser-known plays. This drama presents a classic Islamic portrayal of the Muslim conquest of Iberia that focuses on the glory of Islam. Although there is an explicit theme of paradox in the text, one of the paradoxes implicitly upholds traditional concepts of masculinity and power. Some of the characters philosophize about the paradoxical nature of human life and mirroring this Taymur imagines Tariq as a man who is "completely masculine" (Taymur 3, 4), yet physically imperfect. Taymur's Tariq has a wandering eye and a paralyzed hand—yet the ladies love him, and he is a respected leader with a thirst for conquest. Rather than question any inherited truths, this depiction of Tariq bolsters his image as the heroic, manly conqueror whose strength comes from within—from his religious conviction.

In Taymur's play, Tariq's Amazigh origins are never mentioned, but there is overt reference to the Arabization of the Amazighs as a beautiful, divinely inspired process. In addition, Count Julian, the Christian governor of Ceuta who went down in history for betraying his Visigoth king by helping the Moors enter Iberia, is an unredeemed traitor. Although Julian betrays his king, Roderick, in vengeance for the rape of his daughter, Julian later betrays Tariq as well and commits one ignoble act after another. Amid the curious dynamics of sexuality and religion present in the play, Taymur has Tariq marry Julian's daughter, Florinda, and although they are in love, he has Florinda ask Tariq for a divorce. Florinda cites as the reason for this request that Tariq is more concerned with war than with her (Taymur 156–58). In this way, the Christian woman conveniently bows out of Tariq's life to allow him to pursue his true passion: war in the name of Islam. The message that emerges from this is that cross-confessional love cannot last because of the different religious missions. Not long after this, the play ends with a new battle beginning offstage, with shouts of Muslim slogans heard by the audience (Taymur 173–74). The battle echoes and reverberates, even when it cannot be seen, just as the glory of the Islamic empire continues to resound even when it cannot be seen, even when its paradoxes have not been unraveled.

Some of the traditional discourses surrounding Tariq ibn Ziyad that are seen in Taymur's 1940s play are still alive and well in Arabic-language cultural products ranging from children's cartoons and books to a prime-time television series. In fact, these discourses are able to circulate much faster and more widely because of the new media. In a genre that is a cross between US soap operas and historical mini-series, the popular TV series *al-Tariq* (*That Tariq*; literally, *The Tariq*) consists of thirty-two episodes written by Egyptian Yusri al-Jundi and directed by Egyptian Ahmad Saqr and tells a fictional version of the life of Tariq ibn Ziyad. The title role was played by established Egyptian actor Mamduh ʿAbd al-ʿAlim, and most of the rest of the cast was made up of Syrian and Egyptian actors, plus some from Jordan, Lebanon, and Morocco. The series was filmed across the Arab world, in both the Mashriq and the Maghreb, and it was a joint Egyptian, Syrian, and Moroccan production ("Ahmad ʿAbd al-Halim [. . .]"). The pan-Arab nature of the creation of the series, along with the fact that like most series set in premodern periods it is done entirely in Modern Standard Arabic (*fusha*), rather than a particular regional dialect, bolsters the series' broad appeal. The series was broadcast for the first time in 2004 during Ramadan (the month with the greatest amount of television viewing in the Arabic-speaking world), has since been shown on a number of Arab satellite channels over the years (Shoup), and is available through various sites on the Internet. Yet, based on comments left by some viewers on the YouTube videos, it has received a warmer reception in the Mashriq than in the Maghreb. Indeed, the vision of Tariq offered by the Egyptian scriptwriter and producer comes out of the dominant Mashriq perspective on the spread of Islam west to North Africa and al-Andalus. The durability of this mythified Tariq is also no doubt linked to the rise in Islamism that began in the late twentieth century. In addition, given that the serial's main source of financing was in the United Arab Emirates (Shoup), it is not surprising that it projects a more traditional take on Tariq.

Although some elements of al-Jundi's series display a more pluralistic stance, overall it crafts a traditional Mashriq perspective on Islam and Amazigh identity. Similar to Taymur's version, al-Jundi's TV version of Tariq is motivated solely by religious conviction and a desire for justice as he liberates Iberia from a corrupt, oppressive leader and church. In the series, Tariq's "Berber [*barbar*]" identity and Amazigh culture in general are much more visible in comparison with the works discussed previously. However, the religious message of the narrative is stronger than that of Taymur's text. In al-Jundi's script, Julian (a Christian) is one of the most noble, likable characters and Tariq is presented as an Amazigh who, though raised Muslim, falls away from the faith and fights for Amazigh autonomy.[20] In this portrait, Tariq is an often anguished, internally conflicted man, haunted by disturbing dreams and a seer's prophesies. The theme of a search for lost loved ones is doubly present in the narrative: Tariq searches for his mother from whom he has been separated and for Luʾluʾa, a childhood friend who was kidnapped and enslaved by the Goths. Longing for reunion with these figures from the past and trying to find his path in life, many scenes show Tariq sitting at the seashore, contemplating the waves or sitting at a campfire and reminiscing. The combination of these scenes, various other ones featuring prescient dreams with voices that call out to Tariq and moments of prophecy, and the musical score create a mystical mood. A pagan seer tells Tariq that he sees him carrying a sword and crossing an ocean and that he will be a leader for his people (episode 1). After frequently recalling the seer's words, Tariq ends up in Hispania, where the local inhabitants tell him that a prophecy said that a leader with a birthmark on his arm would help them: Tariq raises his sleeve to reveal a birthmark that marks him as their savior (episode 28). Years later, when the prophecy has been proven true, the North African seer finds Tariq again, and by this point the seer has been converted to Islam by Tariq's own mother.

In the TV version of Tariq, his mother is the vehicle of Islam. When he and his mother are finally reunited, he watches as she prays; soon after (episode 9) Tariq declares his desire to return to Islam, and his mother, who is the spiritual guide of many, encourages him to dedicate himself to spreading the faith. He is given courage by the unified forces of his Muslim faith and his mother, who appears to him in visions after her death. Tariq approaches Musa ibn Nusayr, and they come up with a plan to do missionary work [*duʿaʾ*] among the Amazighs with Tariq spearheading the effort and many scenes showing him leading converted Amazighs and troops in prayer. In this way, *al-Tariq* makes the military leader into a quasi-messiah or prophet who is linked to liberation and spirituality.

Eventually Tariq not only converts the Amazighs but saves his long-lost friend Lu'lu'a, Florinda, and all of al-Andalus from the Visigoths. The explicit message of the series is that Amazighs are equal to Arabs in the Muslim *umma* and participated in spreading Islam and the greatness of the empire. However, this is undermined by the linguistic homogeneity of the program. Not one phrase is uttered in another language (Amazigh, Spanish, or Romance/vulgar Latin), and there is never any reference to translation. Yes, this is a convention in this type of historical TV series, but because this one deals specifically with Amazigh and Iberian communities, the glossing over is particularly noticeable. Somehow, magically, all are united by standard Arabic, in the same way that they are said to be united by Islam. The message becomes one of submission to the hegemonic religion and language rather than cultural equality. This submission is echoed in the final scenes of the series. After the new caliph, influenced by two malcontents who wish to do Tariq in, strips Tariq and Musa of their rank, Tariq returns to his place of birth (episode 32).[21] In the closing scene, Tariq, wearing a white burnoose that gives him a saintly aura, sits on a rock at the seashore staring out at sea with a *misbaha* (Muslim prayer beads) in his hand. By having Tariq, complete with prayer beads, spend the rest of his days staring out at the sea, at the other side of which lies Iberia, the series creates a hero who is at once Amazigh warrior and Muslim mystic and submits to the Arabo-Muslim authorities. In this way, he is a model of the ideal North Africa from the perspective of the Arab East.

About twenty-five years after Taymur's play, an Arab immigrant to Latin America began to unravel the traditional Tariq story. The *mahjar* poet and journalist Zaki Qunsul (1916–1994) was a Syrian Christian who emigrated in 1929 to Brazil and later Argentina, where he initially worked as a peddler. After publishing several volumes of poetry, he published, in Damascus, the play *Tahta Sama' al-Andalus* (*Under the Skies of al-Andalus*, 1965).[22] Rather than display any explicit concern with the migrant experience, concern for Christian Arab identity is strongly conveyed throughout the text. In fact, I argue that the play is a pro-Christian response to Taymur's play and the discourse that prevails within it.

According to Qunsul's text, the conquest of Iberia was the spreading of Arab civilization and justice, rather than the spreading of Islam. Parallel to this, Tariq is presented not as an ambitious man of war but as a fairly humble man focused on freedom and justice. Not only is Tariq not the consummate macho hero, but he drops out of the play about two thirds of the way through, and the leading man role is taken over by ʿAbd al-ʿAziz, son of Tariq's superior, Musa ibn Nusayr. When Musa and Tariq are called away by their amir (45) they leave ʿAbd al-ʿAziz in charge, and Tariq's parting advice to him is that he should be led by justice and not differentiate between Christian and Muslim in terms of rights (46). ʿAbd al-ʿAziz literally takes this advice to heart and marries a Christian, the widow of King Roderick. In sharp contrast with Taymur's message, at one point the Christian wife defends her marriage by saying, "There is nothing in his religion that goes against the teachings of Christ; for the goal is the same, even if they have different means" (55). To further underscore this message of Muslim-Christian harmony, in the closing scene, in his dying breaths ʿAbd al-ʿAziz warns his successors that they must lead the people with personal and religious freedom, quoting the second half of a Quranic *ʾaya* that is invoked by Christian Arabs to this day to demonstrate affinity and fondness between Muslims and Christians (Z. Qunsul 65): "and you will find the nearest of them in affection to the believers [in Islam] those who say 'We are Christians'" (5:82; http://www.quran.com).

Although it may seem that ʿAbd al-ʿAziz becomes the hero of this play, I propose that it is actually Julian. In Qunsul's version of the story, Julian is redeemed and rehabilitated. This Julian, in repentance for having betrayed his "country," joins a monastery and changes his name (59–60). Thus, although Julian at first is characterized by deceit and betrayal, ultimately he reappears as a noble man and, considering that his transformation as a monk makes him a symbol for Christianity, though he is not physically present in the closing scene, he is nonetheless strongly evoked by it. One could say that in this version of the conquest story Tariq is actually upstaged because Julian steals the show. From his position as an Arab Christian, Qunsul's version is not concerned with remembering and maintaining Muslim glory but with asserting the importance of religious pluralism within the Arab world. While Qunsul's text rewrites the Tariq and Julian story and the history of the conquest in general, more explicit questioning of the Tariq story did not occur for a few more years, and all at the hands of Maghrebi writers.

Driss Chraïbi and Bensalem Himmich: A Hybrid Moroccan Tariq and Sexual Conquest

Francophone Moroccan writer Driss Chraïbi (1926–2007) is considered one of the founding figures of modern Maghrebian literature. In 1954, at the height of the conflict between France and Morocco, Chraïbi published the highly controversial novel *Le Passé simple*, which criticized both French colonial rule and the patriarchal system in Morocco. Decried by Moroccans who deemed that he had betrayed his country during a crucial nation-building juncture, the book was banned in Morocco until 1977. Part of why the novel created such a stir is that it debunks the myth of pure Moroccan origins, paving the way for critical assessments of the indigenous forces at work in the country's colonial histories.

In 1986, roughly the midpoint of his writing career, Chraïbi published *Naissance à l'aube* (*Birth at Dawn*), which is the final work in a trilogy that focuses on the survival of an Amazigh community, the Aït Yafelman clan, through various challenging encounters. The first novel of the trilogy, *Une Enquête au pays*, comments upon late twentieth-century state centralization policies and their effect on rural Amazigh life; the second, *La Mère du printemps* (*L'Oum-er-Bia*), narrates the meeting of the ancestors of those Amazighs, the Aït Yafelman clan, and the Muslim general Oqba ibn Nafi [ʿUqba ibn Nafiʿ]. The third novel, *Naissance à l'aube*, narrates the subsequent encounter between the next generation of Amazighs and Tariq ibn Ziyad, Tariq's conquest of Iberia and establishment of Cordoba, and his "descendant" ʿAbd Allah ibn Yasin's founding of the Almoravid Amazigh dynasty, known for its strict practice of Islam. As Danielle Marx-Scouras aptly puts it: "If many Maghrebian critics never forgave Chraïbi for not attributing the narrator's split identity entirely to French colonialism in *Le Passé simple*, they will be even more disturbed by the global proportions of the identity crisis that he depicts in novels that explore the Arab-Islamic conquest of Morocco and Andalusia. For Chraïbi, there are no pure civilizations" (140–41). Although Chraïbi's trilogy is usually seen by critics as a demystification of official history, few critics have considered why the history of al-Andalus per se is the target of the trilogy's demystification, and none seem to have considered how al-Andalus is played out within the specific textual dynamics of *Naissance*.

Chraïbi's *Naissance* presents a tongue-in-cheek portrait of Tariq as barbaric yet seeking a lasting alternative to war through conquests that will create unity, a Machiavellian strategist who seeks peace, a virile man and committed Muslim whose idiosyncratic practice of Islam includes having sex before each call to prayer, even when his concubine is menstruating and thus ritually impure. This caricaturesque Tariq is later overcome by an Amazigh voice that draws him away from religion and ultimately is salvaged as a hero of sorts by the author's postscript. Although Jacqueline Kaye and Abdelhamid Zoubir view Chraïbi as a supporter of the colonial French policy of treating Amazigh culture as completely separate from and superior to Islamic culture (13), in *Naissance à l'aube*, the situation is more complex. Rather than present an Amazigh culture that is separate from Islam, it presents one that is intimately tied to it, albeit an Islam of subjective interpretation and syncretic character. The novel contains many quotes and allusions to the Quran and hadith, the text of the novel is interspersed with Arabic calligraphy presenting Quranic quotes or the word *Allah*, and, as Carine Bourget points out, Islam serves as a uniting force among characters from various different ethnic, linguistic, and class backgrounds (58).[23] However, the text positions Amazighs as superior to Arabs. Moreover, ousting Arabs from their role as the traditional custodians of Islam, in this text the Amazighs take ownership of Islam. In contrast with the versions of Tariq's conquest written by al-Jundi, Taymur, and even Qunsul, Chraïbi's version presents a clearly syncretic Islam with idiosyncratic interpretations; moments of criticism, sarcasm, and doubt; and an impure lineage.[24]

Chraïbi's unorthodox, hyperbolic Tariq not only burns the boats used to cross the straits but, because God does not need earthly help, he has his soldiers break their swords and throw them into the sea (117). This Tariq, a polar opposite to that of the Egyptian serial, is a brash man of action, not a mystical, compassionate, or contemplative man. Rather than befriend Count Julian, Chraïbi's Tariq considers Julian a traitor and lets an Amazigh soldier strangle him to death (119). Similarly, Chraïbi's Tariq, rather than work out his differences with his Arab superior, Musa ibn Nusayr, responds to Musa's letter criticizing Tariq as ignoble and savage—a barbarian/Berber—by eating the letter and intensifying his "savage" battle tactics, thus beginning a war between the two conquerors (124). That is, he responds to accusations of being a barbarian/*barbar* by embracing the purportedly barbarian characteristics of "Berbers" and thus identifying more strongly as Amazigh. In this way, Chraïbi reappropriates the discourses on the savageness of the Amazighs (created by both French and Arab colonizers) in the creation of a powerful Amazigh identity.

Chraïbi's Tariq serves to deliver a strong pro-Amazigh, anti-Arab message that is evident in various other moments of Amazigh–Arab tension that echo Tariq's conflict with his Arab general. As John Hawley has explained, Chraïbi's earlier focus on the psychological and social fractures created by education under colonialism reach an unexpected level of resolution in part through "a personal return to his pre-Arabic roots in the Berber people of Morocco" (64). In contrast with the narrator in *Le Passé simple*, who identifies himself as an Arab, the narrator and main characters in *Naissance* clearly view the Amazigh community as separate and superior to Arabs. For instance, Chraïbi's Tariq suggests that earthly desires, rather than piety, are what motivated the Arab Muslim conquests (118) and blames the division and destruction of the umma (Muslim community) on Arab avarice (118–19). Tariq, who proudly identifies as a sly "Berber [*berbère*]" (122–23), proclaims to his Bedouin and Amazigh troops, as they start to build Cordoba, that the golden age of Islam in the East is over and now it is time to revive it in the West—the Maghreb and al-Andalus: "Sons of the East and of the Berbers, listen: the East is dying. It is behind you with its Damascus[es], its Bagdads and its endless divisions which inundate the earth with blood and falsify the word of God. Never will you go back there. You are here now, in the West, and it is as if you had just been born" (31 [55–56]). Reworking Tariq's famous words about what laid behind his men, this Tariq declares that the Muslims of the East had failed and sowed division within the umma (90), and now the rebirth of Islam is in the hands of the Amazighs.

At times the rebirth of Islam is quite literally in the hands of Amazighs. A key recurring figure in Chraïbi's trilogy is Azwaw Aït Yafelman, the forefather of the Aït Yafelman clan, who is known for the healing power of his hands and is particularly famous for his skill at delivering babies. Throughout the trilogy Azwaw brings Amazigh beliefs and traditional practices together with the rituals of Islam. When Azwaw first appears in *Naissance*, after his own rebirth generations after his death, he helps a camel give birth to her calf. Not long after he meets Tariq, who decides that in spite of Azwaw's syncretic beliefs, he will be useful to the Muslim enterprise in al-Andalus. Azwaw proves this to be true when he helps his daughter, the wife of the emir of Cordoba, deliver a male heir after many stillbirths. Through a magical, mystical genealogy this male heir, son of the Arab emir and the Amazigh woman (grandson of Azwaw) grows up and marries Tariq's daughter; this union, generations later, produces ʿAbd Allah ibn Yasin (d. 1059), the theologian and founder of the Almoravid Amazigh dynasty.

Chraïbi's inclusion of Ibn Yasin in the narrative, alongside the postconquest life that he imagines for Tariq, make for a potentially ambiguous ending to the novel. In Chraïbi's version of events, Tariq ends his days locked up in chains by Musa, tormented by thoughts of the past and the future, and doubting his faith in Islam (144–46). These thoughts are dominated by the voice of Azwaw, and though we are never told what it is that Azwaw is telling Tariq, we do know that "What he was saying had no words, *no religion*—no hope nor disillusionment" (99 [145]). Thus, Tariq ends his days distanced from religion and hope, but free of disillusionment, reborn to a demystified version of Andalusi, Moroccan, and Muslim identities by the voice of Azwaw. Moreover, through poetic license, Tariq is the forefather of ʿAbd Allah ibn Yasin, who headed the dogmatic Almoravid movement that grew into an Amazigh Muslim dynasty that spanned North Africa and Iberia (1040–1147). The narrator, pointing to the famously puritanical ways of the Almoravids, tells of ʿAbd Allah ibn Yasin's visit to Cordoba and how his strict interpretation of Muslim piety clashed with the lavish, painstaking pleasures of the city. Rather than elicit any appreciation for al-Andalus's earthly delights, the luxuries make Ibn Yasin feel impure. The narrator refers to the spread and duration of the Almoravid dynasty and then closes the novel with a cryptic reference to that dynasty as "the space of a renewal, an infinitesimal spring of sidereal eternity" (130 [186]). What does it mean to say that a dynasty known for its strict interpretation of Islam was a time and space of renewal, a small springtime within the eternity of space? How can this be reconciled with the text's playful yet critical attitude toward Islam and its clear acceptance of syncretic and idiosyncratic religious beliefs? I propose that while the author pokes fun at the rigid, austere beliefs of Ibn Yasin, he sees the Almoravid dynasty as a brief glimmer of regeneration because it was an Amazigh Muslim dynasty that arose in the Maghreb and linked the region to Iberia—rather than a defunct Arab dynasty from the East.

How does the purist, stalwart Ibn Yasin relate to the version of Tariq that *Naissance* offers? After the passage that presents Tariq anguished in chains and references to his paternity of Ibn Yasin's forefathers, Tariq's name is not mentioned again in the novel until we arrive at the author's postscript: "Dreamed in the Middle Ages on the vestiges of a birth, in Cordoba, then in Fès; written in France 1984–1985, at night, sometimes in the afternoon, during the naps of my youngest son: TARIQ" (my trans. [186]). The author's decision to name his youngest son Tariq and the gesture of disclosing this to the reader play a significant role in the message of the text. This gesture is a way of indicating that the author sympathizes more with Tariq than with ʿAbd Allah ibn Yasin, founder of a fundamentalist (albeit Amazigh) dynasty. Chraïbi's Tariq, with his cunning and savagery, nearly becomes a caricature, but is stopped short of that by this gesture, which reveals great fondness toward the brash Amazigh leader. Instead, through this epilogue and his championing of the Amazigh community, Tariq emerges as an incongruous hero. Furthermore, by unexpectedly placing Tariq within the genealogy of Ibn Yasin, the novel tells us that hybridity is there from the start.[25] Through this creative genealogy, *Naissance* not only highlights that one of Islam's earliest "return to purity" movements arose from the Amazigh community, it also gives Ibn Yasin, a symbol of purity, impure ancestors and thus pokes fun at the idea of going back to pure origins. The novel implies that Almoravids and today's Salafist groups cannot return to a pure Islam because syncretism was there from the start.[26] For Chraïbi, religious and nationalist purity are therefore absurd and impossible concepts. In the same way that Tariq questions the possibility of Muslim unity when Musa, another Muslim, imprisons him, Chraïbi's reader is encouraged to question the "pure" origins of Islam and the Muslim empire and the purity of Tariq himself.

Chraïbi's Tariq, more of an amusing rogue than an impeccable champion of Islam, breaks the mold that official history had propagated and Kamil, Zaydan, Taymur, al-Jundi, and Qunsul largely replicated. Chraïbi breaks the Tariq mold by rewriting the history of the Almoravids and juxtaposing the moment of the initial Muslim conquest of Iberia (Tariq's crossing of the strait) with earlier and later conquests of the western Mediterranean. Within the novel, the narrator offers an interpretative key by pointing to the importance of history: Emir Badruddin, the wise Arab Muslim scholar who oversees the building of Cordoba, reads from one of the ancient books in his library: "'Unless you know what has happened before you were born, you will always remain a child…'" (45 [74]). To move his readership beyond childlike innocence, Chraïbi offers a wide-angle view of history. He accomplishes this through small details in the narrative as well as the framing introductory story and its relationship to the main story. A recurring detail in the novel underscores the impurity of certain icons by placing them in a transcolonial frame of reference. On four different occasions the narrator and characters use the term "mosque-cathedral" (32, 94, 104, and 129) to refer to the Great Mosque of Cordoba which, after Catholic conquest, became the Cathedral of Cordoba. Although today the hyphenated phrase "mosque-cathedral" is used as a politically correct appellation for this space, in the context of the novel, it is an anachronism that points to hybridity as well as the ebbs and flows of empire: the structure was first built as an Arian Christian Visigoth church, and after Tariq's invasion, for a few decades the structure was divided between Muslims and Christians until Abd al-Rahman I purchased the Christian half of the building and began to modify the structure to create the Great Mosque. With the conquest of Cordoba by King Ferdinand III of Castile in 1236, it became a Catholic church and later a cathedral, in which Muslim prayers are still banned.[27] Thus, though technically anachronistic because the mosque was turned into a cathedral (rather than simply a church) centuries after Tariq or Ibn Yasin's time, the hyphenated phrase invokes, on one hand, a period of religious coexistence in which the iconic structure had a hybrid symbolic and spiritual value, and, on the other hand, a space that has been the symbolic marker of various conquests and shifts in power. Unbeknownst to the typical reader, during Tariq ibn Ziyad's time the structure was a mosque-church, but the contemporary hyphenated term (mosque-cathedral) within a recounting of the supposed glory days of Islam attests to successive power shifts. The recurring, anachronistic hyphenated phrase draws our attention to the temporal, contingent, and layered nature of even the most iconic sites within the succession of conquests that have taken place in the western Mediterranean.

In another strategy that creates historical juxtaposition, *Naissance* begins with an unnamed, external narrator, focalized on Raho, a twentieth-century Amazigh descendant of the Aït Yafelman tribe. The narrative of his interactions with a French Christian boss and then a new urban, Arab-identified Moroccan boss reveals that Raho has more commonalities and a stronger bond with the former than with the latter. In the midst of Raho's conversation with the French boss, the narrator presents a skeptical view of civilization. He refers to Muslim (Arab) and Christian (French) colonization as a devastation of the land and says "They called that 'civilization'" (10 [24]). By following this criticism of both the French and the Arab Muslim civilizing missions with an inventive retelling of Tariq's conquest of Iberia and the birth of the Almoravid dynasty, Chraïbi breaks a taboo and categorizes the Arab spread of Islam not as a *fath* or opening (as it is known in Arabic) but as a conquest and goes on to show how religious authenticity is a construction. In this transcolonial critique, Chraïbi uses the imperial dynamics of al-Andalus to address the enduring Arab/Amazigh dynamics of today.

Chraïbi's attitude toward official history makes the goals of his writing project clearer. In an interview he expressed great distrust toward history: "I do not believe in History. It is written here and there with various interpretations. It is written after the event and not during. The gaze of imagination joins introspection" (Merino, "Coups de cœur en liberté" 31). Chraïbi's project, then, is to craft narratives that offer alternative histories and an awareness of recurring power dynamics across history. He translates the figure of Tariq ibn Ziyad, sanctified by history, into a barbaric, barely Muslim Berber hero. Tariq, an Amazigh with heroic status in the Arabo-Muslim world, provides the material with which to recast the role of Amazigh culture and insist on its inclusion in narratives of not only Moroccan but also Muslim history. When Chraïbi's Tariq crosses the strait, he leaves behind blind allegiance to narratives that only selectively include him and becomes a symbol of the Amazigh-Muslim-Arab elements of Moroccan hybridity. However, Chraïbi's *Naissance* questions history while retaining a form of hero status for Tariq. In contrast, other Maghrebian works, most of them written later, critique other aspects of the Tariq myth, including the very workings of historiography that lead to sanctification.

Given the details of Chraïbi's *Naissance* discussed earlier, as well as the novel's portrayal of Tariq's concubine as a passive and submissive woman, the one aspect of the heroicized Tariq that Chraïbi heightens even more, rather than dismantle, is that of hypermasculinity. In contrast, through two key references to Tariq ibn Ziyad, the 2007 novel *Hadha al-Andalusi* (*That Man from al-Andalus*), implicitly criticizes hypermasculine versions of Tariq and offers another way to conceive of both intercultural contact and the history of al-Andalus. This historical novel by prominent Moroccan novelist and professor of philosophy Bensalem Himmich [Bin Salim Himmish] (b. 1948), tells the story of the simple pleasures and tragic trials of the Sufi philosopher Ibn Sabʿin of Murcia (c. 1217–1270) and in the process disentangles conquest from hypermasculinity and sexual domination.

Part I of Himmich's novel starts with a quote from Tariq's famous speech taken from a version slightly different from that of al-Maqqari. Recall that in this speech Tariq addresses his troops on arrival at the Iberian shore and enjoins them to fight valiantly and thus reap the benefits of conquest. The specific segment of Tariq's speech that opens Himmich's novel states: "You have already heard about the beauteous maidens that this peninsula has produced, daughters of Greece, bedecked in pearls and coral, gowns embossed with eagles, boudoirs in palaces of crowned kings" (1 [5]). In what follows, the protagonist Ibn Sabʿin conveys his pain on losing one of his manuscripts and declares that his quest at that point in his life is women (23). His trysts, however, are not the conquests of an aggressive male but are connected to shared intellectual interests and mutual consent. His lovers are intelligent women of various faiths with whom he discusses philosophy and who reject other men's efforts at controlling them. The specific fragment from Tariq's legendary speech that Himmich uses to open his novel explicitly links territorial conquest with sexual conquest and partakes in the logic of the gendered discourses surrounding conquest the world over. In contrast, in Himmich's work, Ibn Sabʿin's quest for women does not manifest itself as a series of "conquests," that is, as the assertion of power hierarchies, but as mutual encounters that are intellectual, spiritual, and sexual. In this way, Himmich's *Hadha al-Andalusi* subtly disrupts the paradigm of al-Andalus as a woman subjugated by a male conqueror and offers another model for interpersonal and intercultural relationships.

Tariq ibn Ziyad is invoked again in this fictional autobiography in a way that points to the constructed nature of the mythical figure of the conqueror and of history in general. At the beginning of part II of *Hadha al-Andalusi*, as Ibn Sabʿin recounts his experiences in his first place of exile, Ceuta, which happens to have been Tariq's point of departure for the conquest of Iberia, the protagonist refers to regularly seeing the promontory named after Tariq and the word choice in his recounting of his thought process is quite noteworthy:

> I spent my time here in prayer, contemplation, study, and learning. Whenever I could, I wandered along the shore and up the hills. When the weather was nice, my longing for al-Andalus grew stronger. I looked over the straits at Algeciras and then at the Rock of Gibraltar right in front of me; in my mind I could envision myself climbing to the top of the mountain named after the great conqueror and leafing through the pages of glory and honor. (adapted from Allen's trans. 94 [127])[28]

Here the novel associates the act of scaling the promontory named after Tariq with perusing "the pages of glory and honor," not the pages of history but pages that are the basis of the particular image that has been created of this conqueror. Tariq is presented in terms of textuality, his glory and honor consisting of pages of writing. This metafictional phrasing highlights the narrative quality of history and of the legacy of al-Andalus. While Ibn Sabʿin's longing for the Andalus from which he was forced to flee is heightened by the sight of Gibraltar [Jabal Tariq], he nonetheless maintains an awareness of the narrative quality of the history of al-Andalus, embodied in the heroic Tariq, that has been passed down to him. Unlike Chraïbi's *Naissance*, Himmich's novel does not address Tariq's Amazigh origins but instead offers a commentary on knowledge about Tariq as narrative. Moreover, *Hadha al-Andalusi* transfers Tariq's speech and its call to sexual conquest into a new context, that of Ibn Sabʿin's relationships, and in so doing it rewrites the pages of Tariq's legacy by offering an alternate model of masculinity and cross-cultural contact.

Rachid Boudjedra and Tariq as Translation

While Himmich's novel implicitly critiques the problematic gender dynamics surrounding the mythical Tariq and points to the textuality of that myth, another Maghrebian author, Rachid Boudjedra [Rashid Abu Jadra] (b. 1941) radically dismantles Tariq's mythic status. The renowned Algerian writer explicitly questions the truth value of history and the mode of the linear story itself. Boudjedra's *Maʿrakat al-Zuqaq* (*The Battle of the Corridor*, 1986) and its later French version, *La Prise de Gibraltar*

(*The Capture of Gibraltar*, 1987), are written in a fragmented, lyrical, stream-of-consciousness style reminiscent of William Faulkner and Gabriel García Márquez. Boudjedra is particularly noteworthy because of his relationship to language in the context of Algeria's postcolonial history. In 1981, after nearly two decades of writing and publishing in French, Boudjedra switched to Arabic as a statement of support for Algerian national culture, only to switch back to French again in 1992.[29] Throughout he has collaborated in the translation of his own works between the two languages.

The French version of the novel adds details to *Maʿrakat al-Zuqaq* that can be understood as embedded translator's notes, and it also adds material that makes some of the opaque connections between scenes, images, and characters more evident. For this reason, the French version is not only a translation but a further elaboration of the Arabic version. At the same time, certain nuances of the Arabic text, most notably the title, which refers to the strait by its ancient Arabic name, are not found in the French version.[30] For the sake of expediency, rather than compare the two versions, I largely treat the texts as complementary pieces.[31]

Both versions of Boudjedra's Tariq story include quotes and references in the other language: citations in French in the Arabic version and vice versa. Like Chraïbi, Boudjedra acknowledges Tariq's Amazigh identity and makes it central to the narrative, so the two versions occasionally include transliterated Tamazight (Berber) words. In addition, within the Arabic version instead of using only standard literary Arabic, the text sometimes features Algerian colloquial Arabic (e.g., A 12). The resulting linguistic multiplicity together with the complex style of Boudjedra's poetic prose make his works difficult but ultimately rewarding.[32] Exploring the fascination with Tariq within the context of the French colonization of Algeria, Boudjedra uses his writing style to question the mythology created around Tariq and traditional conceptions of history and narrative in general. As Leonor Merino indicates, Boudjedra's treatment of the conquest of Iberia, in contrast with that of Chraïbi, offers "el reverso del mito"—the flip side of the myth ("Conquista" 92). I would take this further and argue that Boudjedra does not simply invert the paradigm and make Tariq a maligned figure; rather, he presents the inner struggles of the process of demystification and ultimately presents Tariq as a useful cultural tool.

In terms of chronology, Boudjedra's pieces on Tariq ibn Ziyad are centered on events in the mid-1950s, but the protagonist is situated in the 1980s looking back at his youth, and through quoted histories and descriptions of paintings, the texts also take us back to Tariq's battle in Gibraltar that led to the Muslim conquest of Iberia. The novels juxtapose that conquest with a key battle of the Algerian war of independence, the Battle of Philippeville, which spread into neighboring Constantine, pointing to the curious coincidence that both battles took place on August 20, one in 711 and the other in 1955. Boudjedra's texts give us an impressionistic, collage-like perspective on the protagonist's experiences growing up in Algeria during the struggle for independence, raised by a father obsessed with translation and the Muslim conquest of al-Andalus. The two texts present recurring images and memories through jumps in temporality and point of view that include the protagonist's childhood through adulthood and first-, second-, and third-person narration. The storyline, which the reader is responsible for piecing together, follows the experiences of the Algerian protagonist whose father is so obsessed with Tariq ibn Ziyad that he names his son Tariq. This Algerian Tariq grows up amid the independence movement being forced by his domineering father to translate classical Arabic histories of Tariq's victory over the Visigoths, contemplating painted images of Tariq's conquest, remembering his mother and processing her death, contending with an abusive teacher at the Quranic school, recounting the run-in between himself and his cousin and a group of French soldiers when the two boys are caught writing nationalist/anti-French slogans, and learning about Tariq ibn Ziyad in high school. Interwoven with these repeating scenes are recurring passages from the Quran, from the famous Arab historian Ibn Khaldun, and from Tariq ibn Ziyad's legendary speech.[33] These recurring scenes and citations are repeated, with slight variations, along with moments in the life of the Algerian Tariq as an adult (his contemplation of a constantly moving construction crane and his trip to Gibraltar) to create a mélange that is loosely strung together through recurring colors, foremost among them yellow.

The protagonist, the twentieth-century Algerian Tariq, who is also the main narrator, moves from the yellow color of a crane in a modernizing Algerian city, to "Yellow like the horses gathered at the strait of Gibraltar" (A 8–9/F 14–15), to the yellow crayon he and his cousin use to write anti-French and pro-nationalist slogans. Bit by bit, through the accretion of details about the scenes and objects of description, the reader pieces together that the yellow horses are a central image in a thirteenth-century miniature by al-Wasiti that depicts Tariq ibn Ziyad with his cavalry at the moment of his entry into Iberia and that a reproduction of this painting hangs in the office of the present-day Tariq's father.[34] Passages of ekphrasis centered on this painting and on the illustrations in one of the history books in Tariq's father's library, recur throughout the novel. In the often-extensive descriptions of these pieces of visual art, the narrator considers who is doing what in the image and speculates about the significance of particular details.

With regard to al-Wasiti's miniature, the narrator notes that the horses, rather than Tariq, seem to be the centerpiece of the image and links this to the painter's location in Persian-dominated Baghdad. Among the illustrations in his father's history book (the same book from which he is often forced to translate), one miniature in particular interests him: a gruesome scene of invading Muslim warriors and European women fleeing with their children, eyes bulging with terror. This scene of the horrors of war, which leads him to think of his own mother and the violence of French colonization and Algerian resistance, simultaneously makes him recoil and fascinates him (A 145/F 257–58, 301). The protagonist seems to identify with the terrified women and children of Iberia and at the same time relishes the great display of Muslim military strength. Although Thierno Dia Toure (20–21) discusses the presentation of the illustration as a postmodern approach to violence, what strikes me about the ekphrasis in these texts is that it serves to highlight the mediation involved in representation and historiography. The insistence on describing these visual representations of conquest conveys the protagonist's fixation with the Muslim conquest of al-Andalus in counterpoint to the colonization of his country by the French. Yet as he gazes on these images, he questions the motivations of the painter (was al-Wasiti trying to make a pro-Persian statement?) and demonstrates the mesmerizing effect of the scenes. At the same time, readers only access the visual works through the narrator's verbal reconstruction. In this way, alongside the constant comparison of different historical accounts of the conquest of Iberia that also takes place in these texts, the contemplation of these visual depictions emphasizes that there is no certain, unbiased history but only reconstructions of the past. As Hayden White has shown, by plotting events in a particular way the historian inserts a moral, a lesson to be learned that relates to a particular *telos*.[35] Boudjedra's novels on Tariq highlight the fallacious lessons embedded in the historical accounts and legends surrounding this figure.

Two other elements of Boudjedra's Tariq story share in this deconstruction of history as narrative: the revelations made by the Algerian history teacher and the trip to Gibraltar. The Algerian Tariq and his friends and classmates all take pride in Tariq ibn Ziyad's Amazigh origins and revere him as a symbol of Arab–North African power. However, their admiration is cut short when one day their history teacher undoes the mystique of this figure and his legendary speech, which they had to memorize in school. The teacher informs the students that there is no reliable documentation supporting the idea that Tariq ibn Ziyad actually delivered this speech and that in all likelihood it is apocryphal. (The teacher's revisionist history hinges on an issue of translation, to which I return shortly.) This eloquent speech, full of military and political rhetoric that had so inspired the young men in their fight against the French, turns out to be a masquerade, a falsification (F 200). The narrator describes the impact of this revelation as a cataclysmic disaster (F 217). As a result, the Algerian Tariq comes to see the conquest in a new light: not only did Tariq ibn Ziyad not write the speech, but he managed to conquer Gibraltar because of Julian, who was trying to avenge Roderick's deflowering of his daughter. Rather than military glory, it was a story of sex (F 189–91, 202). The protagonist-narrator asks why history is so deformed, disguised, and fragile (F 183/A 99) and reports that the teacher has made them detest history and realize that it is falsified (F 193–94). When his father tells him that he should be proud of his name and its symbolism (F 262/A 147–48), we see that the narrator considers it a mistake to have named him Tariq (F 263). When the Algerian Tariq rejects his namesake, the mythical Tariq begins to die along with the protagonist's faith in history.

Nonetheless, the twentieth-century Tariq is still haunted by his namesake. Interwoven with all the other recurring episodes we find an adult Tariq convincing his friend to go with him to visit Gibraltar, that is, Tariq's mountain. Although he has never been there, Gibraltar is part of the twentieth-century Tariq's mental image (A 45); it is his main ghost (F 92–93), a magical name, and a fixation for him (F 97, 102). In his desire to get over his old phantasm, Tariq convinces his friend to go there with him. But the trip to Gibraltar ends up being another experience of disillusionment. They arrive on the same date that Tariq ibn Ziyad arrived in Iberia, but their attempts to trace his footsteps are frustrated as they search in vain for Arab ruins and an Arab fountain. By repeatedly recalling the crushing effect of the history lesson and the disappointing trip to Gibraltar, the narrator questions the mythology created around Tariq as well as traditional conceptions of history and narrative at large. That is, the narrative structure of Boudjedra's two works themselves point to the slipperiness of language and the difficulty of representing lived reality—let alone centuries-old history. The narrator's unsettling experiences lead the twentieth-century Tariq to state that Tariq ibn Ziyad is a "phantom, an obsession either admired or feared" (F 146). Here the ghostly trauma discussed by Flesler is not only experienced by the conquered—by the Iberians and those who identify as their descendants—but also by one who identifies as a descendant of the conqueror. Upon realizing the degree to which history is fiction, to which an inspiring figure from the past is only a construction, that figure becomes a haunting problem.

Michel Lantelme, in his article on the twentieth-century Tariq's obsession with Gibraltar, states, "what is at play here through the 'fantasy' of Gibraltar is the relationship of Boudjedra with the West, in all its complexity" (518). In my view, however, it is clear in the novel that the twentieth-century Tariq seeks to reject the French and, while he is working out how to go about doing so, what undergoes a major transformation is the protagonist's relationship to Arab cultural heritage and its meta-narratives. Gibraltar is not so much a locale that typefies the West, as Lantelme submits, as it is the site of the lost, ghostly Arab conquest of Europe. It represents elusive Arabo-Muslim power, a trace of past glory that cannot be substantiated.

The protagonist's relationship with the West, and his struggle with his (purported) cultural heritage gets played out through his confrontations with French soldiers in Algeria and also through his relationship to language. When Tariq and his cousin write anti-French slogans, Tariq is preoccupied by the fact that his cousin has misspelled French words and that they are making themselves look like the savages that the colonizers make them out to be. This concern with the linguistic projection of the self, and another form of disillusionment, reverberates throughout these texts. Surprisingly, even though a great deal of scholarly attention has been paid to Boudjedra's choice to write in French, little has been said about other linguistic tensions inherent in this set of texts. To begin with, although there is a wealth of scholarship on *La Prise de Gibraltar*, there is almost none on *Maʿrakat al-Zuqaq*, which seems to have garnered little attention. Although Alfonso de Toro briefly mentions the translation of the novel from Arabic to French as part of its hybrid structure (193), few critics of the Francophone text even recognize that the text is at least ostensibly a translation from an earlier Arabic text.[36] To the best of my knowledge, none make more than a passing reference to the role of translation within the narrative of both versions of the text.

In both versions of the novel, translation has a strong presence and yet striking absence. On one hand, translation is explicitly linked to authority, and on the other, it is implicitly connected to the loss of authority. Translation is at the heart of the protagonist's power struggle with his father, who forces Tariq to translate texts without a dictionary—without recourse to the existing archive—and then contests his son's translations. The protagonist's father requests that he translate (typically between Arabic and French and occasionally from Latin) as a form of intellectual exercise. He asks his son to translate classical texts about the conquest of al-Andalus in particular as a sort of provocation against the French colonial authorities in Algeria, but he is never satisfied with the translations and ends up taking over the task. The translation process itself becomes a key element in the texts with the presence of many different versions of translations and each forced translation encounter ending with the father humiliating and insulting his son for his inadequate transfer of meaning. While the father frustrates the son with his rigid ideas on how to translate, the separation between languages is blurred. For instance, at one point the protagonist discusses a French word of Arab origin (*charabia*) (F 113/A 54) and throughout the French version the phrase *version-thème* is used. The French *thème* refers to a translation into a foreign language while *version* is a translation into one's own language. By using the hyphenated *version-thème*, the text blurs the lines between foreign and native tongue and thus calls into question notions of language-based identity. This manifestation of translation as a fluid process which an authority figure (the father) makes overly difficult and rigid, stands in tension with a way in which translation is seemingly erased from the text.

The crisis occasioned by the history teacher also evokes translation. This major disillusionment hinges on the high school professor's statement that as a recent Amazigh convert to Islam, Tariq could not have delivered the famous speech attributed to him. Given his recent exposure to Arabic, Tariq would not have been able to author this text of exemplary Arabic rhetoric and eloquence. As noted, the history teacher's pronouncement has a profound impact on the protagonist and his classmates. What strikes me is that in spite of the fact that the novel addresses the act of translation and itself is a translation in more than one way, the potential role of translation in Tariq's speech is never mentioned. Is it not possible that Tariq ibn Ziyad delivered this speech in Tamazight to his soldiers (after all, if he addressed them in Arabic they wouldn't have understood much because they themselves were Amazighs recently converted to Islam) and that someone later translated it into Arabic? Curiously, in a text so steeped in translation, this possible translation from Tamazight is never even hinted at. Perhaps this does not happen precisely because the dominance of Arabic is such that the possible Tamazight utterance is not only lost but not imaginable, and not of interest, to the history teacher. In addition, if the speech were understood as a translation, rather than as an apocryphal text, it may still be perceived as "inauthentic"—as inadmissible in a narrative of Arabo-Muslim cultural heritage.

The lost original (the Tamazight speech) thus becomes doubly lost origins: lost Amazigh origins as well as the Arab origins lost with the destruction of the inspirational, mythic conqueror. The phantasm here is the Arabic-speaking Tariq, much like it is the Arabic-writing Boudjedra. Just as, according to the history teacher, Tariq ibn Ziyad could not speak Arabic, and thus cannot inspire mid-twentieth-century Algerian nationalism, Boudjedra struggles with expressing himself in written Arabic and thus supporting Algerian cultural independence. Ultimately, the tensions and omissions surrounding translation are productive because they highlight the many forms of verbal mediation involved in the creation of history, but also because they draw our attention to the transcoloniality of power, that is, the links between the layered past and the conditions of post-colonial expression.

Boudjedra's layering of descriptions of visual images and fragments of historical texts, translations, and memories leads to two pronounced and ultimately converging threads: that of al-Andalus as death and that of Tariq, as an Arabic-speaking Amazigh Muslim hero, as a haunting fiction. At one point the description of the illustrations is interwoven with a translation scene with the narrator's overbearing father (A 10-11/F 20–21). The father gives the son Ibn Khaldun's account of the conquest, and the son translates it literally, amid the smell of death: for him the smell of his mother's death mixes with that of the European women of Iberia. In a recurrence of this scene, the twentieth-century Tariq wonders what the connection is between these deaths, those of the French and the Algerians, and his own mother's death (F 259–60). Rather than maintain any trace of the vision of the inception of al-Andalus as the basis for the creation of cultural vitality in a paradise garden, Boudjedra's work points to the death and destruction that were part of the establishment of al-Andalus. Boudjedra also presents the vantage point of the conquered in Iberia, and in that way he departs from the typical Muslim historical perspective on al-Andalus. With regard to Tariq ibn Ziyad, when the narrator discusses the effect of the history class, he refers to it as "the death knell of their hopes, their certainties, their passions/fanaticisms, and their chauvinisms" (F 181). For the twentieth-century Tariq and his classmates, Tariq ibn Ziyad and the hope he gave them have died. In a very telling detail, the title of the Arabic version of the text erases Tariq completely: rather than use the common contemporary name for the strait—*Madiq Jabal Tariq*—and thereby invoke Tariq's conquest, the title refers to the strait by its ancient, preconquest Arabic name: al-Zuqaq (the corridor or strait). Both versions of the text note that Arabic sources don't say much about Tariq after his departure for Damascus and that nothing is known about his death (F 291–92/A 168–69). Boudjedra's works are the narration of Tariq's metaphoric death, his death as a revered icon.

In a sense the demystification of Tariq is part of what Merino refers to as the "desacralization" of the authoritarian father, a revenge against the father through his beloved Arab heritage (Merino, "Conquista" 90). But this blow to the controlling father is at the same time a blow to the mythical narrative of Arab conquest and to the other layers of colonial power dynamics experienced by the narrator—that of French colonization and postindependence neocolonial hierarchies. In this way, the novel enacts a critique of transcoloniality. This is evident near the end of the narrative when Tariq's father berates his son for being against Tariq ibn Ziyad's "opening" (fath) of al-Andalus. He tells his son that he knows that the history teacher considers that "old imperialism" (A 177) and that he knows that for his son "Tariq ibn Ziyad is a nasty colonizer who was successful, while Bugeaud [leader of the French campaign in Algeria] is a nasty colonizer who failed" (F 302–3). Tariq's unspoken, sardonic reaction is to think that the conquest of Spain can't be considered a success anyway since after eight centuries they found themselves back where they started. Boudjedra's texts state directly that the Muslim empire was also a colonial power and furthermore that it should not be painted as a great success. The moment of conquest, Tariq's entry, is not one of glory and power but one of colonial violence—both the violence wrought on the Visigoth women and children and the violence of the father's imperative to translate. Boudjedra plays with the conqueror/conquered roles, and the protagonist is indirectly conquered by Tariq ibn Ziyad through his identification with the conquered Visigoths as well as his obligation to translate and contemplate representations of the moment of conquest. At the same time, the twentieth-century Tariq is also able to conquer the official history of the start of al-Andalus and the phantom of Tariq, the obsession that his father tries to pass on to him.

Elsewhere Boudjedra has stated quite clearly his understanding of history, of his position as both colonizer and colonized, and of the Muslim dynasties of al-Andalus:

> It is through the reading of history that our own history is called into question. My history as an Algerian, as an Arab and a Muslim. That is to say that I myself was a colonizer one day before being colonized, and that it's necessary to get back to all that. [. . .] And I would not want an Algerian, someone who has suffered 130 years of colonization, to say that the French colonization of Algeria is bad but the Arab colonization in Spain is good. This is what is said, of course.

> That's the official history [/story]. That's the official literature. All Arabs today weep over the lost al-Andalus. They should be told that al-Andalus was an act of colonization that succeeded for seven centuries, but the French colonization was also a colonization that lasted just over a century. But the nature of these colonizations is the same. (Boudjedra, "La fascination de la forme")

This statement is completely revolutionary within Arabo-Muslim discourse, yet Boudjedra does not espouse a wholesale rejection of the figure of Tariq ibn Ziyad. Instead, he suggests that Tariq can be an important source of productive questioning.

Maʿrakat al-Zuqaq and *La Prise de Gibraltar* both close with a quote from Tariq ibn Ziyad's famous, possibly apocryphal speech. One day when the protagonist's father has surprised him while he's looking at the miniatures in the book, the father reads out loud Tariq's speech. The twentieth-century Tariq recalls that his mother, in response to his many questions and sense of disgust at the illustrations of violent conquest, told him that he would understand when he grew up. Yet the grown-up narrator reports: "But I realize again today that I've never understood much from that hodgepodge and mishmash that is commonly referred to as history.... I write 'To where would you flee? [*Ayna al-mafarr?*]'" (F 311/A 184). By having the twentieth-century Tariq appropriate this famous rhetorical question from the legendary speech, Boudjedra indicates that although the speech may be apocryphal, the versions of history that are passed down are all that we have, and like Tariq's troops, our only choice is to move forward—knowing all the while that these histories are a construction. I argue, then, that although Boudjedra presents Tariq as a fiction and a sham, and a colonizer to boot, he suggests that this fantasy Tariq can be inspiring to anticolonialists as long as they take an active role in his deconstruction and reconstruction. In this way, history is indeed a form of translation. De Toro notes, in *Épistémologies, le Maghreb*, that "History is practiced as a giant act of 'translation,' as a result of a textual network (palimpsest) and an exercise in writing and counter/re-writing, a process of reading and counter/re-reading of history [*l'histoire*] where the writing subject, in as much as he is a 'translator,' becomes the true creator of history" (177). Through a process of this type, Boudjedra effectively translates the mythical Tariq ibn Ziyad into usable past, an element of Arab cultural heritage that can be employed to understand imperial conquests at different times and places and thus leave behind remaining colonial relations of power.

Mustafa al-Misnawi's Migrant Tariq

The last three works that I discuss in relation to Tariq ibn Ziyad address the intersection between al-Andalus and migration. In sharp contrast with the discourses about North African migration that Flesler points to as reenactments of the medieval Muslim conquest, the texts by al-Misnawi, Shaghmum, and Lalami do not evoke Tariq to figure a modern-day invasion but to critique the world system that generates desperate migration. Moroccan writer Mustafa al-Misnawi [Mustapha El-Mesnaoui] (1953–2015), similar to Boudjedra, carries out a thorough deconstruction of the figure of Tariq ibn Ziyad, but he does so through a markedly different narrative style and with oblique reference to the contemporary Moroccan émigrés who cross the strait. Al-Misnawi, who was also a translator and literary and film critic, is the author of the short story "Tariq Alladhi Lam Yaftah al-Andalus" ("Tariq, the One Who Did Not Conquer al-Andalus," 1979). The explicit theme of this short story is impotence in the face of power and no doubt the political situation in Morocco at the time when al-Misnawi wrote at least partly conditioned this theme. The period of the 1960s to 1980s in Morocco is called Sanawat al-Rusas/les Années de Plomb (the Years of Lead) because of King Hassan II's declaration of a state of emergency, suspension of parliament, takeover of all executive and legislative functions, and brutal repression of challenges to the political system. The vision of what independence from France and Spain would bring had turned to bitter disillusionment. In this story al-Misnawi uses an absurdist, bare-bones style to point to the lacuna, the gaping breach, between triumphalist narratives of the conquest of al-Andalus and present-day reality in Morocco and in the Arabic-speaking world at large. The story uses a terse, understated style, together with anachronisms and an element of the fantastic, to deftly interweave a modern-day Tariq who talks about conquering al-Andalus and a medieval Tariq who sets out to conquer al-Andalus but doesn't complete the mission. The unexplained discrepancies vis-à-vis history and within the deictic reality can leave the reader with a feeling that something doesn't quite fit. And to be sure, the story aims to tell us that something doesn't make sense when we juxtapose traditional narratives about al-Andalus, and specifically Tariq ibn Ziyad, with present day realities.

Al-Misnawi's story is divided into five sections, each one labeled numerically as a scene or tableau (*murabbaʿ*). The first scene starts with the uninvolved third-person narrator stating: "Tariq kissed his wife on the forehead and said to her: 'Farewell, I'm going to conquer [fath] al-Andalus'" (237 [71]).[37] His wife hides her apprehension and wishes him a safe journey, but after he waves good-bye he withdraws to a corner of their shack and starts arranging date pits and cigarette butts on the dirt floor as his "soldiers." Tariq plays at conquest with bits of trash, like a child or a madman, calling the "soldiers" to the conquest and struggle [jihad] on behalf of God. In the midst of this, a second Tariq emerges who does successfully conquer various Iberian cities.

The shift from the frame story of the poverty-stricken Tariq to that of Tariq's fantasy world, or some form of alternate reality, takes place about midway through the first scene and the following three scenes present the story of the Tariq who set out with his troops. However, we cannot simply interpret this second Tariq as the historical eighth-century figure given that the outcome of his expedition, as well as its historical timeframe, is quite different from that of the historic Tariq ibn Ziyad. The Tariq who emerges out of the date pits and cigarette butts crosses the strait successfully and conquers city after city, but after each victory he sends a telegram announcing it to his superior, Musa ibn Nusayr. Musa, jealous of Tariq, writes the legendary letter in which he asks Tariq to stop moving forward with the conquest. In al-Misnawi's version of the story, though, Musa tricks Tariq by telling him that he has come to an agreement with Roderick; rather than put off Musa's order, Tariq complies and returns to North Africa having reached only as far as the outskirts of Toledo. The fourth scene presents Tariq's reception at Musa's court. Musa offers Tariq Coca-Cola and Black & White whiskey and Tariq is pleased by this warm welcome. But soon Tariq discovers that he has been tricked and is now the laughingstock of Musa and his men. Tariq is filled with rage, feeling that his honor as a man and as a soldier has been insulted. The narrative moves from the fourth scene, which ends with the second Tariq feeling "alone and weak and empty-handed" (239 [74]), to the fifth scene in which the poverty-stricken Tariq of the frame story kicks the pieces of garbage with which he has been playing and then cries bitterly. In an inversion of typical gender roles, his wife, brought over by the sound of his weeping, is surprised to see him and asks when he returned and why he is crying. Tariq doesn't answer but grabs his *sebsi* pipe, fills it with kif, lights it up, and takes a long drag.[38]

How can we understand the relationship between the Tariq living in a hovel of the frame story and the Tariq of the embedded fantasy turned nightmare? The ambiguous temporality of the story makes it difficult to separate the two Tariqs into a contemporary version and a medieval one. The frame story Tariq refers to "al-Andalus" (not "Spain"), but then plays with cigarette butts (the result of filters invented in the 1920s). These two pieces of information stand out, particularly in this text with sparse details, because they point to two distinct periods of time (medieval and modern). The result is that regardless of how we locate the frame tale temporally, there is an anachronism pulling us to the other time period. Similarly, other anachronisms (telegrams and Coca-Cola with Black & White whiskey) link the Tariq of the embedded tale, the duped halfway conqueror, to the modern period. These anachronisms, which are also symbols of Western cultural influence, tie the past to the present and create a doubled Tariq in a story within a story: a present-day, impoverished Tariq whose game gives life to a version of the eighth-century Tariq. What unites the two Tariqs, aside from their ambiguous temporality, is a deep sense of frustration.

The first Tariq never sets out and the second Tariq (the first Tariq's fears of failure come to life) leaves but is unable to reach his goal. Both end up filled with anger and feelings of powerlessness. When we layer this on top of what the historical record tells us—Tariq ignored Musa and kept going, conquering most of Iberia, but less than 800 years later all the conquered lands were lost, and in the late twentieth and early twenty-first centuries hundreds of thousands of Moroccans risked their lives to enter Spain and seek opportunities for sustenance and economic gain—the text's critical standpoint emerges.

When the frame story Tariq announces that he is setting out to conquer al-Andalus, he is (also) a contemporary Tariq setting out to pursue a better livelihood in Spain, to struggle for the riches it has to offer. Although his announced quest is to migrate to Spain and make economic gains there, he is overwhelmed by the potential for failure, which emerges in the embedded story of being fooled and mocked by those in power, and sits in a corner of his hut. There he plays with bits of trash, the debris of food and tobacco that have already been enjoyed, and then, in a fit of despair, breaks up his own game and seeks solace—and further distance from reality—by smoking hashish. This Tariq, amid a life of squalor, initially imagines the conquest of al-Andalus as a figure for immigrant success in Spain, but he soon associates the conquest with failure and robbed opportunities rather than triumph and grandeur. The conqueror/would-be-migrant is emasculated and dishonored. The reality that Tariq is able to see, from within the kif haze, is that there was no great conquest because the end result was that they lost al-Andalus and twentieth- and twenty-first-century North Africans risk their lives to immigrate clandestinely to Spain and other parts of Europe.

Through this medieval-modern Tariq, al-Misnawi rejects conceptions of the self that rely on compensatory, romanticizing narratives of the past and indicts the abuse of power and learned passivity for their role in creating hardship in contemporary North Africa. "Tariq Alladhi Lam

Yaftah al-Andalus," by suggesting that Tariq never did actually triumph, or that other Tariqs have not been so lucky, highlights the disjuncture between triumphalist narratives of the past and present social, political, and economic conditions. This Tariq story indicts the bankruptcy of postcolonial regimes and the idealizations of compensatory narratives about al-Andalus and in the process, Tariq moves from virility to emasculation. This translation of Tariq into the abjection and powerlessness of contemporary Moroccan poverty enacts a critique of transhistorical relations of power and the narratives built around them.

al-Miludi Shaghmum and the Return Migrant: Reclaiming the Past

Whereas al-Misnawi's text obliquely connects al-Andalus to contemporary migration, the last two works I discuss here make that connection very explicitly. The first of these texts, the novel *Nisa' Al al-Randi* (*The Women of the Randi Family*), refers to Tariq not by name but by action—the act of burning boats. Like Nini's memoir, it points to the commonalities between laborers from the Global South. *Nisa' Al al-Randi* was published in 2000 by Moroccan writer al-Miludi Shaghmum [Miloudi Chaghmoum] (b. 1947), but one chapter of the novel was published separately with a Spanish translation in the joint Moroccan-Spanish collection *Cuentos de las dos orillas* (Regàs and Monleón 2001), or *Stories from Both Shores*. For this reason, most of the critics who analyze this text (Schulz and Flesler) focus solely on its second chapter, analyzing it as a stand-alone short story. Although that chapter depicts the protagonist ʿAli's clandestine departure from Morocco and eventual arrival in Spain, the novel says next to nothing about life in Spain and focuses primarily on ʿAli's return to Morocco. Rather than address life in diaspora, Shaghmum's novel depicts the "home country" side of the migration story: the desire to leave, the world left behind, and the process of return. My interest, then, is in reading the chapter on departure within the context of the novel as a whole and reading the novel within the framework of the symbolic value of al-Andalus and specifically its interaction with immigrant departure and return.

Shaghmum's novel encompasses four moments in the history of Moroccan–Spanish migration: late eleventh-century migration from North Africa to southern Iberia as part of the spread of the Almoravid dynasty, late fifteenth-century migration from the fallen Muslim sultanate of Granada to North Africa, the protagonist's late twentieth-century emigration from Morocco to Spain, and then his forced return migration or deportation to Morocco. I argue that through these juxtapositions, as well as the themes of the mythical nature of genealogies and versatility in the face of loss, which are central to the text's invocation of al-Andalus, Shaghmum deconstructs Spanish perceptions of North African attitudes toward al-Andalus and Spain, as well as Arab discourses of empire and loss surrounding al-Andalus. In the process, he highlights Moroccans' and Spaniards' current locations within a system of global political and economic power.

The main character, ʿAli al-Randi, traces his family back to forebears who moved from North Africa to Iberia, and then in a subsequent generation were forced to leave Iberia and return to North Africa. However, al-Randi's family is not simply al-Randi's family—rather, his lineage is made up of deception, legend, ambiguous paternity, and incest. The storyline of Shaghmum's novel can be summarized through two intersecting trios of characters: ʿAli, Walid al-Niyya, and ʿA'isha are university students in Rabat. Walid al-Niyya (whose name means "son of intention or will"), has an amorous interest in ʿA'isha, but doesn't approve of her lifestyle as she basically prostitutes herself to reach a higher standard of living. Walid al-Niyya and ʿAli decide to immigrate clandestinely to Spain. ʿAli arrives in Spain via a circuitous route, and after twenty-five years there he is forced to return to Morocco. The bulk of the novel focuses on ʿAli's family history and his relationship with his abusive brother, Yusuf BuSabʿa, and his sister, Nuzha, all of whom were born in the 1960s. ʿAli and his siblings were adopted by their parents, but Yusuf and Nuzha (and possibly ʿAli) are linked as the biological children of their "adoptive" father and a woman married to another man. The conception of the children is surrounded by an aura of magic and mystery that leaves their lineage ambiguous. ʿAli's father himself is an illegitimate child with an estranged half-brother, and the children are conceived through fantastic, dream-like encounters with a sorceress. Furthermore, there can be no nostalgia regarding family life and childhood because as a child ʿAli is abused by Yusuf and his henchman and later they cheat ʿAli out of his inheritance by claiming that he and his sister were adopted while Yusuf was not (166–67).

Shaghmum, a professor of philosophy as well as a novelist, is described by Moroccan writer Ahmad al-Madini as being the type of writer who mixes philosophical concerns with popular or folk traditions (10). This is precisely what we find in *Nisa' Al al-Randi*, where existential questions are interwoven with popular Sufi traditions, supernatural beliefs (e.g., the *ʿifrit*, or mischievous genie), and the oral tradition of tales of families' Andalusi origins. The novel is a meditation on people's relationships to the past, to their regional political history, their family history, and their childhoods. It points to how all of the lineages that are touted and used to create or destroy social status are made up of legend, stories full of uncertainties and failures—not the glory and honor found in idealized narratives. Overall Shagmum's text asserts that we each choose what to do with our past—to allow it to destroy us or to use it to flourish.

The themes of family lineage and loss are developed through al-Andalus—the paramount symbol of Arab loss. The protagonist's anxiety regarding tracing his lineage and his coming to terms with the loss of his inheritance is parallel to the Arab/North African relationship to their glorious past—the desire to identify with a period represented as the height of civilization and the need to process the loss of that position of power. The novel as a whole is placed under the sign of al-Andalus through its title, the surname of the protagonist, and the content of certain chapters. The surname al-Randi (or al-Rundi) that appears in the title of the novel is a demonym that denotes people from the Spanish city of Ronda in the province of Malaga. Ronda came under North African rule in 713 and is associated with two famous figures within Arab culture: Ibn ʿAbbad al-Rundi, a fourteenth-century Sufi theologian who was born in Ronda and emigrated to North Africa, and Salih ibn Sharif al-Rundi, the thirteenth-century author of the famous "Nuniyya" poem that laments the loss of al-Andalus. In this way, already in the title, the novel refers to the intertwined histories of Morocco and Spain—the layers of movement and shifts in vantage point that link them, and the question of how to face loss and change.

The second chapter of the novel, "Haraq al-Sufun" ("The Burning of the Boats"), develops this invocation of al-Andalus very directly. This chapter narrates the efforts of ʿAli al-Randi and Walid al-Niyya to immigrate clandestinely to Spain by interweaving the two young men's experiences with their recollections of their families' history of crossing the Strait of Gibraltar throughout the centuries. The chapter title is a reference to the famous legend of Tariq's burning of the boats, and the chapter's first sentence mentions "Jabal Tariq" [Gibraltar] as the narrator lists the cities on the other shore that he would like to reach (9). Thus, from the start of the chapter, Tariq is associated with a decision to break with the past and forge ahead. Rather than evoke Tariq to represent migration as a new invasion, Shaghmum suggests a rewriting of one of Tariq's most well-known phrases and in that way points to the forces that drive migration. In the speech after burning the boats, Tariq is famous for having said "Behind you is the sea, before you, the enemy" (al-Maqqari, "Al Maqqari's 'Breath of Perfumes'" 241). But in Shaghmum's text, the characters are facing the sea, with their enemies behind them. As they wait in a cave by the seashore, one of the characters notes that the ocean has been and always will be "the future of humankind" (18).

By focusing on the moment of departure from Morocco and the sea as that which fulfills the desire to move forward, instead of focusing on arrival in Spain and the sea as an impediment to return, Shaghmum's reworking leaves the medieval conflict in the past and highlights the contemporary socioeconomic dynamics surrounding migration.[39] In the novel, ʿAli leaves Morocco to escape his enemies: the horrors of his childhood and the havoc his brother has wreaked on his adult life. In addition, ʿAli and his travel companion see Morocco as underdeveloped and believe that they will find true civilization in the West (11). For this reason, for Shaghmum's characters the sea is the more appealing option—whether or not they have a boat. Burning the boats calls to mind the contemporary practice of clandestine immigrants burning their identity documents. In this novel, burning one's ship refers to trying to let go of what is holding you back. In the case of ʿAli, this is his relationship with his brother and more generally the legacy of the past. Instead of using the trope of invasion to position the Moroccan immigrant as a conqueror, this novel focuses on the shifting identities and positions of power involved in the various crossings of the straits that have taken place over the centuries and on contemporary migrants' motivations for departure.

As they await the guide who will take them across the water, ʿAli and his friend remember their families and neighbors gathering regularly to tell stories about al-Andalus. The elders would teach them poetry, dance, and song; it was "a party to practice remembering and mourning" (18). ʿAli traces his family back to a grandfather from Ronda and recalls that his forefathers emigrated to Iberia and led a comfortable life as landowners before they were forced back to North Africa after 1492. ʿAli and his friend gaze at the enticing yet scary lights of the Spanish cities (among them Gibraltar) on the other side of the strait, in the same way that their ancestors looked from Iberia to the lights of Tangier and Ceuta (9 and 15). The young men's Andalusi families were known for their ability to adapt to circumstances. They changed religion according to convenience: first they were Sabians, then Jews, then Muslims, then Christians, and then Muslims again.[40] This was sometimes seen by others as dishonesty or betrayal (15–16). By emphasizing versatility and the ability to think on one's feet to survive, Shaghmum creates a conception of identity that is fluid and defined by circumstance. The great challenge that the protagonist faces is how to be versatile without feeling like he has betrayed his own honor.

ʿAli's first attempt at reinventing himself is his clandestine migration. But just as occurred in 1492 with his great-grandfather, who was left waiting in a cave on the Iberian shore for a middleman who never showed up, ʿAli and Walid al-Niyya's guide never arrives. Ultimately, the ghosts of ʿAli's grandfather and Walid al-Niyya, who has died during the wait, appear to ʿAli and encourage him to try to make it to Spain on his own. While the grandfather tells him he must take action—either risk crossing on his own or return gratefully—Walad al-Niyya has a vested interest in ʿAli making it to Spain because he had made ʿAli promise that he would spin a tale to make Walad al-Niyya's family think that he had reached the longed-for al-Andalus. Walad al-Niyya's ghost insists:

> "You'll betray me if you return. Otherwise, how will you tell them about 'the last time you saw me in al-Andalus' and 'my adventures with the European Arab girl' and how 'happy' I am there with her? Besides, why would you want to go back? To check up again on your boats, the ones that time has sunk? Burn your sunken ships and put yourself in God's hands!" (20)

Here ʿAli's best friend tells him that his boats—the legacy of the past—have already been damaged by the passage of time and his best option is to burn them—to break his ties with the past and move forward by continuing the journey on his own. ʿAli heeds the ghosts and starts to swim. Both literally and symbolically, the protagonist welcomes the friendly ghosts of the past while ridding himself of the harmful ones.

In an unexpected twist, ʿAli is picked up by a Colombian boat whose crew is made up of North Africans and Sub-Saharan Africans who have been spotted in the ocean (20–22). In ʿAli's conversation with the Moroccan sailor who greets him on the boat, class identity emerges as more important than any other basis for community (21–22). The Moroccan sailor and ʿAli are from different regions of Morocco, but as the sailor puts it: "Morocco is one and the same for the poor; the whole world is one and the same for them" (22). The sailor goes on to emphasize that poverty is a uniting common denominator, across language, religion, and culture, by stating: "oppression [. . .], like poverty, is blasphemy [*kufr*]. Morocco may be similar to Colombia . . . completely!" (22). In this way, the text formulates an identity that has nothing to do with religion, language, nation, or geographic region and everything to do with socioeconomic conditions in the Global South.

After sailing the route between Colombia and Italy various times and marrying a Colombian woman, ʿAli is given the choice between continuing to work on the ship for a wage and being left at any port with a fake passport. He immediately chooses to be taken to Spain and the ship takes him and his wife there. When ʿAli and his wife first step on Spanish soil, they have a conversation about Christopher Columbus that indicates that how we process the past dictates our present.[41] Ultimately, ʿAli's marriage falls apart because he feels that he is a failure, not because he cannot adapt to Spanish life but because in the wake of his brother's abuse he cannot adapt to a role as a successful, confident person. His difficulty with processing the past, rather than his reception in Spain, is what negatively affects his life. The protagonist's trajectory can be understood as a message about the need to actively engage with Arab cultural history and reinterpret it in order to move forward. This message is echoed in the rest of the novel and in the very presence/absence of Tariq ibn Ziyad in the text.

Aside from a few other references to emigration, Spain and al-Andalus appear only obliquely in the rest of the novel.[42] However, in a particular group of chapters the indirect references speak directly to the issue of what to do with remnants of the Andalusi past. At one point in the narrative, ʿAli's father decides that he wants to join his brother Sharif as he fights under Abd al-Krim al-Khattabi (1882/3–1963), the Amazigh leader of armed resistance to Spanish and French colonial rule in the Rif region of present-day Morocco (66). Later, three chapters (99–116) consist of a fictional late nineteenth- or early twentieth-century chronicle written by Sharif about his travels to the Rif in search of help in the resistance against European colonialism. As Sharif travels looking for Abd al-Krim, he carries with him a variety of letters: each one represents a different narrative of who he is so that, according to the exigencies of the moment, according to who intercepts him, he can present a letter that will help him survive. Ultimately, Sharif causes great scandal by marrying a French woman, but this, too, was done for strategic purposes (101). Thus, like many before him, Sharif is a quick-thinking chameleon, he is adaptable but is misunderstood in the process.

Within this fictional travelogue, the figure of the *murabit*, and his band of followers, the *murabitin*, takes on a central role. In a general sense, a murabit is a religious leader. The word comes from *ribat*, the term used for the garrisons or frontier forts built along the North African coast in the eighth and ninth centuries as part of the Islamic conquest. Later, in North Africa the term *murabit* became associated with less military, more ascetic leaders, typically local holy men. These are the holy men or Sufi saints known in French and then English as "Marabouts" (in Standard Arabic: *wali*). They are local ascetics and spiritual leaders who come to be seen as popular saints, their tombs treated as shrines. Nonetheless, arguably the most famous murabit in North African history is ʿAbd Allah Yasin, a figure inextricably linked to the Muslim conquest of Iberia whom we met as a character in Chraïbi's *Naissance à l'aube*. Yasin, the eleventh-century religious leader, founded the highly militarized and strict religious group that developed into a dynasty known elsewhere as the Almoravids—the Europeanization of al-Murabitin. A few decades after Yasin founded the group, they were led by Yusuf ibn Tashfin from North Africa into Iberia, where the Almoravids ruled over southern Iberia from 1085 to 1145.

Within the fictitious chronicle, during the journey to the Rif murabitin care for ʿAli's uncle Sharif and his companions (101), Sharif refers to his forefathers as the head of the murabitin of those who are adaptable and versatile (99), and he describes himself and his band of men as "Marabout fighters [murabitin *mujahidin*]" (116). Sharif also refers specifically to ʿAbd Allah Yasin but in a way that runs counter to the standard narrative of the Arab past in which figures such as Yasin stand for the glory and might of all Muslims. Sharif mentions Yasin in a review of the many trials and tribulations that have affected that region within Morocco, as a way to highlight the valor of the local population (102). Yasin colonized both the Krimat region and southern Iberia. The North Africans and Iberians are linked in their subordinate position vis-à-vis dynastic power. In stark contrast with Chraïbi's depiction, Shaghmum doesn't present Yasin as the founder of a great dynasty that extended into al-Andalus. Rather than place him within a narrative of power vis-à-vis Christian Iberia, Shaghmum's text presents Yasin from a local perspective as an unwelcome conqueror.

The unwelcome conqueror with whom ʿAli must contend is his brother, and a great deal of the novel is focused on the process of ʿAli being forced to return to Morocco and, from the depths of failure and despair, rising to stand up to his brother for the first time in his life. The novel ends with ʿAli, through the help of ʿAʾisha, choosing to create a new life for himself in Morocco (198–99). In a striking parallel to the Arab world's relationship to al-Andalus, Shaghmum's novel considers the loss of lineage, the inability to pinpoint one's genealogy and claim one's birthright. In addition to the distant trauma of familial exile, the protagonist carries the trauma of abuse in childhood and denial of his family ties and inheritance. This abuse and the direct and indirect financial impact of his exclusion from his father's inheritance lead ʿAli to look for a solution in the seductive, bewitching lights of Spain, seen from across the strait. In this novel, then, al-Andalus functions as a symbol for the loss of patrimony, and in its contemporary incarnation as the European goal of many economic migrants, it functions as a symbol for the loss of an escapist dream. But these losses are also gains: the protagonist and readers of the text gain a conception of identity as fluid, a consciousness of socioeconomic and political connections between postcolonial locales, an appreciation of the constructedness of history, and an awareness of the need to re-create oneself in the present.

Shaghmum's *Nisa' Al al-Randi*, makes use of the sign of al-Andalus to comment on the relativity of colonial subject positions and the power dynamics of the present. The novel attempts to understand current socioeconomic conditions in Morocco and the phenomenon of migration through the framing lens of al-Andalus, that is, in relation to the remnants and memories of a more prosperous and powerful period. The oppositional groups that the text establishes are not Christian and Moor but haves and have-nots, colonizer and colonized. Yet as the text itself makes clear, these categories are not essential differences but the product of changeable circumstances and crafted narratives. The novel's trans-colonial perspective transforms the anxiety about proving one's lineage into awareness of the potential for self-creation. The protagonist formulates a fluid identity that recognizes current geopolitical hierarchies as also subject to change. In this way, *Nisa' Al al-Randi* uses medieval Muslim Iberia to present a postscolonial interpretation of power and difference in the contemporary Western Mediterranean. As part of this reframing of cultural heritage, Tariq ibn Ziyad does not have a central role in this novel, but neither is he completely erased. Tariq, who is never named in the text but only invoked indirectly through the concept of the burning of the boats and references to Gibraltar, is refashioned as a sign of the benefits of cutting ties and creating a new relationship with the past.

Lalami's Would-Be Migrant: Rewriting Tariq and Tangier

The Moroccan-born writer Laila Lalami (b. 1968), who has lived in the United States since 1992 and writes in English, also invokes Tariq ibn Ziyad within a work that underscores the socioeconomic conditions that lead to migration and the marginalization of immigrants. Lalami's novel *Hope and Other Dangerous Pursuits* (2005) starts with a chapter that presents the departure of a group of Moroccan and West African migrants headed across the Strait of Gibraltar to Spain on an inflatable boat. Subsequent chapters focus on the lives of four of the passengers, delving into what motivated them to migrate and how their lives were affected by migration or the attempt to migrate. The first and last chapters focus on the same character, Murad, a tourist tout turned aspiring writer. Through Murad, Lalami narrates the transition from would-be migrant with a conflicted relationship to the past and to others' accounts of Morocco to a writer who rejects the conquest/migration dream in favor of creatively reworking his Moroccan heritage.

While crossing the Strait of Gibraltar, from the boat overcrowded with thirty passengers, Murad looks out at the approaching Spanish coastline and his thoughts travel from the treacherous sea to Tariq ibn Ziyad:

> The waves are inky black, except for hints of foam here and there, glistening white under the moon, like tombstones in a dark cemetery. Murad can make out the town where they're headed. Tarifa. The mainland point of the Moorish invasion in 711. Murad used to regale tourists with anecdotes about how Tariq ibn Ziyad had led a powerful Moor army across the Straits and, upon landing in Gibraltar, ordered all the boats burned. He'd told his soldiers that they could march forth and defeat the enemy or turn back and die a coward's death. The men had followed their general, toppled the Visigoths, and established an empire that ruled over Spain for more than 700 years. Little did they know that we'd be back, Murad thinks. Only instead of a fleet, here we are in an inflatable boat—not just Moors, but a motley mix of people from the ex-colonies, without guns or armor, without a charismatic leader.
>
> It's worth it, though, Murad tells himself. (2–3)

Tariq and the legends surrounding him were key components in Murad's spiel for tourists—the tales he told to build and evoke the mystique of al-Andalus and North Africa and thus earn a living for himself and his family. Murad attempts to connect Tariq's invasion to the influx of immigrants but, like Nini, observes that the immigrants have no might, no material support, and no leadership. Regardless, he convinces himself that the risks involved in arriving empty-handed by inflatable boat are worth it. Atef Louayene, basing his reading on the same passage cited above, insightfully observes that Lalami's novel "parodies the fantasy of a redemptive Moorish return, since the returning Moors are not the Arab invaders of yore, but rather their postcolonial descendents [*sic*], the flotsam and jetsam of the former colonies disgorged by the *mare nostrum* onto European shores" and that "more importantly, it imputes the plight of the Arab immigrant, at least in part, to the enduring failures of the postcolonial Arab polity" (39). I agree completely with these remarks and in what follows will explain how Lalami uses the figure of Murad as an emerging writer to carry out her critique of both mythical visions of al-Andalus—including fantasies of immigrant "return"—and the socioeconomic predicament of contemporary Morocco.

Murad has a university degree in English and speaks Spanish fluently, but has been trying to eke out a living selling his services as a tourist guide in Tangier. Feeling the pressure to provide for his family after his father's death, he succumbs to the promises of a better life offered by a human smuggler and sells his mother's jewelry to pay for the trip. In spite of Murad's desperate optimism on the boat, he is intercepted by the Spanish Guardia Civil and sent back to Morocco. Similar to the twinned Tariqs in al-Misnawi's story, on arriving back in Tangier Murad feels humiliated by his failed attempt at emigration (or Tariq-like conquest) and insists on staying home to avoid being seen (184–86). Eventually, he starts to work in a shop that sells Moroccan handicrafts and souvenirs to tourists, but he still daydreams about emigrating to Spain (186).

The last chapter, titled "The Storyteller," is full of metafictional gestures that give Murad power over the conquering image of Tariq ibn Ziyad and enable him to actively shape Moroccan cultural heritage or *turath*. Murad returns to working in the tourism industry, but now, in his packaging of Morocco for foreigners, rather than turn to tales of Tariq or Paul Bowles (the US writer [1910–1999] who lived in Tangier from 1947 on), he finds narrative inspiration in his own father's folk tales. The chapter starts with Murad sitting in the shop reading a novel set in Tangier written by a European or American writer and finding himself thinking about how to rework the wording to better convey his own lived experience of the city (176). Interwoven with Murad's reflections, Lalami's narrative presents the conversation between two tourists who have entered the shop. Their talk of Bowles reminds Murad of how he used to use the aura surrounding this figure to entice tourists to hire him as a guide but then tired of this ploy (180–82). The tourists' conversation, including a statement that Bowles knew Morocco "better than the Moroccans themselves," triggers Murad's childhood memories of his father's storytelling (182–83). At first, Murad only remembers bits of the traditional stories his father used to tell and feels frustrated by how difficult it is for him to reconstruct a single discrete story (183–84). He considers his relationship to the past, including those stories he heard as a child, and noticing that his past had already begun to drift away, he fears he may lose the stories altogether and wonders "if one always had to sacrifice the past for the future" (186). But the tourists' comments continue to trigger Murad's memory and help him recall another of his father's stories (187). Murad then uses their talk of Bowles not as a way to sell his services as a guide but as an opportunity to mesmerize them with a folk tale (189–93). In the tale, a woman and a carpet weaver use the weaver's exquisite tapestry to achieve success in their struggle against a powerful sultan and his henchman.

After this encounter with the tourists, which helps Murad sell them a carpet at a fair price, Murad discards the novel he was trying to read, thinks about his father's nearly forgotten stories, and decides that he needs "to write his own" (195). The novel ends with further metafictionality as Murad weaves a tale in his mind that he will write down that night (195). Murad uses his interactions with foreigners and their texts to tap into his past, maintain Moroccan oral traditions, and embark on creative writing—the production of his own version of Morocco. He rejects both the hero who succeeded through conquest, embodied in Tariq, and the role as the object or parasitic beneficiary of others' stories, represented by the foreign writer's novel and the use of Bowles to sell services to tourists. Instead, Murad identifies with active types of power not built on the (immigrant's) conquest of Iberia: the power of the carpet maker's weaving skills and Murad's father's narrative skills.

Murad's failed migration reveals that modern-day migrants have none of the might that propelled Tariq ibn Ziyad, and thus portrayals of them as invaders are unfounded. At the same time, through his thwarted migration experience and the discrepancy revealed by the figure of Tariq, he is impelled to find other forms of strength. Murad reevaluates his past, including his relationship to the literary figures connected to his city and the cultural legacy handed down to him by his father, and moves from recounting tales about Tariq and al-Andalus to reworking his family folk tales in order to narrate Morocco himself. In this text, Lalami successfully translates Tariq ibn Ziyad into a modern-day Moroccan who rejects the illusory promise of migrant conquest in favor of empowerment through narrative.

Concluding Remarks: On Conquerors and Pizza Dough

Not surprisingly, al-Andalus is a central reference point for Hispano-Maghrebian conceptualizations of movement and identity. What may cause surprise is that in contrast with current Spanish invocations of Tariq ibn Ziyad, many contemporary Arab and North African versions of Tariq enact an erasure of the line between insider and outsider, whether Christian/Muslim, colonizer/colonized, or native/foreigner. Rather than rehearse Tariq's invasion, these authors use Tariq to address Arabness and religious, ethnic, and class identities. Tariq the energetic conqueror and bold border-crosser is employed to address not only differences "outside" of the MENA region (between the MENA region and Europe) but also differences within the so-called Arab world—the "strangers" within, whether Christian, Amazigh, Jew, or the economically disadvantaged (would-be) migrant border-crosser. Sara Ahmed, in *Strange Encounters: Embodied Others in Post-Coloniality*, points to the ways strangers are actually not strange, or unknown to us, but are imaginable and recognizable. She states the following: "It is our task to think through the different *modes* of proximity we may have to strangers in contemporary contexts without assuming that the stranger was distant in the past. We need to ask how contemporary modes of proximity *reopen prior histories of encounter*" (13). In the works I have analyzed here, "inside" and "outside," "conquered" and "conqueror," become relative terms that shift over time and the fixed roles of *moros y cristianos* are not reproduced but reopened. The authors examined here rework the moros y cristianos discourse to use Tariq to speak to each other about Arabness, identity, and power.

The most striking indication that Tariq is used to address identity configurations within the MENA region is the divergence between the works from the Mashriq and those from the Maghreb. In contrast with al-Jundi's and Taymur's accounts, in which the Arabization and Islamization of Amazighs is presented as a sacred act, and with Qunsul's in which the Amazigh population is completely erased, in Chraïbi's and Boudjedra's texts the Amazigh identity of Tariq ibn Ziyad is highlighted and the mythical standing of Tariq is dismantled in those two texts and those by Himmich, al-Misnawi, Shaghmum, and Lalami. Clearly these six Maghrebi writers, while drawn to the figure of Tariq, are more irreverent and questioning in their approach to him, in comparison with writers from the Mashriq (Kamil, Zaydan, Taymur, Qunsul, and al-Jundi). How can we explain this Mashriq/Maghreb divergence?[43] One factor that may be at play is the distance afforded by language: in the case of Chraïbi and partially in the case of Boudjedra it could be argued that the use of French, and the schooling in this language and tradition that this presupposes, creates a cultural outlook that allows for an ironic, if not critical, perspective on Muslim accounts of Tariq as a glorious conqueror. However, given that Boudjedra's base text was written in Arabic and al-Misnawi and Shaghmum write in Arabic, an interpretation based on language in and of itself cannot be taken far. However, the fact that some of these authors use French as their language of expression points to the relatively longer European colonization in the Maghreb in comparison with the Mashriq and the deeper French involvement in Maghrebian educational systems.[44] Moreover, the Maghreb—like al-Andalus—was also the site of Arab Muslim conquest and demographically has more "unfinished" colonization. The indigenous Amazigh communities of North Africa, though highly mixed with Arabs in terms of genetic make-up, still retain linguistic and cultural differences and have a growing cultural rights movement. Evidently these factors make it such that the writers from the Maghreb that write about Tariq understand the spread of Islam as imperial conquest. The divergence between the works from the Mashriq and those from the Maghreb points to their varying relationships to different types of imperial power. Writers from the Maghreb address Tariq, their own conquering hero, from their perspective as a people who have also been conquered. Drawing from the enduring friction between Arab and Amazigh cultures and their modes of religious practice, they disrupt the image of the idealized Tariq and thus the narrative of Muslim unity in the Golden Age of the caliphate on which the image of Tariq is based. In this way, they disprove the Arabic saying that the people of the Mashriq are people of creativity while the people of the Maghreb are people of jurisprudence and footnotes.[45] In this case, the law of the Mashriq's hegemonic narrative is dismantled by Maghrebi creativity.

Since the fall of the Emirate of Granada in 1492, the traditional Tariq story has functioned as a compensatory tale, one that revels in former might and glory to soothe the loss. In the modern reworkings of this compensatory discourse, Chraïbi uses a version of that narrative mode to compensate for Amazigh loss. Himmich corrects Chraïbi's version by calling into question the hypermasculine, sexualized conception of conquest and points to Tariq's textual, narrative nature. Boudjedra signals the compensatory nature of these narratives, decrying the falsifications of celebratory histories and their detrimental role in the decolonization process. Nini, al-Misnawi, Shaghmum, and Lalami link this critique to another facet of the postcolonial condition: heavy migration flows from the MENA region, in particular from North Africa, to Europe. These four authors link Tariq ibn Ziyad to migrants, and thus they denounce the broader context for which stories of glorious conquest try to compensate and, as part of this, indirectly criticize another genre of compensatory tale: the immigrant narratives that frame migration as conquest. As the four authors remind us in their different ways, the realities of immigrant life are usually much more unsavory. Migration draws attention to the holes in the Tariq myth, the compensatory myth of triumphant might that does not address the problems of the present or, within some Islamist ideologies, that addresses them by calling for an illusory return to the past. The migration phenomenon highlights the disjuncture between contemporary lived experience and narratives of glorious conquest; this disjuncture makes it seem like Tariq, in al-Misnawi's formulation, never did conquer al-Andalus. But Boudjedra and Shaghmum's works point to the layers of changes of fortune, conquests and reconquests, and the need to recognize this transcoloniality in order to start telling new kinds of stories. Both Lalami and Shaghmum suggest that one can choose which ghosts of the past one allows into the present and how. Rather than haunt, the past should be used to creatively improve the present.

In one of Albert Memmi's latest works, he states that those in the process of decolonization are akin to migrants: "Faced with a dead-end future, the decolonized dream of escape. They are in effect, potential émigrés, virtual immigrants within their own country, which seems to them increasingly limited and oppressive" (68 [86]). Although some of the decolonized use the narratives of Tariq's glorious conquest as an escape, others have interrogated this imperial past to analyze contemporary forms of imperialism and thus assuage their status as (virtual) immigrants and strangers. As Nini realizes while he kneads the pizza dough, no amount of glorification of past triumphs can change the inequities of the present. However, as Shaghmum's novel proposes, the past, with all of its conquests and losses, is as malleable as pizza dough; following Lalami's lead, we can use received legends and tales to create new stories. Indeed, the North African writers fold and reshape interpretations of the past, kneading them into a narrative that can nourish the present.

CHAPTER 4

Abu ʿAbd Allah Muhammad XII (Boabdil) and Other Migrants

In 1976, after visiting the Alhambra for the last time, Jorge Luis Borges wrote the poem "Alhambra," in which he alludes to Boabdil, the ousted sovereign who (like Borges) is experiencing for the last time the beauty of the palace, gardens, and fortress built by previous Muslim rulers of Granada. Through verses such as "Grata la voz del agua" [Pleasing is the water's voice] and "grato a la mano cóncava / el mármol circular de la columna" [Pleasing to the curved hand / The column's rounded marble], the poem conveys how the already blind Borges experiences the Alhambra through his other senses. Given the author's advanced age at the time of writing, when the poet addresses the "rey doliente" [grieving king] in the second (and final) stanza, he can be understood to also address himself. Like the king Boabdil, who Borges portrays taking pleasure in saying good-bye to the Alhambra in the midst of defeat, Borges focuses on experiencing intensely what he assumes will be his last visit to the Alhambra. The poem closes with reference to the pleasure of sensing "que la tarde que miras es la última" [That the afternoon you gaze upon is the last]. As in this poem, depictions of Boabdil, while sometimes including an element of identification with the displaced ruler, usually link him to inexorable finality—lo último/the last. Hispanic interest in Boabdil is seemingly endless precisely because of the desire to savor that lastness. In comparison, few Arab and North African writers have touched on him in their works. Thus, as with Tariq, the lines of cultural difference are distinctly drawn, and yet in certain works the messages converge.

The numerous narrative and dramatic works, two TV mini-series, and popular songs that form the Boabdil corpus can be roughly divided according to four broad categories: (1) those that focus on the tragic Moorish Other to process Spain's loss of empire and other sources of instability, (2) a few that attempt to innovate and present this figure in a somewhat different light, (3) those that identify with Boabdil and use him as part of the assertion of an Andalusian identity, and (4) those that use Boabdil to conceptualize migration in various ways.[1] In this last category the Arab and North African works converge with the Hispanic works, as the Arab and North African writers who address Boabdil have experienced emigration and invoke Boabdil in relation to migration.

Abu ʿAbd Allah Muhammad XII (c. 1460–c. 1533), of the Nasrid Dynasty, was the last sultan of the Emirate of Granada and thus the last Muslim ruler in Iberia. Through the conquests of Tariq and his superior Musa ibn Nusayr, the Umayyad caliphate reached all but a north-central strip of the Iberian Peninsula that, populated by fleeing Visigoths, became the Kingdom of Asturias. In the centuries that followed, the Muslim-ruled areas became greatly reduced due to a combination of Amazigh revolt, attacks from the proliferating Christian kingdoms in the north of Iberia, and Muslim power struggles largely related to the rise of the Abbasid caliphate. In 756, the exiled Umayyad prince Abd al-Rahman I established the Emirate of Cordoba, which in 912 was assumed by Abd al-Rahman III, who declared it the caliphate of Cordoba in 929, thus breaking allegiance to the Fatimid and Abbasid caliphs. The Cordoba caliphate, considered the golden age of al-Andalus, came to an end as a result of civil war and by 1031 the period of the *taifas* (from the Arabic *taʾifa* meaning "faction"), or mostly independent mini-states, had begun. In the face of the rising power of the Christian kingdoms, the taifas sought help from the Almoravids, the Amazigh Muslim rulers of North Africa. The Almoravids took over the taifa kingdoms and were followed by another Amazigh dynasty, the Almohads, and then another taifa period. These small states and principalities were soon taken over by the Christian kingdoms of Portugal, Aragon, and Castile. By 1249 the only Muslim state left in Iberia was the Emirate of Granada, and it was already a tributary state to the kingdom of Castile.

Boabdil, also known as El Zogoibi, from the Arabic *al-zughabi* meaning "the unfortunate one," and as El Rey Chico (the Younger King), a nickname used to distinguish him from his uncle, who was also named Abu ʿAbd Allah, came of age during a challenging time for the Nasrid Dynasty. In 1482 he took the throne of Granada as Sultan Muhammad XII in the midst of power struggles and court intrigue and when the joined forces of Castile and Aragon were seeking to conquer Granada. Soon after taking the throne, he invaded Castile and was taken prisoner in battle.[2] Boabdil obtained his freedom in 1487 in exchange for Castilian support to recover his throne and his agreement to maintain Granada's status as a tributary kingdom, hand over to the Castilians his eldest son and members of the Arab nobility as guarantee of his compliance, and not intervene in the Castilian conquest of parts of the Emirate of Granada, then held by his uncle. Castile and Aragon, taking advantage of the Nasrid succession struggles, laid siege on the city of Granada, and on January 2, 1492, Boabdil turned over Granada to Queen Isabella and King Ferdinand. The Treaty or Capitulation of Granada that Boabdil signed guaranteed a set of rights to the Muslims of Granada, including fair treatment and religious tolerance. However, by 1499 the terms of the agreement were directly violated by Cardinal Cisneros, leading to successive revolts by the Muslims and *moriscos* (Muslims converted to Catholicism) of the region and their eventual expulsion starting in 1609.

Various legends surround Boabdil, the last sultan of Granada. For instance, it is said that his misfortune was predicted by a Muslim astrologer who proclaimed that Boabdil would be the last Nasrid ruler of Granada; that before he left Iberia he hid a portion of his wealth in the Alpujarra region (a treasure that has yet to be found); and that he never actually left because an enchanted Boabdil still lives in the Alhambra or inside a mountain in the region. But the legend that circulated far beyond the Mediterranean and is still well known today is the Spanish legend of *El suspiro del moro*, or the Moor's last sigh.[3] As part of the terms of the capitulation agreement, Ferdinand and Isabella granted Boabdil a fiefdom in the Alpujarra. According to legend, when Boabdil and his entourage were leaving Granada for the Alpujarra, Boabdil looked back at the Alhambra and cried and his mother, ʿA'isha [Aixa] (also known as Fatima), said "Cry like a woman for what you were not able to defend like a man." To this day that mountain pass is still known as El Suspiro del Moro.

As detailed by María Soledad Carrasco Urgoiti, within the Moorish theme that has run through Spanish letters since its inception, various works feature Boabdil as a primary or secondary character. During the late medieval and early modern period several frontier ballads (*el romance fronterizo*) depict Boabdil.[4] These fifteenth and sixteenth-century ballads present him as a figure of misfortune, weakness, and nostalgia and thus set the stage for most Hispanic depictions to follow. Sizen Yiacoup notes that the depiction of Boabdil in the romances as a sad, weak king is parallel to that of Roderick: in both cases a single man's ills are responsible for the fall of an empire (102–3). Yiacoup argues that the ballads about Boabdil are a way to deal with anxiety regarding the state of another empire, that of Castile: "Thus the dismay expressed at the loss of Granadan power manifested in the ballads [. . .] can also be viewed as an expression of anxieties concerning the loss of Castilian power, the collective awareness of which would have been particularly acute in the closing decades of the sixteenth century" (Yiacoup 103). I return further on to this context of the rise and fall of empires as it dovetails with my interpretation of later depictions of Boabdil.

Carrasco Urgoiti notes that starting with Ginés Pérez de Hita's historical novel *Guerras civiles de Granada* (1595), representations of Boabdil shift to that of a cowardly tyrant. The figure of a sanguinary Boabdil prevails throughout the following centuries with eighteenth- and early nineteenth-century neoclassical works tending to present him as tyrannical and ignoble, cruel yet cowardly. However, during the Romantic period the literary conception of Boabdil returns to that seen in the *romancero*—a sad, ill-fated man—and emphasizes even more the fallen monarch's nobility of spirit. This shift is exemplified in the 1838 poem "Al último rey moro de Granada, Boabdil el Chico" (To the Last Moorish King of Granada, Boabdil the Younger) a lyric poem by the famous Spanish Romantic José Zorrilla (1817–1893).

The typical depiction of Boabdil that emerged in the Romantic period and predominates in Spanish discourses until today is that of a Moorish Other who is wrapped in pathos and bound by destiny. This figure, which I refer to as the tragic Moor, is marked by a passivity that is part of both melancholia and submission to fate. In his 1917 essay "Mourning and Melancholia," Sigmund Freud describes melancholia as "pathological mourning" (250). In Freudian psychoanalysis melancholia emerges when, rather than acknowledge the loss and disconnect from the lost object of desire, the subject internalizes the lost loved one, thereby entering an unhealthy (i.e., pathological) state of ongoing mourning, as well as an unhealthy definition of self that is built on the loss. Roger Bartra, in his study on the broad sense of Spanish melancholy that has as its epicenter the Spanish Golden Age (roughly 1492–1681), asserts that in sixteenth-century southern Iberia, in areas recently incorporated into the rising Christian kingdoms where the challenge of morisco rebellions was still ongoing, melancholy arose among both the conquered and the conquerors as "a frontier malady, a disease of transition and disruption" (31). Building on this, I would say that Iberian melancholy is traditionally projected onto the two key Others of this frontier space: Jews (a topic Bartra discusses at length) and Muslims. While diaspora has forged especially deep links between Jews and melancholy, Muslims in particular are associated with the related notion of being oppressed by a belief in fate.

Paradoxically, in the figure of the tragic Moor, although the Moor, due to his melancholy, does not accept separation from the beloved, he accepts his suffering as his fate. Following Orientalist views of Muslims as strong believers in submission to destiny, understood as

God's will, Boabdil's story is typically presented as the unfolding of fate and specifically his attitude is one of surrender to his destiny—the sad destiny which, according to legend, was proclaimed by an astrologer at the start of his life. With a life that has been proclaimed the victim of cruel fate, Boabdil is a tragic figure par excellence. Not only is his melancholic attitude pathological, it incites pathos. As a pathetic figure, he can give rise to compassion or contempt. Whether viewed as a figure to be pitied or one that is so miserable and so accepting of fate as to be disdained, the tragic Moor serves to support and strengthen the version of the Spanish self that views Spain as destined for greatness. The belief in destiny is based on the conviction that there is a fixed natural order in the world. Interestingly, the figure of Boabdil, while possibly portraying a Muslim submission to fate, works to support the Spanish idea that al-Andalus was destined to fall and Spain was destined to be formed, and indeed, according to the Francoist ideology of "the eternal Spain," was being formed since antiquity. Thus, Boabdil, as tragic Moor, is an Other who embodies loss as well as personal gain. Similar to the workings of melancholy and race in the US context analyzed by Anne Anlin Cheng in *The Melancholy of Race*, both the Spanish construct of the melancholic Boabdil and Spaniards who consume the image of the tragic Moor are shaped by the lingering presence of what has been lost.[5] Although the ethnic immigrant context that Cheng focuses on is obviously quite different from that of colonization and counter-colonization in Iberia, this ghostly presence also pertains to the Iberian context. The Spanish tend to attribute melancholia to the Moor who cannot overcome his loss—even when it is still a preordained loss not yet come to pass—and must simultaneously negotiate the ghostly presence of the Moor (Boabdil and all his subjects). The instability that this phantom incites is often assuaged through and transformed into a reaffirmation of Spanish dominance.

Significantly, the shift toward the projection of Boabdil as a noble and tragic Moor occurred soon after the Spanish Empire gave clear signs of having crumbled: in the first decades of the 1800s Spain lost all of its colonies in the Americas except for two Caribbean islands, and by 1833 it had abandoned attempts at reconquest. By the time Zorrilla's poem about a weak yet sensitive and refined fallen king was being received with accolades in Madrid,[6] Spain's once vast empire had been reduced to Cuba and Puerto Rico, the Philippines, the beginnings of colonial holdings in Morocco, and what later became Equatorial Guinea. The death of the Bourbon King Ferdinand VII in 1833 put an end to military efforts at regaining the colonies in the Americas and led Spain from Ferdinand's tumultuous reign to the fight for succession known as the Carlist Wars. This conflict was akin to the struggle for succession in which Boabdil and the Nasrid Dynasty were embroiled in the late 1400s. Thus, the Romantic version of Boabdil is intimately tied to the fall of the Spanish Empire: by turns, and even simultaneously, the figure of the tragic yet noble king functions in different ways to process Spain's new weaker position in world politics. On one hand, Boabdil serves as a stand-in for the tarnished Spanish monarchs of Zorrilla's time to whom the poetic speaker demonstrates compassion and respect. On the other hand, Boabdil can also function to shore up Spanish power by reviving a historical moment in which Castile was first consolidating its Iberian empire and was able to overpower the last Moorish king, a figure so tragic that in comparison the nineteenth-century Spanish monarchy might seem strong. Here recalling the tragic grandeur of those vanquished by emergent Spain mitigates the weakness of Spain at the time of writing. While Zorrilla and other Spanish Romantics may suggest—even if indirectly—a comparison between the Bourbon and the Nasrid dynasties, they do so to assuage the loss of stability and imperial power. Either way, the Romantics use Boabdil as part of a compensatory logic to ease the political instability of their time. Later, in the wake of the loss of Cuba, Puerto Rico, and the Philippines in the Spanish-American War, the Generation of 1898 directly questioned Spanish cultural identity and its relationship to empire, but without invoking Boabdil. After Spain's heavy losses in the Spanish-American War and the effective end of their empire, these writers sought to critically examine Spain and break from certain traditions, including apparently the tradition of remembering the tragic Boabdil.

Boabdil resurfaces in the late twentieth and early twenty-first centuries, during which Spanish representations of him are legion, with most taking their cue from the Romantic writers and crafting the last Moorish king of Granada as some form of melancholic figure. Thus, a recurring manifestation of Boabdil is that of the king of sadness: a romanticized, mournful, destiny-bound figure that might serve to express compassion but at the same time externalizes weakness by projecting it onto the Other, and thus affirms the power of the Spanish self. In what follows I trace appearances of the tragic Moorish king in works from Spain, Argentina, Syria, and the Spanish region of Andalusia and appearances of divergent versions of Boabdil in works from Spain, Morocco, and Lebanon.

To my knowledge, the earliest twentieth-century representation of Muhammad XII is *Boabdil* (1939) by Fidel Fernández Martínez (1890–1942), a prominent Granadan cultural figure of the time who was a medical doctor, an avid Sierra Nevada trekker, and an active conservationist of the Alhambra. Fernández, who was born two decades or more after the Generation of 1898 writers, produced a work of ambiguous genre. It can be considered a novelized history: a history with occasional descriptions of the historical figures' feelings and a handful of dialogues. Although the text's genre is unclear, its depiction of Boabdil is certainly not. Here the Romantic vision persists: Boabdil as the tragic, yet regal soul. In this text, after Boabdil has accepted his court's recommendation that he capitulate to the Catholic Monarchs, we find this description of him:

> Boabdil bowed his head under the weight of that definitive declaration, that snatched from it in one blow the imperial crown; and after a brief pause he raised it again, more solemn and majestic in its disgrace than it had been on the splendor of its throne.
>
> "All right," he said with strong bitterness. "The crown of Islam will soon leave the head of Zogoibi, and destiny has sealed my brow with the most horrific of signs. Tomorrow my emissaries will go to the royal camp at Santa Fe. (197)

Clearly, Boabdil's suffering only serves to intensify his splendid nobility. The narrator goes on to refer to "the pain that was destroying his soul," "noble resignation," and "the valor and tempered serenity of the young King of Granada" (197). On the final page of the text Boabdil's fate as one born under a bad sign is sealed. The narrator states that Boabdil died heroically in a battle in North Africa, but like countless others, his corpse was dragged by a river into the sea. This leads the narrator to proclaim: "Unfortunate even after death, his ashes did not rest on earth" (251). In this way, even after death, Boabdil is still the king of misfortune.

According to Fernández's prologue, he wrote the text in the summer of 1937 (9); this places its creation one year into the Spanish Civil War (July 1936–April 1939). Neither in the prologue nor elsewhere in the text is there any reference to the contemporary strife in which Spain was embroiled. Perhaps focusing on distant history, and specifically a time in which the newly unified Castile and Aragon were ascendant and victorious, a time associated with nobility and valor—even in the face of dark destiny—was an antidote to the war raging while Fernández wrote. At the same time, the book's place of publication ties it to contemporary political realities that were part of Franco's rise to power. Fernández's *Boabdil* was published in Tangier. This Moroccan city had been made an international zone under the joint administration of Spain, France, and Britain in 1923 and it was in northern Morocco that General Francisco

Franco initiated his military career in Spanish colonial campaigns. Furthermore, during the Civil War some of Franco's troops were Moroccans conscripted into the Spanish army. Although Fernández's *Boabdil* does not contain any direct reference to contemporary events, its place of publication plants it firmly as part of Spanish colonialism over the Moor. Read in this light, the text, without declaring a side within the Civil War, is a celebration of Spanish military might over its enemy Other. More specifically, it offers a narrative in which the Moor is destined to graciously accept defeat while Spain is destined to rise in might.

The era during which there seem to be no depictions of Boabdil coincides with the Franco dictatorship, which lasted from the end of the Civil War until 1975. During this period survival became a more pressing concern, and most likely the pathos of defeat intrinsic to the figure of Boabdil was, for all those on the losing side of the Civil War, not a welcome topic. The war had a devastating effect on Spanish literary culture, with major writers dying during the war and others going into exile. Throughout the early years of the dictatorship, hunger, repression, and censorship prevailed alongside state-sponsored neo-Baroque poetry and praises of Franco's Spain. The 1950s saw the emergence of social realist narrative followed by literary experimentation that included *Reivindicación del Conde Don Julián* by Goytisolo.[7]

Musical Interlude: Boabdil in Post-Franco Popular Music from Andalusia

During the 1970s, Boabdil did not appear in Spanish prose works but in song, and possibly for the first time, the tragic Moorish king is not posited as completely Other but as part of the Andalusian self.[8] In 1974, Los Puntos, a Spanish pop and rock group from a small town in the province of Almería (in Andalusia) released a hit single titled "Llorando por Granada" ("Crying for/over Granada") in which they mobilized Andalusian identity politics—a myth of Moorish origins that allows for political organizing.[9] Although the sound and look of the band was very much in keeping with international inspirations such as the Beatles, the song does have a subtle motif that ties it to Middle Eastern music. The lyrics of "Llorando por Granada," without naming Boabdil, tell a condensed version of the legend about an enchanted Boabdil who remained in Granada, eternally crying for his loss. Here the king of sadness is condemned to roam the Alhambra under a spell, crying for it and for Granada.

Similarly, another hit song by Los Puntos, "Tierra Cristiana" ("Christian Land"), which was released as a single in 1976 (roughly a year after Franco's death), presents a crying Moor bidding farewell to the lands that have just become Christian.[10] This figure can be interpreted as an unnamed Boabdil or an anonymous Moor who echoes Boabdil in the legend of El suspiro del moro: lamenting as he says his last goodbye ("su último adiós") to Granada, someone sees him look back and cry like a child ("volviéndose hacia atrás / alguien lo vió como un niño llorar"). Moreover, the only verse in which there is a speaker in the first person observes Boabdil's state and sympathizes with him deeply: "tiembla al hablar, tristeza hay en su voz / tanto dolor me rompe el corazón" ("he shakes as he speaks, there is sadness in his voice / so much pain breaks my heart"). This song also features subtle Oriental (or Orientalist) musical phrases.

These songs can be interpreted as a problematic appropriation of the sounds and historical figures of a conquered culture. Yet they can also be read simultaneously as an identification with the figure of the sad Moor. A current within the literary modernism (*modernismo*) of Andalusia sought to eschew the image of Andalusia as a space of boisterous festivals and instead identify the authentic Andalusian *volkgeist* as one characterized by a deep sense of suffering. The idea of an Andalusian ethos of tragedy and pain came to the fore with the signal work *Tristeza andaluza* (*Andalusian Sadness*, 1898) by Nicolás María López (1863–1936), which presents, with the symbolist style of modernismo, sketches and anecdotes highlighting the melancholy of Andalusia.[11] Given that López was friends with the prominent Granadan intellectual Ángel Ganivet (1865–1898), who is seen by many as a precursor to the *andalucismo* movement, this Andalusian ethos is surely tied to the figure of the tragic Moor.

The period during which Los Puntos produced the above-mentioned songs, and in which they first attained popularity, further elucidates the identificatory process between *andaluz* and *moro* via melancholy. In the second half of the twentieth century, emigration has been one of the defining characteristics of Andalusian culture. After the late nineteenth- and early twentieth-century wave of Spanish immigrants to Hispano-America (primarily Cuba, Puerto Rico, and Argentina) and the Civil War–era exile and emigration of many Republicans to other parts of Europe and Latin America, the 1950s saw the start of an overall Spanish pattern of emigration from the countryside to urban centers that included a massive emigration flow from the most economically depressed parts of Spain—the regions of Andalusia, Extremadura, and Galicia—to urban centers in other parts of the country that were experiencing economic growth, that is, Madrid and (for Andalusians in particular) Barcelona. Additionally, although the Franco government had previously impeded immigration to other countries, the government's 1959 *Plan de Estabilización* (Stabilization Plan) authorized extranational emigration. This produced an exodus from Andalusia and the other depressed regions to other Western European countries (mainly France, Switzerland, and Germany) during the 1960s and early 1970s. With changing economic circumstances on the individual and regional levels, many of these labor migrants returned after several years in Catalonia or abroad.[12] For these reasons, the theme of migrant nostalgia for Andalusia was strong throughout the second half of the twentieth century. This sense of displacement was explicitly linked to the figure of the exiled Moor: in newspaper columns that Antonio Gala wrote in the 1970s and 1980s, he identifies the fate of the exiled Moors with that of the Andalusians of his day.[13] Thus, when Los Puntos sing about crying for Granada and express empathy for the Moor who says good-bye to it, they express the homesickness of Andalusian migrants and the feelings of those who stayed behind, observing their emigration process and missing them.

Intertwined with this emigration phenomenon, recall that the postdictatorship period saw a rise in cultural and political movements centered on regionalisms and nationalisms, among them the andalucismo movement. In addition to the Andalusian identification with the disenfranchised, mourning Moor suggested by some of the songs by Los Puntos, the case of another singer of the same period makes this identification clearer. The music of Granadan singer-songwriter Carlos Cano (1946–2000) demonstrates a folkloric style, a marked influence of Arab music, and a pronounced connection to Arabo-Amazigh Muslim culture. In particular, his 1978 album *Crónicas Granadinas* (*Granadan Chronicles*) includes an instrumental song titled "Suspiro del moro" ("The Moor's Last Sigh"); the song "Canto del Amanecer" ("Song of the Dawn"), which features Cano singing the Muslim call to prayer in Arabic; and a piece dedicated to Boabdil, titled "Casida del Rey Chico" ("Ode to the Younger King").[14]

The title of this last song, "Casida del Rey Chico," uses a loanword from the Arabic *qasida* (a traditional form of monorhyme, strictly metered poetry). Given that Cano's song does not approximate the classical qasida form, the word is used here as a broad reference to Arabic poetry. The beginning of the song, similar to the songs by Los Puntos, uses Boabdil as symbol of loss and nostalgia that encompasses and expresses the melancholy of Andalusian migrants to other parts of the country and Spanish émigrés to other parts of Europe. Like thousands of other Andalusians, Cano himself went to work in Switzerland and Germany as a young man. In the first three verses of the song, the speaker tells us how, at the bottom of an *aljibe* (Arab cistern), "me encontré la tristeza / que matara al rey Boabdil" (I encountered the sadness / that once killed king Boabdil). But the mood of the song changes from sadness to hope in the next verses when the speaker tells us that he left that sadness behind to see if "la luz del pensamiento diera flor / y el pueblo recobrara su color verdiblanco / de origen bereber" (the light of thought would bloom / and the people would recover their green-white color / of Berber origin). Here the speaker hopes that the Andalusian people will recover—that is, return to a consciousness of—the colors of the Andalusian flag, which were chosen in 1918 by Blas Infante, founding figure of andalucismo. Infante explained his flag design by indicating that green was the color of the Umayyads and white that of the Almohads, the caliphates that represent periods of grandeur and power in that region. In case the connection to Muslim dynasties might be lost on listeners, Cano's song directly names the Amazighs, from whom rose the Almohad dynasty. The rest of the song calls the children of the countryside to tell "la tierra / que el pobre la espera al amanecer" ("the earth / that the poor man waits for it at dawn"). Thus the song instructs the children to let the land of Andalusia know that the poor await it, longing to be reunited with it. Whether the reunification of the poor Andalusians with the soil of their region refers to migrant return, or more broadly to the recognition of their supposed North African roots, Cano's "Casida del Rey Chico" posits an identification with Boabdil. Through this song and those by Los Puntos, Boabdil collectively grieves for al-Andalus/Andalusia and also offers Andalusians a grand heritage of which to be proud.

On one hand, through Cano's *Crónicas Granadinas* album, it is easy to see why Spanish journalist Juan Jesús Armas Marcelo refers to Cano as "an ideological mestizo." On the other hand, the pop music uses of Boabdil remain problematic. In the songs by Los Puntos, Boabdil remains a symbol of melancholy—even if Andalusian melancholy—and this opens the door to a role for the songs in the gloating of the conqueror. Reception in Andalusia may have consisted of identification with Boabdil's (émigré) nostalgia, whereas in the rest of Spain it could easily involve a voyeuristic pleasure in the melancholy of the defeated other. Nonetheless, the scale seems to tip in Cano's "Casida del Rey Chico": here the first-person encounter with Boabdil's sadness, at the bottom of an Arab cistern, no less, establishes a stronger identification and transitions to a hopeful call to consciousness for the downtrodden. The suffering is shared, and moreover, it is left behind to pursue a reencounter with the Muslim North African past of the area. Cano's stance is a radical departure in particular from the traditionalist conception of Spain as a Roman-Visigoth Catholic culture corrupted by Muslims and Jews—a vision espoused by Franco's *nacionalcatolicismo* ideology. In fact, the music of Los Puntos and Cano delineated an Andalusian ethos in contemporary popular music that developed into a musical genre called "rock andaluz" (Andalusian rock), a genre that, however problematically, embraces Andalusi culture as Andalusian counterculture.

Even Cano's call for reengagement with al-Andalus, contestatory as it is, has its limitations. "Casida del Rey Chico" glosses over certain historical facts, such as that Boabdil's Nasrid Dynasty was founded not only after the fall of the Almohad caliphate in 1212 but in 1238 as one of the splinter polities of the third taifa period. Although this could be interpreted as a way to leave behind the tragedy of Boabdil and embrace earlier periods of glory, it creates a simplified version of events that whitewashes the power struggles and in-fighting of al-Andalus.

In addition, "Casida del Rey Chico," as well as the rest of Cano's Andalusi-inspired works, maintains the myth of an Andalusian genealogy that directly connects the region to al-Andalus. Given what is known about the expulsion and repopulation projects and what is suggested by modern-day DNA testing, the same *andalucistas* calling for a revival of Almohad spirit, or even simply that dynasty's color scheme, are most likely the descendants of Christian Iberians who appropriated the lands of expelled Muslims. The andalucista call, then, while raising the status of the expelled and proscribed Muslim culture, ignores Andalusians' role in the process of (re)colonization. This disavowal is key to the appropriation of Muslim cultural elements within the cultural and political strains of andalucismo. Yet fully naturalized, it allows Cano and other practitioners of cultural andalucismo to embrace a Muslim ethos in order to reject the oppression of Andalusians by economic inequity and marginalization within the nation. In conclusion, although still problematic in the context of colonizer/colonized relations, the examples of popular Andalusian music express a type of identificatory Orientalism for political and countercultural aims.

Many Requiems for One King: The 1980s and On

Since the late twentieth century, the nobly tragic Boabdil has appeared multiple times in Spanish narrative and popular culture, with a primary role in at least one play, two television series, four novels for adult readerships, and three juvenile novels. In contrast with the songs linked to the Andalusianism movement, in nearly all of these works Boabdil is the tragic Other. Although lighter versions of an Andalusian ethos are glimpsed in the works of Antonio Gala, a more marked reframing of Boabdil occurs in one of the children's novels that invokes him, tears and all, in the context of North African migration to Spain. Before discussing these works and Arab representations of Boabdil, which are all linked to migration, I examine the ways standard Spanish versions of Boabdil are connected to empire and more specifically to attempts at reviving feelings of imperial power.

The connection to Spain's loss of empire, that is, Boabdil's role within Spanish compensatory rhetoric that was pointed to above in Zorrilla's poem, is particularly salient in a 1984 play by Spanish author Antonio Gala. After writing the screenplays for the TV series *Paisaje con figuras*, Gala wrote additional pieces on specifically Andalusian historical figures which were published under the title *Paisaje andaluz con figuras* (1984).[15] Within this collection, the piece titled "Si las piedras hablaran: el fruto coronado (La Alhambra)" ("If Stones Could Speak: The Crowned Fruit [The Alhambra]") focuses on Boabdil and the fall of the kingdom of Granada. In the theater piece, Boabdil, his wife, Moraima, a troubadour [*juglar*], and a narrator, with occasional appearances by the Catholic Monarchs, recount the story of Boabdil. Like its medieval and Romantic predecessors, the piece refers to destiny, lamentations, and the sadness of loss. Using elements of medieval literary stylistics (repetition and citation of well-known romances by the troubadour) the play seeks to stage not only the same message about Boabdil but also the ambience of the era in which he lived.

The message at the end, in Boabdil's voice, is that all empires that rise must fall. This explains not only Granada but the history of Spain and its loss of its empire. The conclusion of the play offers a specific message in Boabdil's voice: "Everything that ascends to its greatest height begins to decline. Don't let yourselves be seduced by life and the love of life . . . [. . .] Only Allah is victorious: you are already seeing it . . . Can there be a homeland [*patria*] for a man who has lost Granada? Cry, cry . . . Because everything that rises, rises up in order to sink down" (40). The message that all empires must inevitably fall applies to Spain: it rose with the help of Columbus, who is referred to in the play, to become a great empire and then like Granada and al-Andalus, it fell.

Recall that the postdictatorship period was one of tremendous political and cultural change in which Spain questioned its relationship with Europe and North Africa, while its regional nationalisms simultaneously found expression after suppression under Franco. Gala wrote "Si las piedras hablaran" during the early part of that period. Soon after, the measures taken during the 1980s to integrate Spain into Europe led to a notable upsurge in North African immigration to the country. The 1990 European Schengen Convention made entry through Spain more enticing for migrants and put more pressure on Spanish border authorities vis-à-vis their European partners. In addition, the quincentenary of 1492 stirred things up further by drawing international attention to Spain's (re)conquest of al-Andalus and its colonization of the Americas. I argue that the focus on the inevitable fall of empire in Gala's theater piece responds to the early phase of the process of reconciling Spain's past and present that was already under way in the early 1980s. Likewise, the various Spanish depictions of Boabdil produced in the 1990s and early 2000s, which I detail in what follows, are responses to the issues raised by the increasing questioning of Spain's identity and the sense that the country's future depended on establishing its Europeanness.

The 1990 Spanish mini-series *Réquiem por Granada* (*Requiem for Granada*) presents the image of the tragic Boabdil, makes it clear that the Spanish public still enjoys savoring the end of Muslim Spain 500 years later, and provides a trope—the requiem—for understanding this enjoyment. The series consists of eight fifty-minute episodes, many of which focus on the relationship between Boabdil's father, Muley Hasan (Abu al-Hasan ʿAli; d. 1485), and his concubine-turned-wife, Isabel de Solís, a Christian captive who converted to Islam and took the name Soraya (Thurayya in Arabic). The show was a major joint production of the public television stations of Spain (Televisión Española) and Italy (Radiotelevisione Italiana). The first episode begins with a caravan crossing the desert and finding a lone traveler on the verge of death. A letter that accompanies the mysterious traveler states: "He pays the price of wanting to be faithful to himself and to Islam."[16] One of the first things the traveler utters is a repetitive statement about death. When the leader of the caravan asks whether his people ("los tuyos") abandoned him in the desert, the traveler says: "My people [*los míos*] no longer matter. They are dead. They ride through the desert, but they are dead. Nobody knows it. Not even them, but they are dead" (4:40–5:10). This traveler turns out to be Boabdil and thus the phrase "los míos" stands for the Moors of Granada, and his statement confirms over and over that they are dead, even if they don't look it. Boabdil goes on to mutter that he himself is dead and repeats for a fourth time that "they" are dead. The caravan leader takes the living-dead Boabdil to his encampment to recuperate and there Boabdil recounts his life story—one destined to end in misfortune.

Boabdil explains that the Granadans went against Allah's will and tried to enjoy paradise on Earth, referring to Granada and the Alhambra as the Garden of Eden. Thus, the Moors of Granada suffered due to their own sins and the Christians are exculpated. The camera soon leaves this elderly Boabdil and takes us to Boabdil as a boy. As if the opening scene of the encounter in the desert and the audience's probable familiarity with Boabdil's fate weren't enough, the first episode is laden with dramatic irony. When the young Boabdil is leaving the Alhambra with his uncle El Zagal (Abu ʿAbd Allah Muhammad al-Zaghal) on a diplomatic visit to the court of Ferdinand and Isabella, Boabdil is worried about leaving Granada and says "It would be sad to not see Granada again." El Zagal encourages him by responding "Granada won't move; it will always be there waiting for us" and boasting about the wonders of the Muslim kingdom created by his people. To this Boabdil replies, "I will never leave Granada! [¡Yo nunca me separaré de Granada!]" (27:30–28:18). The viewing audience, however, knows that he will be definitively separated from Granada and has been reminded of this by the opening scene in the desert. This dramatic irony heightens the pathos surrounding the figure of the unfortunate Moorish king. For example, in the second episode, when viewers first encounter an adult Boabdil, a Castilian Christian who has just met him states: "No wonder they call him the unfortunate prince. Never in my life have I seen a sadder soul [criatura más triste]" (31:30). The viewer and the Castilian character, in analogous positions, observe the extreme piteousness of the Arab prince through the lens of the pathos that precedes him.

In a very loose version of the Boabdil story, this mini-series heightens the tension between Boabdil and his father by having Boabdil have a secret romance with Isabel de Solís before she is captured and sold to his father as a slave-concubine. The father–son tension surrounding Isabel de Solís leads to various conversations expressing Orientalist versions of Muslim views on love, desire, and women. The imagined love triangle serves to emphasize Boabdil's weakness and passivity: when he finally comes to tell Isabel that he will take her away with him, she asks where he was when his father took possession of her, calls him a "subservient dog," and orders him to leave, reproaching him for not standing up to his father. Boabdil flees and when encouraged to avoid cowardice and take what is his—the kingdom and the captive Christian woman—he replies that is it useless because "I'll always be *zogoibi*, the loser" (18:22). Thus, in this version of the story, Boabdil's perdition is caused by his love for a Christian woman and his inability to fight for her against his father. Woman and land (kingdom) are explicitly and implicitly paired, and thus the tragic hero's flaw is a doubled lack of masculine valor.

As the series continues, the depiction of Boabdil takes on Christ-like characteristics. In Episode 5 Boabdil says he must accept his destiny (21:15) and a few minutes later, echoing Jesus's invocation of the will of his Father, Boabdil lets his father's soldiers take him prisoner stating: "Carry out my father's orders [Cumple la orden de me padre]" (33:35). In the following episode, Boabdil, echoing Christ in the Garden of

Gethsemane, prays to God, asking for his guidance, stating that God knows his agony, and wondering how he can save his people. After this, in episode 7, presumably following God's will, Boabdil focuses on ending his reign with honor. When his counselors convince him that they must surrender to the Catholic Monarchs' siege, he insists that he will be the only one to draft the capitulation agreement and attempts to protect the rights of the Granadan Muslims. When the capitulation has been signed and the symbolic key to the city handed over, the mini-series ends with Boabdil, his mother, and their entourage leaving Granada while church bells ring. These church bells tie together the submissive and Christ-like depictions of Boabdil to establish an image of noble submission and sacrifice for the greater good. The ringing bells are at once the celebratory bells of the conquerors and the bells for Muslim Granada's funeral mass or requiem.

Although the bells are ringing, Boabdil and his entourage are never seen dead. *Réquiem por Granada* ends without ever circling back to the Boabdil who is found in the desert in the opening of the first episode. The frame story is incomplete, and the viewer doesn't know how Boabdil moves from being "dead while alive" to actually dying. How can there be a requiem if we don't know about the end of his life? The Latin term *requiem* primarily refers to a Catholic mass for the repose of the souls of the dead and by extension refers to a musical composition used in a requiem mass or related to mourning, and to an act or token of remembrance. This mini-series enacts a remembrance of Boabdil that is a highly ironic gesture: a Catholic mass for the Muslim Boabdil and his people. This irony underscores who the victors were in that conflict. Given that we never see the physical death of Boabdil, the death that is actually being commemorated is the death of a threat: Boabdil and Muslim Granada as a threat to Catholic Castilian identity. In the context of the Boabdil story, the requiem is a ritual that calms fears regarding identity boundaries and power. The mass is not so much *for* the dead as it is an incantation to make dead that which threatens the viewer—whether it is North African immigration within Spain or the place of Spain in geopolitics. As a soothing ritual, the repetition of this requiem heightens its stabilizing, empowering effect. For this reason, the tragic Boabdil keeps appearing again and again in other television programs and popular novels.

Boabdil has appeared again on Spanish television as part of the more recent series *Isabel*, which focuses on the Catholic Monarch Isabella I of Castile and includes Boabdil as one of the main characters throughout most of the second season. The series, produced by Diagonal TV for Televisión Española, began airing in September 2012 and entered its third season in 2014. The 2013 season, in which Boabdil appears in ten episodes, depicts the Nasrid king as a poet who prefers dialogue over war and chooses rendition to save his family and the Alhambra. Following typical portrayals of Boabdil, in this series his mother, Aixa, is an ambitious, intransigent woman who would rather destroy the Alhambra and herself than capitulate.[17] Contrary to most depictions, here Boabdil confronts his mother and goes ahead with the capitulation. His last scene reenacts the famous legend of El suspiro del moro with his mother reproaching him for crying like a woman over what he wasn't able to defend like a man. As an added layer of pathos and defeat, after hearing his mother's words, Boabdil falls to his hands and knees, sobbing. Though he was able to stand up to his mother once, here he is knocked over by her words. The *Isabel* series maintains the commonplace representations of Boabdil but adds another sign of weakness and downfall, thereby creating an opportunity to remember—that is, savor—the moment of Spain's great victory against the Moorish Other.

The novels focused on Boabdil are part of the burgeoning of the historical novel genre since the last decades of the twentieth century in Hispanic letters in general, especially in writing from Spain. Luis Veres explains this broader phenomenon as a sign of mistrust in postmodern and academic conceptions of history that counters such interpretations with a belief in the capacity of fiction to present truth, and to present it in a way that feels more legitimate and believable. Thus, most of these works share the aim of reviewing the past to address issues of the present and have an unquestioning attitude toward the truth claims, or at least the aura of truth, that arises from history/historical narrative. This attitude explains what Fernández Prieto describes as little interest within the Spanish historical novel in the contestatory project of the postmodern historical novel (176). Fernández Prieto's observation is certainly borne out in most of the Spanish novels I treat in this study, especially those about Boabdil.

Two such novels are Magdalena Lasala's *Boabdil: tragedia del último rey de Granada* (*Boabdil: Tragedy of the Last King of Granada*, 2004) and Antonio Soler's *Boabdil: un hombre contra el destino* (*Boabdil: A Man against Destiny*, 2012). Lasala (b. 1958), a prolific writer from Aragon, has published several works that are set in al-Andalus, many focusing on women characters.[18] The cover of her novel about Boabdil displays a section of a famous work by Spanish painter Francisco Pradilla Ortiz (1848–1921) titled "El lamento del moro," which depicts the scene of the Moor's last sigh. The cover image and the reference to tragedy in the novel's title announce the traditionalist portrayal of Boabdil that the narrative fashions. Amid melodramatic portraits of the relationships between the characters, the book emphasizes Boabdil as a figure who passively accepts his fate. This is manifested in the relentless repetition of the words for fate and destiny (*destino*, *sino*, *fatalidad*, etc.) which appear nearly fifty times in the 353-page text. Thus, Lasala's Boabdil is a sensitive, melancholic poet who has a gift for languages and a great appreciation for the arts, but is largely passive in the face of the political machinations of others. When he plunges into battle with energy, it is because he hopes to die and end his sorrowful existence. He accepts the astrologer's prediction (which is portrayed with Orientalist excess [142–47]) that he will be the last king of Granada and only seeks to lessen the blow for Granadans and find a way to enjoy his family in peace. Similarly, Aixa, in keeping with her statement in the famous legend of El suspiro del moro, is a cold calculator: precociously intelligent but masculine, unfeeling, and ambitious. Although Aixa and Isabel (Isabella I of Castile) are explicitly compared and presented as very similar (179 and 263), Aixa, through the repeated use of the term *vientre* (womb) in relation to her, is reduced to her supposedly embattled relationship with her womb and the womanhood for which it stands. The message that emerges is that as a Muslim woman with ambition, she is destined to be conflicted and embittered.

Throughout, the novel suggests that it was God's will that the kingdom of Granada should fall and the Catholic Monarchs take over. The emphasis on destiny culminates in a comparison between Ferdinand and Boabdil in which the difference between them is that while the Aragonese grabbed hold of fate and took action to make of it what he wanted, the Moor accepted fate passively (332). To further underscore the idea that the Christian victory was meant to be, a passage toward the end of the novel proclaims that these lands will never change hands again (327), affirming that the story is over, that no type of Muslim threat—whether in the form of migrants or terrorists—can destabilize Spain. *Boabdil: tragedia del último rey de Granada* was published in the same year as the Madrid train bombings (2004), thus this affirmation of stability is not likely to have been written as a response to that terrorist act, however, it may reflect a general climate of fear of Muslim terrorism in the wake of the September 11, 2001, attacks.

Lasala's novel includes a bibliography but no specific citations or notes, and thus the text conveys the idea that everything it recounts is taken from the historical record. Clearly the sometimes lurid details about the sex lives of some of the last Nasrid sultans and other intimate aspects of their lives and their feelings are the product of the author's imagination or the collective Spanish imagination. This pseudo-historical format serves to imbue the novel with truth value, while never considering the relationship between historical truth and the construction of narrative.

Antonio Soler (b. 1956) is a writer from Málaga who has won national literary prizes. The title of his novel *Boabdil: un hombre contra el destino* might suggest that in this account Boabdil struggles against his purported destiny, but the novel presents, through different means, a message similar to the destiny message of Lasala's Boabdil novel. Through a less melodramatic and less Orientalist style of writing than that of Lasala, Soler's book tells the story of an impossible "bromance" between Boabdil and Gonzalo Fernández de Córdoba (1453–1515), a Spanish military officer who was nicknamed El Gran Capitán (the Great Captain) due to his military prowess. Fernández de Córdoba fought in the campaigns to conquer the Emirate of Granada and partly because of his fluency in Arabic was chosen as one of the officers to arrange the surrender of the kingdom.[19] Soler's novel consists of recounting Boabdil's life, Fernández de Córdoba's life, and the close homosocial bond they form, as well as the realization that their relationship cannot endure because they are on opposite sides of history. Soler's Boabdil story attempts to establish and make sense of a model for respectful distance between Spain and North Africa/the Arab world by recasting the conflict as a something of a gentlemen's disagreement.

In many ways, *Boabdil: un hombre contra el destino* repeats the clichés regarding Boabdil seen in previous works. For instance, destiny is mentioned often (though still only about half as much as in Lasala's text) with Boabdil remembering a few times *la maldición* (the curse) that is on him. Boabdil tries to flee from his misfortune (41 and 313), but he is not able to escape fate (315). In addition, the omniscient narrator describes Boabdil as full of foreboding (17), interested in poetry and considered effeminate by his father (38–39), anxious and sensitive (61), and delicate and ethereal (142). Several times he is described as having a sad smile or melancholic look on his face, and ultimately the narrator presents this as a smile of absolute, almost "animal" sadness (265). In this way, Boabdil's sadness is so profound that it makes him like an animal, devoid of reason.

Soler's novel breaks from the typical Boabdil mold by having Gonzalo Fernández de Córdoba demonstrate great respect and interest in Islam and Andalusi culture and exhibit tastes, such as a love of reading, that are considered effeminate by others (55).[20] When the two men come into contact with each other through Boabdil's Castilian captivity and the negotiation process, Boabdil shares details about his fraught relationship with his mother (161), and the two men find that they have much in common (163 and 165). Boabdil's respect for Gonzalo is so strong that he only agrees to deliver his firstborn son to the Christians as a hostage if his son will live with Gonzalo and be under his tutelage (168). Their star-crossed bond is so deep that even after Boabdil's captivity they maintain their friendship (197–98). Another fresh approach the novel offers is the repeated criticism of the (mis)use of religion in politics on both sides of the conflict. Both men end up feeling defeated because they have a common enemy: religious fanatics, whether Christian or Muslim (59). Similarly, both heroes are disillusioned by the outcome of the war and Fernández de Córdoba believes that understanding between the groups is the best solution (201).

In spite of the interesting departures involved in presenting these heroes as men of honor who share a bond, one core difference remains: unlike Boabdil, Gonzalo Fernández de Córdoba is intent on imposing his will on destiny (54). For this reason, their fates are very different: one is a dethroned king, and the other becomes El Gran Capitán (315–17).

After mentioning legends surrounding Boabdil and Gonzalo, the text concludes as follows:

> In any case, what was truly certain was that Gonzalo had suffered a serious disappointment during the capture of Granada. He saw with embarrassment the humiliations that followed the surrender of the city and how all parties tried to abuse the figure of Boabdil. But he didn't do anything. [. . .] Gonzalo knew that Boabdil felt betrayed by that attitude of his. That period always had a bitter taste in Gonzalo's memory. Parallel lives that became more and more distanced, connected only by the threads of memory and the already smoking embers of an impossible friendship. (317)

Here the narrator conveys how their relationship ended due to the Castilian's betrayal and explains that theirs was an impossible relationship. The closing lines of the novel go on to state that Boabdil, once in North Africa, was said to have died battling valiantly and free of fear. This detail about his end, together with the entire narrative dedicated to the unviable bromance, conveys the idea that mutual respect, but at a distance—with each side in its "proper" place—is the best approach to intercultural relations, since they are fated to be impossible.

The novels by Lasala and Soler demonstrate a tendency that Daniela Flesler identifies in her analysis of other historical novels, focused more broadly on medieval Iberia, as well as of the festivals of Moors and Christians that reenact medieval Christian victories. Flesler notes that the works she studies "constitute an example of the effort at performatively constructing a clear boundary between the two groups" (97). However, she interprets these works as failing "to delimit two clear spaces of separation" and explains that "Moors and Christians become simultaneously guests and hosts in what Homi Bhabha calls a 'third space' that is neither one of complete separation nor one of homogenization" (Flesler 97–98). In the Boabdil-centered works I examine here, the sheer weight of destiny and the reiterated impossibility of Boabdil and Gonzalo's relationship do seem to create separate spheres for Moor and Christian, but the very insistence on retelling Boabdil's story belies this. The fact that Boabdil lingers in Spanish consciousness indicates that the phantom of the Moor and concomitant anxieties surrounding Spanish identity persist. González Alcantud has stated, "With the aim of chasing off the Moorish phantasm, the inhabitants of Granada—who really carried out the process of conquering the city and the kingdom, house by house, street by street, throughout more than a century, until the definitive expulsión of the moriscos from Spain—created different rituals and myths" ("El canon andaluz y las fronteras imaginarias," 370). The role of the performance of ritual and myth within Spanish practices and discourses aimed at containing that Moorish phantasm cannot be overstated. Indeed, spectacle was central to Boabdil's official defeat. Historian L. P. Harvey points out that the public ceremony of January 2, 1492 (known as La Toma de Granada), in which Boabdil handed over a set of keys to King Ferdinand and Queen Isabella, was all a performance because as a result of political concerns, the Alhambra had already been handed over to Castilian control the day before: "What took place on January 2 was a splendid pageant, a piece of memorable street-theater" (322–23). It was a staging of the subjugation of tragic Moorish Otherness. Continuing with that impulse, the works studied here seek to calm the anxieties provoked by the Moorish phantasm, to construct self/other boundaries, by ritually staging the death of Boabdil.

Among the Spanish novels on Boabdil, there are two that move away from the commonplaces that are part of the narrative requiems for the last Muslim ruler of al-Andalus, albeit with limitations. One of these is *El último suspiro del rey Boabdil* (2007) by Leonardo Villena, a school teacher and writer from the province of Granada. Villena's text attempts to historicize the legendary figure, but without any attention to the role of narrative in historiography. The novel, which consists of limited characterization and a choppy narrative, presents a creative reinterpretation of the concept of the Moor's last sigh, by having the narrative end with Boabdil exhaling "his last sigh [su último suspiro]" (185) as he dies in Fez. Similarly, it is the only text that gives Boabdil something of a happy ending as he is able to die content because of the warm reception afforded him by the sultan of Fez. According to the novel, in implicit contrast with his dishonorable treatment by the Catholic Monarchs, Boabdil and his family are so well received in Fez that his son marries the daughter of the North African sultan (133–34). Through this marriage into another royal family, Villena makes it such that Boabdil's nobility is saved and perpetuated. Yet this creative revision that reduces Boabdil's pathos runs counter to the main objective of the novel, which is to disprove historical inaccuracies. For instance, Villena quotes at length from other texts, adding footnotes to point out discrepancies with the historical record. This method is not only confusing and inconsistent with Villena's vision of the suspiro and Boabdil's reception in Fez (which cannot be documented), but it never considers the way narrative plots history, that is, the way it imbues it with a message. In sum, Villena's text is an awkward attempt at historicization that never considers historiographic method or the creative potential inherent in reformulating legends.

The other novel that departs from the typical requiems for Boabdil is that of best-selling author Antonio Gala. Gala's *El manuscrito carmesí* (*The Crimson Manuscript*, 1990) takes us back to the same year as the airing of the mini-series *Réquiem*, yet the project is quite different from that of the TV series. Many critics have noted the innovative narrative technique Gala uses in *El manuscrito carmesí*, which is his most acclaimed work and won the Planeta Prize in 1990.[21] This innovation consists of presenting Boabdil's life story as a first-person narrative from the perspective of Boabdil himself. The fictional autobiography, especially in 1990, was a groundbreaking way of representing Boabdil and the Moorish Other in general; nonetheless, I contend that this innovation is quite limited by colonialist translation dynamics. Fatma Benhamamouche points out that by positioning Boabdil as the narrator, Gala situates the Muslim world as the center, and the Christian world as the periphery, thereby deconstructing dominant discourses. Benhamamouche goes on to assert that "Antonio Gala, in bringing us other voices that give testimony to their own vision of the world, inverts the nature of a Historiography that won't accept any divergence regarding the discourse of Spanish hegemony" (194). I disagree with this assertion because the novel's attempts at providing an alternate history and questioning the very foundations of historiography are undercut by reiteration of the figure of the sad, destiny-bound Moor and by the (colonial) appropriation that is part of the presentation of Boabdil's narrative voice.

As Benhamamouche phrases it, through this novel Gala tries to recuperate "the amputated memory of Spanish History" (200). To some extent the novel rewrites Spanish history by adding a degree of nuance to the narrative of *convivencia* through emphasis on the complexity and hybridity of cultures. Here Boabdil demonstrates that he is not a detached coward but someone who, amid various tensions, seeks what he believes is best for his people and makes observations about the power dynamics and cultural misconceptions that surround him. Through the voice of Boabdil, the reader finds criticism of discourses about fixed difference, in favor of religious, racial, and cultural pluralism (63–67, 139, 179, 558). In tandem with this, the fictional autobiography presents Boabdil as bisexual, and at various points the narrative depicts homosexuality among both Christians and Muslims, and thus it could be argued that the net result is a more fluid conceptualization of sexuality.

El manuscrito carmesí is the only Spanish representation of Boabdil that, at least discursively, questions the narrative process of constructing history. First, in this novel Boabdil presents an alternative version of the Muslim conquest of Iberia that includes proposing that Tariq ibn Ziyad was actually a Vandal (326–30). Second, and more important, at certain points Boabdil shares his views on history: "Even the most beautiful city, Granada among them, has brutal slums, and it is impossible to tell one's own story without telling those of others, since History with a capital H—if it exists, and it isn't that it is invented once it has already passed—is made up of the lower case ones, the same way that the cover of a regal tent [*una jaima regia*] is put together with the bits and pieces of humble patches" (241). Using *jaima*, a loanword from the Arabic *khayma* that is not part of common usage in Spanish, Boabdil describes history as a sort of nomad's quilt made up of smaller, marginalized bits and pieces. In the process, he undermines the credibility of History—with a capital H—as a stable narrative of truth. Similarly, after spending hours drafting a history of the Nasrid Dynasty, Boabdil decides to burn it and, while watching the sheets of paper being consumed by the flames, he reflects on the process of writing those pages:

> Before starting to write them, I reflected: "Who backs up the chroniclers? Maybe one of them chose a long time ago a scapegoat emissary to load up with blame, and the rest transfer the mistake from one to the other the way you transfer an opulent inheritance. History almost always accepts it. Because it is easier to not contradict oneself and not alter the disorderly order that someone established, most probably to get out of an accusation or increase his gains." But after finishing my tale, upon re-reading what I'd written, I understood that I had turned into another chronicler, into one who denounces in order to free himself from blame or share it, and that the exact same reproaches could have been made against me as the others (255).

Boabdil becomes so skeptical of the history-writing process that he decides that he is no more able to guarantee his claims than chroniclers and burns his attempt at a history of his dynasty. Later, similar views are expressed by his wife, Moraima, via reported dialogue (583). Curiously, in spite of these views presented via Boabdil, the style and structure of the text does not perform a "burning of history," that is, it does not question narrative truth claims through its form.

Instead, this novel is based on the topos of the found manuscript, famously used by Cervantes in *Don Quijote*. This topos presents the reader with a text that must be translated and, as François Delpech asserts, serves to make the text that is in the hands of the reader more authentic and prestigious.[22] I would like to probe how this authenticity and prestige are constructed in *El manuscrito carmesí*. Boabdil's fictional memoir is prefaced by an introduction in italics that explains the provenance and translation of the "found" manuscript (7–10). The introduction is written in the first person, but is unsigned. This creates the illusion that the speaker, who says he found the manuscript in a library in Rabat and had a team of Spanish and Moroccan specialists translate it, is Gala himself. This in and of itself lends a greater aura of veracity to the memoirs. In addition, the author figure explains that the manuscript was first discovered in 1931 by a pair of French architects who were commissioned by the French protectorate to study the mosque of al-Karaouine [al-Qarawiyyin] in Fez. While carrying out their project, which was part of a broader study of the city done by various experts, the architects found a hidden room in which there was a cache of manuscripts, among them that of Boabdil. Colonial power and knowledge—the architects' measurements and powers of deduction, as well as the team of translators—make it possible for Boabdil's words to reach us.

The speaker, who oversaw the translation of the manuscript, tells the reader that he chose "to adapt [*trasladar*] the chronology, the names of persons and places, the dates and other references to a language that is more intelligible for today's Western readers" (9). He notes that because of him the translation is "not as faithful" as the scholars would have insisted on. He has made "this sacrifice" to make the text "more accessible to our eyes and our ears" (9). This translator figure then immediately shifts from his quick explanation of his domestication of the text to the question of the text's authenticity. He states that in spite of his "passionate" research efforts, he has not been able to find emphatic proof that the memoir was truly Boabdil's (9). Yet clearly, he believes that it is, because in the next sentence he says "I don't know if what Boabdil tells is all true, or if it veers in his favor" (9). This speaker who carries authorial weight vouches for the manuscript's authorship by Boabdil and simply wonders whether Boabdil wrote in such a way as to present himself in a favorable light. Thus, not only is Boabdil able to speak to us through the colonial system of acquisition of knowledge about the other, he is "author-ized" to do so—legitimated—by the Spanish presenter of the text. Finally, the speaker thanks all those historians and writers, including Boabdil, who have written about Boabdil and goes on to say: "They loved him like I have loved him. Hopefully I've managed, and them too, for my love to be requited [*correspondido*]" (10). By telling readers that he has loved Boabdil and hopes he is loved by him in return, the speaker reveals his desire for the vanquished king to not only forgive but even love Spaniards. This suggests that he makes a demand of Boabdil in the beyond: he requests that in exchange for the care and passion with which he has brought the text to the public, Boabdil should love him back. This wish for Boabdil to return the authorial persona's love creates an eternal Boabdil (still enchanted in the Alhambra?) who defies the passage of time to potentially bestow his approval and authenticity on the author figure and all Andalusians.

However, Gala's Boabdil (though he lives on in the present) does not live up to his potential to vindicate himself. In this version of the Boabdil story, as in all the others, the Boabdil that the preparer of the manuscript loves (and loves to love, and wants to be loved by) is the sad and ill-fated Boabdil who is thrust into a leadership position by his domineering mother.[23] In spite of the efforts to highlight complexity and the at least superficial questioning of history, the traditional image of Boabdil prevails: "Sunken here, I am hounded by the anguish that my destiny may be that of the supreme loser: the loser with whom everyone loses" (210). Here and elsewhere in *El manuscrito carmesí*, readers hear from Boabdil about his nostalgia, melancholy, adverse horoscope reading, and resignation. The myth of the tragic Boabdil is so entrenched that even when he is imagined to speak for himself, and as an Andalusian [andaluz], he presents himself as tragic.

In this novel, the tragic Boabdil is employed to meld together Andalusi and Andalusian cultures. Ignoring the passage of many centuries and the intervening, often violent cultural shifts, Gala has Boabdil use the terms *andaluz* and *Andalucía*, rather than *Andalusí* and *al-Andalus*, "el reino nazarí" [the Nasrid kingdom] or "el Emirato de Granada" [the Emirate of Granada], which are the more historically precise terms used in other texts depicting the period. Boabdil declares "I am the King of Andalusia [Andalucía]" (227) and "I'm andaluz; I was born in Andalusia from an infinite lineage of Andalusians [*andaluces*], and I will die in Andalusia" (558). The terms are used throughout the novel (236–37, 268, 332, 481, and 577) and are emphasized in one of the final paragraphs when Boabdil wonders rhetorically: "what am I, if not andaluz?" (609). As Gardner puts it, Boabdil "serves as Gala's bridge between 20th-century Andalusia, one of Spain's poorest and most neglected regions, and its more glorious Islamic past" (29–30).

On one hand, it is laudable that Gala moves away from the religious dichotomies so common in discourses on al-Andalus (i.e., moros y cristianos) and toward ostensibly shared cultural categories. On the other hand, the use of modern-day terms (Andalucía, España) establishes a fabricated continuity between Boabdil and Spaniards from Andalusia in the twentieth century and beyond. Within the complex relationship between Andalusi and Andalusian identities, Gala strategically appropriates Boabdil—tragedy and all—to imbue modern Andalusian identity with, on one hand, grandeur, nobility, and refined culture, and, on the other hand, the hybridity that is paradoxically used to characterize the essence of Andalusians and reject the essential purity of Castilians. Egea Fernández-Montesinos notes the paradox of using a peripheral nationalism based on heterogeneity to counter a nationalism based on purity; while undermining the latter, the text inevitably points to the constructedness of the former (189–90, 197–98).

I propose that this type of contestation of Castilian purity and dominance is limited by its blithe translation of Boabdil into the twentieth century, so much so that the novel never calls into question the constructedness of Andalusian identity. Upon recalling the role of translation as framing device in the novel's introduction regarding the found manuscript, a parallel emerges. Like the French architects who brought to light the immured manuscript, the speaker in the introduction wields ultimate editorial power over the transmission of Boabdil's autobiography. Although the novel presents interlingual contact in interesting ways, there is no questioning of the author-figure's adaptation of the language and dates to contemporary styles of expression. The authorial voice explains that he decided to domesticate the text without recognizing that this is a form of appropriation. This type of translation creates the illusion that the text was always culturally and linguistically one's own. It whitewashes the complexities of difference. Analogous to this, the novel in no way questions the transformation of the melancholic Boabdil into a timeless "Andalusian." Gala's novel questions the writing of history in general, but not the creation of mythical figures, such as the tragic Moor. In this way, *El manuscrito carmesí* accepts unquestioningly that Boabdil can be made accessible to modern-day Spaniards, without considering the role of the inherited figure of the tragic Moor in this translation process.

In Gala's work we see the impasse of contesting Castilian centralization and any concept of a Spanish essence, while establishing that heterogeneity is the Andalusian essence, and moreover that this essence has existed since Muslim Granada, virtually unchanged in 500 years. *El manuscrito carmesí* stands as a testament to the ways even a seemingly disempowered figure—that of the tragic Boabdil—is employed to construct more culturally powerful identities. Yet in the process of speaking for andalucismo, Boabdil is not able to "speak" for the Andalusis or speak back to those who insist on his pitiful, predestined nature. It would seem that Boabdil's clichéd passivity leads him to accept speaking for others. Articulating the degree and nature of Gala's appropriation of Boabdil, Martínez Montávez refers to the narratorial voice of *El manuscrito carmesí* as "Galabdil"—a fusion of Gala and Boabdil (*Significado y símbolo de Al-Andalus*, 25). Gala's novel does try to highlight the hybridity of Andalusi/Andalusian culture, and in that way dismantle long-standing Spanish cultural myths about racial, ethnic, and religious purity, but at the same time, it leaves the mythicized figure of Boabdil untouched. In contrast with several of the Arab and North African works on Tariq, neither this nor any other of the Hispanic Boabdil texts interrogates the symbolic role of Boabdil in Hispanic culture.

Boabdil and Migration: Convergence and Divergence of Discourses

In chapter 2's discussion of Gala's Averroes and this chapter's discussion of Gala's Boabdil and the songs by Carlos Cano and Los Puntos, I examined forms of identification with exiled figures from al-Andalus in relation to the intertwined phenomena of andalucismo and working-class labor migration. Part of what creates the pathos of Boabdil is his position as an exile. For this reason, one branch within the Hispanic archive of representations of Boabdil consists of works that implicitly or explicitly invoke Boabdil to address migration. At the same time, among the few contemporary Arab and North African prose writers who treat Boabdil, all have experienced some form of migration, and all link Boabdil to the figure of the migrant.[24] Thus, the intersection of Boabdil and migration is the site of divergences as well as convergences between texts by Hispanic and Arab/North African authors.

First, I would like to examine a node of intersection that is geographically distant from the Strait of Gibraltar, but culturally still quite steeped in questions of Hispanic/Arab identities and specifically the iconic figure of Boabdil. Early twentieth-century Argentina witnessed the consequences of immigration recruitment and industrialization projects that began in the nineteenth century. Argentina's founding fathers actively recruited European immigrants to boost the labor supply and the "whiteness" of the population, which consisted of *criollos* (those of Spanish heritage born in Argentina), indigenous peoples, mestizos, and some of mixed African heritage. During the late nineteenth and early twentieth century a deluge of immigrants arrived in Argentina, but they did not fulfill the dreams of progress of the political elite. Most of the immigrants were not the desired Northern Europeans, but instead Southern Europeans, Eastern European Jews, and Levantine Arabs. Rather than arrive to work the land, most joined the process of urbanization that was under way and ended up in cities working in commerce. During the late 1800s, foreign investment interests in Argentina had grown, and criollos regarded this with much distrust. Thus, by the early twentieth century, there was strong xenophobia, much of it directed specifically at Semitic immigrants. The anti-immigrant sentiment grew as part of a broader cultural nationalism. This Argentine *criollista* movement produced discourses that sought the promotion of rural gaucho customs as the national culture. Intertwined with this, the Hispanism movement promoted cultural ties with Spain and revived interest in Spanish history, including Muslim Iberia and the Reconquista.

Within this context, criollo Argentine writer Enrique Larreta (1875–1961) became famous for his novel, *La gloria de don Ramiro* (*The Glory of Don Ramiro*, 1908), about a Spaniard in the post-Reconquista Spain of Felipe II who thinks he has "pure" Christian blood but is actually the son of a Moor.[25] Although that novel was considered a paragon of the literary style known as modernismo, Larreta was criticized by criollistas for focusing on a Spanish rather than Argentine context. Years later Larreta published a novel that is set in early twentieth-century rural Argentina, but nonetheless refers repeatedly to Boabdil: *Zogoibi* (1926).[26] The protagonist of this novel is Federico Ahumada, a rich, young Argentine landowner who, after gaining refinement through education in Buenos Aires, has felt the tug of his fondness for rural Argentina and returns to his family's *estancia* or ranch. Federico's beloved is Lucía, a young woman from a landowning family who, very knowledgeable of the pampas (Argentine plains), has close ties to the ranch hands and country folk and is presented as pure, noble-hearted, and angelic. Lucía clearly represents idealized Argentine values. The problem that pains her is that her aunts, who are her guardians, do not approve of her marrying Federico because he is not religious enough for their traditional worldview. The character who serves as Lucía's confidante and intercessor and Federico's counselor—the voice of reason in the text—is Father Torres, the local priest, who hails from Andalusia.

In a conversation with Federico about his relationship with Lucía, Father Torres reminds him of Boabdil, cites Aixa's legendary admonition as a cautionary example, and closes the conversation with a warning: "Watch out!, Federico! Watch out!, Zogoibi!" (47). The Andalusian priest uses Boabdil to tell the young Argentine to be careful not to lose what he loves—Lucía and the authentic criollo Argentina she symbolizes—without fighting for it. Afterward, Federico's cousin Pepe, a dissolute who has recently returned from Europe an opium addict, decides that "Zogoibi" will be his new nickname for Federico and helps him look up the term in an encyclopedia where Federico sees that this Arabic nickname for Boabdil means "desventuradillo," or "little unfortunate one" (48). The theme continues when Pepe explains his Orientalist reasons for picking the nickname (136) and Father Torres thinks of Federico as "his poor Zogoibi" (148).

The plot thickens when a North American industrialist arrives in the area with his European wife, Zita, and wants to buy some of Federico's land. Zita represents European debauchery, while her husband, Wilburns, represents Anglo-American concern with progress and money over love and enjoyment. Federico succumbs to the cosmopolite's seduction, sells some of his land, and, in the midst of this, asks Zita not to call him "Fico," because that's the nickname his mother and Lucía use, but instead to call him the nickname his cousin has given him: Zogoibi (123). After actively taking on this sobriquet in his affair with Zita, Federico comes to see that the relationship will lead to losing Lucía. Having decided to break off his relationship with Zita, Federico thinks that they will have to change his nickname, though he almost was el desventuradillo (176). However, as with the mythic Boabdil, apparently fate is too strong. As Federico leaves one last rendezvous with Zita, he accidentally kills Lucía and, when he realizes what he has done, commits suicide.

In addition to criollista nostalgia for gaucho ways, the conflict between forces understood as civilization and barbarism that runs through Argentine letters pervades this novel. With that conflict at play, the novel demonstrates a racialized conception of the barbaric Moor: the narrator describes the gauchos as "Moorish [*moruno*]" (19 and 139) and associates Lucía's rich mulatto cousin Cecilio with Moorishness as well through the saying "el oro y el moro" (the gold and the Moor: [he promises] the sun and the moon) (147). Federico, in contrast, is a sort of frontier figure that brings together elements of all the sides that are encountering each other: the gaucho, the Spaniard, and through his nickname and "Berber" horse (195), the Moor. As Joan Torres-Pou aptly phrases it, Federico is presented as a "mozárabe moderno" (95) or a modern version of a Christian living under Muslim rule in al-Andalus.

Thus, the battle between civilization and barbarism is not only an exterior, societal battle but an individual inner struggle, as seen in Federico's inner struggle. Here Boabdil symbolizes the tragedy of not being able to withstand temptation and fight for what one knows is right. Beyond that, the encounter between Arabs/Amazighs/Muslims and Iberians/Christians is used as an analogy for the encounter between indigenous, mestizo gaucho, Spanish, European, and North American elements in Argentina. Larreta's *Zogoibi* is an indictment of the landowning aristocracy of Argentina and their inability to protect the country from foreigners. The foreigners who are explicitly referenced here are cosmopolitan investors, but immigrants are present as the unspoken shadow that inspires criolloismo. Together both types of foreigners are the force of destruction in the face of which Argentines must try to avoid repeating the errors of Boabdil. Boabdil himself, then, with all the character flaws that he represents as the Zogoibi, is an element that Argentina must defend against.

Among the foreigners understood as a threat to Argentine authenticity were Arabic-speaking immigrants from the Levant. Decades after the publication of Larreta's *Zogoibi*, one such immigrant referenced Boabdil in an essay on the status of Arabic within the Arab diaspora in the Americas. Ilyas Qunsul (1914–1981), brother of Zaki Qunsul, left Syria in 1925 at about eleven years of age, settled in Argentina after a few years in Brazil, and with the exception of three years spent in the Middle East, lived the rest of his life in Argentina. Nonetheless, Qunsul wrote his poetry, essays, and novel in Arabic. His 1980 essay *Ma'sat al-Harf al-ʿArabi fi al-Mahajir al-Amirkiyya* (*The Tragedy of Arabic in the American Mahjar* [place of exile or migration]) is a report on the sad state of Arabic letters in Argentina and a plea for monetary and institutional support from Arab countries. Qunsul laments the disappearance of Arabic in Argentina and sees this as the disappearance of a conceptual or spiritual nation that transcends the borders of the Arab states: "the conceptual mahjar nation" (51).

In the last section of *Ma'sat* Qunsul refers to the legend of El suspiro del moro: "And if we are not able to stop [the process of the disappearance of Arabic in the mahjar] then let us reinvigorate it in order to extend its life a bit: 'we do not want to cry like women for a reign we did not protect like men'" (95). Qunsul's final words are a plea to God to not let these words be the last breath of mahjar literature. By evoking the symbol par excellence of Arab loss—the loss of al-Andalus—and speaking of last breaths, Qunsul presents the loss of the Arabic language as a loss of self and of group identity. Thus, on one level, the text is an Arabic-speaking immigrant's last sigh for the loss of his language. At the same time, the work is an entreaty and a call to action. By writing this essay, and in particular in a highly ornate Arabic meant to demonstrate his classical literary skills, Qunsul is doubly rejecting the role of Boabdil. Rather than adopt Boabdil's clichéd passivity by writing in Spanish and doing nothing to promote Arabic in the diaspora, Qunsul chooses to write using elaborate Arabic rhetoric and to publish his essay in Damascus to try to persuade Syrians to join him in defending his cause.[27]

Other rejections of the passive Boabdil emerge from Spanish and Arab writers. The title of Jacinto Gil Sierra's *El retorno de Boabdil* (2009), in the context of Maghrebi immigration to Spain, sounds like it is part of the discourse that figures the Maghrebi migrants as returning Moors. However, the text is actually about the loss of traditional rural life in Spain as a result of emigration and modernization. Gil Sierra (b. 1954), a professor of agricultural engineering in Madrid who is originally from the region of Extremadura northwest of Andalusia, branched out from writing technical works on agronomy to writing fiction centered on his home region and agricultural life. His novel *El retorno de Boabdil*, through a fictional first-person narrator, tells the story of the effects of an actual Francoist modernization project on the small town of Granadilla in Extremadura.

Originally a Muslim village called Granada, in 1160 the settlement was conquered by the kingdom of León. After the conquest of the Emirate of Granada in 1492, to avoid confusion the small town began being called Granadilla (little Granada). Given this onomastic connection to the kingdom of Granada, Gil Sierra uses the figure of Boabdil to frame the story of the Franco government's takeover of the town to build the Gabriel y Galán dam and reservoir. In the early 1960s the government organized the complete abandonment of the town because with the construction of the dam it was expected to become a flood zone. The town center never flooded, it was converted into a peninsula, but all of the residents had already departed, only to return for annual festivals. Gil Sierra's novel details the townspeople's reactions to the exodus, ranging from passive resignation to only being concerned with the monetary compensation. Through the novel's title, he labels the townspeople as returned Boabdils. Thus the novel critiques them by saying that like Boabdil, they passively abandoned their place of birth.

Like Andalusia, in the second half of the twentieth century Extremadura witnessed a massive exodus of the rural population to cities and other regions of Spain and other countries in Europe, and Extremaduran academic Manuel Pecellín has suggested that in this novel Gil Sierra uses the medieval town of Granadilla as a "prototype of all of Extremadura." By using "little Granada" and Boabdil as a model for the resigned emigration of hundreds of thousands of Extremadurans, the author at once characterizes the rural population's loss as tragic and criticizes them for their acceptance of this misfortune. The loss of traditional Spanish rural life due to emigration is understood through the figure of Boabdil—who returns in the form of Christian townspeople who allow themselves to be victims of modernization. Thus, once again Boabdil is a tragic symbol of loss, but he is invoked not as part of a self-aggrandizing ritual but as part of a self-criticism.

In the first half of the twentieth century, al-Andalus was the topic of several Arabic-language plays, and a few of these focus on Boabdil. In each case, Boabdil, presented with romantic touches, serves as the target of Arab self-criticism in a period of definition in the face of crumbling Ottoman control, rising European power, and emerging nationalism. Fawzi Maʿluf (1899–1930), a Lebanese poet who immigrated to Brazil, wrote *Ibn Hamid, aw, Suqut Gharnata* (*Ibn Hamid or the Fall of Granada*, 1916), a play that is a mix of prose and verse and gives more prominence to Ibn Hamid, a member of the Bani Sarraj [Abencerraje] clan, a powerful faction in fifteenth-century Granada. Maʿluf modeled his play after works by French Romantic writers Jean-Pierre Claris de Florian and François-René de Chateaubriand (5). Similarly, Anis al-Khuri al-Maqdisi (1885–1977), another Christian Lebanese poet of the same period, depicts Boabdil in the prose drama *Ila al-Hamra'* (*To the Alhambra*, 1930). Here Boabdil is described as bold, but also vain and greedy (3). In the closing scene to this play, Isabella addresses Boabdil as "the sad prince [*ayuha al-amir al-hazin*]," Boabdil bids farewell, and Isabella calls her people to give a prayer of thanks for their victory (61). The 1952 verse drama *Ghurub al-Andalus* (*The Sunset of al-Andalus*) by Egyptian pan-Arabist poet ʿAziz Abaza (1898–1973) presents a similarly scorned Boabdil. Here Boabdil is a wretched human who submits to the Europeans because he covets the throne, and the hero is Musa ibn abi al-Ghassan [Musa ibn Abu al-Gazan], a Granadan military leader who is little known in European sources but is known among Arabs and Muslims as the one who insisted on continuing to resist the Castilian forces. Abaza's play concludes with a rendering of the famous scene of El suspiro del moro (193).[28]

More recent works from the Arab world view the figure of Boabdil through the lens of migration and even use him to criticize romanticizing relationships to al-Andalus. The Lebanese author Amin Maalouf (b. 1949) presents a critical view of the figure of Boabdil but adds criticism of those who hang onto the Romantic legends surrounding him. Maalouf, who writes in French and has lived in France since 1976, hails from a family that includes Maronite Christians and Melkite Greek Catholics. He is the award-winning author of several novels. Among these is the fictional autobiography of the medieval traveler al-Hasan ibn Muhammad al-Wazzan al-Fasi (c. 1494–1554), who was born in Granada, raised in Fez, and taken as a captive to Rome where he was baptized into Catholicism and took the name Joannes Leo Africanus. In Maalouf's *Léon l'Africain* (*Leo Africanus*, 1986), Boabdil appears as the crystallization of the corrupt elite who leaves behind a harmful legacy and from whom other émigrés wish to distinguish themselves.[29] Additionally, Maalouf uses Boabdil and his legacy to comment on how the past is perceived and impinges on the present. In relation to Édouard Glissant's critique of the myth of origins, Hamid Bahri and Francesca Sautman state:

> Similarly, Maalouf's work blends migration and displacement from one place of origin to new ones with political opposition to the terrors founded on firm adhesion to the root. He thus opens the possibility of a theorization of the distant past (European and Middle Eastern) as antithetic to stable origins and rigid timeframes, as a place of shifting and interlocking spaces. [. . .] Rather than idolizing that past as a monolithic counter-monument of lost grandeur, Maalouf stresses its enormous capacity for mix, hybridity, cultural crossings, and reproducibility across vast expanses of time and space teeming with networks and communication. (198)

In *Léon l'Africain* in particular, those who cling to the past of Boabdil's opulence are placed in opposition to those who, like the hero Hassan/Léon, create a fluid, multiple identity.

In one chapter of *Léon l'Africain*, Hassan/Léon's maternal uncle, who had had an administrative position in the Alhambra and is something of a surrogate father to the protagonist, explains to his nephew why he decided to leave Granada.[30] The uncle, referred to by the protagonist using the transliterated Arabic term *Khâli*, recounts the decisive moment that took place within the Alhambra palace. In Khâli's presence, Boabdil received the bad news about a leading figure of the emirate who had converted to Christianity and joined the Castilian forces, but Boabdil's reaction to the news is shaped by his rivalry with that leader and his own mean-spiritedness and shortsightedness:

> But, while the officer was speaking, the sultan's face swelled into a broad, indecent and hideous smile. I can still see those fleshy lips opening in front of me, those hairy cheeks which seemed to stretch to his ears, those teeth, spaced wide apart to crunch up the victory, those eyes which closed slowly as if he was expecting the warm kiss of a lover, and that head which nodded with delight, backwards and

> forwards and forwards and backwards, as if he was listening to the most languorous of songs. As long as I live, I shall have the image of that smile before me, that terrible smile of pettiness and small-mindedness. (27 [36])

The grotesque repulsiveness of Boabdil's smile is a window onto the hideousness of the sultan's soul. Khâli explains that he was not surprised because he knew of Boabdil's frivolity and feebleness of character, and he knew that their princes were corrupt, "But I had to see with my own eyes the bared soul of the last sultan of Andalus in order to feel myself forced to react" (27–8 [37]). This encounter forces his uncle to face his situation and take the decision to leave Granada: soon after he settles his affairs and leaves for Fez. Thus, in this novel, Boabdil epitomizes corrupt power and symbolizes corrupt elites.

Boabdil appears again in the text when, already in exile in Fez, Hassan's grandmother dies and Boabdil comes to the funeral. Hassan recounts that Boabdil has become fat and is not respected by the other attendees, but they still show him deference because of his titles. The shaykh, by referring to the choice of dishonor over death, makes critical comments directed at Boabdil, and Boabdil eventually slips out through a side door. Hassan concludes the vignette by stating that luckily because of this uncomfortable experience, Boabdil never again showed up at an Andalusi funeral and the Granadans of Fez were able to die in peace (104 [112]). Here Boabdil is once again a pathetic figure, but now as a double exile: not only did he accept his own exile from Granada, but in responding to criticism by sneaking out, he has accepted his ostracism from the community of Granadan exiles in Fez. In this way, he is reduced to an uncomfortable, rejected part of the Granadan exile community.

In her essay on exile and representations of al-Andalus, Denise Filios analyzes the protagonist of *Léon l'Africain* as a reflection of Maalouf's position as an exile who fled the Lebanese civil war (1975–1990) and settled in Paris.[31] Filios argues that Hassan serves as a mouthpiece for the type of fluid, intercultural identity that Maalouf espouses and proposes a model for the "migrant, transnational subject" (101). Filios also notes that the novel's secondary characters represent specific cultural stances and worldviews and suggests that these reflect positions found in Lebanon and the Arabo-Muslim world (98). Building on Filios's astute observations, I submit that Maalouf, while using al-Andalus to tell his own story, uses his depiction of Boabdil to distinguish his departure from Lebanon from that of the bulk of the Christian elite and thus to defend his position as one who left. In Maalouf's text, Boabdil is a foil for the complex identity of the self-exiled migrant subject, specifically one who is a religious minority in his country of origin and an ethnolinguistic minority in his adopted home.

In addition to this reading of *Léon l'Africain* as a working through of Maalouf's own situation, another aspect of the text's portrayal of Boabdil suggests a broader commentary on how Maghrebi and Arab societies relate to the idealization of al-Andalus. At one point in the novel, Hassan recounts the legends he has heard surrounding Boabdil. One of these is that Boabdil had hidden his riches somewhere and put them under a spell. Hassan then describes the *kannazin*—people who dedicate their lives to trying to find the enchanted treasures supposedly left by Boabdil and others. These treasure-seekers continue their pursuit within the city of Fez, and their excavations weaken the foundations of buildings (56–57 [65]). Read allegorically, the kannazin, in their pursuit of the golden age of al-Andalus, damage the edifices of the present and hopes of progress. Oblivious to this destruction, they are convinced of the existence of the treasure and see the barrier to its acquisition as one that is magical and mystical: "It is impossible to have a conversation with a *kannaz* without him swearing that he has already seen heaps of gold and silver in an underground passage, but could not lay his hands on them because he did not know the correct incantations or because he did not have the proper perfumes on him" (56–57 [65]). The kannazin stand for those who are deluded by the fantastical stories of Boabdil's treasure and the grandeur of al-Andalus to the extent that they ruin the present and future.

Bringing this together with the commentary on migrant subjectivities in Maalouf's text, the treasure-seekers are those who are trapped by their nostalgia for the homeland of the past. Without realizing it, they themselves, and not the treasure, are locked in the past by mystical incantations. Hassan/Léon states, "my innocence still flourishes in Granada" (1 [9]), but in contrast with the treasure-seekers, he does not destroy his present and future searching for that innocence or Boabdil's treasure. Thus, in *Léon l'Africain*, Boabdil is not a man to be pitied because he lost greatness; rather, in the words of Hassan's uncle, he was born a vassal and only aspired to die a vassal (25 [34]). This vassal is a vehicle for criticism of both the corrupt elite that destroy cultures (whether al-Andalus or Lebanon) and the beguiled former subjects who continue to search for the gold of the past at the expense of present and future.

Rashid Nini in his *Yawmiyat Muhajir Sirri* (*Diary of an Illegal Immigrant*, 1999), discussed earlier in relation to Tariq ibn Ziyad, brings Boabdil to bear on another facet of contemporary migration, one closer to Boabdil's "home": labor migration from North Africa to Spain. Discussing relatively low racism in Spain vis-à-vis the rest of Europe,

Nini reflects on Spanish oral transmission of legends about Moors: "In some of the remote villages that we went to, to work in their fields, the people there barely knew anything about Moroccans. Everything that they knew goes back to the old legends about the moros that had penetrated their land and that they had forced out in a bad way. These stories are passed down between father and son and narrate a fantastic history full of fallacies" (64). Soon Nini finds an opportunity to showcase one of these fallacious stories—that of Boabdil. While he is working in a pizzeria, his Spanish co-worker Alfonso looks at him with a smile and asks him if he knows about Boabdil. Nini purposely plays dumb to see what Alfonso will say (88). Alfonso, "like a star student," (89) tells a fantastic version of events in which King Ferdinand cuts off Boabdil's ears and throws him to the other side of the sea. As Filios notes, Ferdinand takes the role of a bullfighter who mutilates and humiliates Boabdil in the role of bull (103). Nini responds by suggesting that the situation was not so simple, banters with Alfonso about the Moors having returned in the form of Maghrebi immigrants, and reflects on the contrast between the migrants and Tariq ibn Ziyad.

What interests me here is the way Nini initially manipulates the conversation with his co-worker. Alfonso's smile indicates that he is mischievously trying to poke fun at and perhaps even humiliate Nini and Muslim culture in general, but Nini takes the upper hand in the situation by feigning ignorance. This ruse invites Alfonso to present his supposed knowledge of Boabdil. The Spaniard proceeds like a proud schoolboy, but presents a version that is so far from the historical record that he only succeeds in displaying his flagrant bias, and then Nini reports this to his Moroccan readership in a work that carries the memoir's weight as a source of testimonial truth. Thus, Nini ultimately turns the humiliating gesture in his own favor by revealing Spanish biases toward Moors and contemporary North Africans. He uses Spanish ritual rehearsals of the defeat of Boabdil to highlight how Muslims are maligned in misinformed Spanish discourses. Rodríguez López comments on the Boabdil pizzeria scene as follows: "The former grandeur of al-Andalus is only remembered [. . .] as a defeat in which the Andalusi, the same as the Moroccan immigrant in Spain, is alone. The author establishes in this way a symbolic link between the last king of Granada and himself. Both face up to a destiny of loneliness and uprootedness, and the probable molding or silencing of their memory by time" (9). However, this interpretation imbues the scene with a pathos that is not found in the passage and does not take into account the ways Nini manipulates the conversation for his own gain. Although Alfonso may suggest an identification between Boabdil and Nini, Nini does not accept this type of link and instead points to Boabdil as a topic of Spanish lore whose story has been misshapen by Spaniards. Although Nini may lose at the verbal sparring that takes place in the pizzeria, he attains some type of victory through his published account of his experiences.

Significantly, in contrast with many Spanish accounts of Boabdil, neither Nini nor Maalouf describe him in terms of either pathos or destiny. Rather, difficult circumstances and self-serving choice, respectively, are at the center of their projections of Boabdil. Furthermore, Nini's text makes a gesture toward questioning the narrative process of constructing history and the image of Boabdil in Spain. Steven Gardner, in his essay "The Andalusia of Antonio Gala," argues that the idealization of al-Andalus propagated by the Andalusian nationalist movement and manifested in Gala's *El manuscrito carmesí* is an impediment to the integration of modern-day immigrants from North Africa because it creates a barrier to tolerance and understanding. Indeed, as I demonstrated, Gala's novel does not question the mythical version of the history of al-Andalus, and this allows for the maintenance of static, essentializing conceptions of history and identity that ultimately create divisions. In contrast, Nini and Maalouf propose fluid conceptions of identity and history. In particular, Nini counters the historical inaccuracies in Alfonso's version of history by citing the version of events that he read in Maalouf's *Léon, l'Africain* (89–90). Nini notes that he can't be sure of the Boabdil story because he did not finish reading Maalouf's text, and Filios indicates that this leaves Nini in a position of uncertainty because he is acknowledging that he cannot substantiate a different version of events (103–4). Nonetheless, by critiquing Spanish versions of Boabdil and al-Andalus as fallacious and pointing to other versions of the story, Nini acknowledges that what is considered history is actually a collection of narratives, full of biases. Moreover, he manipulates the situation created by his co-worker as best he can to demonstrate that through such narratives Spaniards attempt to use Boabdil for self-exaltation. In this way, he eschews the passive attitude that Spanish discourses ascribe to Boabdil and instead takes an active role as evaluator and rewriter of narratives about the past and the past's implications for identity in the present.

As the invocation of Boabdil in the pizzeria and the various textual requiems for him make evident, Spaniards use different aspects of the history of Muslim Iberia to redraw lines of identity in the face of Maghrebi immigration to Spain. As with Muslim depictions of Tariq ibn Ziyad, these discourses are present in cultural products made for juvenile audiences as well. The rehearsal of a tragic Boabdil is found in Spanish children's novels from the early twenty-first century.[32] However, one such text uses the teary-eyed Boabdil as part of the presentation of a much more inclusive attitude toward North African immigrants. In Mercé Viana's *Las lágrimas de Boabdil: un paseo por Granada* (*The Tears of Boabdil: An Outing in Granada*, 2010), Boabdil is used to assuage fears regarding North African immigrants and to normalize migration. Granted, the text's progressive message is circumscribed by the fact that the title focuses attention on Boabdil's tears and the book is part of a series featuring a genie who takes a brother and sister on a magic carpet to visit other times and places. This reiteration of Boabdil's pathos and the Orientalist premise of the series aside, the text represents a major change in typical Spanish invocations of both Boabdil and Maghrebi migrants.

Las lágrimas de Boabdil starts with a fight between two classmates in twenty-first-century Spain. One has learned anti-immigrant attitudes from his parents and picks on the other, Yusuf, an immigrant from North Africa. In the process of defending himself, Yusuf says, "Some of my ancestors were born and died in Granada. The last ones had to abandon their house, 500 years ago, to take refuge in the country where I was born" (9). When this is met with disbelief and escalates the conflict, the teacher intervenes. In the process, Yusuf explains that his family still keeps the key to that house (13). The teacher decides to turn this conflict into a teachable moment. First, she explains, "Everyone, wherever they may be from, had the right to look for respectable work, inside or outside of their country. Spaniards also, in other times of need, had had to emigrate [. . .] in search of a better life" (13–14). Here the polemic issue of immigration to Spain is directly connected to the phenomenon of Spaniards emigrating for work in the 1960s and '70s, as well as in the early 2000's after the start of the Spanish economic crisis in 2008. In a parallel fashion, journalist Marvine Howe reports that Federico Mayor Zaragoza, a Spanish politician and former Director-General of UNESCO, alluded to the late twentieth-century Spanish emigration when he stated: "We must be more sensitive to immigrants because we are immigrants too" (175). These comparisons are used to indicate that migration is a process, indeed, a right, that responds to economic need and in which Spaniards have also participated.

In Viana's children's novel, the teacher asks Yusuf to share the stories about his ancestors that he has heard from his father. Among other things, Yusuf says that his father explained that Boabdil surrendered to save his beloved Granada from destruction (17). Taking advantage of the students' interest in Yusuf's stories, the teacher decides to start the class on a research project on the history of the Emirate of Granada, with the incentive that they may take a class trip to today's city of Granada.

The narrative then shifts to focus on a set of twins in the class, Lucía and Víctor, who, with their friend the genie Proscenio, are the common thread throughout the book series. In the course of their online research, the twins find a letter discovered by a Granadan association in which a teary-eyed Boabdil explains his decision to surrender Granada and asks not to be judged harshly (60–64). In class, the twins, Yusuf, and others present their findings. Eventually the twins time travel with Proscenio to visit Boabdil in the Alhambra. They find Boabdil absorbed in thought, trying to make tough decisions (132). Forced to make difficult choices and facing his own exile, he is similar to the labor migrants about whom the teacher has spoken. Before the twins leave, Boabdil gives each of them a decorated box [*cofrecillo*] to take as a gift, and says that they can use them to keep their "most precious jewels" (151). Thus, rather than return with colonial plunder, they are given something for holding their own treasures. Before returning to the present day, Proscenio takes them to the spot of El suspiro del moro, recounts part of the legend, and emphasizes that the story is a legend and there is no way to know if it really happened (153).

In the various ways detailed here, *Las lágrimas de Boabdil* attempts to give both Boabdil and contemporary Maghrebi immigrants the opportunity to voice their perspective on the history of al-Andalus and its end. It emphasizes Boabdil's difficult choice over and above the image of an ill-fated, weak, and passive figure. Moreover, it emphasizes that another element of what is considered common knowledge about Boabdil—the scene of El suspiro del moro—is simply unsubstantiated legend. Instead of invoking fear of conquest or relishing a predestined triumph over Boabdil, this didactic children's book uses the past to reconceptualize Maghrebi immigration to Spain. It uses a revised version of Boabdil to undermine xenophobia by naturalizing and historicizing the immigration process and promoting inclusivity. Translating Boabdil into a common denominator between Maghrebis and Spaniards through the shared experience of the difficult choices inherent in migration creates new perspectives—and new horizons of hope—regarding the past, present, and future of Maghrebi-Spanish relations.

Like the enchanted Boabdil of the legend featured in the song by Los Puntos, Boabdil still lives in Spain, and he appears when he is useful to Spanish needs. He has become a commodity who is consumed as part of a cultural industry of remembrance. Largely, Boabdil has been remembered in a staging of power that confirms that Spain has been "theirs" since at least the fifteenth century, and that in the face of loss of empire and the contemporary social changes brought on by migration, it still is "theirs." The figure of Boabdil externalizes loss, including the loss of the Spanish empire and the losses inherent in Spanish emigration and Maghrebi immigration. At the same time, identification with the tragic Boabdil is used within andalucismo to express the cultural displacement that arose from Andalusian emigration and to shape a particular Andalusian identity.

Although the Arab/North African perspectives on Boabdil often contrast Spanish depictions of him, there are still strong points of convergence. The economic crisis that began in 2008 has led many Spaniards to seek work outside the country. This emigration trend, mostly made up of professionals seeking employment elsewhere in Europe and Latin America, has caught the attention of the Spanish public not only because the number who migrate continues to rise but because some are migrating to Morocco, the longtime source of desperate immigrants to Spain. In fact, as of 2012, after Europe and Latin America, Morocco is the third most frequent destination for Spanish migrants (Bloomberg, Otazu).[33] This has caused surprise among Moroccan observers as well, one of whom commented, "It's as if tomorrow [Americans] started going to Mexico for jobs" (Hustad). This major shift in socioeconomic circumstances, together with the texts by Nini and Viana, points to an emerging mutual need: that of reevaluating both economic systems and attitudes toward migration.

Another apparition of Boabdil, and a possible continuation of the reevaluation of attitudes toward migration, is found in the painting "El regreso de Boabdil," by Spanish artist Salva Bracco (b. 1960). This 2008 painting, which is part of a series of works in acrylic on mail sacks from the Spanish postal service, carries reproductions of the stamps used by border control authorities and depicts a North African figure viewed from behind as he walks. Bracco has done at least one other work on a Moroccan mail bag, portraying poverty in the former Spanish Sahara, and others on Cuban and Chinese mail bags. The series painted on Spanish mail bags all depict images of Spanish-ness: bullfighting, a flamenco dancer, a guitar, and so on. By depicting a Maghrebi migrant on one of the Spanish sacks and referencing Boabdil in the piece's title, the artist suggests that the "return" of Boabdil—his reappearance in Spanish discourses as well as the Maghrebi migrants he represents—is also quintessentially Spanish.

Indeed, Boabdil's Spanishness was cleverly used by the Lebanese Argentine Ibrahim Hallar when, in a 1962 essay that sought to delineate an empowered Arab Argentine identity, the Muslim Argentine pointed to Boabdil's stronger claim to Spanishness than Charles V [Carlos V], the Flemish-born ruler of the Spanish empire, the Holy Roman Empire, and Habsburg Netherlands.[34] Similarly, Hispanophone Equatoguinean writer Francisco Zamora Loboch, in an acerbic 1994 essay, signals the contradictory power dynamics inherent in the crafting of dominant Spanish identity by stating: "The first Moor to whom Spain applied the Foreigners Act [*Ley de Extranjería*] was Boabdil" (11).[35] Like several of the narratives analyzed here, including Boabdil among symbols of Spain, highlighting the generations of Boabdil's forebears who had been born and died in Iberia (in contrast with the case of Carlos V), and wryly observing that Boabdil was the first Other to be expelled by Spanish immigration law create openings for new understandings of the figure of Boabdil, an exile who carries heavy cultural baggage. Rather than an external threat whose melancholy and fated demise should be ritually rehearsed, or from a Muslim and/or Arab perspective a symbol of passive weakness or a romanticized past, Boabdil can serve as a foil to fluid identities that question and take control of narratives of the past. Boabdil can be a multilayered reminder of the lessons learned from a transcolonial view of history: all empires meet their end, but migration is a constant, and the loss of empire and the immigrant condition are common denominators among Spaniards, North Africans, and many others around the world.

Coda

Columbus and Coloniality

> When one of the sailors from Christopher Columbus's ships yelled "Land, land, land!," it was as if three blows announced the opening of the gates of hell.
>
> From that moment, the 12th of October, 1492, the year of the Discovery of America, the world changed and a new world order was inaugurated: that in which we still live together with all of its consequences. [. . .]
>
> I don't like speaking of the "discovery" of America because, from my point of view, America was not discovered; it existed long before European eyes saw it. There was already a culture, or rather, cultures—a civilization—rather, civilizations.
>
> But the new European order would change all that. In fact, the first move was to re-baptize it. [. . .]
>
> Barbarism spread, since the new order needed to continue its implementation. Colonialism reached its era of splendor in the rest of Europe, they went to look for other cultures in Africa and Asia to turn into victims. They went to look for other "savages."
>
> —Jabbar Yassin Hussin *(Memorias olvidadas)*

Another border-crosser often appears in tandem with Boabdil and connects al-Andalus to the Americas and other manifestations of conquest: Christopher Columbus. The renowned Syrian poet Nizar Qabbani reflects on the identification between al-Andalus and the Americas in his poem "al-Andalusi al-Akhir" ["The Last Andalusi"], in which the speaker declares:

> I am the last Andalusi,
> Who begs on the sidewalks of Granada.
> I am the last Red Indian
> Who escaped the teeth of Christopher Columbus. (200)[1]

Indeed, Columbus met with the Catholic Monarchs of Spain in the outskirts of Granada as they were carrying out their siege of the emirate, and his arrival in the Americas signaled for Spaniards the culmination of the transition from colonized to colonizer, and for Arabs and Muslims the opposite: the end of cultural ascendancy in the face of European hegemony. In works from the Middle East and North Africa (MENA) region, Columbus is a lightning rod for thinking about alternatives to the trajectories of Muslim and Spanish-Catholic empire. My analysis of these works leads to a reflection on a contemporary "voyage of return" from the Americas to al-Andalus: the positioning of US Hispanic converts to Islam who refer to their conversion as a return to the religion of their forebears in al-Andalus.

As noted by historian of Spain L. P. Harvey, 1492 is known for three major events: the Christian conquest of the Emirate of Granada, the expulsion of the Jews from Iberia, and Columbus's arrival at the islands and continents that came to be known as the Americas. According to Columbus's extant logbook, which actually begins in Granada, he witnessed the January 2, 1492, surrender of the Emirate of Granada to the Catholic Monarchs, and within that same month the victorious monarchs decided to support Columbus's proposed voyage to India (Harvey 324–25). Columbus departed from the city of Granada in May 1492 to head to the port of Palos; from there, after several weeks at sea, he stumbled on the islands of the Bahamas and Cuba.

Columbus and all that is symbolized by the fall of al-Andalus are closely tied together. After years of lobbying and negotiations at the Spanish court, Columbus followed the Catholic Monarchs to their camp outside of the Emirate of Granada where finally, after the Castilian and Aragonese triumph over Boabdil, he was successful in getting support for the voyage. Many have pointed to the riches acquired as booty from Granada as being what gave Columbus his opportunity to sail. Thus, this opening for him and Spain, and eventually much of Europe, was a moment of double closure for the Arabo-Muslim world. Harvey explains its impact as follows:

> The discovery of the New World may seem altogether more remote from the history of the Muslims of the Peninsula. From the enterprise of America, Muslims (and Jews) were, in theory at least, completely excluded. The indirect impact that Spain's possession of a New World empire had was considerable. Spain's economic and military power and its prestige in international affairs grew immeasurably. The victory at Granada in 1492 might have been expected to evoke a military response, a counter-attack from somewhere in the Islamic world. Not only was Islamic North Africa weak, but Spain's might was increasing all the time. Before long its superiority over any Islamic state within striking distance was overwhelming.

> Thus all three of the events of 1492 combined to make the Christian victory at Granada a final and conclusive one. (325)

In 1492 the Arabo-Muslim world lost both the last Muslim state in Iberia and its moment of political and cultural ascendancy. Just as it strengthened the Spanish empire, Columbus's arrival in the Americas was the final blow to Muslim power. For this reason, references to Columbus in the works that depict Boabdil are tantamount to references to empire and a shift in the balance of power.

In addition, Walter Mignolo and Anouar Majid, among others, have pointed to the birth of modern systems for codifying and rejecting difference—religious, racialized religious, and racialized difference in general—in Reconquista Iberia.[2] Majid emphasizes the roots of the religious zeal and racial hierarchies of colonial mind-sets by referring to the era since 1492 as the "post-Andalusian" period (in the sense of post-Andalusi). Both Mignolo and Majid point specifically to the Iberian concern with *limpieza de sangre* (cleanliness of blood), which viewed Jewish and Muslim lineage as a biological impurity that must be ferreted out and (literally and metaphorically) expelled. This approach to religious and ethnic difference was the basis for the treatment of indigenous peoples and Africans taken to the New World as well as broader racial dynamics that have become global. Nicolás Wey Gómez focuses specifically on Columbus and, drawing from classical and medieval European and Mediterranean sources, documents how the renowned sailor shaped enduring conceptions of the physical and moral characteristics of the inhabitants of the tropics. Thus, for many, as the figure who made this ideological transfer possible and even contributed to it directly in his own writings, Columbus is a symbol of the expansion of devastating racist ideologies.

Among the Spanish works analyzed in chapter 4, the mini-series *Réquiem por Granada* lingers for some time on the figure of Columbus. The Genoese sailor is featured in the last two (out of eight) episodes of the series. The series portrays Columbus in the city of Santa Fe, the staging ground for the Castilian siege of Granada, meeting with King Ferdinand and Queen Isabella. When the king asks him for exact distance calculations that Columbus can't provide, the monarch tells him to develop his idea more and return later. The queen's confessor tells the dejected Columbus that Boabdil, during his captivity with the Castilians, had told him that there is a cosmographer in Granada who can provide those calculations. In the final episode of the series, Columbus risks life and limb to enter the besieged kingdom and meet with that cosmographer and ship designer, amid the latter's astrolabes and other instruments. This learned man explains that Columbus has miscalculated the size of the Earth (due to a conversion error from the Arab to the European mile) and that the distance to India is much greater than what Columbus thought. The Granadan cosmographer provides important navigation tips and explains that he will die soon and he wants his theories to be realized: "Granada is sinking and it shouldn't drag this secret down with it." To this end he gives Columbus his own maps and tells him to realize what "we" were not able to accomplish. Columbus kisses his hand fervently and the Muslim blesses his trip: "May Allah accompany and guide you" (Episode 8: 5:40–11:40).

In this way, *Réquiem por Granada* not only presents the common conception that Muslim navigational knowledge and instruments helped Columbus carry out his voyage but goes further and conveys the idea that the Spanish victory over the Emirate of Granada enabled Columbus to use advanced Arabo-Muslim knowledge to start the European colonization of the Americas. In the series the imminent "discovery" of the New World is presented as a purely positive event and is framed by the passion and goodwill between Columbus and the Granadan cosmographer; the Moor who is witnessing his world crumble helps Columbus achieve great things. The 1990 Spanish mini-series bares no hint of critical commentary on the Spanish expansionist endeavor, but instead presents the passing of the baton (of power and of knowledge) from the Muslims to the Christians as an epic and inevitable moment in history. This type of portrait of Columbus no doubt inspired Syrian author Qamar Kilani to comment, in her memoir about her trip to Spain, that Columbus was treated like a messiah by Spaniards (85) and had been consecrated by them as a national symbol (86).

Around the same time that *Réquiem por Granada* was produced, writers from the Global South were expressing critical perspectives on Columbus's voyage that dismantle the figure's heroic status. In Latin America some of the authors of "the Boom" (a burgeoning of experimental works that started in the 1960s) focused their creative energies on deconstructing Columbus. The most well-known works in this regard are *El arpa y la sombra* (*The Harp and the Shadow*, 1979) by Cuban Alejo Carpentier (1904–1980) and *Vigilia del Almirante* (*Vigil of the Admiral*, 1992) by Paraguayan Augusto Roa Bastos (1917–2005). Through innovative narrative techniques, these two novels point, respectively, to the role of power-hungry members of the Catholic Church in shaping Columbus's legacy and to the violence of the European encounter with the indigenous peoples of the Americas.

Similarly, some Arab-authored texts use Columbus to comment on the conquest and colonization of the Americas within the wider frame of geopolitics. One of these is *Gharnata* (*Granada*, 1994), a work that I analyze in depth in Chapter 6. In this novel, which focuses on the lives of Muslims after the fall of Granada, Egyptian author Radwa Ashour [ʿAshur] (1946–2014) depicts a parade of the returning Columbus and one character's subsequent voyage to the New World colonies to point to parallels between the Castilians' conquest of al-Andalus and of the Americas. When the main characters in the novel witness a parade welcoming Columbus back from his first voyage, one of these characters, Naʿim, a young Muslim from Granada, sees a bedraggled indigenous woman who has been brought back as a captive to be exhibited and is completely taken by her beauty (37–41). One of Naʿim's companions, Saʿd, wonders if the Castilians attacked the New World the same way they did his native Malaga and thus establishes a parallel between the expansionist wars (42).

Later, Naʿim, who has converted to Christianity to avoid expulsion, accepts a position as assistant to a priest who is going to the New World as a missionary. There Naʿim witnesses firsthand the abuse of the indigenous people by the Castilians, identifies himself and his fellow Granadans with the oppressed natives, falls in love with an indigenous woman, and learns her language (219–24, 257–66). As Nezar Andary points out, "Ashour adds global connections to the representation of al-Andalus by creating unity among the victims of modern European colonialism and the Arabs who lost al-Andalus. The marriage between Native American and Arab is clearly not coincidental in Ashour's prose and this in itself must be interpreted as a form of resistance in terms of creating affiliations against a singular colonizing power" (85). This Arab-Amerindian love story ends with Spanish conquistadores killing Naʿim's beloved and thus intensifies the critique of European colonialism. In Ashour's novel, the storyline that connects Columbus's enterprise with Naʿim's amorous life also connects the subjugation of the *moriscos* with that of the indigenous peoples of the Americas.

The 1990 novella "Le nouveau monde" ("The New World") by well-established Tunisian author Chams Nadir (pen name of Muhammad Aziza, b. 1940) is a rewriting of exploratory history in which Columbus wasn't the first, he was simply the worst.[3] Like Ashour's text, this work establishes a parallel between the fall of al-Andalus and the fall of the indigenous Americas. However, in the case of the Tunisian narrative, the entire work focuses on this idea via an imagined back story of precursors to Columbus. "Le nouveau monde" tells the story of how members of the international medieval maritime community (a Northern European Christian, a Muslim Arab Andalusi, and a crypto-Jew) found the New World, saw what havoc Europeans could wreak there, tried to protect it from Old World intervention, but failed when Columbus followed the same route thirty years later, without as much self-reflection and sense of ethics.[4] This leads to a second Granada—a repetition of the fall of the Emirate of Granada.

Nadir's novella features a fragmented point of view that shifts between an omniscient third-person narrator, dated entries from admiral Johann Vogado's personal diary, and the first-person perspective of "Jaber le Maure" (Jaber the Moor).[5] Jaber is a Muslim cosmographer whose family has been exiled from Toledo and Cordoba and who senses that the fall of Granada is near: "But Granada would fall, of that he was sure, and then, everything would turn upside down. He would be deprived of even the memory of what it had been in glorious times, Paradise lost. Al-Andalus would be nothing more than a mirage in the desert of defeat" (24). In an expedition organized by the legendary fifteenth-century Portuguese prince known as Henry the Navigator, Jaber the Arab polymath helps the Christian admiral arrive in the New World, thirty years before Columbus. While the other members of the expedition give in to their base instincts, representing greed and the abuse of military and ecclesiastical power, Jaber, the admiral, and the admiral's servant observe the destructive effects of their arrival with horror. The money and power-hungry members of the expedition meet violent ends that reek of poetic justice. In contrast, Jaber, after healing an indigenous chieftain, is treated like a god and is received by the Aztecs as their awaited god. He decides to stay in the New World, because although he knows that his role as a deity is a farce that will inevitably end, he also expects Granada to fall soon and feels that his position among the Aztecs has given him a new life. Jaber knows that the civilizations of the New World will be vanquished, just like his people in al-Andalus, but hopes that it will take several decades for that to occur (60).

For his part, the admiral, during his return voyage to Europe, decides to cover up their discovery. In honor of Jaber and for the good of humanity, he wants to avoid a second Granada: "And then, how could one forget Jaber and his second life. The relentless wheel of destiny must be detained, through crime and lies, if necessary, and Granada must be prevented from falling for a second time" (64). At first, the admiral's decision to pretend they never found the Americas, in order to protect those lands from contact with Europeans, or at least delay the inevitable, seems to meet with success. But after the admiral's death, his faithful servant, the crypto-Jew Escrivado, hears that Columbus's expedition was funded by the Catholic Monarchs and that he has returned triumphant. This makes Escrivado feel as though his master has died again and prompts him to recall Jaber: "He also gave a sorrowful thought to Jaber whose fears were coming to pass. Granada, for a second time, would fall" (68). The impending destruction of the New World is understood as the second loss of Granada. Beïda Chikhi, in an essay focusing on the figurative use of the sea to counteract loss in Nadir's work, points out that "Le nouveau monde" is the story of the disappearance of an Eden, in this case, al-Andalus, viewed through the loss of the mythical spaces of the New World (175, 180). She states that Jaber's voyage unfolds within a meditation on "the why and the how of loss" (181) and goes on to characterize Nadir's work as follows:

> This issue of loss and mourning, in its maritime and maternal manifestations, unloads and then reloads a centripetal force, that makes of suffering a place of pleasure [*jouissance*] and fecundity as shown by the motifs of whirling, submersion, and cosmic flight, where everything ends up floating, where historical protagonists are mixed with legendary figures, spatial dimensions with temporal dimensions, and where hierarchical principles are totally drowned. (182)

The storyline and narrative style that Nadir brings together certainly turn loss and grief into a potential for the pleasures of rebirth; however, Chikhi's formulation regarding the consequences of this for hierarchical structures remains ambiguous. Within the novella the negative consequences of Columbus's expedition are foreseen, mainly by an exile from al-Andalus, and are presented as an inevitable part of the human process. Within this unstoppable process, the Americas and Granada (and perhaps the Tunisia of Ben Ali, in which Nadir wrote) are equated as victims of violence, religious fanaticism, and the desire for money and power gone mad. Nadir's text does not simply submerge or blur hierarchies; rather, it clearly indicts the abuse of power and intensifies that indictment by pointing to the parallels between the structures of power put into practice in Iberia and in the Americas.

Al-Miludi Shaghmum's *Nisa' Al al-Randi*, which I discussed in chapter 3, presents a critique of the effects of Columbus's voyage with an added layer of commentary on the place of the traumas of the past in the present. The protagonist ʿAli, after being picked up by a Colombian ship during his attempt to emigrate from Morocco to Spain, works on the ship for the required timeframe and is dropped off in Spain with his Colombian wife and a fake passport. When they have finished with the entry process, ʿAli and his wife have a conversation about Christopher Columbus. ʿAli says that he himself could have been part of the discovery of America, if his forefathers had not "been spoiled by their riches, the magic of al-Andalus" (23). For that reason he considers the year-long celebration of the anniversary of Columbus's discovery, 1992, a year of mourning. ʿAli's Colombian wife has a different reason for hating Columbus: she feels that "he destroyed the civilizations of two continents" (24). ʿAli then tries to explain to his wife that he was joking, because Arab civilization had destroyed itself long before Columbus, and those discoveries had broadened humankind's horizons. He tells her that like his ancestors, she is also among the quick-thinking, adaptable ones. But since she continues to insist ʿAli finally gives up and tells her she is right, he is no longer one of the quick and adaptable (24).

Barbara Schulz sees the chapter as ending on a "happy note" that "conveys a sense of reconciliation with history" (23, 24). However, I see an inherent tension in the situation: the narrator is unable to make his wife understand his perspective and decides instead to placate her. Eventually, ʿAli's marriage fails because he has not yet recovered from his brother's abuse in the past. The conversation between ʿAli and his wife about Columbus demonstrates that the famous sailor and the rise of European imperialism are not in and of themselves problematic, but how we process the past dictates our present.

Another work, this time by a Syrian writing in English, takes a creative approach to the processing of the traumas of the past by using elements of the fantastic and a carnivalesque atmosphere to critique and reimagine the role of Columbus in world history. Riad Ismat [Riyad ʿIsmat] (b. 1947) is a prominent Syrian playwright, short story writer, theater director, and literary critic who also served as ambassador and then Minister of Culture under Bashar al-Assad before leaving that post and Syria in 2012 in opposition to the regime's violent repression of the Arab Spring. Ismat has written all of his extensive publications in Arabic, except for the unpublished play "Columbus," which he wrote in 1989 while pursuing graduate studies as a Fulbright Fellow in the United States.[6] The cast of characters in this two-act play includes an Old Columbus and a Young Columbus and displays the Old Columbus's process of looking back at his life and legacy. Through Old Columbus facing Young Columbus, history looking back on itself, the play investigates the figure's mythic status and proposes an alternative present and future.

The play starts with a prologue in which Old Columbus is waiting to see the ailing Queen Isabella at the royal palace, amid a statue of a young, heroic Columbus and a group of noblemen and courtiers. These men, representing specific historic figures, debate whether Columbus deserves his status as a celebrated explorer and largely disdain him. Old Columbus defends himself by pointing to the importance of imagination. In the first scenes of act I, Old Columbus continues to request permission to see the queen and, despairing, begins to doubt his faith in God. Then his old friend and supporter, the Prior, who acts as his conscience, shows up. The Prior tells Old Columbus "You have to discover your guilt, in order to seek salvation" (11) and leads Old Columbus through his past. The following scenes feature Young Columbus's struggles with his own arrogance amid his efforts to convince Ferdinand and Isabella to support his enterprise. Eventually, the monarchs agree to fund the voyage and, as Columbus prepares to set sail, we see Young Columbus's arrogance and anti-Jewish attitudes. The first act closes with a repentant Old Columbus crying over what he did.

Act II presents the travails of the voyage, how Columbus loses control of his men, and how their greed and lust lead to disaster. Observing this, Old Columbus regrets his men's treatment of the indigenous peoples they encountered (79). The occasional anachronisms used in the play increase and on Columbus's return to the Old World in the middle of act II, various screens show TV news reporters announcing Columbus's discovery through skewed, Euro-centric accounts. Yet the hybrid welcoming procession includes indigenous music mixed with a jazz band (87). The chaotic celebration of Columbus's return impedes him from fulfilling his aim of complaining to the monarchs about his men's conduct. After the celebration, the Prior offers another lesson: stop living in the past, for "He who lives in the past has neither present nor future" (92). When Old Columbus is jailed by a rival, he has the opportunity to further process the past. He is put in a jail cell with two men he had wronged: a Muslim sailor from the first voyage and the gay Jewish convert to Christianity who served as the expedition's interpreter. In a conversation among the three that offers a commentary on the Palestinian–Israeli conflict, the Muslim and the Jew forgive Old Columbus, band together, and offer to help him escape.

When Old Columbus finally gets to see the ailing Isabella, he too practices forgiveness. After Columbus and Isabella declare their love for each other, regretting not having pursued a romantic relationship, she asks what he needs. Rather than pursue his complaints, Old Columbus tells her that he is satisfied with what he has and only wants to see her get better. Although Isabella dies, this gives way to a carnivalesque epilogue. In the grand finale, a din of music and hypocritical mourning rituals are halted by Columbus's anger. Then the lighting changes to allow Columbus to see, high above him, the Rabbi and the indigenous chief Guacanagari, both of whom Young Columbus had mistreated, opening their arms to welcome him. Finally, with harmonized drum and violin music rising, Columbus and Isabella are glimpsed climbing out together hand in hand, between the Rabbi and Guacanagari. Thus a repentant

Columbus and his beloved queen escape the madness together amid the resurging power of those they once oppressed. Ismat's "Columbus" is a fantasy of the redemption of Columbus: the mythic figure recognizes the errors of his ways and forgives himself and others to enjoy a reimagined, more equitable outcome. By moving from a repentant Columbus to one who departs accompanied by a rabbi, an indigenous leader, and Queen Isabella, the work carries the broader message that it is never too late to reinterpret history and, out of the injustices of the past, create a new, better future.

Depictions of Columbus from the MENA region point to the creation or reconfiguration of socioeconomic disparities, but also gesture toward creative approaches to overcoming such disparities. These works use Columbus not only to criticize empire but to create alternate versions of history in which less destruction and greater equity are imagined. They suggest a conception of the Arab as both colonizer and colonized that allows for the formulation of fluid identities. As per Shaghmum, this state of flux establishes a framework in which creative adaptation to change is understood not as a loss of tradition but as the continuation of a tradition. According to Ismat's vision, even former opponents can reevaluate their identities and legacies and move forward toward more just and harmonious relationships.

Columbus's voyage enabled and intensified the global power dynamics that create migratory flows, and a steady current within these flows moves from Hispano-America to the United States. Ironically, within US Hispanic communities, the three key events of 1492 have led to the phenomenon of conversion to Islam as a recuperation of al-Andalus and/or a rejection of all that Columbus symbolizes. While Castilian support for Columbus's journey was a result of the victory over Boabdil and the Emirate of Granada (and, in turn, that victory and the financial success of Columbus's expedition influenced the Spanish monarchs' imposition of Catholicism and expulsion of Jews and Muslims), the economic and racial systems these shifts built have led to the phenomenon of Latinos who respond to their cultural dislocation and socioeconomic disenfranchisement by embracing Islam. The rise in the number of Latino converts to Islam since the early 2000s is part of a global trend toward more conversions to Islam that is one aspect of what has been dubbed "the other September 11 effect."[7] However, the Latino converts, in spite of being a diverse group, often espouse, whether on their own or through the efforts of proselytizers, a view of al-Andalus as part of their identity as Hispanic Muslims.[8] Although most US Hispanics are still Catholic and significant numbers have joined evangelical churches, a small but growing group of US Hispanics are converts to Islam. In terms of the number of Latino Muslims, there are widely varying estimates, ranging from 50,000 to 200,000, which, although rising more rapidly than in the past, is still a small percentage of the total Latino or US Muslim populations. Figures aside, the phenomenon is tangible in the existence of Latino mosques in the largest US cities, such as Los Angeles, New York, and Chicago. Across the United States, the Latino Muslim population is made up of diverse countries of (family) origin, age groups, educational levels, and socioeconomic strata (Agosto 127–28).[9] Nonetheless, many see themselves as "reverts," rather than converts, to Islam. In part this is because of the Muslim belief that all people are born Muslims, that it is their natural state, but this is also due to the genealogical narrative, manifested in different versions, that the Latino reverts share.

Similar to African Americans' arrival at Islam through identification with Muslim Africans, particularly those brought to the Americas as slaves, many Hispanic Muslims trace their link to Islam as far back as al-Andalus. This account of history positions Hispanics as the descendants of Andalusi (whether Iberian or North African) Muslims and thus views their conversion as a reversion to the faith of their Andalusi ancestors. While this understanding of the trajectory of Hispanic Muslims is informed by broader references to cultural links between Latinos and Arabs, such as those found in the poetry of renowned Nuyorican poet Victor Hernández Cruz, it is also cultivated by leaders within US Hispanic Muslim communities.[10] This narrative is quite palpable in the Alianza Islámica (Islamic Alliance), the United States's first Latino Muslim association, which was founded in New York in 1975 by Puerto Rican converts. The imam of the Alianza Islámica, Ramón Omar Abduraheem Ocasio, stated at a 1999 Alianza event, "We are reclaiming our history after a 500 year hiatus. [. . .] We are the cultural descendants of the Moors" (Aidi, "Olé to Allah"). Aidi describes the banner outside of the Alianza's headquarters as follows: "The Alianza's banner [. . .] unabashedly celebrates this revisionist view of Latino history: against a red, white and blue backdrop stands a sword-wielding Moor, flanked by a Taino Indian (one of the indigenous inhabitants of Puerto Rico) and a black African. The Spanish Conquistador—'who raped and pillaged'—is simply left out" (Aidi, "Olé to Allah"). Similarly, a 2012 public event, featuring Ocasio and others and held at America's Islamic Heritage Museum in Washington, DC, was titled "Latino Muslims: Letters from Al-Andalus" and presented itself as an opportunity to "Learn about the Muslim cultural legacy from Islamic Spain to the US."[11] Imam Ocasio has explained this Latino Moorish heritage as follows:

> Most of the people who came to Latin America and the Spanish Caribbean were from southern Spain, Andalusia—they were Moriscos, Moors forcefully converted to Christianity. The leaders, army generals, *curas* [priests] were white men from northern Spain . . . *sangre azul*, as they were called. The southerners, who did the menial jobs, . . . servants, artisans, foot soldiers, . . . were of mixed Arab and African descent. They were stripped of their religion, culture, brought to the so-called New World where they were enslaved with African slaves.... But the Moriscos never lost their culture . . . we are the cultural descendants of the Moors. (Aidi, "'Let Us Be Moors'")

This is a revisionist history that recognizes the causal links between the three events of 1492 but adds an emphasis on the arrival of Muslims and moriscos to the New World as part of its colonization. There are documented cases of such arrivals, and the architecture of colonial Latin America certainly supports their presence, but since they were seeking to hide their faith and/or origins there is (thus far) no certainty regarding their approximate number. More important, this historical narrative establishes an analogous relationship between the oppressed morisco, the oppressed indigenous American, and the oppressed immigrant/ethnic minority.

The variations of the Moorish Latino narrative contain two sometimes interwoven threads. One of the narrative threads relies heavily on idealized images of al Andalus as a space of cultural development and religious tolerance and focuses on the achievements of the Muslim Golden Age.[12] Agosto notes that "Many Latino/a Muslims described the study of this Spanish-Islamic history as an act of recovery, of retrieval of a cultural memory that had been denied them" (157). In addition, like the characters in Nadir's "Le nouveau monde," many of the Latino converts who subscribe to this historical narrative are aware of the links between the destruction of Granada/Andalusi culture, the destruction of New World cultures, and nascent Spain's rejection of non-Catholic faiths. In this vision of history, that world of relatively peaceful coexistence ended primarily or solely due to Spanish Catholic monoreligious zeal in the form of the Reconquista and the Inquisition.

Consequently, the other main thread in this genealogy is the conversion to Islam as a rebellion against Spanish, European, and Euro-American authority.[13] The Mexican American convict turned writer Joe Loya observes that "Latino Muslims were common in prison" and explains this phenomenon as follows: "There reside in the Latino consciousness at least three historical grudges, three conflicting selves: the Muslim Moor, the

Catholic Spanish and the indigenous Indian. [. . .] The old Latin American revolutionaries converted to atheism, but the new faux revolutionary Latino American prisoner can just as easily convert to Islam. In the end, both choices are a sort of adolescent rebellion against authority—in this case, the Catholic Church." The theme of rebellion that Loya highlights indicates that the phenomenon of Latino converts to Islam is intertwined with contemporary youth culture's view of the embracing of Islam as an anti-establishment, antiglobalization stance.

Thus, US Hispanic converts understand the conversion to Islam as a return to one's illustrious roots and/or a countercultural act. Roots in a mythical al-Andalus can offer US Hispanics the hope of harmonious coexistence, a cultural and linguistic plurality that is celebrated precisely because of its hybridity and multilingualism. Alternately, an identification with the subjugated Moor can foster a stance of refusal to submit to Euro-American cultural norms and racial and economic systems. Either way, US Hispanic converts to Islam invoke al-Andalus to carry out acts of cultural translation that are part of the construction of narratives of identity.[14] For these converts, Islam is a way to contest socioeconomic, racial, and ethnic inequalities symbolized by Columbus and the European hegemony for which he stands.

The Latino Moor narrative can be useful if it leads to flexible formulations of identity and solutions to contemporary intolerance. Many of the reverts see their path as a return to a true or authentic identity, a perspective that risks creating dangerous, essentialist barriers between communities. At least one, however, has a stance akin to that of Moroccan writer Shaghmum. On mainstream Hispanic communities' lack of acceptance of conversion to Islam, because of the links between Catholicism and Hispanic cultures, Mexican American Muslim Juan Galván maintains that "Defining culture by religion is not very effective, because our ancestors were Christian, Muslim, Jewish or pagan. Many Hispanics think that leaving Catholicism means rejecting their identity. We should re-evaluate how we traditionally define culture. Although some people define culture as something static[,] I think defining culture as a dynamic process is more accurate" (Viscidi 58). Galván's conception of culture and identity echoes that expressed by Shaghmum in *Nisa' Al al-Randi*, where the Andalusi-Moroccan protagonist is proudly aware of his protean lineage. Ultimately, the texts that address Columbus, alongside the phenomenon of Latino converts identifying with al-Andalus and the moriscos, point to the connected histories that shape the present and that are rewritten to attempt to transform the present and the future. By adopting a transcolonial view of history that takes into account cross-cultural and imperial encounters over time, these texts and the Latino reverts highlight shifts between religious identifications and between the positions of colonizer and colonized—dominant power and subaltern, as well as enduring patterns of subjugation. That is, they emphasize the destructive capacity and short-lived nature of empire (yesterday's conqueror may be tomorrow's conquered), the persistence of the disenfranchisement of immigrants from the Global South, and the possibilities for imagining and establishing new patterns and realities.

* * *

Tariq and Boabdil are the bookends of al-Andalus, and both are implicated in the process of using the Andalusi past to define and redefine the identities designated as Muslim, Arab, North African, Christian, European, Spanish, and Argentine, as well as exilic and migrant. The role of Columbus in the end of al-Andalus highlights the extent to which the shifting roles of colonizer/colonized and host country/immigrant population are part of the nexus of Spanish, Arab and Maghrebian, and North and South American cultures around the chronotope of al-Andalus.

Through my analysis of the works centered on Tariq and Boabdil, I identify significant temporal and regional differences. I clarify that the temporal differences in the works on Tariq and Boabdil are linked to specific cultural shifts: on one hand, the rise in Islamism and the resulting interest in figures of heroic Muslim power, and, on the other hand, Spain's questioning of its identity as it uneasily integrated into what became the European Union, went through the quincentenary of 1492, and experienced a simultaneous rise in North African immigration. Furthermore, I argue that the regional difference in attitudes toward Tariq is the result of the Maghreb's experience of conquest by Muslim Arabs from the Arabian Peninsula and the Levant. Maghrebian writers, drawing from the friction between Arab and Amazigh cultures and their modes of religious practice, disrupt the image of the idealized Tariq and thus the narrative of Muslim unity in the Golden Age of the caliphate on which the image of Tariq is based. Just as many of those contestatory works link Tariq to labor migration, the only contemporary prose works from the MENA region that represent Boabdil link him to issues of migration and exile. Thus, on one hand, representations of Tariq and Boabdil have become cultural commodities that are part of a staging of nationalist and/or religious power that further cements difference and hierarchical dynamics. On the other hand, there are works like Lalami's, with her would-be migrant protagonist's reference to Tariq, and Viana's children's novel on Boabdil that connect the historical figures to contemporary migration to reimagine the past and its role in the present and thereby help audiences work through contemporary issues of tolerance and difference within an increasingly polarized world.

Tariq and Boabdil are part of a cultural industry of remembrance; paradoxically they are intertwined with the present realities of migration. Their own positions as Tariq the colonizer and Boabdil the colonized and the rotating role of immigrant can serve as a useful equalizer: I have been (or soon may be) in the other's shoes. Thus, migration reveals the falsehoods of triumphalist narratives (whether the triumph of Tariq or the triumph over Boabdil) and can also open the way to shared narratives of al-Andalus. Al-Andalus emerges as a central reference point for Hispano-Arab conceptualizations of movement and identity and points to an erasure of the line between insider and outsider, whether colonizer/colonized or native/foreigner.

PART III

Florinda, Wallada, and Scheherazade, or the Women of al-Andalus and the Stories They Tell

> Whenever a woman is a writer, she is able to face the power of society that imposes a marginal position on her, with another power: the suggestive power of the imagination.
>
> —I'tidal 'Uthman

> Writing is a retrieval of a human will negated. I write, the space becomes my own, and I am no longer an object acted upon by history but a subject acting in history.
>
> —Radwa Ashour (quoted by Youssef Rakha)

In the previous two chapters, I demonstrated how migration as well as constructions of masculinity and femininity are intertwined with the figures of Tariq ibn Ziyad and Boabdil. If Ibn Rushd, as icon of cultural (un)translatability, and Tariq and Boabdil, as masculine conqueror and feminine "surrenderer," respectively, are the main male figures from al-Andalus still invoked today, who are the female figures, and how are they constructed and reconstructed? The two women most frequently associated with al-Andalus are Florinda, the legendary figure whose rape/seduction is said to have led to the Muslim conquest of Iberia, and Wallada, an eleventh-century poet who lived through the fall of Umayyid Cordoba and is known either as the beloved of a famous poet or an audacious poet and lover in her own right. The link between al-Andalus and seduction/sexual impropriety for which these two figures often stand is a salient feature of twentieth-century Arab culture.

For instance, al-Andalus as seduction is seen in the classic postcolonial novel *Mawsim al-Hijra ila al-Shamal* (*Season of Migration to the North*, 1966) by Sudanese writer Tayeb Salih [al-Tayyib Salih] (1929–2009). In this novel, Tariq ibn Ziyad and al-Andalus make a brief but paradigmatic appearance. Salih's novel examines the impact of British colonialism and time spent in Britain on two Sudanese men and their village. One of these men, the unnamed narrator, becomes obsessed with uncovering the mysteries surrounding the other man: a newcomer to his rural Sudanese village, Mustafa Saʿid [Sa'eed]. Mustafa is trying to live incognito in this village after experiencing colonization and he himself becoming a colonizer of sorts in England. After having grown up in Sudan and Egypt under British rule, Mustafa establishes himself as an academic in England, but his success in the colonial center is marred when he is humiliated and tormented by a British woman with whom he has fallen in love. Eventually, he kills her with her complicity and sets out to seduce other local women. Mustafa's sexual conquests of European women can be read as a form of revenge against European colonization, and his standard method is to appeal to the women's Orientalism by citing Arabic poetry and preparing his apartment with Oriental decor and incense. In pursuit of his third conquest, Isabella Seymour, he invokes al-Andalus in particular, not only to woo his prey but to create for himself a scene of desired conquest.

When Mustafa meets Isabella, she is a church-going mother of three who has been happily married for eleven years. She tells Mustafa that her mother is Spanish and he immediately plugs in a romanticized tale of their having met centuries before in al-Andalus:

> "'That, then, explains everything. It explains our meeting by chance, our spontaneous mutual understanding as though we had got to know each other centuries ago. Doubtless one of my forefathers was a soldier in Tarik ibn Ziyad's army. Doubtless he met one of your ancestors as she gathered in the grapes from an orchard in Seville. Doubtless he fell in love with her at first sight and she with him. He lived with her for a time, then left her and went off to Africa. There he married again and I was one of his progeny in Africa, and you have come from his progeny in Spain."
>
> 'These words, also the low lights and the wine, made her happy. She gave out throaty gurgling laughs.
>
> "'What a devil you are!" she said.
>
> 'For a moment I imagined to myself the Arab soldiers' first meeting with Spain: like me at this instant sitting opposite Isabella Seymour, a southern thirst being dissipated in the mountain passes of history in the north. However, I seek not glory for the likes of me do not seek glory.

'After a month of feverish desire I turned the key in the door with her at my side, a fertile Andalus; after that I led her across the short passageway to the bedroom where the smell of burning sandalwood and incense assailed her, filling her lungs with a perfume she little knew was deadly. (42 [39])[1]

The passage goes on to describe their first sexual encounter which led to an impassioned affair that, like all of Mustafa's conquests, ended in the ambiguous suicide of the seduced woman (was she driven to suicide because of him or because of other factors in her life?). In this accomplished novel about seduction/subjugation between East and West, al-Andalus has a dual function. On one hand, the protagonist uses al-Andalus to entice his sought-after object of desire. Al-Andalus heightens Mustafa's allure by creating an aura of idealized desire between cultural opposites, and it serves to lower Isabella's guard by presenting their illicit relationship as something inevitable, an encounter that continues a desire that was first sparked centuries before. On the other hand, Mustafa uses al-Andalus to heighten the thrill of the chase for himself. Through the positing of their relationship as that of a Muslim soldier and a Christian peasant, and the figuring of the grape-picking peasant as "fertile Andalus [*Andalus khasib*]" the text explicitly links sexual conquest with territorial conquest.[2] In the gendered discourses from which Salih's protagonist draws, al-Andalus is the lost beloved of the Arabs, who some dream of reconquering. Salih's text presents a measure of irony with regard to the seductive power of the East/West encounter in al-Andalus, but other texts seek to explicitly disrupt the paradigm of al-Andalus as a woman subjugated/seduced by a male conqueror.

In part III, I examine the dynamics of sexual and sexualized conquest with regard to the figures of Florinda and Wallada and alternate manifestations of "fertile Andalus": texts authored by women that point to the fecundity of creative narratives about al-Andalus and its women. In chapter 5, I analyze the representations of Florinda and Wallada in twentieth- and twenty-first-century Arab and Spanish cultural production and consider how the largely static representations of these two women as subjugated and/or seductive are reworked in certain texts that consider the discursive construction of cultural icons and the connections between sexuality and power. In chapter 6 I continue to explore issues of narrativity in other works that address al-Andalus and women more broadly: an Iraqi short story and an Egyptian novel trilogy. By focusing on the transformative power of storytelling, including storytelling as survival and al-Andalus as a narrative, these texts suggest a Scheherazade figure who recasts conceptions of gender as well as of al-Andalus.

CHAPTER 5

Florinda and Wallada

Subjugation, Seduction, and Textual Transformation

Florinda and Wallada are associated with seduction and empire, whether they are seducer or seduced and whether they are part of a shift in power or part of the glory days before a shift. Within both Spanish and Arab discourses, aside from Isabella (*Isabel la Católica*) who brought an end to Muslim rule in Spain, Florinda and Wallada are the most prominent female figures in historical accounts of al-Andalus and are still portrayed in twentieth- and twenty-first-century texts. Like Tariq, Florinda is part of the moment of Muslim conquest, but in contrast with the active "masculine" conqueror, representations of her oscillate between that of a passive victim (akin to Boabdil) and that of a dangerous seductress. Wallada, as part of the last days of glory of Umayyad Cordoba, is associated with the initial decline of al-Andalus, but in contrast with the passive "feminine" Boabdil who marks the end of Muslim sovereignty in al-Andalus, Wallada is either active, independent, and even outright masculine or she is relegated to a muted, ornamental, secondary role. I argue that although many of the works on Florinda and Wallada reinscribe the paradigm of al-Andalus as a subjugated or seducing woman, some critique those power dynamics, using the mythology of al-Andalus itself to offer alternate narratives about the women of al-Andalus.

Florinda as Foil

In my discussion of Tariq ibn Ziyad in chapter 3, I introduced the figure of Florinda. According to legend, she was the daughter of Julian, governor of the Visigoth outpost at Ceuta. When Julian sent Florinda to the court of the Visigoth king Roderick, Roderick raped her (or was the victim of her seduction?), and thus Julian decided to seek revenge by helping the Muslims invade Hispania. On both sides of the Strait of Gibraltar, the interpretation of Florinda has varied between that of object of subjugation to be avenged and agent of seduction to be reviled. At least to the north of the strait, Florinda's ambiguous ethnocultural identity played a part in her transformation from victim to seducer. Although Florinda was Christian, since she was raised in North Africa, certain Christian sources present her as Arabized. Yiacoup notes that in medieval Spanish ballads on the fall of Visigoth Iberia, "the female figure is once again the site of moral and cultural ambiguity" and Florinda functions "as a personified trope of the frontier" (46). In a key fifteenth-century Spanish text (Corral's *Crónica sarracina*) Florinda is presented as a temptress and as linked to the Arabo-Muslim world, and thus she is exotically seductive (Drayson 37–38, Yiacoup 47). To quote Yiacoup, "As La Cava is designated by Christians as being Arabized, and by Arabs as being Christian, she becomes the archetype of the yielding feminine principle." In this way, Florinda is alternately Self or Other, a victim that serves as a rallying cry for group identification or a dangerous woman whose rejection establishes group boundaries (48). Either way, her agency is rejected and she remains an object—whether of pity or of scorn.

Elizabeth Drayson, Patricia Grieve, and Marjorie Ratcliffe (17–62) have carried out detailed analyses of the medieval and early modern sources that refer to Florinda and the evolutions the figure has undergone.[1] Grieve notes that although Florinda is not mentioned in the earliest extant Spanish chronicles, in Spain "historians have reinforced as the central event of the collective national myth of the fall of Spain—often called, plaintively and with great longing for an irrecoverable past, the 'loss of Spain' or the 'destruction of Spain'—the sexual scandal between King Rodrigo and a young girl from North Africa" (15). Early Arab chroniclers are the first to mention Florinda, though not by name. In texts such as the mid-ninth-century *Futuh Misr* (*The Conquest of Egypt*) by Ibn ʿAbd al-Hakam, the Christian king's rape of an army commander's innocent daughter is offered as the motive behind Julian's collaboration with the Muslims (Grieve 25, 40). Christian historians began to mention Florinda in the thirteenth and fourteenth centuries as the victim of sexual aggression. In the medieval and early modern periods, female chastity was analogous to political order, and thus invasion was figured as rape (27, 36–37). However, Grieve indicates that by the sixteenth century the climate of misogyny in Spain had resulted in a recasting of Florinda as the guilty party, as either innately seductive by virtue of being a woman or as an outright shameless temptress (21–22, 25, 37–38). Thus, in the traditional Spanish perspective, al-Andalus is the reconquered beloved known as "Spain," although in the process of recuperation, Florinda, the figure who embodies sexual(ized) appropriation by the Other, is rejected as a tainted woman who is to blame for her own downfall.

Although Grieve states that Arab sources present Julian as a dishonored father who takes understandable action (44), there is some indication that there was also a less favorable view of Florinda in circulation in the Maghrebian and Arab world. Florinda was first known in Christian accounts as la Cava Rumía, a term most likely derived from the Arabic *al-qahba al-rumiyya*—the Christian whore.[2] This, together with two 1940s Egyptian texts that I address below, suggests that there was also an Arab discourse about Florinda as a woman of loose morals.[3] Nonetheless, most depictions of Florinda from the modern Arab world are more invested in demonstrating her honorableness, and all of them use her to highlight the accomplishments of Tariq ibn Ziyad.

A number of Arab authors have depicted Florinda, in historical novels, plays, and a television series, yet their portrayals never attempt to creatively imagine her subjectivity or question received history. The portrayals primarily serve to highlight the heroicness of the figure for whom Florinda serves as a foil: Tariq ibn Ziyad. The most well known of these works is also the earliest: *Fath al-Andalus* (1903; translated as *The Conquest of Andalusia*), the historical novel by Jurji Zaydan I discussed in chapter 3.[4] Although the original title of the novel included the name Tariq ibn Ziyad and Tariq appears in the novel as a stalwart Muslim and a courageous hero, he is not a main character, at least on the surface. Rather, the novel's outward focus is the political intrigues of the end of the Visigoth kingdom. Yet the original title, with its reference to Tariq, provides a clue regarding how to interpret the work, regarding who and what takes on the most significance in Zaydan's version of history.

Although much of *Fath al-Andalus* is dedicated to Florinda, she has little agency and is first and foremost a carrier of male honor. Thus the core of the novel is the value of her honor as seen in the relationships between Florinda; her beloved, the Visigoth prince Alfonso; Alfonso's uncle the Bishop Oppas [Ubas]; Florinda's father, Julian; King Roderick; and Tariq. Zaydan's version of events is quite clear with regard to who was at fault in the sexual advances between Florinda and Roderick: Florinda is repeatedly presented as chaste, honorable, pure, modest, and of strong religious faith, whereas Roderick is an evil, lustful tyrant. In this version of the legend, Florinda is successful in fending off Roderick and defending her virginity, which becomes central to the narrative. The concept of virginity appears repeatedly throughout the novel. For instance, when Florinda is trying to fend off Roderick's advances she tells him that all she has is this one jewel ["hadhihi al-jawhara," 44]. Similarly, the impersonal, omniscient narrator and Florinda refer to chastity as more valuable that what is in the treasure vaults of kings ["al-ʿiffa athman mima fi khaza'in al-muluk," 43] and to virginity as a jewel, worth more than all the treasure vaults of the world [e.g., "hadhihi al-jawhara, fa'innaha athman min khaza'in al-ʿalim bi-usrihi," 45]. Florinda's body, given the need to protect it from trespass, is analogous to this symbolic vault and violated spaces that appear elsewhere in the novel.[5] Later she declares that her virginity is more valuable than her life and that it is what makes her worthy of notice by her betrothed, Alfonso (94–95 [98]). Finally, as Florinda tries to encourage Alfonso to rise up against Roderick and join Julian in the Arab camp, she refers to "that precious jewel that belongs to Alfonso more than to me" (319 [338]). This conception of a woman's worth, quite consonant with the time in which Zaydan wrote, is further emphasized through Florinda's devotion to the Virgin Mary and the comments of other characters. For instance, Badr, who had been raised as Tariq's younger brother, and then Tariq refer to a captured Iberian woman as "booty" [*ghanima*] (221 [223]). Similarly, in the scene depicting Tariq delivering his famous speech encouraging his troops just before they head into battle, Tariq suggests to his men that one of the spoils of war will be the famous bejeweled maidens [*hur*] of Iberia (312–13 [330]). Thus, maidenhood is repeatedly presented as a precious commodity, one that inspires hope in Florinda through the Virgin Mary and one for which men vie.

Once Florinda's "jewel" has been threatened by Roderick, it is up to Alfonso, Julian, and Tariq to protect and avenge her. Although she was able to defend herself from Roderick's advances and initially escape his clutches, the male characters must ultimately save her. Thus the few moments in which she demonstrates agency end up with her reclaiming her role as damsel in distress. This depiction of Florinda and the role of her honor as an object of exchange between men justifies the Muslim invasion of Iberia and explains the actions of the male characters. This power dynamic is reflected in a single line of the novel. Close to the end of the narrative, when Alfonso, Julian, and Tariq are facing Badr, who has captured Florinda and wants to marry her, Alfonso declares that he should be the one to challenge Badr to a sword fight and states: "Whoever wins [the sword fight] will get the girl." (343 [364]). Getting the girl and her jewel is a symbol of power. In this way, much of the novel centers on Florinda's honor as a commodity exchanged between men, and she is reduced to the value of her sexual possession.

Significantly, though not as visible in the sociopolitical struggles depicted, it is Tariq who is instrumental in setting things right in the denouement of the novel. He first appears more than halfway through the novel, but he does so to save the day. Ultimately, he saves Florinda from harm by negotiating her release from Badr and placing her and her family under his personal protection. In the process, Julian is reunited with Badr, who turns out to be Julian's long-lost son, Tumas.[6] Thus, by conquering Iberia, Tariq reunites a family (Julian, Florinda, and Badr/ Tumas), creates filial links between himself and Christians via Badr/ Tumas, reunites lovers (Alfonso and Florinda), and offers an alternative to Roderick's corrupt rule. Zaydan's novel has a didactic purpose and in addition to presenting the message that it is important for each people to maintain their cultural identity and religion (lest they end up like the Visigoths), it seeks to transmit the idea that the conquering Arabs offered just rule and religious freedom. This message is conveyed via Tariq's protection of Florinda. That is, in Zaydan's *Fath al-Andalus*, Florinda's threatened virginity gives Tariq the opportunity to shine as a just and honorable leader and gives the Arabo-Muslim world something to bring its constituents together and feel good about. By highlighting the value of (Christian) Florinda's virginity and adding ties between the Christians and Muslims of nascent al-Andalus and Tariq as a heroic savior for all, Zaydan uses Florinda's jewel to further the goals of pan-Arab nationalism.

In 1940s Egypt there seems to have been some doubt regarding Florinda's virtue, but all the same, she is employed to further the heroic stature of Tariq ibn Ziyad. In chapter 3 of this study, I analyzed Egyptian Mahmud Taymur's *Tariq al-Andalus* (*Tariq of al-Andalus*), a play published circa 1940. One of the prominent characters in Taymur's play, which presents a largely traditional view of Tariq as manly hero par excellence, is Florinda. Taymur's text presents a Florinda who is less virtuous and more complex than that of Zaydan, but ultimately it puts her in the same position of being a foil to Tariq.

In Taymur's version of events, Roderick does rape Florinda, but as Julian seeks retribution for the dishonor, the Muslim characters have doubts about his honor and honesty (44). Sure enough, later he plots against Tariq (68). In parallel fashion, Florinda is not clearly chaste. After Roderick's sexual aggression, Julian, seeking to establish an alliance with the Muslim camp, convinces Florinda to start a relationship with Tariq. The sexually suggestive scenes include Julian telling Florinda that Tariq was staring at her and mentioning that people say that women run after him (48–49), Julian purposely leaving Florinda alone with Tariq so that she can be charming and enticing (50), and Florinda flirting with Tariq while she is dressed as a knight (50–53). The questionable morals she displays by flirting alone with Tariq to further her father's agenda are quickly eclipsed when Tariq saves Florinda from a Goth soldier who was trying to assassinate her (54). The next time she appears she is in Arab clothes (69), symbolically having switched sides and declaring allegiance to Tariq through her clothing. Florinda later declares her love for Tariq, and they marry. By this point in the play Florinda's allegiances have shifted to such an extent that when Julian, humiliated by Tariq's success, tries to kill Tariq, Florinda saves him (107–9, 113) and defends Tariq even in the face of Julian's threats as he brandishes a dagger (129, 148). In an unexpected turn, Florinda asks Tariq for a divorce, citing that he's a man of war and hasn't made time for her (156–58). They part ways, and Tariq goes to meet with Musa and explains his disobedience to him as a gift to Islam (161–65). Thus, in the end, Florinda is neither an innocent victim nor a corrupt seductress but something in between in that she leaves Tariq because she is more concerned about how much attention he pays to her than about the welfare of the Islamic state. In Taymur's text the discourse on virginity is absent and Florinda is a flirtatious and self-centered figure. Her sudden exit from the storyline of the play allows Tariq to focus on being a military hero. With Florinda conveniently out of the way, Tariq can become the fully realized, uber-masculine hero.

In another Egyptian work from the same period, a Florinda figure emerges who is of clearly corrupt morals. In *Hatif min al-Andalus* (*A Voice from al-Andalus*, 1949), a text which I will discuss again below in relation to Wallada, ʿAli al-Jarim (1881–1949) creates a character who is a stand-in for a noxious Florinda. In his novel, which takes place a few centuries later in Cordoba, a female Castilian character is called Florinda and another character remarks on her name and refers to the legendary Florinda (64, 72–73). The eleventh-century Florinda marries a distinguished Arab of Cordoba and supports their daughter ʿA'isha's efforts to seek retribution against the Muslims for their takeover (91). ʿA'isha works as a spy for the Christians against the Umayyad state in Cordoba and seeks to destroy the famous poet and vizier Ibn Zaydun, who had broken off their romantic relationship. ʿA'isha is first sent into exile and then imprisoned for her work against the Umayyad regime. Florinda and her daughter are cast as traitors, and in this way biculturalism or a plurality of affiliations is suspect and punished and Florinda symbolizes the perils of duplicity. Ultimately, *Hatif min al-Andalus* uses Florinda, even in a work set centuries after the time of the legendary figure, to accentuate the travails and perseverance of Ibn Zaydun, a male figure who represents the cultural zenith of al-Andalus.

While Taymur and al-Jarim were, like Zaydan, writing within the context of Arab nationalism, they did so in a later period that was also witnessing the rise of Egyptian nationalism. At the time of the publication of Zaydan's *Fath al-Andalus*, British control over Egypt was still being formalized under a de facto colonial protectorate. But by the time

Taymur and al-Jarim wrote, tensions and internal Egyptian conflicts were on the rise. The British protectorate had become officially recognized in 1914 and, due to Egyptian nationalist resistance, the Anglo-Egyptian Treaty of 1936 was signed to limit (but not put an end to) British military presence in Egypt. Meanwhile, certain Egyptian nationalist groups continued to push for full independence, and this led to conflict with the British and with the Egyptian Wafd Party that had supported the treaty. It was not until 1954 that the British agreed to withdraw their troops from Egypt. The negative depictions of Florinda found in the works of Taymur and al-Jarim reflect a moment of nation building in which women's sexuality and their demands for male devotion had become dangerous and burdensome, respectively. British–Egyptian tensions find their analogue in Arab-Iberian tensions, yet in the historical period that is portrayed, the Arabs are the triumphant invaders. This triumph—a military one in Tariq's time and a political and cultural one in Ibn Zaydun's time—is made possible by having Florinda and the Florinda proxy ʿAʾisha leave the scene, whether by choice or by force. Although these Florindas are granted subjectivity and agency, these qualities are cut short by the need to distance them from the heroes. With the power of the Florindas with dangerous and demanding sexuality contained, the greatness of the men that remain center stage is enhanced. Silencing Florinda empowers the male heroes.

An Arab depiction of Florinda from later in the twentieth century does not go any further in granting the figure lasting subjectivity or agency. A couple of decades later, Argentine *mahjar* writer Zaki Qunsul, in his play *Tahta Samaʾ al-Andalus* (1965), which I analyzed in chapter 3, only briefly provides Florinda with a voice. Qunsul's text presents an innocent Florinda akin to that of Zaydan, but has her shame at dishonor overpower her before she ever appears as a character. Only Julian's reference to a letter she wrote gives her a brief say in the events of the text. In this text, Julian recounts to Tariq and Musa's son that Florinda was raped by Roderick and then committed suicide to cleanse her dishonor with her blood. He tells them about a letter she left in which she asked Julian to swear to avenge her. Although Zaydan's Florinda is able to protect the jewel of her virginity, this Florinda is overcome by Roderick as well as by dishonor and shame (26).

Rather than be one of the links between Iberia and the Arab world and between Christians and Muslims, as seen in Zaydan's text, this Florinda reflects the moment of dishonor and aborted unity that followed the short-lived merging of Egypt and Syria as the United Arab Republic (1958–1961) and the resulting instability that led to the 1963 coup that put the Baʿath Party in control of Syria. Qunsul's Florinda is a martyr figure whose disgrace and death must be avenged and made worthwhile by Tariq. In this way, her silencing through death allows Tariq, and the hope of unified Arabo-Muslim power that he offers, to shine.

I now turn to Florinda in the modern Spanish context. Although the historicity of the various figures in the Florinda legend has been disputed, she is one of the figures from the medieval period who are central to the narratives of Spanish national identity (Grieve 24–25, 235). The so-called fall of Spain was linked not to male political actors but to Florinda, the "Eve" of Spain (Grieve 24), and by the sixteenth century she had been transformed from virginal victim into blameworthy whore. During the Romantic period, there were a few attempts to rehabilitate Florinda, but mostly the texts that treated her aimed to recuperate Rodrigo [Roderick] as a valiant Visigoth forbearer in order to support the nation-building project (38, 125). As Francoist nationalism promoted legendary figures of triumph, Florinda, the figure blamed for the "fall" of Spain, was pushed out of the limelight and has not been the subject of any major twentieth- or twenty-first-century Spanish works.[7] Hence, her erasure in post-Romantic Spanish culture is most noteworthy. This erasure is particularly salient in Goytisolo's *Reivindicación del Conde don Julián* (*Count Julian*, 1970) which I discussed in chapter 3. This novel focuses on the characters of Julian and Tariq but reduces Florinda to an absence only made present by repeated reference to a grotesque, menacing grotto-vagina.

The common Spanish epithet for Florinda, La Cava, though derived from an Arabic term, also takes on a Latin-derived meaning due to its coincidence with the Latin *cava*. From *cava*, the Latin term for "cave," Spanish derives both *cava*, referring to a cave in which sparkling Spanish wine (*un cava*) is made and *cueva*, the more general term for a cave. These two words, which are either identical or nearly identical to the alternate name for Florinda, link Florinda La Cava to the space of the cave, a space Goytisolo uses throughout his novel as a symbolic referent for female genitalia. In chapter 3 on Tariq ibn Ziyad, I presented the critique of Spanish tradition that Goytisolo carries out in his text and its limitations. The novel offers a radical alternative to constraining conceptions of Spanish masculinity and national identity, but through problematic portrayals of Arabized and homosexual masculinity. In addition, as Brad Epps has masterfully argued, in the process of rejecting the traditional construction of Spanish identity in this way, Goytisolo reinscribes the misogynist attitudes that led to the vilification of Florinda.[8]

Early in Goytisolo's *Reivindicación*, the narrator, identifying with Julian, thinks about his plans to destroy Spain and lays out who from among the historical and legendary figures will play a part in his invasion: "reviving the memory of your humiliations and affronts, accumulating drop by drop your hate : without Roderick, nor Frandina, nor Cava : new Count Julian, forging somber betrayals" (89). The narrator makes explicit his plan to exclude Roderick, Frandina (Julian's wife/Florinda's mother), and Cava (Florinda herself) from the story as he focuses on his own experiences and recurring assault on Spain. Indeed, in the rest of *Reivindicación*, while Julian and Tariq have prominent roles, Florinda is subsumed within the figure of the child version of the narrator, within the figure of Potiphar's wife, within Spain as invaded motherland, and within the physicality of female sexuality through the space of the cave.

Through oneiric fragments that are cyclically repeated, Goytisolo's text brings the figure of Florinda to mind without naming her. Florinda as innocent victim of sexual aggression is suggested by the child Alvarito, who is raped by Julian. Although Florinda as dangerous seducer can be seen in the references to Potiphar's wife, who in the Book of Genesis (39:1–20) is the wife of an officer of the pharaoh who buys Joseph as a slave. Potiphar's wife tries to seduce Joseph and then falsely accuses him of having assaulted her. Through Alvarito, the victim of violent sexual aggression, Florinda is stripped of any power; as lying temptress she is associated with traditional views of women as dangerous sexual aggressors. Either way, she remains unnamed and her perspective on the encounter with Roderick, or the legend about it and any potential agency are completely silenced.

In *Reivindicación*, Florinda is also present under erasure, that is, in a silenced form, as the invaded motherland. The text revolves around Julian's vindictive invasion of Spain, figured as a sexual assault on a gendered nation that deserves retribution. In this way *Reivindicación* replays the legendary rape of Florinda while denigrating her as worthy of punishment and as a nonentity, a figure not worthy of being named or listened to. In addition to being subsumed under the nation, Florinda is reduced to her genitals, which are presented as menacing and abhorrent. One of the recurring spatial elements of *Reivindicación* is the grotto or cave that within the symbolic system of the text, represents the vagina as a repulsive and rejected—that is, abject, space. Thus, not only are Florinda and women in general reduced to the physicality of female sexuality, but their physical and sexual aspects reflect a relationship to the feminine that is built on repulsion and fear.

Through intertextual references to historical and literary works and a fragmented, nonlinear narrative, Goytisolo aggressively counters the traditional historiography and symbols of Spain, but his deconstruction simultaneously suppresses and denigrates the story of Florinda. Epps explains the consequences of this dynamic as follows: "seeking revenge—that is to say, narrating—without Cava, Frandina or Rodrigo,

Goytisolo's reinvigorated Count Julian only partially betrays the (established) History of Spain. In fact, the story that Julian remembers is one that faithfully reaffirms the silent history of women, one that remains loyal [. . .] to an entire narrative tradition that is almost exclusively male" (Epps, "Politics of Ventriloquism," 280). By not telling Florinda's story, the author misses the opportunity for a comprehensive revision of Spanish history. Instead, "Goytisolo, vindicating Julian while dismissing Cava, continues to operate within a phallic economy that construes women as the repository of male desire and honor and as the site of male conflict and exchange, as little or nothing, that is, in and of themselves. Women, subjugated and silenced by history, are also subjugated and silenced by Julian's critique of history" (Epps, "Politics of Ventriloquism," 287). Ironically and tellingly, in a work that purports to rewrite history and dismantle dominant Spanish ideology, Florinda La Cava is relegated to the position of abject Other.

Furthermore, in *Reivindicación* Florinda is present/absent as the raped text of the Spanish legends that Goytisolo seeks to destroy. As the author explains elsewhere, in this novel he attempts to use the phantasmagoric Spanish image of the Moor as a sexual aggressor to symbolically invade nationalist Catholic Spain and attack the myths and legends on which it is built through the sodomization of the Christian boy/younger narrator, Alvarito: "to give betrayal a dynamic and positive meaning, to extend it to language, to invert the attacked value system, to 'take' the legend from behind, to sodomize the myth" (*Crónicas sarracinas* 40). In *Reivindicación*, the narrator, using the second person to talk to himself, refers to how the Golden Age poet Góngora inspires him to attack language as well: "with the wondrous verses of the Poet inciting you to betrayal : encircling the word, breaking the root, forcing yourself upon [*forzando*] the syntax, violating [*violentándolo*] everything : one step away from the tempting Strait" (158). Clearly Goytisolo himself is enacting this attack on standard, traditional language usage through the unconventional syntax and punctuation with which he writes this novel. Moreover, by using the verb *violentar*, which can mean *to force, to disort,* and *to rape*, among other related meanings, Florinda La Cava is also substituted by language as the object of sexual(ized) attack. Goytisolo destroys traditional language, whether medieval texts revered as the medulla of Spanish origins or realist texts respected for their "faithful" reflection of reality, but in the process he also obscures the violence that the traditional texts wreak on Florinda. For this reason, Epps concludes:

> Hence, if Goytisolo is truly revolutionary, it is, at least from my position, in a way decidedly *different* from what the vast majority of his critics think. His radicalness lies not, as I see it, in the way

> he violates language, but in the way his language violates itself, in the way his language throws itself into something different. Reiterating the silent history of women's oppression, *Conde Julián* slips a scandalous truth into the body of the text and trips itself up in the process. ("Politics of Ventriloquism" 295)

Ironically, it is in an otherwise traditionalist narrative of the Muslim conquest that the most empowered Florinda emerges. A more recent work from the Arab world, the 2004 television series *al-Tariq* (discussed previously in chapter 3), allows more room for Florinda's subjectivity and has her overcome her experience of sexual aggression with the help of Amazigh Muslims. This Florinda echoes that of Zaydan in her innocence and virtue, but not in the reduction of her value to the maintenance of her virginity. Episodes 19 and 20 of *al-Tariq* show that Florinda is raped by Roderick, becomes suicidal as a result, but is saved by Roderick's servant ʿAbad, an Amazigh who was a childhood friend of Tariq. In episode 22, Julian and Florinda's Visigoth beloved, Sizut, try to help the depressed and dissociative Florinda. Though they are supportive, Florinda only wants to see Luʾluʾa, the Muslim Amazigh servant who was another childhood friend of Tariq. Luʾluʾa returns to Julian's household and by talking with her about what happened, Florinda recovers her mental health. Later, in episode 31, when Florinda is being held captive by Roderick in Hispania, Julian and Sizut seek Tariq's help in rescuing her and Tariq reassures Sizut by declaring: "She will return! That innocent girl will return, her freedom regained, just as tyranny will disappear, young man, from the lands [*diyar*] of al-Andalus" (14:30–14:40).

On one hand, while not departing radically from the basic storyline offered by the legend or giving her a particularly strong role, the TV series does manage to create a Florinda that both overcomes her victimization at the hands of Roderick and is reunited with her Visigoth beloved, largely due to the help of Amazigh Muslims. However, the window into this Florinda's thoughts and feelings is limited in comparison to the access offered to other characters' subjectivity. Although voiceover monologues are used to present the interiority of various other main characters, this never occurs with Florinda. In addition, ʿAbad and Luʾluʾa, who are instrumental in helping Florinda survive and recuperate, serve as extensions of Tariq. At the start of the series, the viewer sees a definitive moment in Tariq's childhood in which ʿAbad and Luʾluʾa are kidnapped to be sold as slaves in Iberia. In subsequent episodes, Tariq recalls that event and is haunted by his desire to save his friends, in particular his beloved Luʾluʾa. Consequently, ʿAbad and Luʾluʾa function as Tariq's proxies and their relationship with Florinda serves to glorify Tariq's conquest, extending the reach of his liberating influence, which in the context of this series is the liberating influence of Islam. In keeping with this, after Tariq and Lu'lu'a have been reunited, Tariq is called on to help Julian and Sizut save Florinda from Roderick, and his assurance that she will be saved places Florinda on par with the oppressed places of al-Andalus. Thus, although this representation does give Florinda more subjectivity and agency and allows her to successfully heal from trauma, the various stages of her recovery all exalt Tariq's role as liberator of Iberia and reduce Florinda to a symbol for the lands that he "liberates."

The various versions of Florinda in Arab and Spanish cultural production include an innocent near-victim whose value is reduced to her virginity—a treasure that is the right man's possession, a victim who is so overcome with shame that she commits suicide, a dangerous woman of questionable morals, nothing more than an abject cave, and a survivor of sexual assault who overcomes trauma. In all of these cases, the narratives subjugate Florinda by subsuming her to a broader ideological project, whether the promotion of a particular vision of al-Andalus through the figures of Tariq as consummate hero and Ibn Zaydun as symbol of cultural peak, or the iconoclastic destruction of constrictive Spanish nationalism. In each case Florinda is pressed into service to construct a particular type of male figure and is thus silenced.

In Search of Wallada: Sources and Discourses

In some ways, the figures of Florinda and Wallada, the most famous woman poet of al-Andalus, are complete opposites. The figure of an innocent, besieged Florinda contrasts with the prevailing image of Wallada as independent and witty, if not opinionated and sexually promiscuous or liberated (depending on one's perspective), and even with the high-culture version of Wallada from the Arab world, which sanitizes her as the beautiful beloved of a famous poet. Even the seductress version of Florinda is a despicable woman who does not have the refinement and artistry associated with most representations of Wallada. Whereas Florinda can be understood as more passive—whether as raped/conquered or set free by others, Wallada is often outspoken and active in the realms of literature, love, and possibly politics, and in one work in the realm of sexual politics. In addition, although there is no strong evidence to support the historical existence of a Florinda figure (whether by that name or any other), there is documentary evidence proving the existence of Wallada, scarcity of details notwithstanding.[9] What the historical record offers regarding Wallada presents an extremely intriguing figure, but because she is coopted for different purposes, details about her life are either cut out or embellished to suit certain needs. What emerges are two basic versions: a whitewashed Wallada who occupies a secondary, supportive role and has little to no voice and an embellished version of Wallada that reflects Orientalist projections and rigid conceptions of gender and sexuality. However, there are two works that depart from these patterns of representation.

According to what the historical record offers, Wallada bint al-Mustakfi (c. 1010–1091) never married and never had children; instead, she was a prominent figure in the cultural life of Cordoba because she ran a literary salon frequented by writers and members of the nobility, because she wrote her own poetry, and because she was the subject of many poems by Ibn Zaydun (1003–1070), perhaps the most famous love poet of al-Andalus. In her palace and salon gatherings, Wallada instructed younger women, such as Muhya, in the literary arts. Wallada lived during the end of the Umayyad caliphate of Cordoba and the beginning of the first *taifa* period—or period of smaller, independent Muslim-ruled states. She was the daughter of the penultimate Umayyad ruler of al-Andalus, Muhammad III, who ruled from 1024 to 1025. In 1031, after the abdication of the last Umayyad caliph, the prominent citizens of Cordoba granted power to Abu al-Hazm ibn Jahwar, a leading Cordoban sheikh, who soon developed a republican system of government. Ibn Zaydun served as a vizier for Abu al-Hazm. Wallada abruptly broke off her relationship with the poet-vizier, and at one point Ibn Zaydun was imprisoned for reasons that are unclear. He subsequently went into exile in the taifa of Seville and was only able to return to Cordoba near the end of his life. Although few of Wallada's poems were anthologized and preserved, what has survived includes erotic allusions and sexual explicitness in the forms of *ghuzal* (love poetry) and *hija'* (satire).[10]

Based on these facts about Wallada, she clearly does not fit common views of medieval women or Muslim and Arab women of any period. The unexpectedness of her profile and the limited and filtered medieval sources about her have given rise to a great deal of inference regarding other details about her life and her character. The popular image of Wallada, on both sides of the Strait of Gibraltar, is that of a refined, clever, strong-willed woman and even a seductive libertine. On one hand, the historical record presents little information and already includes a layer of interpretation. Teresa Garulo Muñoz notes the difficulties in corroborating and interpreting Wallada's biography according to medieval Arabic sources: the Wallada found in these sources is seen through the eyes of male biographers and historians who criticized her and asked for God's forgiveness on her behalf, without pointing to specific misdeeds (106–7).[11] On the other hand, in the face of what medieval historians and biographers do not specify, many have sought to fill in the gaps with what poetry suggests. For this reason, the extant literary corpus has led to a great deal of extrapolation and supposition.

Within the extrapolation from poetry, Arabic literature exhibits the more traditional, patriarchal tendency to consider Wallada to be a secondary figure. Given that the corpus of extant poems by Ibn Zaydun is much larger than that of Wallada, and that Wallada's corpus contains material considered unseemly—especially for a woman, many writers have dwelled on her as the object of desire, the muse for the more famous male poet. For this reason, in many Arabic literary histories and literary representations Wallada is considered part of Ibn Zaydun's story, not worthy of a story in her own right. Out of this perspective arises a common epithet for her: *habibat ibn Zaydun* (Ibn Zaydun's beloved). When this perspective is fused with a focus on the opulence of the Cordoban nobility and their cultivation of the arts, Wallada is referred to as *amirat Qurtuba* (princess of Cordoba).

The second tendency has been to piece together a biography, often on shaky interpretive ground, based on Wallada's and Ibn Zaydun's poems and references made in various sources. This has produced narratives along these general lines: Wallada refused to wear the veil and enjoyed flaunting her beauty. She had tempestuous relationships with two men: Ibn Zaydun and the wealthy Cordoban political figure Ibn ʿAbdus.[12] While Ibn Zaydun and Ibn ʿAbdus were rivals for her affections, Wallada was jealous of the attention Ibn Zaydun paid to one of her slaves, the singer ʿUtba. An incident related either to ʿUtba, to Ibn ʿAbdus, or to Ibn Zaydun's anti-Umayyad activities led Wallada to end their relationship and Ibn Zaydun's imprisonment was instigated by his rival, Ibn ʿAbdus.

Based on her autonomous lifestyle and outspokenness, many interpreters have seen Wallada as a proto-feminist.[13] In addition, in a related interpretation, starting in the nineteenth century some European scholars and writers have understood the obscene invective poems that Wallada's protégée Muhya directed at Wallada as proof that the two women had a lesbian relationship.[14] The verses in question suggest that Wallada had a child out of wedlock and lampoon her for her pursuit of sexual encounters with men. The reasoning behind the deduction is something like this: if Wallada and Ibn Zaydun had strong feelings for each other that they expressed in poetry (of longing and of insult) and this reflects an amorous relationship, then if Wallada and Muhya had strong feelings for each other that they expressed in poetry, they also had an amorous relationship. This false parallelism is based on a rigid understanding of relationships in which impassioned feelings are identical to romantic and erotic love. Since Muhya and Wallada's relationship seems to have been intense, rather than understand their interactions on a continuum comprising heterosexual and homosocial possibilities, including poetic and social rivalry, it is assumed that the two women had a homosexual bond, whose rupture or betrayal is reflected in Muhya's scathing verses on Wallada. Furthermore, this interpretation doesn't take into account the characteristics of the hija' genre—invective poetry that regularly included sexual allusions and developed from its original function of attacking enemy tribes to being used as a political tool or for social entertainment. Wilheim Hoenerbach alludes to this when he calls for critics and readers to interpret Wallada not as a courtesan who broke the moral code of her time but as a poet who was writing within the literary currents of her time and place (473).

The interpretation of Wallada as a feminist and/or a lesbian has been conditioned by Orientalist perspectives. For some critics and observers, for a woman with her (supposed) attributes and attitudes to have existed in a medieval Muslim setting, she must have been a pioneer and a rebel. Hoenerbach points to this problem when he states that "Westerners" are so used to the notion of passivity typical of the harem that they tend to locate active figures outside of their milieu and as part of the twentieth-century language of female emancipation (470–71). Layered on top of these assumptions is the Orientalist tendency to see the Orient as a space of sexual liberty and transgression. For these reasons, Garulo Muñoz rightly observes that in Western representations Wallada is wrapped up in Orientalist and feminist fantasies (98). The lesbian interpretation has been taken up by at least one Arab scholar, As'ad AbuKhalil, who conjectures that Wallada wrote love poems to Muhya that were suppressed because their content was considered immoral.[15] This line of reasoning, although not implausible, does not have any documentation to support it. Out of this interpretation of Wallada's life, she gained the title of "the Arab Sappho."

Wallada in the Arab World Part I: Ibn Zaydun's Beloved and Cordoba's Ornament

Although there is a tendency in Arabic letters to "clean up" Wallada by suppressing the bawdiness of her extant poetry and eschewing the libertine image that has grown from it, the image of a beautiful, witty poetess from the Cordoban caliphate has proven to be quite alluring. Wallada's appeal has yielded a plethora of literary works which are, at least ostensibly, focused on her.[16] Given the stature of Ibn Zaydun within the Arabic literary canon and the place of Wallada as part of the world of Andalusi poetry and refinement he represents, there are several male-authored Arabic verse plays that feature Wallada, though they are not exactly about her.[17] Although many of these plays refer to Wallada explicitly in their titles, Ibn Zaydun is consistently the main character. Wallada is relegated to the status of habibat ibn Zaydun (his beloved), and as such her notable characteristics are her beauty and elegance and her position as Ibn Zaydun's object of affection. In these works, Wallada has little to no interiority or agency.[18]

In the case of prose works by Arab authors, Wallada does not fare much better than she does in the male-authored verse plays. Her voice remains quite muted in the prose play *Sizif al-Andalusi* (*The Andalusi Sisyphus*, 1981) by Nadhir ʻAzma (b. 1930). This play, which was performed in Rabat in 1975 (165), invokes Sisyphus and his hubris together with the taifa period of al-Andalus to carry out a political commentary on the contemporary Arab world. The play presents a Wallada who, though clever, is also extremely jealous (29, 44). Moreover, in this work focused on political intrigue and the imprisonment of Ibn Zaydun, Wallada is largely a secondary character, appearing in about three scenes of the five-act play. Given that most of her lines consist of declarations of love, once again she is reduced to the role of habibat ibn Zaydun.

An Arabic novel that features Wallada functions similarly to silence her subjectivity. Rather than imagining what thoughts and feelings motivated her and considering the significance of her actions, let alone questioning typical representations of her, the author relegates her to a supporting role. *Hatif min al-Andalus* by al-Jarim, which I referred to in the discussion of Florinda, is one of many historical novels written by this Egyptian neoclassical poet and literary scholar. *Hatif* is a novelized biography of Ibn Zaydun, and thus from the outset it is clear that he will be the main character. What is striking in this text is that Wallada does not even occupy a secondary position but is eclipsed by the three other female characters of the novel: first, the Florinda stand-in, a woman named Florinda who has a gift for dancing and singing; second, Florinda's daughter, the dangerous ʻAʾisha (18), who is Ibn Zaydun's rejected beloved and a spy for the Castilians; and third, Naʾila al-Dimashqiyya, a crafty older Arab Cordoban lady who knows everything that's going on in the city and uses her cleverness to save Ibn Zaydun from ʻAʾisha's plot to ruin him.

William Granara points to the sociopolitical context that gave rise to *Hatif min al-Andalus*, indicating that al-Jarim "read[s] the rise and fall of Arab cultural superiority and political sovereignty in medieval Spain against the ongoing struggle throughout the Arab world for independence, the loss of Palestine, and the fragile state of pan-Arabism and political infighting" ("Nostalgia" 63). He argues convincingly that this context explains the prominence of "the themes of jealousy, disunity, and betrayal that are woven into the narrative" (66). Yet in my view, he overstates the shift from East–West conflict to internal Arab-Muslim struggles when he asserts that

> The biographical structure of *Hātif min Al-Andalus* pits the individual against society, where the east vs. west binarism is backgrounded, and the bifurcated Arab self takes center stage. The protagonist's obstacles are not those of the Christian enemy or the Reconquista, but fellow Arabs and Muslims, whose jealousies and petty rivalries provide both the novel's tensions of plot and its political messages. (Granara, "Nostalgia" 67)

This statement does not take into account the role of ʿA'isha, Ibn Zaydun's nemesis throughout the narrative. ʿA'isha is the daughter of an Iberian Christian (Florinda) and a Cordoban Arab, but she chooses to spy for the Castilians against the Cordoban state. In many ways she steals the show. For instance, Ibn Zaydun is so concerned about how she may try to seek revenge on him that he is haunted by her image (95–96). Also, throughout the novel the reader has access to Ibn Zaydun's thoughts and feelings and at various moments the same occurs with ʿA'isha. In contrast, Wallada has little to no interiority.

In *Hatif min al-Andalus*, al-Jarim whitewashes the risqué elements of Wallada and Ibn Zaydun's relationship and their poetry and wipes out the tumultuous end to their relationship. The novel ends with Ibn Zaydun and Wallada reunited in Cordoba: as he dies reciting poetry, Wallada cries at his side (240). The end result is that rather than simply relegate Wallada to the position of Ibn Zaydun's foil, as so many others have done, al-Jarim's novel makes her a marginal figure next to the dynamic Florinda, ʿA'isha, and Na'ila. Typically, Wallada stands for much of what is alluring about al-Andalus: beauty, nobility and its luxuries, and accomplished literary expression. But al-Jarim's novel, as Granara indicates, is aimed at portraying the sociopolitical problems of the taifa period and its *fitna* or internal conflict, in order to encourage readers to embrace pan-Arab unity. Rather than highlight the cultural grandeur of the Cordoban taifa by giving Wallada even a secondary role and some level of depth as a character, al-Jarim uses political intrigues and ʿA'isha's biculturalism to present the dangers of disunity and offers a *Dimashqiyya*—a Damascene and by extension a Syrian alliance—that saves the day. Avoiding the figure of amirat Qurtuba, the novel creates a very muted habibat Ibn Zaydun.

The 2005 Syrian *musalsal*, or one-season dramatic television series, *Muluk al-Tawa'if* (*The Taifa Kings*) gives Wallada a fairly prominent position, but it also circumscribes her in her established roles of princess (refinement and luxury) and beloved (mute object of longing). This series, written, directed, and produced by Syrians with a Syrian and Moroccan cast, focuses on the political and romantic intrigues of the taifa period in Cordoba, Seville, and Granada and the rise and spread of Almoravid rule from North Africa to Iberia. *Muluk al-Tawa'if* is the third in a sequence of historical series in Modern Standard Arabic, each focused on al-Andalus, by the same writer (Walid Sayf) and director (Hatim 'Ali).[19] Given the time period it covers, *Muluk al-Tawa'if* presents an al-Andalus of political intrigue and inner conflict, but one that nonetheless is a paragon of high culture.

Muluk al-Tawa'if consists of thirty episodes, and the character Wallada has speaking parts in five of these episodes (episodes 2–6), with a visual appearance in a sixth (episode 9). Ibn Zaydun is featured in the same episodes and a few more. The series opens with a scene of Marrakech's famous square, the Djemaa el-Fna, at the time of filming and labeled "Marrakech 2005 m." as a group of people in bedraggled medieval robes walk through the square singing. This chorus passes through an archway to an open-air marketplace and, as indicated by the new label "al-Andalus 427 h./1036 m.," it thus travels to the other side of the strait and into the past.[20] At various moments in *Muluk al-Tawa'if*, the chorus reappears in different locations. Calderwood, noting the role of the chorus in classical theater, discusses the chorus in this series as a mechanism for inviting viewers to participate in the projection of al-Andalus ("Proyectando al-Andalus" 239–40). At first, the image of al-Andalus to which the viewer is invited by the chorus to participate in projecting seems to be quite innovative. The chorus often appears singing the refrain "Despots were always the condition for invaders" [*In al-tagha kanu da'iman shart al-ghuza*]—a surprising and truly audacious message to be coming from Bashar al-Assad's Syria. The Wallada created by this narrative is quite audacious in many ways. She has more agency, with clear ideas about what she wants and demands in a relationship. She has strict boundaries regarding the behavior she will accept from a romantic partner and voices the difficulty of her decision to break off her relationship with Ibn Zaydun, in spite of still loving him. When Ibn Zaydun is imprisoned, even though the couple is already estranged, she is concerned about his welfare and suggests that she will help him escape. This Wallada starts out as an outspoken woman of action.

In episode 2 Wallada makes a dramatic entrance among the men gathered at her literary salon, with the music stopping and all eyes on her. She banters with the men and then meets Ibn Zaydun for the first time, talking politics and flirting with him. We then see them bidding each other farewell as he leaves her house at dawn. In the next episode, Ibn Zaydun demonstrates his jealousy over Ibn ʿAbdus's attempts at wooing Wallada, and Ibn Zaydun refers to her as "his." Wallada immediately replies that she belongs to no one, that there is parity between them (7:55). In a similar assertion of Wallada's autonomy and self-worth, in episode 4, again at a salon gathering in her palace, she asks which ghazal poems are the best. Ibn Zaydun replies, with veiled references to his relationship with Wallada, and concludes by saying that he follows his own *madhhab* (school of poetry and way of life). Then Wallada is asked her opinion regarding the question she posed. She replies that she believes in variety (just as there is no one ideal form of love poetry, there is no one ideal type of love) because not every woman wants the same thing. When pressed to say what she looks for in love, she replies:

> Audacity that is not mistaken for imprudence,
> Self-assuredness that is not obscured by arrogance,
> Delicateness, not confused with weakness,
> Patience that is not mistaken for powerlessness.
> A man that I give myself to as much as he gives himself to me,
> That doesn't see himself as being above me or beneath me.
> He isn't beyond me and he isn't striving to reach me. (14:08–15:41)

Later in the episode, out of jealousy Ibn Zaydun sends Ibn ʿAbdus a letter with an insulting poem, which he signs as if it were from Wallada. The invective poem circulates in Cordoba and is laughed about by many. Wallada takes Ibn Zaydun to task for being arrogant and speaking in her name. As she finishes telling him off, she speaks about possession and, making a play on words with *malaka*—meaning to possess or own and also to rule—she says: "It's easier for you and those of your ilk to run a kingdom [*al-mulk*] than to have a woman like me who no longer owns [*tamlik*] anything but herself" (34:50). After this strong declaration of her autonomy, their conflict escalates and Wallada kicks Ibn Zaydun out of her house.

In spite of her assertion of agency, ultimately in *Muluk al-Tawa'if* Wallada is relegated to the role of the silent beloved. In episode 5 Ibn Zaydun knocks on Wallada's door asking to see her. Her servant, following orders, sends him away, but Wallada silently watches him through the window as he stands in the courtyard entrance of her mansion. Later in the episode, Wallada tells her servant that she is closing her literary salon and that, though it pains her, her separation from Ibn Zaydun is final. Wallada and Ibn Zaydun appear next in a scene that echoes that of her framed behind her window. Here Ibn Zaydun sits in a corner of Wallada's courtyard, staring at the door, thinking about Wallada, and reciting to himself a famous poem he wrote: "She is absent from me, yet present with me [*Agha'ibatan 'anni, wa-hadiratan ma'i!*]" (33:55). As he gets up to leave, Wallada is looking at him from inside through the window, crying with her hand covering her mouth. Here Ibn Zaydun expresses his feelings at length in verse while she silences herself with her hand. He gets the last word while, in an ironic inversion of the poem, she is present yet absent.

Wallada does not appear in episodes 7 and 8 (though Ibn Zaydun does); in episode 9 Ibn Zaydun, who has been imprisoned and then escaped to Seville, reminisces about their relationship. While listening to musicians at a party, he recalls the image of Wallada looking at him through the window as he stands in her courtyard, and the viewers see the scene of her crying with her hand over her mouth. Wallada does not appear again in the series, and thus she is left in the position of being Ibn Zaydun's silent object of longing. In *Muluk al-Tawa'if*, although Wallada initially articulates complex ideas and demands equality, she is later silenced in the sense that Ibn Zaydun gets the last word while she repeatedly occupies the position of mute suffering.

This Wallada also bears resemblance to many of the previous versions in the sense that she functions as an ornament, a beautiful object that sets the scene of an opulent, cultured, and enticing al-Andalus. She always appears wearing very ornate, exquisite clothing and expresses herself in witty verse, though in the end, as we have seen, her active role in society ends on her break-up with Ibn Zaydun. As amirat Qurtuba she not only represents the exquisiteness of that age gone by, but she is a rare gem. In other words, in this TV series and other works she is portrayed as a complete exception with no female peers. Although the historical record shows that there were other women poets at the time, including at her salon (e.g., Muhya), the author of this script erases them.[21] The only other women who appear are servants who may sing but don't participate in the discussion or recitation of poetry. The contemporary Spanish representations of Wallada generally do not present her as reduced to the role of Ibn Zaydun's beloved. However, they do reiterate the vision of Wallada as a rare gem, as an exquisite ornament that completes the scene of a magnificent, thriving al-Andalus that in turn completes seductive cultural narratives. In so doing, they also silence her, although in different ways. This attitude toward Wallada is evident in Qabbani's "al-Andalusi al-Akhir" ["The Last Andalusi"], in which the speaker claims his right to elements of his familial and cultural legacy declaring "I am the last Andalusi / The one who came to ask for his share" and includes among the sentimental items and cultural artifacts sought "A poem by Ibn Zaydun / One of the rings of Wallada bint al-Mustakfi" (199).[22] Whereas Ibn Zaydun is remembered for his poetry, Wallada is remembered for her many rings. This poem's reduction of Wallada to a prized object, exquisite adornment, is paradigmatic of her role in the Arab and Spanish imaginary. In most works Wallada is either subjugated to Ibn Zaydun or as part of an alluring Andalusi scene.

Wallada in Spain: The Fictions of Rebellion

In twentieth- and twenty-first-century Spain, Wallada is still a recognized site of historical memory. Especially in the province and city of Cordoba, her name is synonymous with poetry and specifically women's poetry, as witnessed by the existence of the Asociación Literaria Wallada (Wallada Literary Association), a women's poetry group founded in Cordoba in 1982, and its annual publication, the literary magazine *Wallada: Revista de Poesía*. In terms of Spanish fictional works featuring Wallada, there are two plays and three novels that center on the Cordoban poetess using different literary styles and narrative techniques. In spite of their heterogeneity, four of the five point to and even foreground the hypothetical claim that Wallada was bisexual or homosexual. At the same time, they present problematic conceptualizations of gender and sexuality.

The earliest of the five Spanish works is *Wallada o los poetas* (*Wallada or the Poets*, 1986) by Jesús Riosalido (b. 1937), which is part of a series of three dramas about women and the role of Santiago Matamoros, or Saint James the Moor-Slayer, in their lives. Santiago is of great symbolic significance as the patron saint of the Christian Reconquista of Spain. This mythical figure is understood to be the Apostle Saint James who, legend has it, arrived in Iberia in the 800s to help the Christians battle the Moors. Thus, the Santiago element in the play is quite incongruous alongside a rebellious Muslim princess, and although it could have been used in an ironic or farcical fashion, it seems to be presented at face value. On one hand, this play establishes an intriguing Muslim-Christian syncretism; on the other hand, the level of fusion in the work leads to a lack of recognition of the connection between Santiago and anti-Muslim sentiment and action, plus a lack of distinction between different poets and periods of al-Andalus. Although the play presents Wallada as a rebel, she is not a model of the "emancipated," autonomous woman, but rather a victim of her own inflexible idealism. The text carries out this commentary through a process of generalization in which the violence associated with Santiago Matamoros is erased and Wallada is interchangeable with other Andalusi poets.

The pilgrimage to the shrine of Santiago Matamoros in Santiago de Compostela (Galicia), known as El Camino or the Way of St. James, began by the ninth century. It soon became one of the most important Christian pilgrimages of the Middle Ages and is still a popular spiritual exercise to this day. Pilgrims have long linked the Camino to the path traced by the Milky Way in the night sky, which is said to point travelers to Santiago de Compostela. In Riosalido's play, Wallada's unnamed servant, who is ostensibly Muslim, is a devotee of Santiago and makes constant references to him and the stars in the night sky, whether to encourage Wallada to seek the saint's guidance or to commend her soul to him on Wallada's death. Wallada refers to the saint by his Arabic name, Mar Yaʿqub, and although she never demonstrates faith in him, the drama does not pass any judgment on her for this, but presents her tragic end as a result of perfectionism.

In Riosalido's version of the story, Wallada has one failed amorous relationship after another—first with her protégée, Muhya, then with Ibn Zaydun, and finally with Ibn Abdus. In despair over the impossibility of finding a perfect, lasting relationship on Earth, Wallada commits suicide. Her declaration just before suicide—"My life is mine, understand? And I'll do whatever I want with it" (69)—could be read in isolation as a way of presenting suicide as a heroic choice. However, in the context of her servant's comments, it is presented as a misfortune that could have been avoided. Given that the servant is Wallada's moral guide, her reference to Wallada's life as a "tragedy" (71) frames it as an act of wanton willfulness. At this point, the servant asks Saint James to protect Wallada and take her to her loved ones, and the curtain closes as the servant sings a lullaby in Arabic.

Wallada o los poetas, which was performed in Madrid in 1986, is greatly informed by the author's background as an Arabist, yet that background did not keep him from falling into various cultural blind spots. Riosalido has a degree in Islamic law and, in addition to publishing various literary works, has served as the ambassador of Spain to Syria, Kuwait, and other countries. Much of the dialogue is made up of poems, a few by Wallada, some by Ibn Zaydun, and many by other poets of al-Andalus; the author notes that he himself translated these poems from the Arabic into Spanish using Spanish versification (6n1). Riosalido also explains that he divided the play into three main parts that follow the three thematic units of a traditional Arabic ode [*qasida*] (9). The mix of poems by different authors creates a cultural and poetic pastiche in which Wallada and the rest of the poets of al-Andalus are somehow interchangeable. The title of the play itself indicates this.

Furthermore, in spite of the author's expertise and his efforts to pay homage to the Arabic poetic tradition, he seems to not notice the incongruity of having an eleventh-century Muslim be devoted to Santiago Matamoros—the Moor-Slayer. Including the saint's name in Arabic does not in any way address the anti-Muslim sentiment for which he stood nor the political conflict in which he was taken up by the Christian side as the icon of triumph over the Muslim enemy. In addition to not mentioning what a Muslim perspective on Santiago Matamoros might be during the violent conflicts of the Reconquista period, the play coopts Ibn Zaydun as part of the Spanish tradition—not Hispano-Arabic but simply Spanish. A character in the play refers to him as the greatest poet of all of Spain (40), although Spain as such did not exist at that time and Ibn Zaydun never lived under Castilian or Christian rule. This cultural appropriation of Ibn Zaydun, alongside the generalization of Arabic poetry and lack of attention to the cultural politics behind the figure of Santiago, results in a portrait of Wallada that lacks specificity and merges her with other poets. Here Wallada is reduced to a needlessly idealistic poet as she is pressed into service to make a statement about Spain's cultural transformation in the postdictatorship period. That period was known for its countercultural movements, such as La Movida Madrileña (the Madrid Scene), responding to years of oppression with a reconfiguration of Spanish cultural expression and identity. This transformation included an explosion of culture and critique from the margins that included feminist and gay perspectives. Riosalido, who is slightly older than those who participated in the movement, seems to use this version of Wallada to criticize the idealism of Spanish women of the postdictatorship period. In the process, he silences various elements of Muslim-Christian cultural history in Iberia and ironically, in a work centered on Wallada, strips Wallada of her specificity and fashions her as one of many poets—or one of many idealists.

Another Spanish play about Wallada from just a few years later presents a very different version of the Cordoban poet's life story but ends up creating an equally constricted figure. The play *Wallada* (1990) by Jesús Alviz (1946–1998), is a lurid Orientalist vision of a Wallada who is celebrated for her sexual liberation, but one that is based on rigid conceptions of gender and sexuality and fantastic visions of the Orient. This play, which won a local theater prize, depicts Wallada as a lesbian who hates men because they have created a society that doesn't accept lesbianism, but who dresses and wears her hair in a masculine style.[23] The play opens with a graphic scene in which a group of Muslim eunuchs and a Muslim doctor carry out the bloody castration of a Catholic priest (5–6). Later it emerges that Wallada has ordered this castration and requested that the man's genitals be delivered to her. She feeds the excised organs to a panther as she complains to Ibn Zaydun about how problematic men are and tells him of her inner turmoil, which she expresses with the phrase "I want to love myself [*Quiero quererme*]" (10). As the play proceeds, it emerges that what troubles her is that she is in love with Muhya but cannot reveal this secret because of fear of social censure. Thus, in Alviz's work Wallada is a caricature of the man-hating, closeted lesbian. Once she emerges from the closet, though, she instigates a sexual and social revolution.

Against the backdrop of a Cordoba whose state of political and cultural decline is highlighted, Wallada is troubled by her love for Muhya. Eventually, perhaps taking a cue from her father—who is openly gay, appoints his male lover of humble origins as vizier, and then stabs to death one of the nobles who opposes this appointment—Wallada begins to take bold steps.[24] She reveals to Ibn Zaydun that she has rejected him because she is in love with a woman. In spite of his incredulity and derisive laughter, Wallada explains that she was raised with certain morals and it has been difficult for her to construct a new moral code for herself. Finally, she declares her love to Muhya and literally forces her to display their love in public (44–45). Muhya reciprocates Wallada's feelings but is not comfortable demonstrating this at a gathering of the nobility. Nonetheless, Wallada pushes her to do so, and in the face of negative reactions, she criticizes all the male guests for their hypocritical, closeted homosexual relations with Christian slaves, to which she ascribes the destruction of the once powerful Muslim kingdom. Wallada vows to make lesbianism as accepted as love between men and tells the nobles that their wives can forget about seeking pleasure with their eunuchs because there is greater pleasure elsewhere (45–48). Her actions actually instigate a change in not only how the women of Cordoba seek sexual pleasure but how they relate to men: women now go out without veils and look men in the eye, and some have sex among themselves (53).

The understanding of sexual orientation and gender roles as paired (i.e., lesbian = butch), persists in the play. Wallada explains to Muhya that as a girl her passions were horseback riding and archery, and she was pushed to leave those pursuits aside and be educated as a woman, but on meeting Muhya the Wallada of the bow and horse had been reborn (48–49). Similarly, she assumes that Muhya, as a woman, is especially adept at manipulating the feelings of others (50). Toward the end of the play Muhya complains of Wallada's domineering ways and jealousy—Wallada is worse than men—and says she is no longer in love with her (56–57). Muhya ends their relationship while the castle is being invaded by hordes who want to kill Wallada's father. As her father flees disguised as a woman and accompanied by a terrified Muhya accompanies him, Wallada insists on standing her ground. The last thing that is heard from her is a cry of impotence, presumably at her role in having suffocated Muhya's love (57, 60).

On one hand, this play presents a revolutionary Wallada who is able to inspire her contemporaries to end their subjugation to men, whether socially or sexually. On the other hand, this version of Wallada is built on both an essentialist conception of sexual orientation and gender roles and an essentialist view of the Orient as a space in which violence and sexual freedom are intertwined. Recall that the rationale behind interpreting the relationship between Wallada and Muhya as homosexual is based on assuming that that is the only logical explanation for the intensity with which Muhya rejects Wallada in her invective poems. Similarly, the false logic behind this depiction of Wallada is that frustrated lesbianism and an envious hate of men are the only ways to explain her fierce independence and that her irrepressible lesbianism is necessarily tied to masculine proclivities in hairstyle, clothing, and domineering treatment of others. This rigid formulation that pairs sexual orientation and gender roles ironically places the presumably liberated Wallada under the yoke of a traditionally male gender role. In this play lesbianism is not a sexual orientation, but the result of wanting to be a man, that is, wanting to have autonomy and power.

The vein of Orientalism in which Europeans negotiate their own relationships to sexuality and political conquest by viewing Arabo-Muslim spheres as havens for sexual freedom and/or aberration is well documented.[25] In Alviz's text this relationship with the Orient manifests itself particularly in the perverse fascination with the figure of the eunuch and in the idea that not only male homosexuality but (thanks to Wallada) lesbianism were widely practiced and somewhat accepted.[26] This view of al-Andalus in particular allows Alviz to use Wallada to create a "Spanish" tradition of homosexuality. But this creative construction of a tradition that can support late twentieth-century practices is carried out by masculinizing Wallada and exploiting the tradition of fascination with the supposedly aberrant Orient.

The three twenty-first-century Spanish novels centered on Wallada do not echo the themes of Oriental lasciviousness and masculinized lesbianism found in Alviz's play, but two of them, Magdalena Lasala's *Walläda la omeya: la vida apasionada y rebelde de la última princesa andalusí* (*Wallada the Umayyad: The Passionate and Rebellious Life of the Last Andalusi Princess*, 2003) and Matilde Cabello's *Wallada, la última luna* (*Wallada, the Last Moon*, 2000) are similarly problematic in that they present Wallada as a symbol of al-Andalus and savor its end. The third text, Miriam Palma Ceballos's *La huella de las ausencias: un relato sobre Walada* (*The Trace of Absences: A Tale about Walada*, 2009) offers the most innovative Spanish representation of Wallada.[27]

In Lasala's novel, Wallada is a rebellious woman along more classical lines. First, with regard to the form of the novel, it is rendered in the third person with an omniscient, uninvolved narrator. The novel does not directly identify Wallada as a lesbian but alludes to it through a leitmotif of Greek culture: the novel posits that Wallada's mother was a Greek-speaking Persian slave who refused to speak Arabic because it was the language of her owner, and that Wallada recites Greek poetry, wears Grecian robes, wishes to be like Aphrodite, and is educated through the poetry of Sappho, the seventh-century poet from the island of Lesbos (33, 38, 185, and 259–60). Moreover, Wallada is compared with Sappho and identifies with her (146, 193, and 278). Here Lasala gestures to an ambiguous sexuality: like Sappho, Wallada has been interpreted in subsequent eras as being homosexual and even a symbol of lesbianism, but there is no clarity regarding the sexual categories and practices of her time or her own life. At the same time, Lasala presents Wallada as a champion of feminism in that she credits her with facilitating women's education and liberty (226–27). Nonetheless, Wallada's student, Muhya, does not fare well in Lasala's account. Rather than portray mutual attraction between the two women, the text racializes Muhya and presents her as the archetypical vengeful mulatta (181–82, 228). Considering in tandem the Grecian theme and Muhya's racialized demonization, Lasala's novel works to create a Wallada who is affiliated with the ideals of classical Mediterranean antiquity, rather than the Arab world. At the same time, though, it focuses on Wallada and Ibn Zaydun's relationship representing the last hurrah of a decaying Cordoba and in this way dwells on the agony of the dying Muslim caliphate and relishes its death. The theme of classical Greek antiquity serves to make it easier to incorporate Wallada into the Spanish tradition, but the ambivalence regarding what to do with al-Andalus in the Spanish national narrative is quite strong. For this reason, the novel emphasizes beyond all else the scene of waning Muslim power.[28]

Lasala's novel, following the common gendered trope of equating woman to land/nation/empire, presents Wallada as a symbol of Muslim Iberia. Wallada and Ibn Zaydun's love is explicitly presented as a symbol of the resurgence of the crumbling Cordoba (16, 19, 236), but just as the happy days of their relationship are short-lived, so is the renewed flourishing of Cordoba: "What was more of a fantasy, their love or the hope of Cordoba?" (24). The narrative then establishes a direct correlation between Wallada and Cordoba: "Wallada is Cordoba, Cordoba could be called Wallada" (177). Just as Cordoba is extended to refer to all of al-Andalus, Wallada is equivalent to al-Andalus in its entirety: "Al-Andalus could have been called Wallada, the last princess of its splendor" (290). In this way, Lasala limits Wallada to the role of a splendid place, an object of desire that may be conquered and may crumble but will be longed for, an object that cannot take action but can only be acted upon.

The death throes of Cordoba, and metonymically all of al-Andalus, that are described often in the novel are repeatedly linked to the idea of "lastness" that is manifest in the subtitle: "The Passionate and Rebellious Life of the Last Andalusi Princess." Although Wallada was technically not the last Umayyad princess and was certainly not the last Andalusi princess, Lasala labels her as such because she was the last prominent Umayyad princess and extending this to the level of al-Andalus heightens the pathos of her figure and the extent of the finality of Muslim rule.[29] Throughout the novel the narrator refers to the protagonist as "the last princess," and in this way Wallada becomes a key prop in the staging of the scene of the end of al-Andalus. Similar to Lasala's 2004 *Boabdil: tragedia del último rey de Granada*, discussed in chapter 4, the continual reiteration of Wallada's finality is a way to emphasize and savor the end of Arab Muslim ascendance in Iberia and the inauguration of Castilian Christian ascendance.

Wallada, la última luna by Matilde Cabello (b. 1952), a journalist, poet, and novelist who was born in Cádiz but has lived in Cordoba since the 1990s, has a narrative structure that lends itself to foregrounding Wallada's subjectivity. Nonetheless the novel participates in the same objectification of Wallada as symbol of al-Andalus that manifests in Lasala's novel.[30] Cabello's text consists of Wallada's reminiscences and reflections, from the distance of old age, on her amorous relationships with Muhya, Ibn Zaydun, and Ibn Abdus. Wallada speaks in the second person, addressing an absent Muhya. In this version of her life story, she had a lesbian relationship with Muhya, who was her slave, but became infatuated with Ibn Zaydun and started a relationship with him and then sold Muhya, who had sought a new owner. The protagonist declares that Muhya was still her true love and laments her decision to sell her. Through this storyline, Cabello, like Lasala, points to the agony of Cordoba's demise, but rather than emphasize that demise and identify Wallada with al-Andalus, Cabello presents her as a symbol of Andalusia, understood as the inheritor of the Iberian Christian and Muslim Andalusi legacies. In the process, the fraught power dynamics of *andalucismo*'s embracing of *lo andalusí* comes to the fore.

In Cabello's text, much like in Lasala's, there is reference to the anguish of the end of the caliphate and the identification between Wallada's life and that of Cordoba. However, here the death throes of Cordoba are more readily apparent in the author's historical introduction than in the narrative itself. In the introduction there are references to "the agony of the Caliphate" (9, 11), whereas in the narrative the distress that pervades the text is Wallada's longing for Muhya. Moreover, the narrative highlights Wallada's realization that she did in fact inherit a great treasure from her Umayyad father.

Whereas in Lasala's novel Wallada makes references to the importance of leaving history in the past (25–26 and 283), by contrast, Cabello's Wallada notes that whatever injures or cures us in the past leaves a mark on us, affecting our present (21). This prepares the ground for her statement about the importance of her Arab father's legacy:

> For a long time I went around believing that I had no inheritance other than the jewelry and coins salvaged from plunder when the Caliph's palace stopped being my home. But by the light of those lamps that time turns on in our thoughts, I saw that there were many more treasures that the blood of my father had left in my heart. I knew then that the exquisiteness of my taste, my love for beauty and my passion for poetry and art were seeds that had flowered with the heat from the splendor that had surrounded my childhood. (21–22)

Given that the text refers to Wallada's mother's blue eyes, and many of the Umayyads had consorts from the Christian kingdoms, Wallada emerges as the daughter of an Umayyad caliph and a woman of Christian Iberian origin who is evaluating her dual cultural heritage. In this way, her realization is offered to all Spaniards, especially Andalusians, as a framework for understanding the role of the past in the present: the past that at first may be disdained as fruitless is actually the source of Andalusia's appreciation for all that is refined and artistic, that is, its sense of aesthetics.

Significantly, Cabello's novel is tied to the andalucismo movement via the date stamp on the last page. After being self-published in 2000, in 2005 *Wallada, la última luna* was published by Almuzara, a publisher that carries many titles related to Andalusian culture and history. With the publishing information typically found in the back matter, Almuzara included a note indicating that printing was completed on the same date on which Alfonso Lasso de la Vega y Jiménez-Placer, a prominent figure of cultural and political andalucismo, was born more than 100 years before and explaining how Lasso de la Vega is related via intellectual genealogy to two of the most important figures in andalucismo. This tagging of Cabello's novel as linked to the champions of andalucismo makes the weight of the text's message clear: Andalusia is the inheritor of al-Andalus's cultural talents, and both the inheritance and the inheritor should be recognized as such.

Within this allegorical presentation of Wallada, what is the role of her longed-for lover, Muhya?[31] Like Lasala, Cabello racializes Muhya, referring to her as having brown skin (37, 38). However, rather than create a vengeful Other, Cabello's brown Muhya is constantly pined for. The object of Wallada's taboo love is like the *moriscos* from the perspective of a certain vein of andalucismo: expelled and then longed for. Tellingly, in this narrative Muhya may receive Wallada's reminiscences and reflections on love, but she never responds in any way. Wallada calls her former slave over to help her reconstruct her life story (16) and even commands her to speak, saying, "Break your silence, Muhya" (28), but Muhya never speaks. Her silence is so complete that it seems that she is in fact not present but a figure conjured up by the imagination of the aging Wallada. Thus, Cabello's narrative reproduces the dynamics of Spanish–morisco relations; Muhya, though the contributions of her culture are prized, has no voice. As Pilar Moyano notes, Cabello's text sets out to rectify male-authored versions of history in which Wallada is only deemed important by virtue of her relationship to Ibn Zaydun (13–14). In the process, though, Cabello creates a narrative about Andalusia carrying the rich inheritance of the Arabo-Muslim past while symbolically silencing voices from that past.

One of the most innovative elements of Cabello's approach to representing Wallada is that she offers a portrait of Wallada in old age, during her "last moon" as the subtitle indicates. Cabello thus avoids re-creating the figures of the ornamental princess and the poet's beloved. Similarly, the lyrical novella *La huella de las ausencias* by Palma Ceballos, a professor of German literature at the University of Seville, depicts an aged Wallada. Rather than focus on the agonizing caliphate or its celebrated yet suppressed inheritance, this narrative critiques the objectification of women and uses metafiction to question the creation of historical icons.

Like Cabello's text, Palma Ceballos's novella is presented from the perspective of an aged Wallada, this time speaking to Ibn Zaydun. This ethereal Wallada, who at the end of the narrative is moribund, elucidates the relationship between women's age and objectification: "Old age is the best veil for women, because it exempts us [*nos redime*] from the burden of being valuable merchandise. Old age is the best veil for women, because it finally throws us into a space of acrid freedom by knowing we are not owned by anyone" (145). At another moment in the text, Wallada expresses regret at not having appreciated her mother more, not having seen her through eyes other than those of her father, who viewed her mother like a valuable object (30). Though ghost-like, Wallada remembers her years of vigor: she enjoyed scandalizing people, but when she asked sincere questions they were seen as brazenness (20–21, 36–39). Rather than occupy the position of Muhya's owner, as in Cabello's text, this Wallada remembers Muhya as a close friend, not a lover, and repeatedly recalls her rejection of women's subjected role as a man's possession.[32] In this way, Palma Ceballos's Wallada dismantles the very bases of the constructions of Wallada as Ibn Zaydun's beloved and as ornamental princess.

While Cabello's Wallada receives the gift of poetry from her father, Palma Ceballos's protagonist, like that of Lasala, learned about music and poetry from her mother and the other slaves (30). Using that knowledge, Wallada sets out to tell her own story in order to reach her final resting place: "I feel that if I am able to delimit with words my history [*mi historia*] or my fiction, I will be able to rest at last" (15). The novella points to Wallada's story as fiction; it does not subject her story to constructions of truth as History and thus avoids repeating the subjection of Wallada. Breaking with the model of the historical novel that aims for linearity and an accuracy that accesses the truth, Palma Ceballos's work recognizes that Wallada's story is just as much history as it is fiction. The title of her novella alludes to the only Wallada available in the twenty-first century: a trace of absence. Indeed, the epigraph to the novella places the whole work within an awareness of the fictionality and narrative construction of Wallada. Taken from the Uruguayan Spanish writer Cristina Peri Rossi, the epigraph reads: "Women are books that must be written / before dying / before being devoured / before being left castrated [*Las mujeres son libros que hay que escribir / antes de morir / antes de ser devorada / antes de quedar castrada*]" (7).[33] Wallada is a story, but one that must be written to try to keep her memory alive and maintain whatever power she may represent.

Although all of the Spanish texts on Wallada give her more agency, with the exception of Palma Ceballos's *La huella de las ausencias*, they all subject her in other ways. Some of the Spanish works, namely, those of Riosalido and Alviz, also subject the figure to limiting conceptions of gender and sexuality. Like many of the Arabic-language works, some of the Spanish works (those by Riosalido, Alviz, Lasala, and Cabello) use Wallada to stand in for al-Andalus, a compendium of everything that it represents, except for convivencia: power and glory, political intrigue, beauty, passion, jealousy, and indulgence in love and pleasure. Although a pronounced trend in Arabic literary discourses has been to suppress Wallada as too obscene or as demonstrating too much agency, Spanish writers typically understand her writing as identical to her being and meld these extrapolations based on false logic with the rhetoric of their own agendas. However, Palma Ceballos's work suggests that texts about historical figures must maintain an awareness of their status as reconstructions: whether based on the figure's writings or not, fictions about these legendary and historical figures are artifacts that reflect their own moment of conception.

Wallada in the Arab World Part II: Time Travel and Textual Construction

The 1997 novel *Wallada bint al-Mustakfi fi Fas* (*Wallada, Daughter of al-Mustakfi, in Fez*) centers on Wallada in a way that radically departs from other representations of her precisely by recognizing her as a textual construction. This novel by ʿAbd al-Rahman Muhammad Yunus (b. 1955), a Syrian literary critic and novelist who spent several years living in the Maghreb as a university student, is a postmodern folktale in which the main element of the fantastic is the unquestioned presence of Wallada and other historical figures in late twentieth-century Fez, Morocco. By playing with the mythical constructions of historical figures and traditional popular narrative forms, Yunus creates a novel that employs Wallada and a pastiche of historical periods to criticize the intertwined power dynamics of politics and sexuality.

In *Wallada bint al-Mustakfi fi Fas*, four historical figures from three different time periods are presented as visitors from al-Andalus in modern-day Fez. The historical figures are magically transferred into the twentieth century in that during their visit to Fez they carry Spanish *pesetas*, drink cocktails made of Black & White whiskey and Coca-Cola, and ride in cars. The four figures are Wallada and Ibn Zaydun; ʿAbbas Ibn Firnas (810–887), an inventor, physician, engineer, and musician who is said to have attempted flight with wings that he constructed; and ʿAbd al-Rahman I (731–788), the son of an Umayyad prince and Amazigh mother who fled from the Abbasid revolution in Damascus to Iberia, where he proclaimed himself emir of Cordoba, thus establishing a government that splintered off from the caliphate of Damascus and that his progeny turned into the caliphate of Cordoba. These figures are somehow immortal and live simultaneously with twentieth-century characters in a world that blends together modern technologies and consumer goods (such as television, remote control curtains, and Coca-Cola) and powerful men who own opulent palaces, odalisques (female slaves or concubines), and eunuchs. This combination of elements gives the novel the flavor of a modern version of the *One Thousand and One Nights*.

In the fantastical world of the novel, ʿAbd al-Rahman I (known as "al-Dakhil," the one who entered) is the political rival of a Moroccan leader, the Wali Qarqush al-Iskhariyuti.[34] The administrative title Wali was used during the caliphate and in the Ottoman Empire to refer to governors of administrative divisions. In Morocco, King Hassan II started to use the term *Wali* in the early 1980s to refer to regional leaders, and by 1997 it was an official title used to designate the governor of a region.[35] In this novel the Wali is a despised dictator figure who can be interpreted as representing King Hassan II, whose reign (1961–1999) is known for its poor human rights record and near-dissolution of parliamentary democracy, Syrian President Hafez al-Assad whose regime (1971–2000) was similarly marked by autocratic militarism, or despotic rulers in general.[36] For this reason, the novel can also be read as a political allegory. The Wali character's name adds to the narrative's strong criticism of despots. The character's surname, al-Iskhariyuti, is the Arabic form of Iscariot, as in Judas Iscariot who betrayed Christ with a kiss in exchange for money.[37] Thus the Wali symbolizes ultimate betrayal against one's people in pursuit of personal gains. Along with money and power, the Wali obsessively pursues sexual pleasure, and it is through sex that his conflict with Wallada is played out.

In the same way that the novel compresses time to bring together historical and fictional characters from different periods, it presents an ambiguous notion of space. In addition to the multiple possibilities for the allegorical referent of the Wali, Fez works well as the setting because it is a city associated with Andalusi culture via the various waves of exiles who settled there and still identify as Andalusi. In that sense it is an Andalusi city in Morocco. Furthermore, Wallada is frequently referred to as a princess from "Gharnata" (the Arabic name for Granada), though she is also linked to Cordoba, al-Andalus, and Alicante. Granada functions as a metonymic equivalent to al-Andalus and as a sign of the persistence of al-Andalus into the present day. In the same way that the novel is a pastiche of historical periods and geographic spaces, it is a heteroglossic mix of registers. The book intersperses quotations from the Quran, classical Arabic poetry, Sufi poetry, an erotic treatise, Wallada's bawdy poems lampooning Ibn Zaydun, French, and Moroccan colloquial Arabic (*darija*). These juxtapositions highlight the connections between seemingly disparate times, places, and discourses. This dynamic is seen in microcosm in a brief reference to the modern social issue of clandestine emigration to Spain. On the third page, one of the characters hears a song that offers a guide to understanding the rest of the novel. The song is a lament in which "We are crying for the last friends that were swallowed up by the ocean while traveling in the direction of

Alicante to look for light, the North Star, and the virgins of paradise in al-Andalus" (14). Space and time are compressed, and Alicante and al-Andalus become synonymous to suggest that just as desperate North African migrants risk their lives to cross the Strait of Gibraltar in search of an idealized paradise on Earth, Arabs and Maghrebians sustain losses when they idealize al-Andalus. By compressing and melding temporal and territorial spaces and the rhetorical styles of different registers, Yunus's novel makes a statement about the romanticization of al-Andalus as well as the power dynamics and resulting socioeconomic oppression that have endured since that time.

The storyline of the novel centers on the main male characters trying to use Wallada to satisfy their sexual desires and/or to reach their personal and political aims and on her responses to these efforts and the power dynamics in which they are enmeshed. The main male characters include Ibn Zaydun, Ibn Firnas, the Wali, and a twentieth-century Moroccan *faqih*, or expert in Islamic jurisprudence, named al-ʿAwmari. The novel begins by showcasing the hypocrisy of Shaykh al-ʿAwmari, who is known to frequent bars and brothels. The many vignettes related to him criticize male objectification of women and double-standard patriarchal norms regarding sexuality. At the same time, al-ʿAwmari is haunted by the situation of his wife, which, while suggesting that women are complicit in their objectification and subjugation, reveals the role of socioeconomic disparity in gender oppression.

The wife of al-ʿAwmari, Fatima al-Idrisi, has been imprisoned by the Wali, who became jealous when she married al-ʿAwmari and is charging Fatima with threatening state security by spreading socialism. From captivity Fatima calls out to Abd al-Rahman I for help as if he were a saint (108, 12–13, 146). The mythical ruler visits her in her prison cell but initially says that he cannot help her because he needs Wali Qarqush's support for political reasons (120, 124). In an effort to gain her freedom, Fatima tempts Abd al-Rahman with her body, but later, in the face of the Wali's sexual aggression, she tells him that she would rather die than give him her body and that she won't sell her body for her freedom (141–42). This may seem like a contradiction, given that this is what she was trying to do with Abd al-Rahman, but Fatima has provided the key to understanding her seemingly incongruous statements and the unorthodox treatment of historical figures in the novel as a whole.

In an earlier conversation, Fatima criticizes Abd al-Rahman for allowing prostitution and drugs to flourish in his lands, and he responds wryly that she is gambling with her body by offering it to him. Fatima retorts that "poverty is what degrades women" (117). She is the last Idrisid princess (141), but since that dynasty is defunct, she no longer has monetary power and is willing to offer her body to Abd al-Rahman to avoid impending rape by the Wali.[38] Interestingly, her comment about the nexus between women's degradation and economic inequity arises from Abd al-Rahman's boastful citation of a poem about the wondrous mosque he built in Cordoba. Fatima criticizes poets' accounts of Abd al-Rahman vis-à-vis the reality of his rule. Perhaps to spur Abd al-Rahman to take action on her behalf, she criticizes poets for having "falsified history" in exchange for payment; they wrote about his glorious feats when he also "turned the peninsula into a big bordello" (117). As the conversation continues, Abd al-Rahman explains that the poetry about him is like that because of Arabic rhetorical flourishes and that the Arab gift for words cannot be denied. Fatima responds by once more pointing to the ways writers have idealized historical figures: "What pains me and makes my head spin is that with the fabrications of this language and its gyrations we transform defeat into heroism. … Here we have that language has made a hero out of you . … But where is your courage?" (118). Fatima's stance toward historical figures and the discourses about them echoes that of *Wallada bint al-Mustakfi fi Fas* as a whole. In this narrative, the figures as they appear in historical record and collective memory are understood as textually constructed and thus open to textual reconstruction. Words have the power to distort and also creatively reshape iconic figures.

Later in Fatima's conversation with Abd al-Rahman, he asks her why her family or husband are not trying to set her free, and she tells him that "a prostitute named Wallada bint al-Mustakfi" arrived in Fez and put a spell on her husband, doing away with his ability to reason (137–38). On one hand, in a comical moment typical of the novel, on hearing Wallada's name Abd al-Rahman roars "who gave that harlot [*ʿahira*] an exit visa to leave Granada?" (138). He explains that he had banned her from travel because of the havoc she had wreaked there: corrupting women's morals, giving women ideas about equality, turning her house into a brothel, and so on. Abd al-Rahman says he will go right away to establish a "joint defense agreement" with the Wali and settle his accounts with "that whore" [*qahba*], and promises to return after that to free Fatima (138). On the other hand, Fatima does not know that while al-ʿAwmari has certainly indulged in many distractions and cannot conceive of confronting the Wali himself, he has asked Wallada to steal the Wali's sword and free Fatima.

The only sword in Fez is that of the Wali and, while Ibn Zaydun wants Wallada to steal the sword to resolve his own conflicts in "Gharnata," Shaykh al-ʿAwmari wants Wallada to steal the sword to free his wife. The sword can be read as a phallic symbol in that it represents both the

Wali's sexual power and the power of the phallus, that is, patriarchal authority, in general. Ibn Zaydun brings up the sword in the context of his jealous complaint that Wallada steals men from their wives and so she might as well steal the Wali's sword (29). Given this context, the text suggests that Wallada stealing the sword is tantamount to her having sex with the Wali. Yet true to their double standards, Ibn Zaydun and al-ʿAwmari hold it against Wallada when they think that she has submitted to him sexually. I return to the encounter between Wallada and the Wali later, after addressing the portrait of Wallada created by Yunus.

In relation to the patterns of representation seen in other works, on the one hand, Yunus's novel disrupts the habibat Ibn Zaydun paradigm in that in this text Ibn Zaydun has a decidedly secondary role as compared with that of Wallada, and their relationship is more complex. The omniscient, uninvolved narrator criticizes Wallada for having sex with Ibn Zaydun even though she feels hostility toward him (182), and Ibn Zaydun is frequently criticized by the narrator, Wallada, and other characters for his excessive jealousy, which can be understood as a form of dependency on Wallada. On the other hand, the novel plays up—and arguably plays with—the image of Wallada as the princess of Cordoba. Yunus's novel characterizes her as wealthy, fond of opulence, and concerned by aesthetics, yet at the same time she enjoys hanging out in a bar full of the city's riff-raff and exploring working-class restaurants (180). With regard to Wallada as a representative of feminist ideals, Yunus's version is equally ambiguous. I argue that in this novel just as the princess is brought down to Earth, so is the mythical feminist heroine.

Wallada's legendary beauty is integral to images of her as Ibn Zaydun's beloved and as the symbol of Cordoban splendor. In contrast, in *Wallada bint al-Mustakfi fi Fas*, although Wallada's proverbial beauty is a central element of her persona, the beauty myth writ large is dismantled. Similarly, conceptualizations of women's sexuality are reworked in the course of the novel. Beauty and sexuality are the tools with which Wallada will ostensibly take possession of the Wali's sword. At first Wallada dreams big and fantasizes about taking over control from the Wali and putting an end to his oppression. She thinks of stealing the sword and freeing the Wali's women, slaves, and prisoners, mentioning by name actual political prisoners such as the poet Abdellatif Laâbi, a writer from Fez who was imprisoned and tortured (1972–1980) by the government of Hassan II (42). Having noted earlier that cultural tastes had declined in Fez, if she were to gain control she would replace unjust imprisonment with cultural development: "If God were to give her authority, she would tear down all of Fez's prisons, build a new Okaz, and fill the markets with every type of book, newspaper, and magazine" (42). Okaz [ʿUkaz] in modern-day Saudi Arabia was the site of a renowned marketplace where pre-Islamic poetry competitions were held. Here the famous site of cultural exchange and flourishing is invoked as an alternative to oppression for which there is an Arab precedent. Nonetheless, before carrying out that grand vision, Wallada must capture the Wali's sword, but having sex with the Wali would confirm all of the negative stereotypes surrounding Wallada and women in general in this text.

Although a few of the Spanish representations of Wallada present her as sexually liberated in a positive sense, in Yunus's novel, the image of Wallada as a loose woman—one who is too sexually available—is toyed with and eventually rejected. Recall that Abd al-Rahman I refers to Wallada as a harlot and a whore, using the same term sometimes associated with Florinda (*qahba*). Ibn Firnas maintains this association between Wallada and loose morals and expresses negative views about women in general. When Ibn Firnas meets Wallada, he thinks that she's a slave girl [*jariya*] and offers al-ʿAwmari the wings he has invented in exchange for her. Wallada harshly sets Ibn Firnas straight, explaining that she is Wallada, the princess and poet: "I am not bought nor sold ... I give myself when I wish to" (39–40). Similarly, she asserts her autonomy when she tells Ibn Zaydun that she is a free woman, no one owns her (151); when an undaunted Ibn Firnas asks al-ʿAwmari to give him the gift of just one night with Wallada, al-ʿAwmari wonders why some people still view women as a "sweet thing" and tries to explain that she is a princess, not somebody who can be given as a gift (166). Here Ibn Firnas's misogyny come to the fore as he responds that it doesn't matter what title she carries, he needs her and she is a woman no matter the title, so she must know how to "spread her legs swiftly on a bed" (167). Ibn Firnas makes an attempt at explaining his attitudes by referring to his experiences of rejection by women on the basis of his lack of good looks. But the misogyny continues when Wallada subsequently lies to Ibn Firnas about what she is doing that night and he thinks about women and their deceptive ways and judges Wallada as sexually promiscuous (182–83). When he once again asks al-ʿAwmari to give him Wallada for one night, al-ʿAwmari explains that she is the one who chooses when she will give herself (184).

In a turn in the course of Ibn Firnas's attitudes, although he knows that al-ʿAwmari and Wallada are leaving to have sex with each other, he playfully quotes a text that offers advice for al-ʿAwmari on foreplay—to be sure to satisfy the woman he is with, because if not it will be a waste of her energy—and states that "pleasure must be mutual in order to satisfy all of the senses" (186–87). A footnote indicates that this quote is taken from *The Perfumed Garden of Sensual Delight* (*al-Rawd al-ʿAtir fi Nuzhat al-Khatir*) by Muhammad ibn Muhammad al-Nafzawi (187), which was written in the fifteenth century in what is now Tunisia. By pointing to the importance of women's sexual fulfillment, even in jest, Ibn Firnas rises above his misogynistic attitudes and shares an understanding of women as subjects who deserve to pursue and attain pleasure. In parallel, by referencing a classical sex manual and work of Arabic erotic literature, Yunus is reclaiming sexuality, and specifically women's right to sexual pleasure without being labeled immoral, as part of Arab tradition.[39] Wallada responds by praising Ibn Firnas's expertise and recommending that he put it into practice, which he does with a prostitute whom he treats so well that she decides not to charge him and to leave the profession for good. Thus, though the quote from al-Nafzawi's erotica is introduced jokingly, in keeping with the mood of the novel, through Ibn Firnas's subsequent actions the validity of women's right to sexual pleasure is affirmed.

Furthermore, rather than the idealized or critiqued "emancipated" woman found in most of the Spanish texts, Yunus's Wallada emerges as an autonomous woman caught in the web of the patriarchal system's accumulated absurdities and contradictions. This situation is most prominent when Wallada comes face to face with the Wali and meets her greatest challenge: overcoming her own sexual desires. The Wali proclaims that he will humiliate Wallada just as he did Fatima (175), that is, he will subjugate her sexually. The Wali's chief of staff knows that if the Wali treats Wallada in that way, given her standing, it will lead to negative repercussions with Abd al-Rahman I and other leaders. For this reason, he transforms the arrest order into a dinner invitation, warns Wallada that the Wali hates poets and is incapable of containing his sexual urges, and promises to help her escape if necessary (177, 206). The Wali is aware that he should not treat Wallada with his usual aggression and sets out to seduce her. Wallada's initial challenge—how she can capture the mythical sword without becoming the proverbial whore—is transformed into how she can survive her evening with the Wali without submitting to her own sex drive and the aggressive insistence of a man she finds loathsome. Paradoxically, to prove that she is not a harlot (not willing to have sex with a despicable despot), she must forgo the sword and focus on controlling herself. Thus, by viewing the despot as despicable she has already proven her worth.

The contradictions and compounded conflicts created by the patriarchal system are further illustrated by the contrast between Wallada, Fatima, and the unnamed odalisque who was originally scheduled to spend that night with the Wali. The slave girl who was supposed to sleep with the Wali was looking forward to it and had spent the whole day preparing. When she is warned by one of the servants that the Wali is harsh and ill-tempered and that she should humble herself before him, she replies "I will be the ground and a shoe ... so that, God willing, I can enjoy him" (176). In a sense, by being as subservient as possible, she is complicit in her own subjugation, yet like Fatima, she has no choice and is trying to make the best of the situation. In contrast, Wallada is repulsed by the Wali, his inability to appreciate culture, and his unjustified imposition of his power, and her social standing allows her to reject him. In confirmation of Fatima's statement about the effect of poverty on women, the Wali violently rapes Fatima but initially only attempts to seduce the wealthy, well-connected Wallada.

When Wallada arrives at the Wali's palace, she soon notices the power of the sight of her body over the Wali. In another of her comparisons between Granada and Fez, she observes that the people of Granada are "more balanced and logical in the way they deal with matters of the body and sexuality" (209). Another social commentary arises when Wallada insists that the Wali call in the chief of staff to join them, and he is visibly nervous and unable to relax in his tyrannical boss's presence. Wallada notes this and ascribes it to the lack of democracy and freedom of thought in the Arab world (211). Meanwhile, the Wali is aware that he is before the legendary beauty, and as usual, he is having trouble controlling "the always awake beast of his body" (212). Because Wallada is a princess, he tells himself that he needs to go about things the "civilized" way and asks her to marry him (212). Trying to trick him, Wallada says that she can't because she is already married and three months pregnant. As the Wali, infected with the "bacteria" of sex, nonetheless continues to try to seduce her, he gives her a tour of his palace that includes a hall of naked dancers and his opulent, pleasure-dome bath (212, 214).

The narrative then jumps to Wallada, looking ill, picking up her three friends from the bar and whisking them away to return to Granada with her and thus escape the Wali's rage. Once they are on the "Andalusi" ship heading for Alicante, she tells her friends about her experience in the palace and how the chief of staff and one of the slaves saved her from imminent rape. Ibn Zaydun doesn't believe that she could resist her own lust, and al-ʿAwmari is also skeptical. Wallada admits that the bathhouse affected her, but insists that in the face of that loathsome man, she controlled her sexual appetite (222). Still not believing her, Ibn Zaydun uses a metaphor about a dog licking a food container to say that Wallada is now ritually unclean and needs to be purified. When Ibn Firnas defends her by saying that the Wali didn't "lick the container" but only her clothes (224), al-ʿAwmari says that they should wash her caftan. Hurt by the attitude of Ibn Zaydun and al-ʿAwmari, who themselves have been "implanted with the bacteria of sex, lust, and doubt," Wallada asks herself rhetorically, "Even if the Wali had been successful in taking my body and spirit, would that have turned me into a prostitute [ʿahira]?" (224). Thus, through Wallada, Yunus's novel raises questions about what constitutes proper behavior for a woman and how this interacts with sexual violence.

In the denouement of the novel, the beauty myth and misogyny are undone through Wallada and Ibn Firnas's relationship. On the ship (back) to al-Andalus, Wallada notes that Ibn Firnas, who calls her "a holy, pure woman [*al-tahira al-muqadisa*]," (225) immediately believed her account of her encounter with the Wali. Consequently, Wallada appreciates him greatly and wants to devote herself to making him happy. When she invites him to a dark corner of the ship, which incidentally is called "Liberty [*Libarti*]" (224), to make love, he offers himself to her as an "obedient husband," and she accepts his marriage proposal (226). In the same way that Ibn Firnas's vision of women is transformed in the course of their escapades, Wallada comes to value his honorable character in spite of his unattractive physique. After Ibn Zaydun and al-ʿAwmari stand before "the legendary woman" to ask for forgiveness, al-ʿAwmari expresses his sadness over the fact that Wallada did not steal the sword and free his wife (226–27). Ibn Firnas steps in, promising to save al-ʿAwmari's wife from the Wali, presumably by means of his winged flying device. This raises the issue that Wallada was able to save herself but not another woman, as Fatima is still suffering in the Wali's prison, but simultaneously ignites the hope that she will be saved via the regeneration of Ibn Firnas and thus indirectly through Wallada's triumph over the Wali. This hope, together with Wallada's ability to withstand the Wali's attempts at seduction and her ability to appreciate Ibn Firnas for his good character, make it such that Wallada, although not reaching the status of a perfect heroine, does reach redemption.

In keeping with the novel's critique of the rhetorical idealization of Andalusi figures, via Fatima's comments and the configuration of the novel as a whole, a complete heroicization of Wallada is eschewed. Unlike Florinda, she does not sacrifice herself (her body) to capture the sword/phallus and renew Arab culture. At the same time, Wallada is not relegated to the status of loose woman. Instead, she gains control and thus true ownership of her sexual desire by rejecting the Wali's seduction and choosing a relationship with the faithful Andalusi polymath, regardless of physical appearance.

The novel closes with the ship arriving in al-Andalus at dawn as Ibn Firnas sleeps on Wallada's chest, dreaming of building the most beautiful airport for his planes that will continue to fly "until God exchanges these times for new times" (228). This compression of time that brings hope via a new dawn of future inventions is followed up by an announcement from the ship's captain that further melds timeframes. The "captain of the ship [*rabban al-bahira*]" replicates the welcome statements made by airplane pilots (also *rabban* in Arabic) on landing, welcoming the passengers to Alicante, home of "the most desirable women on Earth and in history" and wishing them a pleasant stay with their "family, loved ones, and lovers" (228). The linked meanings of *rabban* support the play between time periods that simultaneously highlights the continuity of the past into the present and a playful, irreverent approach to history and its mythical figures. The novel uses fantastic elements and bawdiness that are reminiscent of Arab folktales to translate Wallada and other historical Andalusi figures into contemporary settings and thus comment on various forms of oppression in today's world. In Yunus's narrative, although Wallada does not become the heroic agent of change that she initially dreams of being, her adventures across time and space highlight the many obstacles to this change that are created by the mechanisms of the patriarchal system and by the rhetoric surrounding historical figures. This Wallada is transhistorical in the sense that she exists across time periods and also in the sense that she cuts through and lays bare the construction of historical icons.

* * *

In contrast with Florinda, who is only the object of discourse and is thus created (or in the case of Goytisolo's novel, destroyed) through that discourse, Wallada herself produced texts. However, given their bawdy nature, Wallada's extant verses have led to efforts at suppression or convoluted interpretations of her life. Nonetheless, her position as poet has perhaps made it more likely for modern-day writers to imagine her interiority and give her a stronger voice. In Spanish texts, while Florinda embodies the fall of "Spain" (a predated Spain), Wallada usually embodies the fall of the splendor of al-Andalus. In both Spanish and Arab traditions, whether Wallada is largely an accessory or the protagonist of the narrative, she typically functions to set the scene of al-Andalus, to complete the image of its refinement, beauty, and intrigue. By the same token, she is symbolically silenced (or complicit in the silencing of others in the case of Cabello's text), and an exception among other women of her time. Regarding why Wallada (and not any of the other female poets of al-Andalus) is still a prominent icon today, two factors jump to the fore. She is remembered because of her affiliation with the renowned Ibn Zaydun and for being the "last" princess. That is, paradoxically, her subordination to Ibn Zaydun has kept her alive in cultural memory, but usually as an accessory figure. Regarding the allure of being the "last," Wallada is either the last to be dismissed to make way for the rise of Spain or the last to hold a place of power and prestige that did once exist. This gives her a seductive power over audiences all around the Mediterranean. Nonetheless, in literary representations of Wallada, analogous to the scene of Andalusi desire in Salih's *Mawsim* (*Season of Migration to the North*), in which the beautiful woman completes the scene of seduction but is also its victim, in most instances, Wallada functions to complete the enticing scene of a flourishing or declining al-Andalus, but suffers limitations in the process.

Although many of the works on Florinda and Wallada reinscribe the paradigm of al-Andalus as a subjugated or seductive woman, the novels by Palma Ceballos and Yunus transform that pattern of representation into a critique of the discursive bases of historical icons and the role of sexuality in the establishment and maintenance of power. Palma Ceballos's *La huella de las ausencias* not only gives Wallada narrative voice but also destabilizes the typical objectifications of her as Ibn Zaydun's beloved, as ornamental princess, or as a paragon of feminism. Palma Ceballos's version highlights at once the importance of Wallada's story and the constructed nature of any version of her. In this way, it attempts to strike a balance between the need to write women's stories and the need to recognize that they are narratives: they are subjective accounts that create meaning and not fixed truths. Similarly, Yunus's version of Wallada comments on the objectification of women, the nexus between economic disparity and patriarchy, and the role of all of these in oppressive autocratic regimes. Furthermore, Yunus's text, through its comments on the rhetoric of heroicization and its playful approach to revered figures, highlights not only how idealized historical figures are constructed through words but how they can be reshaped to address the present and the future. While the figure of Florinda remains objectified or subjugated as the foil of a male hero, both Palma Ceballos and Yunus translate the figure of Wallada into a protagonist that comments on contemporary uses and abuses of history and critiques a long tradition of objectification and control or judgment of women's sexuality. In sum, these authors use the often quite seductive mythology of al-Andalus to reflect on the mythification process and offer alternate narratives about al-Andalus and its women. Along the way, they suggest that al-Andalus is a collection of narratives.

CHAPTER 6

Scheherazade

al-Andalus as Seduction and as Story

Many of the works discussed in the previous chapter point to how women are subjugated in the formulation of seductive narratives about al-Andalus, but the last two novels, by questioning the textual construction of historical icons, suggest that al-Andalus itself can be understood as a narrative. The set of works that I analyze here—a short story from Iraq and a novel trilogy from Egypt—work with these elements to point to al-Andalus at large as a narrative that defines identity and can provide sustenance. The authors of these works reappropriate the feminized al-Andalus that is both subjugated and seduces and present al-Andalus as a narrative. Al-Andalus is not a fixed history of rape or seduction but a site of creativity, a story that can be rewritten.

al-Andalus as a Seductive Tale and a Tale of Seduction

The short story "Qissa Andalusiyya" ("An Andalusi Tale," 1964) by the prominent Iraqi writer Dayzi al-Amir (b. 1935) presents al-Andalus as a means of seduction through narrative and also a narrative whose authorship and ability to deliver fulfillment are in question.[1] This deftly nuanced, metafictional story portrays the encounter between a female student from the Arab world and a male Spanish immigrant working in the student lounge at a university in an unnamed northern European city during the mid-twentieth century.[2] The story is told by a third-person narrator, focalized on the young woman, the only character whose thoughts and feelings the narrator can access. The Spaniard's job is to help customers with a vending machine that dispenses coffee. When the young woman arrives to buy coffee, he tries to strike up a conversation by asking where she is from in a witty way. She experiences this as a test because normally she would never converse with a strange man, but she had come here to learn and disconnect from her past and her future, and for that reason she decides to respond (101). He says he hopes that she is Spanish and then asks where she got her olive complexion. She proudly replies that she is an Arab, and the Spaniard continues, "Well, I am Arab too" (100). She is filled with pride by this Spaniard's recognition of his link to the Arab world and its implicit acknowledgment of its illustrious past. From that moment on the Spaniard insists on pressing the buttons of the machine for her each time she comes to get coffee between her classes. Each time he also talks to her about al-Andalus, Spain, and the Arab world.

Starting from the first time they speak, when he places her order from the machine, he uses coffee to impose his own definition of Arabness. That first day he intercepts the student's finger when she is about to press the cream button and tells her that Arabs drink their coffee black (100). Each time he orders her coffee, he points out that he will not press the buttons for cream or sugar because Arabs never drink their coffee that way (101). With this repeated gesture the Spaniard enforces a particular definition of Arabs as a people with a true appreciation for coffee that allows them to savor its bitterness. Moreover, the young woman's acquiescence suggests that she is unsure of how she defines Arabness and, in her effort to live in the present, is willing to accept his "Andalusi" definition.

Throughout al-Amir's story, the Spaniard's interactions with the student include declarations of kinship with Arabs. He calls himself her cousin (102) and her only relative at this foreigners' school (104), and he refers to his home country as "al-Andalus" (105). These expressions of shared heritage partly reflect his sense of camaraderie with the student as someone from an economically depressed Mediterranean region vis-à-vis an economically thriving Northern Europe. When the immigrant speaks of his plans to improve his English and of the socioeconomic problems in his country, the student feels as if she is speaking with one of her countrymen about his aspirations and struggles (105). However, the invocation of shared heritage is also an assertion of affinity that stems from his efforts to woo the Arab student. He tells her about the mark of Arab culture on contemporary Spain, and this satisfies her national and feminine pride (102). She can tell that he looks forward to their conversations, and she notices that she does as well, so she takes herself to task and decides that the next day she won't let him speak to her with such liberty. But the next day he returns to "the talk about al-Andalus [*hadith al-Andalus*]" and she continues to listen (102). The phrase "hadith al-Andalus" has a rich doubled meaning: among other related meanings, *hadith* can mean a long, rambling story; a narrative in general; or a conversation. Through this phrase the narrator implies that the Spaniard's talk about al-Andalus is something of a tall tale and also constantly reminds the reader of the workings of narrative.

The narrator notes that the student suspects that the Spaniard, rather than speaking factually, is spinning a yarn, but she decides to go along with it, in part to try to train herself to focus on the present. In another gesture of kinship, he complains of the smell of the non-Arabs around them—identifying with Arabs and their love of bathing and cleanliness, and she glances at his grungy-looking clothes and doubts this to be true. However, having been burned by people's lies in the past, she no longer cares whether he is telling the truth. She decides she will take his words for what they are, casual talk, and will accept the amusement that the moment offers without any greater expectations (103). This is one of several instances of the narrator making opaque references to the student's past and future. Generally, she seems troubled by the pain of the past while longing for elements of it. These ambiguous references to past and future can be read as references to failed amorous relationships but also more broadly to disappointed hopes, such as those arising from an ideology of Arab unity based on the grandeur of the Arab civilization of the past. As a Christian Iraqi, al-Amir may have initially supported secularist pan-Arabism. But she wrote this story soon after the violence of the Ramadan Revolution, also known as the February 1963 coup d'état, in which the Baʿath Party's Iraqi branch overthrew the prime minister of Iraq with a military coup. Shortly afterward party leaders organized a massacre of suspected communists and other dissidents and the ousted prime minister's execution was broadcast on television. Although al-Amir had been living in Beirut since the early 1960s, she worked at the Iraqi embassy there and surely must have been acutely aware of the political and ideological battles raging in Iraq, with repercussions beyond. Although the Arab student in the story intends to focus only on the present, not on the disillusionments of the past nor apprehensions about the future, the denouement of the story indicates that this was not yet possible.

In al-Amir's text, the use of narrative and storytelling to incite desire comes to the fore again when the narrator reports that the Spaniard has offered to keep the Arab student up to date on news from the Arab world. Although she knows that some of those news items do not deserve the enthusiasm with which he presents them, she enjoys finding a Spaniard who takes pride in the Arab world. Here al-Andalus and specifically the narrative of *convivencia* makes it possible for her to ignore the undue significance with which he endows certain news items and, instead, enjoy a feeling of pride and the seducing Spaniard's company. Furthermore, the Spaniard takes on the role of Scheherazade of *One Thousand and One Arabian Nights*. Each day when the conversation has gone on for too long, she looks at her watch and he stops his story midway, knowing that she will come to hear the rest the next day (103–4). By cutting his story short at the first sign of boredom, he uses narrative to manipulate the student and keep her coming back for more. Noting his certainty that she will return, she begins to play games with him, staying in the classroom instead of going to get coffee. He then comes to the classroom looking for her and makes flirtatious remarks about what they will look like when they are old (104). Although she had been hoping for such flirtatious banter—referred to by the same key word: *hadith*—she fends it off by saying that she is not interested in the past nor the future, only the present moment (104–5).

One day the Spaniard tells her that he will soon be returning to his country and, though she only laughs, saying that they shall meet again in "al-Andalus" (105), when she returns to the lounge area another day and finds his chair empty, she is distraught. She pushes the buttons on the coffee machine herself "and the empty chair tells her a thousand tales [*alf hadith*]" (107). Here the term *hadith* is used to convey that his absence is even more evocative than his presence: now that he is gone, she allows her imagination to create narratives about the past and future. As she starts to shed tears, she notices that by mistake she has put cream in her coffee. Thus, the story indicates that her very identity as an Arab has been shaken by the Spaniard's passage through her life and his departure. Feeling confused and directionless, she observes that she is sure of one thing: "What she knows is that she hopes that she has not added to the storeroom of her past an Andalusi tale [*ila makhzan al-madi qissa andalusiyya*]" (107).

In al-Amir's "Qissa Andalusiyya" there are (at least) two Andalusi stories. First there is the Spanish man's story of seduction: trying to use al-Andalus and storytelling to woo the Arab woman. Second, there is the woman's story of this encounter: what starts out as an attempt to live in the moment and take it all as an amusing experience leaves her longing for the continuation of the tale and fearing having accumulated another story of heartache in her storeroom-library of relationships, this one labeled "Andalusi." The word *makhzan* ("storage room," "repository," etc.) is related etymologically to *khizana*, which denotes a smaller storage space and thus is used as "wardrobe," "storage locker," "vault," "treasury," and so on. In the phrase *khizanat al-kutub* it means "bookcase" and thus by extension *khizana* can also mean "library." Thus, *makhzan* in the context of this story suggests the image of the student's past existing as an archive or library of story-experiences. Incidentally, it contrasts with the khizana, or treasure vault, that appears a few times in Zaydan's novel about the conquest of al-Andalus. In Zaydan's text, Florinda's virginity is worth more than a king's treasure room and she hopes to gift it to her beloved, whereas in al-Amir's story the protagonist has her own storeroom of treasures: the treasures of her past experiences, figured as stories.

In al-Amir's metafictional short story, al-Andalus is used to seduce through stories—hadith al-Andalus—and it is in and of itself a seductive story, that is, a narrative that manages and incites desires. Although the Arab student was trying to live in the present and not experience another romantic entanglement, the Spaniard's glowing accounts of al-Andalus and Arab-Spanish kinship affected her. Through the play between hadith as talk and as story and the phrase "Andalusi tale [*qissa andalusiyya*]" in the final line, the text suggests that just like the Spanish man's words, stories of a glorious al-Andalus are narratives that arouse desire, sometimes of a surprising intensity, but don't deliver fulfillment in the present. Soon after its establishment as a sociopolitical entity, al-Andalus became a cultural sign that functions like a set of narratives, and attention must be paid to who controls the narration and what type of story is told. In this case, the male Spanish immigrant has led the joint writing of the tale, but the Arab student, by adding it to her repository/library of experiences, catalogs it as an Andalusi tale and thus intervenes in the archive of al-Andalus.

al-Andalus as a Story to Be Rewritten

The concept of al-Andalus as a narrative is also manifest in the award-winning *Thulathiyat Gharnata* (*The Granada Trilogy*, 1995) by Egyptian writer and academic Radwa Ashour and in this work the storytelling is not only about women but carried out by women characters.[3] Two of the novels in Ashour's trilogy focus on female members of the family and all of them, through different metafictional gestures, highlight the role of storytelling. This set of novels, rather than retell the life of a famous woman—Florinda or Wallada—presents the trials and triumphs of everyday life for an Arab family, their friends, and neighbors during the dissolution of al-Andalus. As William Granara notes, this set of works departs from the much more common focus in Arabic letters on the apogee of al-Andalus:

> The temporality of the novel is quite unique in the modern Arabic literature of "remembering Al-Andalus," in that the obsession with the glorious past, with the Muslim conquest and the Golden Age of the Umayyad Caliphate of Cordoba, is diminished by the powerful sense of the now, the actual moment when the nostalgia for paradise lost is silenced by the political immediacy of defeat and survival, not obsessing on what was but what is, and more importantly, what will be. ("Nostalgia" 68)

Thulathiyat Gharnata recounts the struggles, fears, and difficult choices of Muslims during and after the fall of Granada. With the rise of the Inquisition, they face increasing restrictions that outlaw Arab clothing, Arabic books, and the use of Arabic in conversation; force them to convert to Christianity or leave; and ultimately, in spite of (at least outward) conversion, expel them from Spain. The trilogy presents these challenges through an innovative narrative style that consists of shifts between an omniscient third-person narrator and moments of narration from the perspective of the characters via dreams and memories. In what follows, I demonstrate that throughout the retelling of these events and how they affect a Muslim Arab family, there is a leitmotif centered on the power of books and narrative that reformulates the role of al-Andalus in Arabo-Muslim discourses. Caroline Seymour-Jorn notes that "In *Granada*, the strongest element of hope resides in the form of texts and female oral narration" (126). I take this further by arguing that throughout the trilogy texts and storytelling are the source of cultural resiliency and al-Andalus itself, rather than reiterate subjugation or seduction, is understood as one of the stories that can provide resilience.

The first novel in the trilogy, *Gharnata* (*Granada*, 1994), starts in 1491 and recounts the vicissitudes of the family of Abu Jaʿfar [Jaafar], focusing primarily on his granddaughter, Salima [Saleema] who disdains typical women's chores and instead pursues knowledge through reading. The second novel in the trilogy, *Maryama* (1995), focuses on the title character, who joins the family by marrying Salima's brother and is an example of the ingenuity of crypto-Muslims who must feign Christianity to remain in Spain. As ʿIzzat Jad points out, the second novel is not named after a geographic location or a historical event, but one of the characters (150). This is indicative of the central role of Maryama, and by extension her trunk or chest (*sunduq*), in the trilogy. The third novel, *al-Rahil* (*The Departure*, 1995), narrates the life of ʿAli, Salima's grandson (and thus great-great-grandson of Abu Jaʿfar), who was raised by Maryama in Granada during the years leading up to the 1609 Spanish decree that called for the expulsion of the *moriscos* from Spain. Having already been forced to leave Granada for other parts of southern Iberia, at the end of the novel ʿAli witnesses the exodus of many moriscos from Spain but decides to stay in defiance of the decree. In this way, the departure with which the trilogy closes is a departure from the imposition and expectation of exile.

Books are central to Ashour's trilogy from the start. The patriarch of the family, Abu Jaʿfar, is a *warraq*, a bookbinder who prepares and sells manuscripts. He takes in two apprentices to help him in his shop, and the novel describes in detail their careful craftsmanship (e.g., 6–7).

Gharnata presents books as a treasured craft and a source of material, intellectual, and spiritual sustenance. But these valued objects that convey and symbolize all forms of riches are soon threatened by the rise of the Inquisition. The first work in the trilogy depicts the role of Francisco Ximenes (or Jiménez) de Cisneros (1436–1517), a Spanish cardinal who became the Grand Inquisitor of Spain and wielded a great deal of political power. In 1499 Cisneros arrived in Granada as part of the Inquisition and brought with him an aggressive and oppressive approach to converting the city's Muslim inhabitants to Christianity, which included forced mass conversion and the burning of Arabic manuscripts.

When the Castilians start requisitioning Arabic books, Abu Jaʿfar and his friends hide their volumes in his country house to save them (55–57). Although they have managed to save some books, Abu Jaʿfar, his two young apprentices, and his two grandchildren are overwhelmed with grief on witnessing a book burning in a central Granadan plaza.[4] Abu Jaʿfar the bookmaker is so horrified that he stops believing in God and dies that night (57–62). Later his granddaughter Salima, who was raised by her grandfather, recalls the flames consuming the books and becomes ill. When she recovers, the first thing she does is travel to their country house, enter the cellar where the books were hidden, and make a detailed catalog of all the volumes (64–65). As Seymour-Jorn notes: "With the death of the patriarch, Abu Jafar, early in the narrative, there is a transfer of textual authority to his granddaughter, Saleema. It is Saleema, rather than a male heir, who symbolically carries on his legacy: she has inherited his love of books and his passion for knowledge" (122). Salima's embodiment of this textual tradition is seen in the remainder of the first volume of the trilogy in which she clandestinely buys Arabic books about medicine and becomes a respected healer. Similarly, her interest in acquiring and understanding classical Arabic scientific, philosophical, and narrative texts leads to various intertextual references that place her within the tradition of Arab knowledge and Arabic letters. In keeping with this, Abu Jaʿfar and Salima's books and manuscripts remain the most treasured possessions of the family.

In the second volume of the trilogy, Abu Jaʿfar's grandson Hasan reveals to his sister Salima's young son, ʿAli, that the cellar of their country house is full of Arabic books. He explains that to keep the books safe from the Castilian authorities, Salima and Maryama once hid them in a trunk in their house in Granada and that "these books are a rich treasure" (37). Although the young ʿAli is not ready yet to appreciate their value, with time he recognizes it, as witnessed by his acts on returning to Granada and being forced to leave it again. When ʿAli wishes to live in Granada, he makes a deal with a powerful morisco,

José [Khusayh], who was given special permission to stay; as part of their arrangement ʿAli signs the deed of the country house over to José. But first he makes sure to have his great-great-grandfather's books brought to his family's house in the Albaicín area of Granada (127). Later, the night before escaping José's plot to have ʿAli arrested, ʿAli buries the books in Maryama's trunk in the garden of the Albaicín house, for safekeeping (153). As I explain further on, Maryama's trunk full of books takes on a central role in the final novel.

Returning to the first volume, the centrality of books leads to an extended metfictional simile. Books are so vital to Salima that when she imagines her impending death, she sees herself as a book. The last chapter of *Gharnata* presents Salima in jail, being held for further investigation by the Inquisition. A guard tells her that she will be sentenced to burn at the stake in an auto-da-fé and Salima, as she imagines the scene of her execution, links her burning at the stake to the burning of the books she had witnessed years before with her grandfather. As she conjures up the devastating images of burning pages, she wonders: "And people, aren't people written on like paper... a string of words, each one indicating a meaning and its totality too, doesn't the inscription of words reveal the whole person? She is Saleema bint Jaafar, and in one split second she wanted to defeat death, but then she changed her mind and accepted a mission less impossible. She read books, treated the sick, and deliberately disregarded the injustice of the Castilians" (303).[5] As Salima thinks about the suffering ahead, her thoughts turn to her young daughter, ʿAʾisha, but she pushes thoughts of her away, feeling that they will drive her to madness. Instead, she thinks about Abu Jaʿfar: "her grandfather, Abu Jaafar, the grown up who inscribed the first word in her book. . . . The grandfather who announced that he would provide her with an education just as he would for Hasan, and who whispered to his wife that Saleema would be like the educated women of Cordova. Her grandmother laughed and repeated those words to Saleema. And so it was inscribed" (224 [304]). In these passages, the reference to Cordoba alludes to Wallada and her contemporaries. But by the time Salima is an adult, book learning in Arabic is construed as a crime in nascent Spain. Moreover, by connecting the burning of books with the burning of people condemned by the Inquisition, Salima develops a view of humans as books on whose pages words—both written and spoken—are inscribed, thus creating the chain of signification, or narrative, that constitutes the person. In Salima's case, the stories that her grandparents tell regarding their wishes for her become inscribed in her "pages" and create her sense of self.

In *Gharnata*, in another metafictional gesture, the theme of books is interwoven with that of storytelling as Maryama emerges as an important storyteller. When Maryama joins the family as Salima's brother Hasan's wife, although her mother-in-law is not happy with her because the young woman doesn't know much about domestic matters, Salima gets along well with Maryama and teaches the clever young woman how to read. Although Salima is more of a serious figure whose intellectual pursuits lead her to question God and religion and Maryama often serves to provide comic relief through her wily solutions to problems, the women work together to achieve their common goals. When Maryama joins the family she brings her trunk, which has been handed down for generations in her family and contains heirlooms such as an embroidered handkerchief and a decorated copy of the Quran. Jad indicates that these items represent Arab heritage (150), while Iqbal Samir points to passages that describe Maryama appreciating and enjoying the chest and its contents as a child, particularly when she climbed inside it to tell stories (175–76). Afterward Maryama and Salima add to this trunk a central element of Arab heritage: books. In the events later recounted to ʿAli in the second part of the trilogy, when the authorities decree that all Arabic books must be brought in for inspection, it is Maryama's trunk—the site of sacred texts and storytelling—that they use to hide their books (188–89 [253–55]). In the final volume of the trilogy ʿAli associates the trunk with Maryama and her stories. In these ways, Maryama becomes the character who transmits Salima's book-based legacy and the power of narrative to the next generations.

The value of books and the transformative capacity of stories are particularly salient in the conclusion of *Gharnata*, which consists of Maryama telling a story to ʿA'isha. While Salima is being led to the woodpile to be executed like a banned book, Maryama is at home, worried about why Hasan and Salima's husband, Saʿd, have not returned yet and wondering if Salima would be sentenced that day. In spite of her anxiety, she cannot say no to ʿA'isha's request that her aunt Maryama tell her a story. Maryama begins to tell a story about a fantastic tree that grows in the sky and whose branches carry, for each person on Earth, a green leaf—or a "page" since the Arabic *waraqa* (plural: *awraq*) carries both meanings: "leaf" and "page." This giant, magical tree continually sheds leaves [awraq] and grows new ones, and once a year it sprouts a strange and wondrous flower (310). Maryama's preoccupation over Salima causes her to pause her storytelling, but the girl urges her to continue the tale, and the book ends with the omniscient narrator stating, "Maryama looked into the face of the little girl and she took a long deep breath. She let it out and continued [the] story" (229 [310]).

Thus, *Gharnata* ends without narrating Salima's actual burning at the stake. Instead, while Salima is being executed, the reader, in the position of ʿA'isha, receives Maryama's story counteracting death by conveying a sense of the ongoing renewal of life and its wonders, including the inscription of lives on leaf-pages. The sense of hope that this open-ended conclusion offers is augmented by the multiple names of the narratee of the story. The legal name of Salima and Saʿd's daughter, which the authorities require to be a Christian name, is Esperanza, Spanish for "hope." However, at home the child is called ʿA'isha, Arabic for "she who is alive" and well known as the name of the Prophet Muhammad's favorite wife, who, along with his other wives, carries the title of "Mother of the Believers" (*Umm al-Mu'minin*). But at home Salima's daughter is also nicknamed Amal, Arabic for "hope." Thus, her names carry a rich symbolism in that her Arabic nickname circles back to the meaning of her official Spanish name, passing through a name that celebrates life. The recipient of the story, then, who has urged Maryama to create and continue her tale, represents hope and life across languages, religions, and cultures. In this way, Ashour's *Gharnata* conveys the idea of continuity and survival, and specifically resilience, through bookmaking and storytelling.

In the second volume of the trilogy, *Maryama*, books and storytelling continue to have a crucial role in the unfolding of the morisco characters' lives. In addition to the treasured books hidden for safekeeping and the stories told by other characters (Hasan and Naʿim), Maryama has a central role as a storyteller whose tales have a positive impact on herself and ʿAli. Maryama's family has been fractured by their difficult circumstances, and she is raising her niece ʿA'isha's son, ʿAli, who refers to her and her husband Hasan as his grandparents. The second volume begins with a beleaguered Maryama telling a story to a different sort of narratee: she tells what she saw in a vision and a dream to a dream interpreter, who declares that it is a sign of change, the end of hardship, which will come about in seven years (7–8). The positive interpretation of the vision and dream—the idea that their misfortune will come to an end—transforms Maryama, who no longer feels knee pain, becomes sprightly, laughs more, and goes back to tending her garden. The narrator explains that while neighbors and passersby admire Maryama's revived garden, she looks out to the end of the street, thinking about those who had left: "She knew that the time had not come yet, but, as she awaited, she was seeing with the eyes of the imagination the return of those who were absent" (10–11). This passage demonstrates the power of narrative and creativity to change one's experience of reality.

As seen at the end of *Gharnata* with the story Maryama tells her niece, in the second part of the trilogy Maryama uses storytelling to entertain, teach, and protect ʿAli. Early in this novel, when she is concerned that Hasan is about to tell a visitor the story of how ʿAli's grandfather died after the horror of seeing his wife burned at the stake, to protect ʿAli from knowledge of that event she offers to tell him a make-believe story in another room. The bedtime story she tells features a Scheherazade-like heroine who uses her cleverness to evade angels that have come to take her to heaven. The heroine tells the angels that she can only go to heaven if her loved ones accompany her, and her loved ones are all the victims of injustice in the world. The heroine begins to give the angels a list of names, and a thousand years later she is still giving them names (17–18). Maryama tells a never-ending story in which the protagonist uses words to save herself and simultaneously point to injustices in the world. The list of names, when understood through the metaphor of people as pages that appears twice before in the trilogy, is also a list of stories. Maryama's bedtime story to ʿAli serves then as a metafictional *mise en abyme* of Ashour's trilogy itself.

Within the trilogy, the stories told by Maryama continue to reverberate years later. At certain moments in *Maryama*, the narrative points to the importance of these stories in ʿAli's life (26–27 and 113). For instance, when ʿAli grows older and is forced to leave Granada with Maryama, who dies during the forced march, a legend that his "grandmother" Maryama had told him years before helps him escape (107–8). In addition, just as part I of the trilogy ends with an unfinished tale (Maryama's tree story for ʿA'isha), parts II and III have open endings with ʿAli departing Granada for a second time with no known destination and ʿAli deciding to stay in Spain, facing an uncertain future.[6] The perpetuation of stories in the trilogy, like the Scheherazade-like heroine of Maryama's bedtime story, offers the hope of using ingenuity to triumph against injustice.

In the final book of the trilogy, *al-Rahil*, the centrality of storytelling continues with the mature ʿAli remembering nostalgically how as a child he listened to Maryama's stories (221–22). Moreover, the novel, and the trilogy as a whole, culminates with ʿAli being inspired by Maryama's trunk and the desire to understand "the story" of his people. In the final pages of *al-Rahil*, Maryama's sunduq—Arabic for "trunk," "chest," and also "box"—functions to link books, stories, and the effort to understand the rise and fall of al-Andalus. As Nezar Andary aptly notes, in reference to the efforts of Abu Jaʿfar and his descendants to protect their books, "The trunk is Scheherazade's strategy to survive" (74). This becomes particularly salient in the conclusion of the trilogy, when the trunk full of books has a central role in ʿAli's life journey. In this closing passage, Maryama's trunk symbolizes both the high culture writing of the classical texts that Abu Jaʿfar prepared in book form and Salima studied, and the folk tales, often inspired by religious texts, that Maryama told. Like Scheherazade, to survive, the women—and men—of this family must maintain their connection to their stories: the written and oral narratives passed down and the interpretations of life stories still to be comprehended. As Samir indicates: "The trunk full of books is a key device in the reading and interpretation of the text" (178). Samir proposes that the books in the trunk are equivalent to Maryama in that both preserve and transfer knowledge. The trunk shelters the books just as it once was the space in which the young Maryama told stories (176). Samir interprets the trunk as a symbol of how much the characters value aesthetics (175) and of Arab and Muslim identity and culture (178). However, my analysis of the trilogy asserts that rather than broadly represent Arabo-Muslim culture and its sense of aesthetics, Maryama's trunk specifically stands for the Arab narrative tradition.

When ʿAli has arrived at the port to leave Iberia as part of the exodus of moriscos, he looks out at the scene of boats, officials, and refugees and wonders if there is any meaning to be taken from what is happening. The narrator tells us: "He knew his story," he knew what he himself had lived and experienced,

> but he didn't know the details of the bigger story about his people, the Arabs and the Muslims, and the humans who killed and were killed on this piece of earth hanging from the sky—what's the connection between heaven and earth? He was incapable of understanding because the story is inside a story inside a story. A box [sunduq] inside a box inside a box and he only had his small chest [sunduq] that he had made with his own hands and in which he had placed papers, keys, and mementos. (255–56)

Here ʿAli yearns to understand the broader situation of the fall of al-Andalus, but identifies that situation as a story—not discrete, knowable history—and one that is difficult to comprehend because of the many layers of embedded narrative. The many stories about al-Andalus are like nested boxes, each one enclosed around another.

As ʿAli thinks about the parallels between the layers of narrative and nested boxes, he recalls the small chest in which he has packed his belongings for departure from Spain—documents, keys, and mementos—and thinks about the process of leaving the village in which he had been living. Soon after, his thoughts move from the small chest he has with him to a large chest, the trunk of books buried in the garden of the family home in Granada. ʿAli consoles himself by thinking that "Maryama's trunk [. . .] enclosed around the books," firmly underground, is not affected by the edict of expulsion [*sunduq Maryama baqa hunak . . . mughlaq ʿala al-kutub*] (*al-Rahil*, 257). ʿAli then rests his head on his small trunk and falls asleep by the shore as the image of Maryama's painted trunk full of books becomes mixed with that of her tomb. On waking he wonders whether departure will actually take him further or closer to death. He wonders where he can find the answer to this question and thinks that perhaps it is buried, like the trunk full of books. He vacillates regarding whether to stay or go, asking how he will start a new life at his age, in a strange place where there is "no grandmother's tomb upon whose 'box' [*sunduqiha*] to plant a garden" (258). These dream-infused thoughts lead him to think about the decisions his ancestors made and he feels the desire to understand "the meaning of the story" (258). Finally, inspired by these thoughts, he turns his back to the sea and runs away from the shore. Later, as he calmly walks inland, he tells himself that Maryama's tomb will offer protection from alienation or loneliness [*la wahsha fi qabr Maryama!*] (258–59). The text fuses the tomb of Maryama, his grandmother and mother figure, with her trunk, which served as her first storytelling space and is full of the family's treasured books. That trunk of narratives gives ʿAli a sense of rootedness, the desire to understand the narrative of which he is a part, and the confidence to choose this difficult path.

On one level, the Granada Trilogy is a commentary on the political and cultural situation of the contemporary Arab world. This interpretation is suggested by the text when Saʿd, Abu Jaʿfar's former apprentice and Salima's husband, is under arrest due to anti-Muslim sentiment and continually wonders: "Was the past repeating itself?" (178–79 [240]). While some have seen the trilogy as an allegory for Palestine, Ashour has deemed this interpretation reductive and recommends that rather than read the work as an allegory, it should be read as "a metaphorical image of loss and resistance in the Arab nation" (Ashour, quoted in Andary 62–63). Indeed, Ashour has indicated that she was inspired to write on al-Andalus by the 1991 bombing of Baghdad during the First Gulf War, which she experienced as part of a string of bombings and defeats that began with the 1967 war (Salwa ʿAbd al-Halim and Rakha). For this reason, Andary concludes that "Ashour's contemporary struggle is about confronting a strong sense of defeat and failure in Arab culture" (80). Similarly, Granara argues that "*Gharnata* posits a new interpretation of Arab nationalism that constructs a community of all those who are linked by the trauma of defeat and subjugation and the longing for liberation and dignity" ("Nostalgia" 70).

However, interpretations of the Granada Trilogy as a commentary on the contemporary Arab world, and even an evolution of Arab nationalism, must be careful to note how the novels reenact the shortcomings of Arab nationalism. Granara goes on to elaborate that in the trilogy, "The collective lived experiences of both the triumphant and defeated Al-Andalus become the paradigm of modernity with its problems and challenges" and that its portrait of an Arab neighborhood post-1492 "eclipses the triumphant Cordoba and the defeated Granada as the locus of the modern Arab nation" (71). Similarly, Andary asserts that "al-Andalus can remain a unifying place because it no longer exists and Arabs from Morocco to Yemen can imagine themselves as Andalusians. Because al-Andalus has ended as a political Arab reality, a writer can use it as a location to realize a unified Arab culture which does not exist" (79). Nonetheless, when we compare Ashour's trilogy to the works by Driss Chraïbi, Rachid Boudjedra, and other North African writers discussed in chapter 3, the tension between the trilogy's pan-Arab spirit (at least as understood by Granara and Andary) and Amazigh consciousness comes to the fore. The main limitation of the Granada Trilogy as a sociopolitical commentary is that it does not go far in addressing the multiple religious, ethnic, and linguistic identities that were part of al-Andalus, even at the moment of its political end. Although there are some complex, sympathetic Christian characters, some critics have noted that many of the Christian characters are one-dimensional bad guys who are simply overbearing, ignorant, or hostile toward Muslims.[7] Beyond this, there are no Jewish characters and no Amazigh characters. The categories of Arab and Muslim are elided to such an extent that the Amazigh presence is completely erased. In this way, the trilogy displays one of the limitations of pan-Arab nationalism: either it does not account for ethnic minorities at all or it positions them on unequal footing with Arabs.

On another level, the Granada Trilogy's commentary on the present is enacted, and gains greater complexity and depth, through the novel's proposal that narrative is a path to survival and resilience. That proposal contains the potential for creating more inclusive and equitable cultural identities, beyond traditional conceptions of pan-Arabism. Andary points out that Ashour's experimental autobiography *Atyaf* (1998) indicates that Ashour wrote the trilogy to process the series of defeats that have been part of Arab politics and personal lives since the 1967 war: writing and imagining allowed her to regain balance and control in her life (Andary 63–65). This process is manifested within the trilogy through its metafictional leitmotif about narrative. Storytelling is a survival tool that allows both narrator and narratee to compensate for and even change reality. Through the prominent role of books, Maryama's storytelling in general, and the heroine of the bedtime story who saves herself and the oppressed of the world with her never-ending list of names/stories, the Granada Trilogy invokes the famous figure of Scheherazade from the *One Thousand and One Nights*. In this way, Ashour participates in a phenomenon that began in late twentieth-century Arabic letters in which various women writers, as well as some men, have taken up Scheherazade to question her position in the famous frame tale of the *One Thousand and One Nights*, celebrate some aspects of it, or reimagine her as a feminist by way of her use of narrative to gain power.[8] In *The Postcolonial Arabic Novel* al-Musawi notes that "The Scheherazade trope has become indeed one of the salient markers of feminism and its centrality to postcolonial theory and politics. The figure of the defiant and daring young woman, with great resourcefulness and manipulation of her womanhood, is to cut across the nation and narration, postcoloniality and postmodernity, and culture and imperialism" (74).

The reappropriation of Scheherazade, in turn, is part of the broader phenomenon of the creative reformulation of *turath*, or cultural heritage, within the (post)colonial cultural production of the Arab and Maghrebian worlds to which I referred in the introduction. Fadia Suyoufie points to the ambivalence of many Arab intellectuals, particularly women writers, between rejecting tradition and embracing it—albeit to rework it. This ambivalence arises from the marginalized position of women writers with regard to the structures of authority that establish and manage turath (219). Although this makes women's appropriation and reformulation of classical texts all the more destabilizing of oppressive power structures, Suyoufie points to one of the contradictions that can arise from feminists using the appropriation of traditional material as part of a subversive strategy for empowerment: "These women writers have reclaimed the art of storytelling by recasting the role of women in a tradition which is mainly a 'male' prerogative. Their appropriation of tradition is intended as a subversion of existing orders that limit women's freedom. Yet in their very subversion of tradition they inevitably revive it" (247). However, this risk of reviving the negative aspects of tradition while trying to reclaim it is greatly diminished in Ashour's text through its metafictional strategy. The Scheherazade trope is, at its core, a reminder of the narrative process and certainly the way Ashour uses it highlights her novels' status as fiction and thus raises questions about the relationship between fiction and reality. Moreover, the self-referential techniques that Ashour uses not only draw attention to the trilogy's status as fiction (and not history) but point to the status of cultural narratives about al-Andalus as artifacts, as constructed stories. That is, the Granada Trilogy highlights the constructed nature of discourses on al-Andalus at large and identifies al-Andalus as a narrative that can be creatively reformulated to improve the present and the future. As ʿAli experiences at the end of the trilogy, today al-Andalus is a collection of stories that, like nested boxes, can be difficult to access. But as the novel suggests, this collection of stories can be continually rewritten in search of hope and renewal, and women can play a central role in retelling al-Andalus.

* * *

From Salih's *Mawsim* to Yunus's *Wallada*, al-Andalus is part of either the reenactment or the dismantling of seduction and subjugation. In part III, I have analyzed the ways narratives about Florinda and Wallada from Spain and the Arab world have largely constrained the legendary and historical figures within gendered and/or Orientalist frameworks as they reinscribe the power dynamics of seduction and conquest. The notable exceptions are the renderings of Wallada by Palma Ceballos and by Yunus, which in different ways critique those power dynamics and bring to the fore the process of the discursive construction of cultural icons. In this way, these two works draw attention to al-Andalus itself as a narrative of seduction.

Al-Andalus as narrative is further developed in al-Amir's short story "Qissa Andalusiya," in which al-Andalus is a tall tale that is used to manipulate and manage desire. In Ashour's trilogy, Maryama and the heroine of one of her stories are Scheherazade figures who show how stories—including the stories of al-Andalus—are malleable artifacts that women, as storytellers and not just the objects of narrative, can use to create equity and cultural resilience. While most narratives about al-Andalus rest on hierarchical and/or restricting conceptions of gender and sexuality, Ashour's trilogy points to how women can use creativity for individual and community survival and also for reworking the myth of al-Andalus. Across the works examined in part III, al-Andalus is transformed from gendered land or a subjugated/seductive woman to be conquered into material to be creatively reworked by a woman protagonist with interiority and agency, and even by a woman storyteller. As suggested by the title of the last volume in the Granada trilogy, *al-Rahil* or The Departure, the works of Palma Ceballos, Yunus, al-Amir, and Ashour constitute an imaginative departure from both discourses of nostalgia and forced exile and the versions of al-Andalus that replay East-West conquest through romantic and/or sexual relationships.

Conclusion

Reweaving Narratives of al-Andalus, Identity, and Tolerance

> Because al-Andalus is not a historical bubble, an inert material, isolated and in suspension [. . .] and this contributes to explaining the fact, perhaps unexpected, surprising, or anomalous for more than a few, that a matter of the past can also be a matter for the present and the future.
>
> —Pedro Martínez Montávez (*Significado y símbolo de Al-Andalus*)

> The decentered pluralism [that W. E. Connolly] advocates in place of liberal doctrines of multiculturalism requires a continuous readiness to deconstruct historical narratives constituting identities and their boundaries.
>
> —Talal Asad

While medieval Iberian scholars translated and commented on the knowledge of other regions and earlier periods, today writers and filmmakers from the Hispanic and Arab worlds "translate" medieval Iberia to rewrite the past and the present and suggest alternate futures in light of transcoloniality and its interaction with migration and gender. Although often the invocation of al-Andalus is understood as a purely nostalgic gesture or a reenactment of medieval conflict, this analysis of the literary and visual texts produced in the era of globalization that portray or invoke al-Andalus reveals two opposing tendencies. On one hand are works that use al-Andalus to further cement religious difference and hierarchical power dynamics, often based on differences understood to be biologically or ethnically determined. Although al-Andalus carries different, sometimes opposing meanings for different cultural, religious, and linguistic groups, similar structures of power are at play in the narratives of identity it is used to produce. On the other hand are works produced by writers and filmmakers from across these groups that reimagine al-Andalus and its role in the present.

Countering works that reiterate fixed, oppositional identities and thus incite conflict, translators of the past and of otherness transform the myths about al-Andalus into new self-aware narratives. Although in *Performing al-Andalus* Jonathan Shannon finds that in Morocco, Syria, and Spain, music that is understood to be Andalusi functions as a source of a sense of authenticity; in contrast, many of the narrative and dramatic works about al-Andalus question or rework the constructs that underlie authenticity. In the case of storytelling about al-Andalus, the past is often not something that is depended on but something that is repurposed. In narrative and dramatic cultural production, al-Andalus is employed to develop secular Islam; establish plural conceptions of national, religious, or cultural identity; imagine new migrant and gendered identities and different types of cultural integration; and enrich the creative processes that support all of these. Sites of memory are always sites of creativity, but what sets these works apart is how much the narrative is reworked and to what end. This analysis of the afterlife of medieval Muslim Iberia in contemporary Arab and Hispanic cultures reveals alternate discourses about the legacy of al-Andalus that take into account the imperial and gendered dimensions of al-Andalus. Beyond those discourses that rehearse established grand narratives for particular sociopolitical objectives, others appropriate and transform such narratives, and still others engage in outright rejection while using metanarrative to point to the constructed nature of al-Andalus as a cultural sign.

Contrary to what views informed by Orientalism and its projection of an immutable, tradition-bound, monolithic Arab and Muslim psyche may dictate, on the whole Arab and Maghrebian authors and filmmakers are actually taking the lead in innovative retellings of al-Andalus. These creators are working through postcolonial cultural and socioeconomic issues in imaginative and even groundbreaking ways, often going further in questioning colonial and imperial dynamics and the mythical nature of al-Andalus than do their Hispanic counterparts. Perhaps because the gap between the rhetoric of triumphant conquest in the past and the current state of affairs in the Arabo-Muslim world is more glaring, many of the writers and filmmakers from the Arab world boldly contest standard accounts of al-Andalus, point to the status of al-Andalus as a constructed narrative, and even translate standard versions of the Andalusi past into transformative creativity.

The 2006 Moroccan box office hit *ʿAbdu fi ʿAhd al-Muwahhidin (ʿAbdu in the Time of the Almohads)*, directed by Saïd al-Naciri [Saʿid al-Nasiri], provides an interesting metaphor for the relationship between modern socioeconomic conditions and al-Andalus.[1] In this film, the title character, ʿAbdu, is a street peddler and tourist hustler in contemporary Marrakech who is on the run from the police. During the chase, ʿAbdu passes in front of the rays emitted by an experimental device used by a team of American, European, and Moroccan researchers. The device's beam sends ʿAbdu into the thirteenth century and the era of the Almohad Empire, where he has various humorous and poignant adventures amid the splendor and cultural advancement of the period, including a scene in which he explains to Ibn Rushd and other learned men from the period the phenomenon of *harragas* (illegal, undocumented migrants) trying to immigrate to what was once al-Andalus and turning the Mediterranean into "a big mass grave" (50:55–51:08). The time traveling ray that zaps ʿAbdu as he tries to escape the police mirrors the way modernity, including its failures, pushes Arabs and North Africans to reconnect with al-Andalus.

Assumptions that may be held about which groups are more likely to break with tradition, to be open to rewriting narratives about the past, are analogous to assumptions about translatability. In addition to expectations about access to meaning and the ability of language to capture reality, cultural positioning (in this case, affiliation with the East versus the West) brings with it associations regarding which mind-sets have access to insight about that which is new or Other (recall Borges's narrator vis-à-vis Averroes/Ibn Rushd) and are generally open to change and innovation. The acknowledgment of the mediation that filters our knowledge about the Other need not result in a belief in the absolute incommensurability between impermeable worlds, and even less so in a belief in the greater impermeability of some worlds over others.

The case of the overt intertextual dialogue between Borges, Kilito, and Hussin demonstrates that translation, in its literal sense, can and does lead to productive intercultural contact. The projects of Spanish institutions such as the new Escuela de Traductores de Toledo (School of Translators of Toledo; founded within the University of Toledo in 1994); Moroccan-Spanish initiatives such as the Al Mutamid Program of the Instituto Internacional del Teatro del Mediterráneo; Spanish publishers Editorial CantArabia, Ediciones Alfar, and Ediciones del Oriente y del Mediterráneo; and the 1980s Moroccan journal *Bayt al-Hikma* serve to facilitate dialogue among/across readers of Spanish and Arabic.[2] If efforts to produce high-quality translations continue to grow and are accompanied by growth in an active readership, or an active TV and film audience, as the case may be, through the expansion of literacy as well as critical literacy (the ability to analyze and interpret discourse), these cultural products can contribute to cultural dialogue and the opening of spaces for more harmonious coexistence.[3] This contribution is particularly robust when the literary or visual texts are reworkings of standard narratives about al-Andalus, that is, cultural translations of the Andalusi past and the selves and others connected to it. Cultural products of this type use al-Andalus as a site for both deconstructive and creative processes and thus generate openings for coexistence.

How can the recognition of al-Andalus as a story and its rewriting contribute to tolerance? Simply put, tolerance is connected to questions of translatability/untranslatability and exposing mechanisms of power and difference through the disruption and retelling of cultural myths. A more detailed response to this question, however, requires that we first consider the concept of tolerance itself and debates regarding its implications. The term *tolerance* refers to an attitude of acceptance held on a personal level toward other individuals or groups, whereas the related term *toleration* is used in political science and related fields to refer to concepts ranging from the institutional measures taken to establish conflict-free coexistence (Michael Walzer) to the extreme degree of aversion and disapproval involved (Bernard Williams).[4] The issue of disapproval is at the core of many critiques regarding the means and even the desirability of creating tolerant cultures.

The political philosopher John Rawls viewed toleration as the pragmatic response to diversity, but many other thinkers have pointed to problems with the concept and practice of tolerance. In his study of Andalusi musical traditions, Shannon considers the possibility of finding a model for tolerance in al-Andalus and notes that tolerance creates a hierarchical relationship between the tolerant and the tolerated: "To tolerate someone (a cultural Other) is to mark that person as an outsider, as distinct, which is tantamount to denying that person's humanity" (172). Shannon cites the work of gender studies scholars Janet Jakobsen and Ann Pellegrini who, in reference to the US legal context, argue that tolerance is a reluctant acceptance in which markers of difference remain intact and us/them thinking thrives (Shannon 172–73). Similarly, political theorist Wendy Brown asserts that tolerating is tantamount to conditionally allowing that which is viewed as abhorrent and abject, while at the same time, especially in colonial and neocolonial contexts, the intolerant are labeled barbaric.[5] Marxist philosopher and cultural critic Slavoj Žižek deems that tolerance, when practiced, is done so in a limited and superficial manner (Daly and Žižek 122–24; Žižek 674). For this reason, as an alternative Žižek calls for awareness of the struggle against oppression that unites us: "The formula of revolutionary solidarity is not *let us tolerate our differences*, it is not a pact of civilizations, but a pact of struggles that cut across civilizations. . . . A better formula would thus be: in spite of our differences, we can identify the basic antagonism of the antagonistic struggle in which we are both caught; so let us share our intolerance and join forces in the same struggle" (674). However, the phrase "in spite of" constitutes a process of toleration. Žižek's proposal is actually a deep form of tolerance, not a superficial multiculturalism rife with contradictions, but a recognition of shared struggles and goals that encourages us to bear differences—to unite "in spite of."

Nonetheless, Žižek's stance can be paralyzing given the outward rejection of tolerance and the unclear relationship between it and the awareness of shared struggle. The critiques of the concept of tolerance can lead to an impasse. How can we cultivate peaceful coexistence while we avoid erasing difference in the name of a false universality, promoting the privileging of one group as arbiter of what should/should not be tolerated, or heightening the rigid sense of boundaries between in-group and out-group that leads to violent conflict? Political theorist Lars Tønder distills the debate as follows: "Contemporary democratic theory has split into two camps [...]: whereas one camp sees tolerance as a practice of restraint, necessary for the existence of a just and fair society, the other sees it as a practice of repressive benevolence needed to reinforce the norms set by the powerful" (2). Given this panorama, how can deep tolerance, an equitable and socially empowering response to pluralism, be sought?[6]

When Shannon's discussion of the contemporary musical genres referred to as Andalusi leads him to a parallel question, he turns to the work of Talal Asad and William Connolly on pluralism. In a seminal essay within political theory, Connolly presents as an alternative to problematic models of multiculturalism, and the attending issues of grudging and/or asymmetrical tolerance, the goal of "a democratic state of multiple minorities contending and collaborating with a general ethos of forbearance and critical responsiveness" (61). Connolly prefaces this statement with reference to the changes that would need to occur to reach such a goal: "This shift in the self-recognition of a dominant constituency works best if it acknowledges the shifting and historically contingent character of, say, the sensualities, language, faith, and canonical texts that have inspired it the most" (61). Anthropologist Talal Asad, while making it clear that he does not advocate a borderless world but one in which the complexity and heterogeneity of boundaries and historical moments are recognized and cultivated (179), elucidates Connolly's proposal as follows: "The decentered pluralism [Connolly] advocates in place of liberal doctrines of multiculturalism requires a continuous readiness to deconstruct historical narratives constituting identities and their boundaries (which, he argues, have a tendency to become sacralized and fundamentalized) in order to 'open up space through which *care* is cultivated for the abundance of life'" (177). Ultimately, Shannon argues that Connolly's model of "'decentered pluralism' [. . .] requires that we deconstruct our cherished historical narratives—like the standard narrative of al-Andalus and its modern iterations—and rethink our identities and the boundaries we construct to defend them" (173). Heightened intercultural contact creates a need for heightened critical awareness of the narratives that create the fabric of identity, an awareness that is enabled by linguistic, cultural, and temporal translation.

The calls to deconstruct the ideologies of narratives of identity that come from Connolly, Asad, and Shannon dovetail with the process that Žižek ultimately offers as a solution. Žižek closes his essay on tolerance by stating that it is only "through hard work on our own ideological underground" that we can identify our shared struggles and thus arrive at a new type of universality. For this reason, he declares that "the motto of every radical emancipatory politics is the same as the quote from Virgil that Freud chose as the exergue for his *The Interpretation of Dreams. Acheronta movebo:* dare to move the underground!" (682). By daring to move the "ideological underground" that is the basis of Hispanic and Arabo-Maghrebian identities, the writers and filmmakers discussed here shift conceptions of identity; they point to their constructed and mutable character and in this way make community boundaries flexible enough to allow for a more self-motivated, less grudging tolerance between communities. Whether the ideology is divinely guided Muslim conquest, divinely guided Catholic reconquest, the privileging of Arabs over other Muslims or of Muslim Arabs over Arabs of other faiths, "Old Christian" *limpieza de sangre*, Spanish nationalism, anticolonial nationalisms (including Argentine settler nationalism, anti-Castilian/anticentralist Andalusian nationalism, and pan-Arabism), Latin American Hispanism, Orientalism, or masculinist conquest of feminized land or of objectified feminine beauty, we can better bear difference by baring the underpinnings of difference that reveal much sameness—Žižek's shared struggles. Shaking the ideological ground underfoot exposes the ways group identities (be they ethnic, religious, national, imperial, class, or gender-based) are based on fictions and how over time different groups have occupied the same positions (colonizer and colonized, host country and immigrant). In the process of disrupting myths, that which was foreign or unintelligible can become intelligible or at least uncannily familiar. Tønder, Fiala, and others point to the sacrifices and suffering required by tolerance. To reach a more equitable, less contradictory tolerance, the process must also include enduring the distress and discomfort of acknowledging that one's identity is made up of narratives—some of which overlap in unexpected ways with those of others. However, the disruption of ideologies that constitute self/other, in-group/out-group, can deconstruct those identity formations without aiming for a homogeneous world and thus maintain the most usable (least noxious) parts of particular traditions.

This deconstructive process is not an end, but a set of new beginnings—of new, more self-aware narrations of identity. In an essay that considers al-Andalus, exile, and Zionism, Gil Anidjar puzzles over the finality and exceptionality associated with al-Andalus and asks: "what if the so-called past had not ended? What if al-Andalus had a future? What if bearing witness to al-Andalus meant to reconsider its being past, to enact its being-present and even future?" (191). Writing against the purported ephemerality and exceptionality of al-Andalus as a space of tolerance, Anidjar suggests that al-Andalus can be an opening to new possibilities for the future. Rather than focus on the finality and inaccessibility of al-Andalus, one can be attentive to how it is being used to critique the present and imagine better futures. The retellings of al-Andalus include a critical consciousness of the role of narrative in ordering reality, masking oppressive power, and forming identity, as well as an empowering awareness of narrative's role in cultural resilience. In addition to the various works already discussed, two brief examples further substantiate this awareness.

Often, the story of al-Andalus in twentieth- and twenty-first century literature is one of manuscripts lost, found, translated, and otherwise rewritten. One novel in which al-Andalus is figured as a text that has been lost but can be compensated through creativity, through the writing of new texts, is Bensalem Himmich's novel *Hadha al-Andalusi* which I discussed in chapter 3 in relation to Tariq ibn Ziyad and gender dynamics.[7] I highlight here another element of this Moroccan historical novel about an Andalusi Sufi philosopher to demonstrate how it establishes the centrality of storytelling in cultural survival. Part I of Himmich's novel is titled "The Search for the Missing Manuscript" and revolves around the protagonist Ibn Sabʿin's discovery that the only copy of a manuscript he wrote has gone missing, his attempts at locating the manuscript, and his grief over its loss. At the end of part I, as Ibn Sabʿin's mourning for the manuscript is coming to a close, or at least his distress over the manuscript is overshadowed by the distress of exile, he carries out his first voyage of exile on a ferry from Iberia to North Africa. On the ferry to Ceuta, a woman sits next to him and tells him the story of her woes, to which Ibn Sabʿin responds by giving her money to help her care for her child. Another passenger, a merchant from Ceuta, criticizes her and reveals that she makes a living out of spending the day going back and forth on the ferry telling new sob stories—with occasional reference to cruel Castilians. Ibn Sabʿin, much to the merchant's surprise, replies that had he known this before he only would have given her more money. Ibn Sabʿin launches into praise for the woman's creativity, saying that "her imagination" is "the one weapon she possesses" and comparing her to a professional poet or storyteller (88 [119]). This crafty woman is a version of Scheherazade—using stories to survive. The anecdote, and part I of the novel, closes with Ibn Sabʿin recounting a nightmare in which the ferryboat Scheherazade has a key role. After disembarking, Ibn Sabʿin falls asleep and dreams that he is on the ferry during a violent storm. As the storm rages the woman with the sob stories tells tales about the horrors and calamities of the sea while the other men on board try to make her stop. Finally the merchant throws the woman and her child overboard into the churning water. Then the boat capsizes and Ibn Sabʿin ends up in the sea, struggling for his life, facing death, and putting himself in God's hands as he feels himself sinking (89 [120–21]). In this metafictional vignette within the story of Ibn Sabʿin's escape from orthodox Muslim authorities in the midst of the advancing Castilian conquests, the woman who uses her creativity to find a livelihood embodies the vital importance of storytelling: Ibn Sabʿin fears the end of her stories because the perceptive mystic knows that once the tales are silenced, all travelers will meet perdition. In the next chapters, after struggling to remember bits of his lost manuscript, Ibn Sabʿin starts a new life and begins writing a new mystical treatise. Thus, he follows the example of the crafty woman on the ferry and turns his woes into creative energy and a new account of his mystical journey.

A more upbeat and playful account of the role of storytelling in resilience is offered by Jordanian American writer Diana Abu-Jaber. Her 2003 novel *Crescent* tells the story of Sirine, an Arab American woman who was raised by her uncle and now works as a chef in a Lebanese restaurant in Los Angeles, and Hanif (Han), an exiled Iraqi man who is a professor at the University of Los Angeles. When Sirine and Hanif meet in the restaurant, the reader witnesses how their romance and various friendships with other immigrants blossom in that space. Nouri Gana's astute analysis of the novel reads it as a commentary on Arab identity and a reworking of the fabled *convivencia* of al-Andalus in a diverse US community. Furthermore, Gana points to the Andalusi symbolism of another storyline in the novel that runs parallel to that of Hanif and Sirine and ends up fusing with theirs. This interwoven story consists of a tale that Sirine's uncle tells and retells her in installments and features as its hero a figure evocatively named Abdelrahman Salahadin. This name melds two prominent figures from Arabo-Muslim history: the Umayyad prince ʿAbd al-Rahman, who escaped an Abbasid massacre in 750 and a few years later founded the Emirate of Cordoba, and Salah al-Din, who recaptured Jerusalem from the crusaders in 1187 (Gana 238–39). Eventually the storylines in *Crescent* fuse and Abdelrahman Salahadin becomes Hanif's name (Abu-Jaber 393–94). The uncle's tongue-in-cheek, mythical tale of his supposed cousin Abdelrahman Salahadin consists of the young man repeatedly selling himself into slavery and then, on receiving payment, pretending to drown in the sea and disappearing by swimming away. This crafty figure is used by the uncle to teach Sirine lessons about love and offer a way to embrace Arab identity while ironically recognizing its complexities:

> Abdelrahman knows he might be free, but he's still an Arab. No one ever wants to be the Arab—it's too old and too tragic, too mysterious and too exasperating, and too lonely for anyone but an actual Arab to put up with for very long. Essentially, it's an image problem. Ask anyone, Persian, Turks, even Lebanese and Egyptians—none of them want to be the Arab. They say things like, well, really we're Indo-Russian-Asian-European-Chaldeans, so in the end the only one who gets to be the Arab is the same little old Bedouin with his goats and his sheep and his poetry about his goats and his sheep, because he doesn't know that he's the Arab, and what he doesn't know won't hurt him. (54)

The Abdelrahman story unites Sirine and her uncle, helps her relationship with Han progress, and gives her another way to be Arab. This story of healing and resilience, together with other more explicit references to al-Andalus and the multiculturalism of the space of Los Angeles and the Lebanese café in which the main characters gather, make the novel hint at an al-Andalus that is created and re-created by storytelling and at storytelling as the source of positive bonds and communal power.

Drawing on Anouar Majid's reference to a "post-Andalusian" perspective on the world in *Freedom and Orthodoxy*, Gana seeks to use *Crescent* to delineate a "post-Andalusian critique" and thus facilitate a broader historical framing and, moreover, "allow [. . .] for a *reactivation* of the *Andalusian* imaginary, at the heart of which there lingers empowering modalities of socio-cultural co-existence" (230–31, emphasis in original). The concept of an "Andalusian imaginary" corresponds to what Shannon, drawing from Crapanzano, refers to as "an Andalusian imaginative horizon" (62). Indeed, al-Andalus is a vital part of the imaginary of the many inheritors of its legacy—Arabs, Muslims, Jews, Spaniards, and

Hispano-Americans—and often forms part of their creative efforts to comprehend the world and imagine it differently. Gana states that "post-Andalusian critique [. . .] emerges in the transformational-generative border space between two competing impulses—the one seeking to recover it and the other to recover from it" (231). Engagement with al-Andalus is linked to recuperation in the form of creatively and critically rewriting—recouping—the al-Andalus story and using those stories to recuperate from the tragic treatment of the *moriscos*. In the best of scenarios, recovering from the morisco experience of oppression and expulsion includes moving away from the ways of thinking that enabled such events.

Muslim Iberia can help us develop a more tolerant and just society, but not in the way that most people think. Not as a model per se but by looking at how the al-Andalus story is told and retold, we can learn about creating more equitable tolerance and more intercultural harmony. The opportunities to apply the insights gained by analyzing the "Andalusian imaginary" are endless. One concrete and pressing opportunity, that created by North African immigration to Spain, is astutely indicated by Gardner: "Ironically, it is at this moment, as people of Muslim and Christian traditions face each other once again in the Iberian Peninsula, that all of Spain has the opportunity to create a level of tolerance and understanding that never really existed in al-Andalus" (36). The usefulness of the past lies not so much in identifying exactly what happened (was it tolerant or wasn't it?) but in using the past—our versions of it—to identify what we want for the future. Thus, romanticized, biased versions of the past, if analyzed to reveal the underlying assumptions and interests at stake, can help us build a better future. In this way, producers and consumers of culture can carry out the difficult work of translating the (supposed) coexistence of the past into a better tomorrow. There is no such thing as an unproblematic, apolitical, or seamless translation process, but if anything, awareness of the cultural narratives that make linguistic, cultural, and temporal translation challenging intensifies the need to continue to struggle to negotiate meaning. Coexistence is possible, but just like textual translation, it requires the hard work of reading hallowed texts with a critical eye, moments of incomprehension, and a strong commitment to finding the best (even if imperfect) solutions. Negotiation of meaning and restructuring of identity narratives across cultural frontiers is crucial to human well-being. It allows us to reach beyond discourses of both idealized convivencia and unresolvable conflict. The convivencia associated with al-Andalus, to whatever degree and in whatever form it existed, cannot be transferred wholesale into the present but can be used to carefully adapt and transform—to translate—desired narratives into realities.

The critical reflection on the past inherent in reworking it and bringing it to bear on the present enables the identification of sources of conflict and of what is desired for the future. By using al-Andalus to address the present, many of the works examined herein transform the concepts of cultural, religious, and gender identity that are the foundation of traditional discourses about al-Andalus, Arabness, Maghrebi, and Spanish identity and East–West relations at large. This group of texts—through which al-Andalus lives on, while alerting us to the dangers of either assuming the direct accessibility of the past or the other, or assuming the radical inaccessibility and unintelligibility of the past or the other—highlights the constructedness of representations of the foreignness/sameness of the past and cultural, religious, and racial others/selves and simultaneously offers the constructs of al-Andalus as narratives that can be retold to improve the present and the future. This body of works attests to the possibility of meaningful cultural contact: not a facile, idealized vision of convivencia or Muslim supremacy but a careful negotiation that considers how power is implicated in the construction of identities.

Notes

Introduction

1. Obama's June 4, 2009 speech can be found at "Text: Obama's Speech in Cairo," *New York Times*, June 4, 2009 (http://www.nytimes.com/2009/06/04/us/politics/04obama.text.html?pagewanted=all&_r=0). On Bin Laden and al-Zawahiri's video statements, released October 7, 2001, see Sachs.

2. The motif of loss in Arab cultural history, which continues with the loss of al-Andalus and the loss of Palestine, has its roots in the classical literary trope of the poet's loss of his beloved and his mourning at her deserted nomadic camp. The mourning over the *atlal* (remains of the desert encampment) is the archetypal image of the *nasib* or opening section of the classical Arabic *qasida* (ode). The most famous poem by Imrū' al-Qays, a pre-Islamic Arabian poet of the sixth century, is his *mu'allaqa* (one of the *mu'allaqat*, or Suspended Odes, which are seven pre-Islamic Arabic poems canonized as exemplary verse and said to have been hung on the Ka'ba at Mecca). It opens with a verse, from which it takes its title, that is well known in the Arabic-speaking world: "Stop, both of you, and let us weep [*Qifā nabki . . .*] over the remembrance of a beloved and her abode." In a similar vein as al-Naqqāsh, Bahraini intellectual Muḥammad Jābir al-Anṣārī, in a 2011 newspaper article titled "Kharā'iṭ al-Wāqi' al-Ijtimā'ī . . . am Bukā'iyyāt al-Andalus?" ("Maps of Social Reality . . . or the Weeping of al-Andalus?"), in which he calls for a critical evaluation of Arab history that will promote assessment of current social realities, specifically recommends moving away from weeping over al-Andalus.

3. Gala's "Averroes," which was aired in 1981 and published in 1984, was an episode of the Spanish public TV series *Paisaje con figuras* (*Landscape with Figures*). I analyze this screenplay at length in chapter 2.

4. On how European colonizing powers viewed colonized nations as being "medieval" and in need of civilization, see Davis and Altschul, 2.

5. See Granara, "Nostalgia, Arab Nationalism, and the Andalusian Chronotope" and González Alcantud, *Lo moro* 183.

6. After Toledo was retaken by Christian forces in 1085, the Christian authorities

continued to foment translation activity in what was later denominated the Toledo School of Translators. For more on this, see the section "The Formation and 'Translation' of Identities" in this introduction.

7. See "al-Andalus in Spain, Andalusia, and Argentina" further on in this introduction for a discussion of the question of how many moriscos may have managed to assimilate and remain in Iberia, and how this is tied to identity and politics in Andalusia.

8. Al-Andalus has clearly also had a formative role in Jewish identity, but this book focuses on the groups who were the main power brokers in al-Andalus, those who at certain points headed conquest/reconquest. For more on this, see the section "The State of the Field and the Parameters of This Study" in this introduction.

9. See Kellner for a cogent theorization of globalization. On globalization and the Muslim world, see Schaebler and Stenberg.

10. Two examples of the invocation of Cordoba are Imam Feisal Abdul Rauf's Park51 project, which was originally named Cordoba House and became the center of a controversy referred to as "the Ground Zero mosque" because it was to be built near the site of the Twin Towers demolished by the September 11, 2001, terrorist attacks, and the virtual rebuilding of the Cordoba mosque by Canadian Pakistani architect Gulzar Haider and his student Zara Amjad (see Sardar, and Amjad and Haider).

11. On the translation activity centered in medieval Toledo, ranging from revisionist to significantly contextualized perspectives, see Vegas González, Santoyo, Burnett (*Arabic into Latin* and "Communities of Learning"), Fidora, and chapters 2 and 3 in Pym.

12. Tamazight or the Amazigh languages are part of the Afro-Asiatic language family; Arabic is part of the Semitic branch of that language family. Tamazight has had a written tradition, on and off, for over 2,000 years, but it has been frequently disrupted by invasions. It was first written in the Tifinagh alphabet, still used by the Tuareg. It has also been written in Arabic script and a version of the Latin alphabet. A modernized form of the Tifinagh alphabet was made official in Morocco in 2003, and a similar one is sparsely used in Algeria together with the Amazigh Latin alphabet. To this day, the Tamazight languages are primarily used in oral literature and songs. See note 14 in chapter 1 on writing in Tamazight.

13. See, for instance, Silverstein and Crawford, and Maddy-Weitzman.

14. Though Arabic and French continue to dominate, the Amazigh movement has achieved significant gains in the form of the official recognition of Tamazight as a national language (2002) and an official language (2016) in Algeria and as an official language in Morocco (2011) and in the form of the limited introduction of Tamazight into the educational systems of both countries.

15. For more on andalucismo, see Martin-Márquez 301–3; Calderwood, "'In Andalucía, There Are No Foreigners'"; and Duran.

16. See Brann, "The Moors?" on the cultural history of the term *Moor* and the concept of "Moorishness."

17. For more on Infante (who is said to have converted to Islam in Morocco in 1924) and his role in andalucismo and the Spanish rhetoric of a Hispano-Moroccan brotherhood that supported the colonial project in Morocco, see Calderwood, "'In Andalucía, There Are No Foreigners.'" For an analysis of Infante's writings, including a play about al-Muʿtamid (last ruler of the taifa of Seville) and essays on flamenco music, see Egea Fernández-Montesinos. On Infante's version of Andalusian history, see Stallaert 95–97.

18. For more on Burgos and Acosta Sánchez and the perception of Castile as colonizer of Andalusia in general, see Egea Fernández-Montesinos and Stallaert.

19. On parallels and overlaps between the rhetoric of Iberian Reconquest and New World conquest, see Baue 47–49; Harris, *Aztecs, Moors, and Christians*; Fuchs, *Mimesis and Empire* 7–8; and Mejías-López.

20. See also Ashcroft, Griffiths, and Tiffin 2.

21. In "*Andalucismo* as transperipheral critique," Calderwood uses the ideas of Lionnet and Shih to analyze the interaction between two of Spain's peripheral nationalisms: that of Catalonia and that of Andalusia.

22. Revisionist accounts of Spanish history assert that the concept of Reconquista is problematic because there was not a unified Christian Spain before Muslims conquered the peninsula and the process took nearly 800 years. As a result, much has been written about the term *Reconquista* itself. See, for instance, Barbero and Vigil; Lomax 1; González Jiménez, "Sobre la ideología de la Reconquista"; Ríos Saloma; and Martínez Montávez, *Significado y símbolo* 30.

23. On these debates, see, for instance, Cohen, Ingham and Warren, and Gaunt.

24. Walter Mignolo and others have pointed to the links between the practices of discrimination and extermination, as well as legitimating ideologies of superiority, found in the early modern Iberian Christian kingdoms' treatment of Jews and Muslims and Spanish treatment of Amerindians and Africans. See, for instance, Martínez. See further discussion of this in relation to Columbus in the coda to part II of the present study.

25. For an extended critique of Nora's lieux de mémoire, see Ricoeur 401–11.

26. On al-Andalus in the contemporary music of the MENA region, see Shannon, Davila, and Reynolds. On its manifestation in traditional Moros y Cristianos (Moors and Christians) festivals in Spain see Albert-Llorca and González Alcantud; Flesler; Harris, "Muhammed and the Virgin"; and Rogozen-Soltar. On monuments and tourism, see González Alcantud and Malpica Cuello; González Alcantud, "Social Memory of a World Heritage Site" and *Lo moro* 81–9; and Calderwood, "The Invention of al-Andalus" and "The Reconquista of the Mosque of Cordoba." On the manifestation of medieval Muslim–Christian conflict in Iberia on official shields in the Autonomous Community of Aragon and elsewhere in Spain, see Fierro, "Decapitation of Christians and Muslims."

27. For more on the Nahda and Zaydān, see Di-Capua and Phillip et al.

28. See Laroui's *L'idéologie arabe contemporaine* and *La crise des intellectuels arabes: traditionalisme ou historicisme?* (*The Crisis of the Arab Intellectual: Traditionalism or Historicism?*), both of which have been translated into Arabic, and more recently *Islam et histoire: essai d'épistémologie.*

29. For more on the relationship of modern Syrians with al-Andalus, see Shannon 52–83.

30. See Bahrami; González Alcantud, *Lo moro* 191–93 and "El canon andaluz y las fronteras imaginarias" 373–74; Shannon 84–118; and several of the essays in *Andalusíes: antropología e historia cultural de una elite marroquí* (González Alcantud and Rojo Flores).

31. Between the late 1990s and the early 2000s there was approximately one fatality, usually due to drowning, per 100 migrants intercepted. Official figures show that 1,035 migrants died between 1999 and 2003 while en route to Spain. However, migrants' rights groups say that the actual number is higher (de Haas).

32. This is particularly salient in Palestinian poetry and especially in the works of Maḥmūd Darwīsh. See, for instance, al-Juʿaydī and García Moreno.

33. For more on the postclassical (1150–1500) and early or premodern (1500–1850) periods, see Allen and Richards.

34. *Adab* is an Arabic term that connotes being well-mannered, cultured, and urbane, and came to refer to a literary genre characterized by its broad humanistic concerns. Adab literature developed during the height of Abbasid culture in the ninth century and continued through the Muslim Middle Ages and includes compilations of poetry, instructive stories, and knowledge considered necessary to be cultured.

35. On the mythification of al-Andalus and its ties to nascent nationalism in their writings, see Paradela Alonso 135–45. See also Martínez Montávez, *Al-Andalus, España* 23–36, as well as Shannon 32–34.

36. Shawqī's "al-Andalus al-Jadīda" ("The New al-Andalus," 1913), reflects on the 1912 Balkan Wars, in which the Ottoman empire lost its Balkan territories. His "al-Riḥla ilā al-Andalus" ("The Journey to al-Andalus"), commonly referred to as Shawqī's "Sīniyya," or S-rhyme poem, and the play *Amīrat al-Andalus* (*The Princess of al-Andalus*) are two of his most famous works written during his exile in Spain. For more on Shawqī's stay in Spain and al-Andalus in his oeuvre, see Makki and Martínez Montávez, *Al-Andalus, España* 39–51.

37. See Grieve, Drayson, Flesler, and Goytisolo, *Crónicas sarracinas*. On the foundational myths about the Moor and the quest for racial purity specifically in the Falange (Civil War and Franco eras), including the Spanish novels of the 1960s and 1970s that parody and reject these formulations of Spanish identity, see Labanyi, *Myth and History in the Contemporary Spanish Novel*. Among these novelists, the one who most directly attempts to contest these narratives is Goytisolo, whom I discuss in chapters 3 and 5.

38. On the medieval and early modern periods see Yiacoup and Fuchs, *Exotic Nation*.

39. On the Black Legend and scientific racism in Spain, see Martin-Márquez 39–42 and Fuchs, *Exotic Nation* 116–17.

40. See Monroe 28–37 and 52, Martín Muñoz 58–59, and Martin-Márquez 17–28.

41. See Labanyi, "Love, Politics and the Making of the Modern European Subject"; Martín Muñoz 58–59; and Martin-Márquez 28–50.

42. On these two generations, or moments in Spanish intellectual history, see, for example, Lima and Menéndez Alzamora. On the Generation of 1898 and their influence on the Falangists in relation to narratives of Spanish identity, see Labanyi, *Myth and History in the Contemporary Spanish Novel*, 35–36, 55–58, 60–62, and 64–65.

43. For more on the concept of convivencia, see Manzano Moreno. On convivencia in Anglophone scholarship, see Akasoy.

44. On convivencia and the three Abrahamic religions in the Spanish tourism industry, see Calderwood, "The Invention of al-Andalus."

45. On the cultural implications of Spanish colonialism in North Africa, the Franco dictatorship's ambivalent attitude toward the Maghreb, and the deployment of the concept of Hispano-Moroccan hermandad, see, Martin-Márquez; Campoy-Cubillo; Labanyi, "Love and Colonial Ambivalence"; González Alcantud, *Lo moro* and *Marroquíes en la guerra civil española*; and Aidi, "The Interference of al-Andalus."

46. Paradoxically, starting in the 1930s and continuing during the dictatorship, Spanish historians began reevaluating the history of al-Andalus and posited that Spain had been the site of a different type of Islam, one that reflected the Hispanic influence. Hence, appropriative terms such as "Muslim Spain" and "Hispano-Arab" became common in academic circles, the media, and popular histories. The term "Muslim Spain," in addition to being a gesture of appropriation, is anachronistic given that the earliest starting point for a politically unified entity named "España" is the marriage of Isabella and Ferdinand in 1469. New academic work has moved beyond the "Muslim Spain" model, though it is still alive in popular discourses (see Martín Muñoz 65). Many studies critique Spanish Arabism, its political deployment, and its historiography of al-Andalus; see, for instance, Rojo and Casares Porcel; López García, "30 años de africanismo español"; Tofiño-Quesada; Viguera, "Al-Andalus y España: sobre el esencialismo"; Fierro, "Al-Andalus en el pensamiento fascista español"; Martín Muñoz; Rivière Gómez; and the classic study by Monroe. For an overview of the interpretation of al-Andalus in the work of European and North American historians, see González Ferrín, "Al-Andalus: un estado de la cuestión."

47. Al-Andalus, and specifically Franquista-style rhetoric about an "eternal Spain," came to the fore in Spanish prime minister José María Aznar's September 21, 2004, lecture at Georgetown University where he stated, "Spain's problem with al-Qaeda and Islamic terrorism did not begin with the Iraq crisis. In fact it has nothing to do with government decisions. You must go back no less than 1,300 years ago, to the eighth century, when a Spain, invaded by the Moors, refused to become one more piece of the Islamic world, and began a long battle to recover its identity" (cited in Domínguez García 125).

48. The geographic boundaries of al-Andalus once covered almost the entire Iberian Peninsula, but began to progressively shrink soon after the Muslim conquest. From 1249 to 1492, all that remained of Muslim Iberia was the Emirate of Granada. (See Figures I.1 to I.4.) For a long time after the Catholic Monarchs' conquest of the emirate, it maintained its character as a political unit, but in 1833

it was made part of the neighboring region of Andalusia with part of the historical emirate forming the province of Granada.

49. On the myth of present-day Andalusians, specifically those from the Alpujarra region, being descendants of moriscos, see González Alcantud, *Lo moro* 90–112. Recent genetic research indicates that the repopulation project led to the vast majority of those living in Andalusia today tracing their origins to Iberia, not North Africa. Genetic testing has demonstrated that Spaniards do carry a 10.6 percent mean proportion of North African ancestry, however, no doubt due to the forced relocation of moriscos to the north of the peninsula before the expulsion decree and encouraged relocation of Christian Iberians to the south after expulsion, in Andalusia the proportion of North African ancestry is actually relatively low as compared to other regions of Spain (Adams et al. 732). At the same time, Soria Mesa's research has found that in Granada as late as the eighteenth century about 300 descendants of Muslims were tried for heresy by the Inquisition. On post-Reconquista Spain and morisco culture, see Childers, Barletta, Perry, García-Arenal, and Dadson. On the repopulation project in particular, see Barrios Aguilera and Andújar Castillo, Bravo Caro, and González Jiménez, *En torno a los orígenes de Andalucía*.

50. For more on purity/heterogeneity and the revisionist histories of andalucismo's ideologues, see Stallaert 70–126.

51. For more on the debates surrounding essentialism, see Fuss, Heath, Spivak ("Subaltern Studies: Deconstructing Historiography" and "Subaltern Talk: Interview with the Editors"), and Schor and Weed.

52. On the quincentenary, see Dotson-Renta 2–3, Stern 1–6, Chaddock, Summerhill and Williams, Riding, and Delgado Gómez-Escalonilla 153–57 and 160. The last two see the quincentenary celebrations as a public relations success for Spain.

53. For an analysis of such maneuvering in the work of a nineteenth-century Chilean intellectual, see Altschul 228 and 230. On how criollo Orientalisms manifest in the Argentine context see Civantos, especially 3–5, 25–26, and 58–59.

54. The polemic Arabist Fanjul criticizes the Andalusian nationalists' mythification of al-Andalus, but at the same time he is known for his opposition to all regional nationalisms within Spain (e.g., Basque, Catalan, Galician, and Andalusian cultural and statist movements) and for his defense of the Spanish colonization of the Americas. For an overview of some of these discourses, see Molina, Manzano Moreno, Marín and Pérez 63–64, Subirats, Flesler 199–200n4, Martin-Márquez 319–23, and Aidi, "The Interference of al-Andalus" 81–82.

55. On the trope of invasion in Spanish and Moroccan texts, see Rueda and Martín 60–61 and Flesler.

56. On ghost imagery, see Rueda and Martín 53–55.

57. See chapters 3, 4, and 5 for analyses of novels that are part of this subgenre.

58. Among the texts I analyze here, examples of novels that cite Arabic texts (documented or fictional) or provide a bibliography include Gala's *El manuscrito carmesí*, Lasala's *Boabdil* and *Walläda la omeya*, Cabello's *Wallada, la última luna*, and Palma Ceballos's *La huella de las ausencias*.

59. On history and literature as forming part of a continuum, see Fernández Prieto 165.

60. On narrative, identity, and reality, see Jameson, D. Carr, Danto, and Mink. See Hanne, in particular 8–36, for an overview of the relationship between narrative and power; on narrative and social actors, see Somers as well as Somers and Gibson.

61. On the postmodern historical novel, see Fernández Prieto 175–81.

62. In addition to Hühn and Sommer, see Elam, Richardson, Fludernik, and Nünning and Sommer.

63. This focus on the dramatic text is largely due to the lack of access to performed versions of most of the plays studied, which were staged, if at all, long before the conception of this project and with no video recording. Similarly, there is one TV narrative, Gala's "Averroes," in which I base my analysis only on the script because I was not able to locate a recording of the televised episode. In the case of Gala's "Si las piedras hablaran: el fruto coronado (La Alhambra)," I base my comments on the screenplay because it was never produced for television.

64. The twelfth- to thirteenth-century Andalusi Sufi and philosopher Ibn ʿArabī is considered the greatest mystical poet in Arabic. Ibn ʿArabī is invoked in the poetry of renowned contemporary Arab poets such as Maḥmūd Darwīsh, ʿAbd al-Wahhāb al-Bayātī, Adunis [Adūnīs; ʿAlī Aḥmad Saʿīd Aṣbar], and Abdelwahab Meddeb [ʿAbd al- Wahhāb al-Madab] who overtly draw inspiration from his poetry, and he also has a role in the novel *Kitāb al-Tajaliyyāt* (*The Book of Epiphanies*) by Egyptian Gamal al-Ghitani [Jamāl al-Ghīṭānī]. The exegetical concepts of Ibn ʿArabī's thought are presented in the film *Ṭawq al-Ḥamāma al-Mafqūd* (*The Lost Necklace of the Dove*) by Tunisian Nacer Khemir [Nāṣir Khamīr]. In a similar vein, the novel *Hādhā al-Andalusī* (*That Man from al-Andalus*) by Moroccan Bensalem Himmich [Bin Sālim Ḥimmīsh] tells the story of the Andalusi Sufi philosopher Ibn Sabʿīn (see my discussion of this novel in chapter 3 and in the conclusion). The Sufi-inflected works sometimes use al-Andalus as a symbol for longing, and specifically *wisal*—the longing for a mystical union with God or a sense of wholeness that leads to the dissolution of the self. In contrast with the tendency toward understanding Ibn ʿArabī as a universal spiritual guide, Ibn Rushd is inextricably linked to his Andalusi context and the life of the mind.

65. Rahman 43–64. See also Snir; Assadi and Naʿamneh; Khalīl 11–36; Martínez Montávez, "Al-Andalus y Nizar Qabbani: la tragedia", and (on references to Granada and Muslim Spain in contemporary Arabic poetry and travel literature) Thomas de Antonio, "Granada en la literatura árabe contemporánea."

66. See, for instance, Carrasco Urgoiti.

67. On the concept of connected history, see Douki and Minard.

68. Sepharad has a prominent role in Jewish studies as a whole, specifically in Sephardic and Mizrahi studies, in that it is used as a trope and source of inspiration in the work of scholars, writers, artists, and musicians. This can be seen in works ranging from the poetry of Mizrahi Israeli Almog Behar to the novel *The Last Jew* (2000) by American Jewish writer Noah Gordon. In terms of relevant scholarship, the essays in Halevi-Wise's edited volume *Sephardism: Spanish*

Jewish History and the Modern Literary Imagination examine how Sepharad has been used by Jewish and non-Jewish writers from around the world since the nineteenth century. In the anthology *The Schocken Book of Modern Sephardic Literature* editor Ilan Stavans brings together literary works on the basis of their engagement with "the Sephardic condition." Ross Brann's *Power in the Portrayal* and his forthcoming *Andalusi Moorings* are comparative treatments of al-Andalus among Muslims and Jews that focus on material from the medieval period. On the role of representations and invocations of Muslim Iberia in modern Jewish–Muslim relations, see Nirenberg.

69. On Moors and Christians in Spanish and Arabic-language children's literature, see García Castañón.

Part I

1. First published in 1947 in the magazine *Sur* 152 (June), then in the collection *El Aleph* (1949).

2. For a critical analysis of Comité Averroes, see López García, "La sociedad civil y las relaciones con Marruecos."

3. The Maliki *madhhab*, prevalent in North Africa, is one of the four major schools of *fiqh*, or religious law, within Sunni Islam.

4. For instance, Sayyid Quṭb (1906–1966), one of the main ideologues of Egypt's Muslim Brotherhood, rejected Ibn Rushd's work as non-Islamic (Kassab 46). For an introduction to Ibn Rushd, see Fakhry. On Ibn Rushd's ideas and reception, see Taylor, I. Y. Najjar, Abū Zayd, and Akasoy and Giglioni.

5. On Ibn Rushd among nineteenth- and twentieth-century Arab thinkers, see von Kügelgen, F. M. Najjar, and Lahoud 110–25. Lahoud analyzes Ibn Rushd's thought as she questions whether the view of him as a standardbearer of liberalism is warranted. She notes, among other things, that romanticized views of al-Andalus condition this type of interpretation of his work and legacy (112).

6. For more on al-Jābirī's use of Ibn Rushd, see Abu-Rabiʿ 265 and Lahoud 45–49.

7. See, for instance, Bahrawi, who argues that Muslims can overcome their fear of secularism by returning to al-Andalus, specifically to Ibn Rushd, Ibn Ṭufayl, and Ibn ʿArabī.

8. One exception to this might be the 2006 Moroccan film *ʿAbdū fī ʿAhd al-Muwaḥḥidīn* in which Ibn Rushd makes a brief appearance as one among a group of thinkers representing the Arabo-Muslim scholarly achievement of al-Andalus and the Muslim golden age. Nonetheless, here Ibn Rushd, together with the film's protagonist who has traveled back in time, bridges a vast temporal distance. See my brief discussion of the film in the conclusion of this book.

Chapter 1

1. For background on the concept of (un)translatability, see de Pedro.

2. For example, the story "Ibn Hakkan al-Bokhari, Dead in His Labyrinth" ("Abenjacán el Bojarí, muerto en su laberinto," 1951) presents the Arab East as a site of radical difference. The lesser known story "The Twelve Figures of the

World" ("Las doce figuras del mundo," 1942), portrays the Syro-Lebanese Druze community in Argentina as inherently different and impenetrable. In both cases the ironization of identity construction that takes place with other characters and cultural manifestations stops short of the Arab characters and Arab culture. See Civantos 100–109.

3. The two terms—*tragedy* and *comedy*—were already mistranslated when they reached the historical Averroes. On the ambiguities surrounding translation in "La busca de Averroes" and the actual Arabic translations of Aristotle's *Poetics*, see Kilito [Kīlīṭū], "Borges et Averroès" and "Yawm fī Ḥayāt Ibn Rushd" in *al-Adab wa-l-Irtiyāb*, as well as Beebee 116 and 122–28.

4. My quotations from Borges in English are from Irby's translation, but here I have adapted Irby's translation in which the Spanish "en el ámbito del Islam" (95) is rendered "the whole world of Islam" (149). Though Irby's wording flows better, for my purposes I wanted to stay closer to the Spanish.

5. For an overview of this issue, see Moreh, "Theater." Moreh argues convincingly that a medieval Arab theater did exist in *Live Theatre and Dramatic Literature in the Medieval Arab World*. See also Ceccato 347–68.

6. I have adapted Irby's translation (148) because it omits the phrase from the Spanish "algo en la carne de Averroes" (94).

7. *Mohalacas* is a Spanish transliteration of *Muʿallaqat*, the Suspended Odes or seven exemplary pre-Islamic poems that were hung in the Kaʿba at Mecca. See note 2 in the introduction.

8. See Macfie.

9. See the seminal work of Alazraki on the centrality of the mirror, as not only a thematic element but a structural technique, in Borges's writing.

10. Merrell's treatment of Borges's "La busca" falls somewhere between these two types of assessments. Through a selective reading of the text that disregards many of its elements, Merrell concludes that it is an example of "meaning approximation" or of communication across "generally incommensurable" worldviews (103). For an interpretation of "La busca" in the context of magical realism and Borges's interest in *The 1001 Nights*, see ʿAbd al-Nāṣir 189–91.

11. Aristotle's *Poetics* had become a marginal text by late antiquity and was even more distant from scholarly activity in the Middle Ages; Averroes's commentary on Aristotle helped bring the Greek thinker's work into the center of European intellectual discourse. Javitch points out that Averroes's version of Aristotle in the Cordoban's "Middle Commentary on the *Poetics*," which was translated into Latin in 1256, seems to have appealed much more to medieval scholars than an accurate Latin translation of Aristotle's own text done in 1278. Javitch explains further that "because the kind of ethico-rhetorical terms into which Averroes recast Aristotle's poetics reflected prevailing notions of poetry well into the sixteenth century, Averroes's commentary on the *Poetics* was published, reprinted, and coexisted with Giorgio Valla's 1498 Latin translation of Aristotle's text (the first to be published) and the 1508 Aldine printing of the Greek original" (54).

12. In this thoughtful and innovative study that treats a wide range of Borges's writings, Waisman addresses the Averroes story on pages 125, 139–46, and 155–56.

13. On language politics in Morocco, see, for instance, Dakhlia.

14. On Moroccan writing in Tamazight, see Pouessel and El Mountassir. On Moroccan writing in Spanish, see Campoy-Cubillo, Ricci, and Chakor and Pérez Beltrán. On changing attitudes toward writing in Moroccan dialect (*darija*), rather than standard *fusha* Arabic, see Elinson, "*Dārija* and Changing Writing Practices in Morocco."

15. Derrida (1930–2004) was born into a Sephardic Jewish family that, when exiled from Toledo, moved to Algeria. He left Algeria in the late 1940s to complete his secondary education in Paris.

16. This passage appears on p. 95 of "La busca de Averroes," p. 149 in Irby's translation of Borges, and p. 174 in Kilito's story.

17. The story first appeared in French translation within Hussin's collection *Le Lecteur de Bagdad: contes & nouvelles* (2000) and then in Arabic, under the name Jabbār Yasīn. In addition to publishing in the Arabic press, Hussin has published several collections of his stories and essays in French translation. His story about Ibn Rushd appeared in an English translation by Randa Jarrar with the title "The Day in Buenos Aires" in *Words without Borders: The World through the Eyes of Writers*.

18. Most of my citations of the story in English are from Jarrar's translation. When I use my own translation, this is indicated parenthetically. The page numbers for the Arabic Dar al-Adab edition are indicated within brackets.

19. Nor does it mirror the French-language title of "La busca de Averroes," which is "La quête d'Averroès" ("The Search of Ibn Rushd").

20. See for instance, Hussin, *Memorias olvidadas*.

21. On the politics of colonial and postcolonial writing in Latin America, including the very definition of literacy, see, for instance, Boone and Mignolo.

22. The issue of the stuttering scribe is at once a confluence between orality and literacy, and between reason and the fantastic: Ibn Rushd responds to Borges's question about the cause of his exile by saying that a stuttering scribe had incorrectly taken Ibn Rushd's dictation, and the mistake—"King of Berber" instead of "King of Ber"—had angered al-Mansur. This odd slippage between oral repetition of a syllable (stuttering), aural reception of the scholar's words (taking dication), and written repetition creates an ambiguous zone between spoken and written words.

23. Hussin was born in Baghdad and as a teenager suffered arrest and torture at the hands of the Baʿathist regime for his political activities. In his early twenties, he fled the threat of another arrest and established himself in France, where he still resides. In 2003, after the overthrow of Saddam Hussein, Hussin was able to visit Iraq for the first time since his departure.

24. In 1195, when he was seventy, Averroes's teachings were condemned, his works were burned, and he was temporarily banished to the town of Lucena, just outside Cordoba. For an overview of these events, sometimes referred to as "Averroes's ordeal," and of the different explanations of the motives behind them (10–13), plus an analysis of Averroes's arguments in *Tahāfut al-Tahāfut*, see Kogan.

25. For more on modernity and epistemology, see, for instance, Castro-Gómez.

Chapter 2

1. On the film's music, see Hoffman 34–36; on homoeroticism in the film, see Hoffman 39–40 and Andary 124–25.

2. *Al-Maṣīr* was directed by Chahine and written by Chahine in collaboration with Khaled Youssef. The 135-minute film was produced by Ognon Pictures (France), France 2 Cinema (France), and Misr International Films (Egypt).

3. Calderwood points to the hybridity of the musical scenes themselves, given their fusion of elements of the music of the golden age of Egyptian cinema and the music and dance of Spanish flamenco ("Proyectando al-Andalus" 217).

4. The historical Ibn Rushd never actually had his day in court; he was tried in absentia by a group of Islamic jurists.

5. Initially, thirteen episodes (directed by Mario Camus and Antonio José Betancor) were aired between 1976 and 1977, with an interruption due to censorship that I discuss later. Another twenty-six episodes, directed by Carlos Serrano and Antonio José Betancor, were aired between 1984 and 1985. The "Averroes" episode was first aired outside of the regular run of the series on February 5, 1981, apparently due to an RTVE decision (Pérez Ornia). The episode was aired again within the comeback of the regularly programmed series on December 27, 1984.

6. The scripts were published in a two-volume edition titled *Paisaje con figuras* (1985). Gala wrote additional pieces on other Andalusian/Andalusi figures that were not part of the RTVE series. Those new plays, together with the ones from the television series that were also on Andalusian/Andalusi figures, were published together as *Paisaje andaluz con figuras* (1984). My references to the "Averroes" piece come from volume 1 of *Paisaje andaluz con figuras*. Later the Cordoban theater troupe Color Persona performed a theatrical version (circa 2009) of Gala's "Averroes" screenplay (see http://www.youtube.com/watch?v=ReFQ266KgBA). In chapter 4, I discuss one of the added *Paisaje andaluz* pieces that centers on Boabdil.

7. Gala's bisexuality is an open secret in the sense that although in his autobiography he does not address it, in many of his works his protagonists are bisexual (see Gardner 30) and in interviews he has expressed the opinion that bisexuality is natural (Bruquetas de Castro). One of the works featuring a bisexual protagonist is *El manuscrito carmesí*, which I analyze in chapter 4. Regarding anti-Jewish sentiment, although many of Gala's comments in the press about Israel are limited to criticisms of Zionism, he has also made statements that are anti-Semitic. See, for instance, Gala, "¿Los elegidos?"

8. Gala was born in the province of Castilla-La Mancha but moved to Cordoba at a young age and explicitly identifies as Andalusian.

9. See the blurb on the RTVE website: http://www.rtve.es/alacarta/videos/paisaje-con-figuras/ (accessed February 2, 2015).

10. Ibn Quzmān (1078–1160), transliterated into Spanish by Gala as Aben Guzmán, is one of the most famous poets of al-Andalus, known for his often bawdy colloquial Arabic poems of the *zajal* genre.

11. The drama was performed (for the first time) on February 20, 1998 in Carthage, Tunisia, as part of the International Averroes Symposium.

12. In this play the historical figure of the late twelfth-century Almohad caliph Abu Yusuf Yaʿqub al-Mansur (also known as Moulay Yacoub) is referred to as "al-Sultan" and by his name, Abu Yusuf Yaʿqub, rather than the title "al-Mansur," perhaps to avoid confusion with other leaders who carried the same sobriquet, such as Abu ʿAmir Muhammad ibn ʿAbd Allah ibn Abi ʿAmir, al-Hajib al-Mansur, also known as Almanzor, who rose from a low rank in the court of Cordoba to become the de facto ruler of the Cordoba caliphate in the late tenth to early eleventh centuries.

13. The two hadith compendiums considered to be the most authentic within Sunni Islam, and which are mentioned by name in al-Madani's play, are *Ṣaḥīḥ al-Bukhārī*, compiled by Persian Islamic scholar Muḥammad al-Bukhārī (810–870), and *Ṣaḥīḥ al-Muslim*, collected by Persian Islamic scholar Muslim ibn al-Ḥajjāj (c. 815–875; also known as Muslim Nīshāpūrī and Imām Muslim).

14. "من مات محباً فله أجر الشهادة." This hadith is reported in the classical collection of biographies of Shafiʿi jurists *al-Ṭabaqāt al-Kubrā* and is rejected in Ibn ʿAsākir's *Tarīkh Madīnat Dimashq* (*The History of the City of Damascus*, commenced in 1134). It is categorized as *maqtuʿ* or "severed," that is, a narration attributed to a successor of one of Muhammad's companions, not to the prophet himself nor to one of his companions (http://library.islamweb.net/hadith/display_hbook.php?bk_no=798&pid=379517&hid=12201).

15. Abū Nuwās (c. 756–814) is a major classical Arabic poet who is famous for his witty, often crude poems that focused on wine drinking and sexuality.

16. On Ibn Quzmān, see note 10 in this chapter.

17. "Le transfert d'Averroès" appears in *Langue d'Adam et autres essais* 59–63 and was published subsequently in Arabic in *Lisān Adam*.

Chapter 3

1. Translation of al-Maqqarī's *Nafḥ al-Ṭīb min Ghuṣn al-Andalus al-Raṭīb* (The Perfumed Breeze from the Tender Branch of al-Andalus), adapted from "Al Maqqari's 'Breath of Perfumes'" in Horne 241–42.

2. On Tariq ibn Ziyad's prominent role in the seventeenth-century travelogue of al-Ghassānī, see Hermes.

3. For more information on the historical figure see Collins, and García de Cortázar and Sesma Muñoz.

4. Muḥammad al-Idrīsī (1100–1165), in addition to his important contributions as a cartographer, produced *Kitāb Nuzhat al-Mushtāq fī Ikhtirāq al-Āfāq* (translated as *The Book of Pleasant Journeys into Faraway Lands and The Pleasure of Him Who Longs to Cross the Horizons*), a compendium of geographical information in which he refers to Tariq ibn Ziyad.

5. See Labanyi, *Myth and History in the Contemporary Spanish Novel* 196–214.

6. In Morocco, kif can refer to either a powder derived from the trichomes (hair-like growths) of cannabis and sometimes pressed into hashish cakes, or a mix

of finely cut dried cannabis flower buds (marijuana) and local tobacco typically smoked in a long pipe called a sebsi [sibsi].

7. On the dynamics surrounding treason in this novel, see Frohlich.

8. In the cases of Goytisolo and Chraïbi, the texts present a hyperbolic masculine sexuality that can easily be read as humor yet leave untouched patriarchal male/female hierarchies. I discuss issues of gender and sexuality further in part III. Goytisolo's novel came out in French as Don Julian (Paris: Gallimard, 1971), and thus Chraïbi may have read it before writing *Naissance.*

9. In *Coto vedado* (38) Goytisolo describes himself as: "Castellano en Cataluña, afrancesado en España, español en Francia, latino en Norteamérica, nesrani [cristiano/europeo] en Marruecos y moro en todas partes, no tardaría en volverme a consecuencia de mi nomadeo y viajes en ese raro espécimen de escritor no reivindicado por nadie, ajeno y reacio a agrupaciones y categorías." (Castilian in Catalonia, Frenchified in Spain, a Spaniard in France, a Latino in the United States, nesrani [Christian/European] in Morocco, and a Moor everywhere, it wasn't long before I became, as a result of my nomadism and travels, that rare breed of writer that is defended/claimed by no one, alien and opposed to groupings and categories.)

10. There is a similar legend about Hernán Cortés in his conquest of Mexico burning his boats so that his troops could not turn back.

11. See Hermes for a list of these sources.

12. Fernández Parrilla, "Breaking the Canon," notes that ʿAbd Allah Kānūn identifies Tariq's speech as the starting point of Moroccan literature in al-Nubūgh al-Maghribī fī al-Adab al-ʿArabī (Moroccan Genius in Arabic Literature, 1938).

13. In the first few years of the 2000s, approximately 30,000 Moroccans emigrated each year with Spain as their primary destination, either to stay there or to continue to other parts of Europe (Abend and Pingree). However, many more than that attempted to cross the waters, with Vermeren reporting in *Le Monde Diplomatique* in 2002 that 100,000 Moroccans were attempting to leave the country each year. Due to the economic crisis that began in Spain in 2008, starting in 2011 the number of immigrants residing in the country and attempting to enter the country has decreased. In addition, in 2006 the Spanish government stepped up its patrolling of Spanish waters and thus, the *New York Times* reports that in 2006, a record high of 39,180 people arrived in Spain illegally by boat, whereas in 2012 the total was 3,804 (Minder and Yardley). These figures, because they include Sub-Saharan Africans who cross through Morocco to try to enter Spain, give a sense of the total number of migrants, among them Moroccans and other North Africans, who have attempted to cross the Strait of Gibraltar over the past few decades. On migration patterns around the Mediterranean and specifically to Southern Europe, see King.

14. Flesler (165–68) discusses the representational issues and hierarchical relations that arise in this collaborative text.

15. On the classification of Nīnī's text in terms of genre, see my comments in the introduction and also al-Gharūsī 82–83 and 93–96.

16. I discuss Nīnī's references to Boabdil (Abu ʿAbd Allah Muhammad XII) in chapter 4.

17. Regarding Nīnī's comments on the Moros y Cristianos festival, see Flesler 100–101 and Rodríguez López 4–6.

18. Like his other works, Zaydān's novel was first published in his journal *al-Hilāl* and thus reached a wide audience. This novel was published in English (translated by Roger Allen) under the title *The Conquest of Andalusia.*

19. For more details on Kāmil's play and its context, see Walker.

20. Jewish characters are included in secondary roles, but they are caricatures of baseness.

21. This is a departure from the historical record, which states that after Tariq and Musa were ordered back to Damascus by the Umayyad caliph al-Walid I in 714, they stayed in Damascus and spent the rest of their lives there, with Tariq dying there in 720 (Reilly 52).

22. For more information on the context in which Zakī Qunṣul wrote, see Civantos.

23. For more on Islam in Chraïbi's works, see Bourget and Hadjadji.

24. In the earlier novel *La Mère du printemps (L'Oum-er-Bia)*, the character Azwaw swears at once on both Allah and the river referenced in the novel's title, the Mother of Spring (214); within the nature worship of the Amazigh belief system springs and rivers have spiritual significance and the Oum-er-Bia in particular is sacred because of the saints' tombs along its banks. In *Naissance*, Azwaw's daughter Yerma (which means "barren" in Spanish) has a son with the Arab emir and he is delivered by Azwaw.

25. This novel and Chraïbi's oeuvre in general demonstrate a great deal of linguistic hybridity by mixing (often without translation) Tamazight and Arabic words into the French text. For more on this see de la Batie.

26. For a discussion of the writings of Chraïbi and other Maghrebian authors as a rejection of religious fundamentalism, see Marx-Scouras 141.

27. Since the early 2000s, Spanish Muslim organizations have been petitioning Roman Catholic authorities to allow them to pray in the Cathedral of Cordoba. So far those requests have been denied. In 2010 a scuffle broke out when a group of Austrian Muslim tourists began to pray in the cathedral and guards tried to stop them. See D. Fuchs, Tremlett, Keeley, Shubert, and Calderwood, "The Reconquista of the Mosque of Cordoba."

28. Allen's English translation of Himmich's novel was published under the title *A Muslim Suicide*. Throughout his translation of the novel, Allen renders the Arabic "al-Andalus" as "Spain." Here I have modified his translation (which reads: "I longed for the Spain I'd lost") for the sake of historical accuracy and a more literal translation.

29. On Boudjedra's decision to write in Arabic, see Lantelme 525–26 and Ruhe 397.

30. The Arabic edition has 184 pages, whereas the French edition has 311, with no preface. This page difference, which cannot be accounted for by font size and translation alone, demonstrates the extent to which the French version contains additional material.

31. I refer to page numbers in both the Arabic and French versions, when there are analogous passages in both, and distinguish between them with an A and an F.

32. For a detailed discussion of the text's postmodern narrative structure and its relationship to the depiction of violence, see Toure.

33. The historian Ibn Khaldūn (1332–1406), who was born in Tunis to an Andalusi family and spent a period of his adult life in Nasrid Granada, is famous for his theories about social cohesion and conflict.

34. The name of the artist Yaḥyā ibn Maḥmūd al-Wāsiṭī (1210–1278) is rendered al-Wasity in Boudjedra's *La Prise de Gibraltar*.

35. See White, *The Content of the Form* and *Metahistory*.

36. The lack of awareness of the original Arabic text is such that Merino mistakenly identifies the Arabic text as a translation from the French (Merino, "Conquista" 90n21). The Arabic text was published one year before the French text, and that French version is labeled with "roman traduit de l'arabe par Antoine Moussali en collaboration avec l'auteur" ("novel translated from Arabic by Antoine Moussali in collaboration with the author") on the title page.

37. "Ṭāriq Alladhī Lam Yaftaḥ al-Andalus" originally appeared in a 1979 collection of short stories that carried that same title and is currently difficult to find. In 2001 the story was published in a bilingual Arabic-Spanish volume that brought together works by various Spanish and Moroccan writers and is titled *Cuentos de las dos orillas* (Regàs and Monleón). My citations refer to my translation into English and the Arabic pages of *Cuentos de las dos orillas*.

38. On kif, see note 6 in this chapter. In both usages of the term kif, there is cannabis involved. However, the Spanish translation of the story renders kif as "tobacco."

39. The reworking of Tariq's line is even more direct in the short story version of this chapter that appears in *Cuentos de las dos orillas*. There the story is preceded by an epigraph stating: "The sea is before you and the enemy is behind you, and before you as well" (27 [Arabic pages]).

40. The Sabians are two distinct religious groups that were present in Mesopotamia during pre-Islamic times and early Islam: a monotheistic sect and a pagan sect. In Arabic the term can also be used more generally to refer to apostates. The ancient monotheistic sect centered on John the Baptist has been linked to the agnostic Mandaeans who still live in modern-day Iraq and Iran.

41. I discuss this invocation of Columbus in more detail in the coda to part II.

42. These other references to emigration include the comparison of a woman's body to that of a *harraq* (a clandestine immigrant or harraga in colloquial Arabic) covered in water (117) and émigrés leaving the country thanks to corrupt politicians (176).

43. The 1994 and 1997 symposia on Maghreb/Mashriq cultural relations hosted by Marrakech's Jamiʿat al-Qadi Ayyad [L'Université Cadi Ayyad] attest to Maghrebi scholars' interest in these issues. See the double conference proceedings, titled *al-Maghrib-al-Mashriq*.

44. The following dates provide a rough idea of the duration of European colonialism in the countries in question: in Algeria the French initiated conquest in 1830 and Algeria gained independence in 1962; in Morocco, Spanish presence

around Ceuta grew in the 1860s, and in 1884 Spain created its protectorate while in 1904 Spain and France established their zones of influence and Morocco gained independence in 1956; Tunisia was a French protectorate from 1881 to 1956; Egypt was under British occupation from 1882 to 1922; in Syria the French occupation lasted from 1918 to 1946; and in Lebanon the French mandate lasted from 1920 through 1943.

45. "أهل المشرق أهل إبداع وأهل المغرب أهل فقه وهوامش."

Chapter 4

1. One work that portrays Boabdil but is difficult to categorize is Paco López Martín's "trilogy," which consists of the novel *El secreto nazarí: la leyenda del juego de las torres de la Alhambra* (2010), the game of strategy Las Torres de la Alhambra (sold exclusively by the store of the Board of the Alhambra and the Generalife), and the novel *La ruta de Boabdil: el presagio* (2012). In this sui generis work, López Martín, a game inventor from the province of Granada, uses an ambience of intrigue to create a legend surrounding his game and thus a fictional Moorish tradition behind it. In the novels, the Sultan Yusuf I (one of Boabdil's forebears) asks his main minister to create something special as part of the inauguration of a new building within the Alhambra. Later Boabdil and his mother play the game. In the second novel, *La ruta de Boabdil*, Boabdil's sons retrace their father's steps in reverse, heading from Fez back to Granada, seeking to uncover secrets.

2. Yiacoup reports that at least one Arab chronicler of the time described Boabdil's capture as a source of great shame (65).

3. The legend of the Moor's last sigh and others surrounding Boabdil and the Alhambra Palace were given international fame by US author, historian, and diplomat Washington Irving in his *Tales of the Alhambra*, which was published concurrently in the United States and England in 1832, with a revised edition in 1851. Salman Rushdie invokes this legend in the title of his novel *The Moor's Last Sigh* (1995). Although the novel is set in the Indian cities of Bombay and Cochin, the title refers to Boabdil, as does the name of the protagonist and narrator, Moraes Zogoiby, an alternate spelling of Boabdil's nickname, Zogoibi. Among other references to Boabdil in Rushdie's novel, the mother of Moraes Zogoiby and a friend of hers make paintings that they title "The Moor's Last Sigh."

4. Carrasco suggests that the Iberian romances may have been influenced by contemporary Arabic songs and poems referring to the heartbreak of Boabdil and mourning the loss of the Emirate of Granada ("Otras Poesías del Siglo XV" in *El moro de Granada en la literatura*).

5. Cheng's analysis includes melancholic self-representations by those racialized as Other within the US context, which although possibly very fruitful in treating other Arab texts, does not arise in the works depicting Tariq and Boabdil.

6. José Luis Várela, *Vida y obra literaria de Gregorio Romero Larrañaga* (Madrid: CSIC, 1948) 74, cited in Carrasco.

7. See my analysis of Goytisolo's *Reivindicación del Conde don Julián* in chapter 3, devoted to Tariq ibn Ziyad, and in chapter 5 in the section on Florinda.

8. Boabdil has been the subject of other musical works, such as "Lamento de Boabdil" (1931), a composition for cello and piano by Spanish composer Gaspar Cassadó; "Elegía a la pérdida de la Alhambra" for voice and piano by Spanish composer Antón García Abril as part of his *Canciones del jardín secreto* (2001); and the musical play *Boabdil, último rey de Granada*, by the Granadan theater company La Butaca Vacía, which was performed in Andalusia in 2010 (http://labutacavacia.es/compania.html and http://fiestasdearmilla.blogspot.com/2010/08/fiestas-desmiguel-2010.html).

9. "Llorando por Granada" was also part of the 1975 album *Feria*, the two 1976 greatest hits albums *Lo mejor de . . . Los Puntos* and *Los Super 20 de Los Puntos*, the 1977 album *Oriental*, and then the 2010 album *Los Puntos: 40 Años*. Los Puntos was active from 1967 to 1978 and then in a comeback period, which resulted from a well-attended reunion concert, from 1998 to the present.

10. "Tierra Cristiana" was also part of the 1976 greatest hits albums *Lo mejor de . . . Los Puntos*, the 1977 album *Oriental*, and then the 2010 album *Los Puntos: 40 Años*. Some other songs by Los Puntos with Andalusi or Oriental themes in the lyrics are "Ciego en Granada" and "Sherezada," both of which have pronounced Oriental musical motifs.

11. See Correa Ramón.

12. With regard to immigration from Andalusia to Catalonia alone, it is estimated that 850,000 Andalusian were living in Catalonia at the beginning of the 1980s (Pérez). For other specific figures on the different aspects of these emigration movements, see Recaño Valverde and Romero Valiente.

13. Gala's column titled "Charlas con Troylo" appeared weekly in *El País* between July 1979 and November 1980, and his column "En propia mano" also appeared there weekly from February 1981 to January 1983. Both columns were later collected and published in book form under the respective column title.

14. This album also includes the song "El bando" ("The Proclamation") that might seem to glorify the Catholic Monarchs with the lyrics repeating the abbreviation of the motto of Ferdinand II of Aragon (*Tanto monta, monta tanto*) and the medieval Castilian-style music, but the various references to the harsh expulsion of the Moors along with the song title make it a clear criticism of the royal proclamations that led to the mistreatment of the newly conquered. In the later album *El color de la vida* (1996) Cano continues to embrace Moorish themes with the songs "Moros y cristianos," a farcical criticism of anti-moro sentiment as expressed in the yearly celebration of the capture of Granada (la Toma de Granada) and "Kalam Garnata," whose Arabic title, repeated in the chorus of the song, means "the language [words/speech] of Granada."

15. See my discussion of the original *Paisaje con figuras*, and specifically the "Averroes" episode, in chapter 2.

16. This series demonstrates the common linguistic "suspension of disbelief" that is seen inversely in the Egyptian series *al-Ṭāriq*. In *Réquiem* every character speaks unaccented Castilian Spanish and the only Arabic heard is the call to prayer. This becomes more awkward when the Granadan Muslims talk with the Catholic Monarchs and then all of a sudden Ferdinand asks Boabdil where he learned to speak Spanish so well.

17. The Syrian writer Qamar Kīlānī contests this typical image of Boabdil's mother by presenting a fictional first-person account of the events from the mother's perspective.

18. For an insightful analysis of a novel cowritten by Lasala and focused on women in Muslim Iberia, *Moras y cristianas*, see Flesler 97–98 and 115–29.

19. The mini-series *Réquiem por Granada* hints at this type of relationship. In episode 7, through the process of negotiations between Boabdil and the Spanish emissary Fernández de Córdoba, the Castilian officer promises Boabdil to take care of the latter's son, who is being held by the Spaniards to guarantee Boabdil's loyalty, and Boabdil declares his respect and affection for Gonzalo. Similarly, in Gala's *El manuscrito carmesí*, Fernández de Córdoba expresses deep respect for Boabdil and treats him as a king and an intellectual equal.

20. Another way in which Soler's novel departs from typical versions of the Boabdil story is that by having Fernández de Córdoba have an amorous relationship with a Jewish woman, it includes secondary Jewish characters and their persecution by the Inquisition.

21. On the narrative innovation in *El manuscrito carmesí*, vis-à-vis the traditional historical novel, see, for instance, Ortega 86, de Toro 177–78, and Benhamamouche, the last of which I discuss later. The Planeta Prize is a major literary prize in Hispanic letters that is awarded by the Spanish publisher Grupo Planeta.

22. This topos is famous because of the (ironic) role of Sidi Hamid Benengeli's text in *Don Quijote*, but it long predates Cervantes's novel (Delpech and Johnson).

23. Although discussion of this issue does not fit within the scope of this study, it is important to note that in the case of Gala, the melancholia surrounding Boabdil may be linked to the theme of nonheteronormative sexuality in Gala's oeuvre. That is, as pointed out by Gema Pérez-Sánchez (personal communication August 2015), this melancholia may be a figure for queerness.

24. Several twentieth-century Arab poets have treated Boabdil in their work, see Khalīl 7, 14, 30, and 80. Also, al-Allaq argues that Maḥmūd Darwīsh's 1992 poem "Aḥada ʿAshara Kawkaban ʿalā Ākhir al-Mashhad al-Andalusī" ("Eleven Planets at the End of the Andalusian Scene") not only refers to Moors in general leaving Granada, but to Boabdil.

25. See Civantos for an analysis of how *La gloria de don Ramiro* uses Orientalism to seek refuge from the reality of immigrant-filled Argentina (89–90) and for more on the context of Larreta's work.

26. The 1941 edition, and most subsequent editions, carry a longer version of the title: *"Zogoibi," el dolor de la tierra* ("Zogoibi," The Suffering of the Land).

27. See Civantos for an analysis of the language politics of this essay (199–200) and for more on Ilyās Qunṣul's other works and the context in which he wrote.

28. Interestingly, al-Maqdisī's play blames scheming women (ʿA'isha and Isabella [rendered as *al-malika*, the queen]) for the fall of Granada, whereas Abāẓa's text glorifies ʿA'isha as a valiant figure whose machinations were efforts to save the kingdom. There is oblique reference to Boabdil in a later play: *al-Akhīr* by Palestinian writer Walīd Abū Bakr (b. 1938). The only thing that situates the play in al-Andalus is the initial stage direction stating that it takes place in "the

king's palace in Granada" (5), and the only thing directing the reader to Boabdil is the title *al-Akhīr* (*The Last One*). The main characters are given only the generic names "The King" and "The Queen," which enables the play to function as a political allegory about legitimacy of power and the transition from autocracy to democracy.

29. For a treatment of the fall of Granada in general in *Léon l'Africain*, and in comparison with two other novels on the fall, see Ortega.

30. In Maalouf's novel the name is transliterated as "Hassan."

31. For a comparison of Gala's *Manuscrito carmesí* and Maalouf's *Leo Africanus* from a narratological perspective, see Khalīl 118–26 and 134–41.

32. Two of these juvenile novels are Josefina Careaga Ribelles, *Boabdil y el final del reino de Granada* (2009) and Brígida Gallego-Coin, *Boabdil* (2012).

33. Although many of those that have left Spain since 2008 are immigrants who returned to their country of origin, within that there are rising numbers of Spanish-born nationals seeking employment elsewhere. See Sanmartín, EFE, and Sánchez.

34. For more on Hallar and his use of Boabdil, see Civantos 61–64.

35. Zamora Loboch states this in the essay collection *Como ser negro y no morir en Aravaca*, cited in Martin-Márquez 342.

Coda

1. The Arabic original reads:

أنا الأندلسي الأخير،
المتسول على أرصفة غرناطة.
و أنا آخر هندي أحمر
نجا من أسنان كريستوف كولومبوس.

2. Mignolo, *Local Histories/Global Designs* 76, 105–106, and Majid, especially 27–28.

3. "Le nouveau monde" is a fifty-page narrative in the collection *Les Portiques de la mer*.

4. Roa Bastos's *Vigilia del Almirante* is based on a similar premise.

5. For more on Chams Nadir's literary style, as well as his use of French, see Ben Hassen.

6. Ismat shared a typescript copy of this play with Pedro Martínez Montávez, who kindly allowed me to make a copy of the work.

7. For more on this global phenomenon, see Aidi, "'Let Us Be Moors.'"

8. In Spain, in addition to immigrants from the Maghreb and elsewhere and the residents of Ceuta and Melilla (the Spanish enclaves in Morocco) who are of North African origin, the Muslim population consists of growing numbers of converts from Catholicism. Many Spanish converts to Islam also identify with al-Andalus and the morisco. But of course, without the link to the Americas and the analogous relationship between the oppressed morisco and the oppressed immigrant/ethnic minority. See Abend and Howe, chapter 8, "Spain's Multiple Muslim Voices" (121–38).

9. For more demographic information, see Abdo and Garrison. More broadly, in addition to Agosto, Abdo (169–86), and Garrison, on Muslim Hispanics see Morales, Martínez-Vázquez, Aponte 36–40, Aidi "Olé to Allah," Wakin, and Viscidi.

10. Victor Hernández Cruz's *In the Shadow of Al-Andalus*, a poetic reflection on the historical ties between Iberia, North Africa, and the Caribbean and their similarities in terms of racial and linguistic hybridity, is full of such references. For example, in the poem "Vicente Espinel—La Decima" the poet describes the commonalities between the song of a Puerto Rican folk singer and traditional Arab music and explains the similarity by stating that the Puerto Rican musician opens his song "as our Arabic ancestors did / in al-Andalus" (90–91).

11. A March 17, 2012, event advertised on Facebook.

12. See http://www.hispanicmuslims.com/andalusia/andalusia.html and http://hispanicmuslims.com/articles/andalusian_past.html

13. A handful of the tens of thousands of Muslim Hispanics have turned to violent expression of counterculture or anti-imperialist attitudes through militant Islam. The most famous of these is José Padilla, who was born in the United States, was raised by Catholic parents of Puerto Rican origin, and converted to Islam in prison while serving time for a gang-related crime. In a highly controversial case, in 2002 Padilla was arrested on suspicion of participating in a "dirty bomb" plot, was designated an enemy combatant, and in 2007 was convicted of aiding terrorists. The media coverage and commentary on the case often reflected the racialization of minorities and Muslims. For more on the role of race and other social factors in minority conversions to Islam, see Aidi, "'Let Us Be Moors'" and "Jihadis in the Hood."

14. See Martínez-Vázquez (131) on how recuperation of a connection to al-Andalus leads to the reformulation of limited conceptions of *mestizaje* or the cultural and racial mixing of Spanish and Amerindian elements.

Part III

1. This is taken from Denys Johnson-Davies's translation, with one small modification: Johnson-Davies translates "Andalus" as "Andalusia," and I have used the term that transliterates the Arabic original.

2. The connection to conquest is even stronger in Arabic given the phonological similarity between *khasib* and *ghasab*—meaning to take by force, compel, rape, or conquer.

Chapter 5

1. The story of Roderick and Florinda made it to Spanish America as well: on an eighteenth-century Mexican drama version of the Roderick-Florinda story, see Ratcliffe 38–41 and on nineteenth-century Colombian and Argentine opera versions, see Drayson 206–10.

2. See Grieve 25–26, Hernández Jubería 177–78, and Segura González 2n2.

3. See my discussions of Florinda in Taymūr's *Ṭāriq al-Andalus* and ʿAlī al-Jārim's *Hātif min al-Andalus*.

4. My citations in English come from Zaydān, *The Conquest of Andalusia* (translated by Roger Allen).

5. See Panier regarding the discourses surrounding closed spaces (the castle, the bedroom, and the casket) in Zaydān's novel.

6. In Zaydān's novel, Badr/Tumas was kidnapped and sold to the Amazighs by Sulayman, a crypto-Jew. Badr/Tumas was then raised by Tariq's father and ultimately, to keep Julian from killing Badr, Sulayman himself reveals that Badr is the long-lost Tumas. In this way, a Jew, albeit through treachery, created filial ties between Christian Goths and Muslim North Africans. The novel suggests that this treachery is the result of Roderick's oppression of Jews and that Sulayman's redemption by revealing the truth is made possible by Tariq toppling Roderick's regime.

7. See Grieve 232–33 on Franco's use of the triumphant figures of Pelayo and the Virgin of Covadonga.

8. See Epps, "The Politics of Ventriloquism." See also Rogers and Epps, *Significant Violence*, chapter 1. For an analysis of *Reivindicación del Conde don Julián* as part of a set of post–Civil War texts that reflect Spanish intellectuals' feelings of being symbolically sodomized by the Franco regime and how later writers reworked the misogynist approach of Goytisolo and others, see Pérez-Sánchez, 61–112.

9. On historians' perspectives on the authenticity of accounts regarding Florinda and company, see Grieve, 235–36 and 238.

10. Iman Darwish suggests that few of Wallada's poems were preserved due to a lack of interest as well as outright censorship (6–7).

11. For more on the historical sources about Wallada and the time period in which she lived, see Shammarī, Aragón Huerta, Bellido, and Marín, especially 238 and 664–65. On Wallada as a courtly poet and the limits of feminist analysis of her work, see Darwish.

12. On Wallada and veiling, see Garulo Muñoz 105–106.

13. Some have cited Wallada as proof that the women of al-Andalus had greater personal freedom than did women in other Muslim cultures (an idea that scholars have since debunked), ascribing the relative freedom and feminism of Wallada and other Andalusi women to contact with Christian influence in the interfaith mix of al-Andalus. Marín discusses the European sources of this interpretation and the fallacies inherent in it, 220–22. See also Bellido 56.

14. For more on Muhya and the lesbianism interpretation, see Garulo Muñoz 108, Marín 678, and Amer 231. As Marín explains (678n307), this interpretation was first propagated by French Orientalist Henri Pérès in *La Poésie andalouse en arabe classique au XIe siècle* (1937), basing the idea on a comment by the nineteenth-century French-Dutch Orientalist Reinhart Dozy.

15. In contrast, in the afterword of one of the plays I discuss later, *Sīzīf al-Andalusī*, the author, Nadhīr ʿAẓma, dismisses sources that say that Wallada was homosexual or bisexual (161).

16. Wallada has also inspired a wide range of dance and musical works, such as the 2003 joint Moroccan-Spanish album *Wallada y Ibn Zaydún: una historia de amor y poesía* by Mohammed El Arabi Serghini and Eduardo Paniagua; the 2004 Spanish

theater production "Wallada, El sueño de un poeta cordobés," with flamenco-based dancing, music by Grupo Qurtuba, and libretto by José María de la Quintana and Javier García-Pelayo; the 2008 song "Wallada la Omeya" by Spanish metal band Saurom in their album *Once romances desde Al-Andalus*; and the 2008 album *La Voix de l'amour* by Syrian oud player and singer Waed Bouhassoun [Waʿd Abū Ḥasūn], in which she sings songs based on the poetry of Ibn Zaydun and Wallada.

17. These include the works by Aḥdab (which alternates between verse and rhymed prose [*sajaʿ*]), ʿAbd al-ʿAẓīm, Sirāj, al-Khiyārī, and Juwayda.

18. In refreshing contrast, more recently in "ʿAwdat Wallāda" ("The Return of Wallada") the woman poet Marām al-Miṣrī (b. 1962), a Syrian living in France, has taken up Wallada as a symbol of a woman who paves her own way. This collection of poems has appeared in a bilingual edition with the Arabic original and Spanish translation and also in French translation. Some of the original Arabic poems can be found at http://www.discover-syria.com/news/1639.

19. The only internal connection between the three mini-series is that they cover successive historical periods in al-Andalus. The first series, *Ṣaqr Quraysh* (2002), tells the story of ʿAbd al-Rahman I, and the second, *Rabīʿ Qurṭuba* (2003), is about the period of the Cordoban Caliphate's flourishing, including the period of de facto rule by al-Mansur.

20. The "m." is an abbreviation for *miladi*, the Christian Gregorian calendar, and "h." is the abbreviation for *hijri*, the Islamic lunar calendar.

21. Some other women poets of al-Andalus who wrote openly about love are the tenth-century Guadalajaran Ḥafṣa bint Ḥamdūn, the eleventh-century Almerian Umm al-Kirām, and the twelfth-century Granadans Nazhūn bint al-Qulaiʾiya and Ḥafṣa bint al-Hājj al-Rakūniyya. See Viguera, "Asluḥu li ʿl-maʿūlī," 709–11, Afsaruddin, and Hammond, "He Desires Her?" and "He Said 'She Said.'"

22. The original poem reads:

أنا الأندلسي الأخير
الذي جاء يطالب بحصته
. . .
وقصيدة من ديوان ابن زيدون
وخاتم من خواتم ولادة بنت المستكفي.

23. The play won the "1er certamen autores de teatro de la Comunidad de Madrid" for 1990.

24. The father of the historical Wallada was al-Mustakfi, but throughout this text his name is written al-Mustakfir.

25. See, for instance, McClintock, *Imperial Leather* and Martin-Márquez.

26. Another recent Spanish historical novel set in al-Andalus, specifically in the Cordoban caliphate, also displays a morbid fascination with eunuchs: Kresdez's *El veneno del eunuco*.

27. Another Spanish novel makes an oblique reference to Wallada: In Cáliz's *Horas para Wallada* the title character is a Granadan sultan's concubine in a later period than that of Wallada bint al-Mustakfi. Upon conversion to Islam, the heroine-concubine is named after the Cordoban poetess because, like her namesake is presumed to be, she is a strong-willed woman. This fictional

intra-Andalusi reference to a major figure is similar to what al-Jārim does with Florinda in *Hātif min al-Andalus.*

28. The ambivalence regarding whether to incorporate and appropriate al-Andalus as part of the line of descent of contemporary Spaniards is evident in the switching back and forth between using "andalusíes [Andalusis]" and "andaluces [Andalusians]" to refer to the citizens of Muslim-ruled Cordoba.

29. Wallada was the daughter of the penultimate Umayyad ruler of al-Andalus, the caliph of Cordoba. He was succeeded by a usurper from the Amazigh Hammudid Dynasty who in turn was succeeded by Hisham III, the last Umayyad ruler of al-Andalus (1026–1031) and the last person to hold the title caliph of Cordoba. Hisham III had at least one daughter (Townson 45). Thus Wallada was not the last Umayyad princess but certainly was the last famous Umayyad princess. The subtitle indicates that she was the last Andalusi princess, which she was far from being, considering that the Nasrid Dynasty in Granada lasted until the fifteenth century.

30. In a parallel fashion, Cabello's novel objectifies the visual aesthetics of the Arabic language while stripping it of the ability to create meaning. The introduction is preceded by the Spanish-language rendering of the well-known Muslim invocation "In the name of God, the Merciful, the Compassionate"; directly below that are three semblances of words in Arabic, but each has a mistake in letter formation and the three together don't form any meaningful phrase, let alone the Arabic original for the prayer presented in Spanish. Cabello has also published a jointly written collection of poems that represents a dialogue between Ibn Zaydun and Wallada: *Epílogo de un sueño* (2004, with Antonio Herrera).

31. Cabello uses an alternate transliteration of the Arabic name: Muhía.

32. Palma Ceballos renders the name Muhcha.

33. The epigraph is taken from Peri Rossi's *Evohe: poemas eróticos*, which caused scandal when first published because of its lesbian erotic content.

34. The fusion of time periods in Yūnus's novel is similar to that of *Concierto barroco* (1974) by Alejo Carpentier (1904–1980), who spearheaded the approach to reality and narrative known as magical realism.

35. On page 43 Wallada thinks of the Wali Qarqush as "the Ottoman Wali," but Morocco was never under Ottoman control. This can be linked to the general melding of geographic locations in the novel.

36. At one point in the narrative, the Wali refers to himself as a member of the Hashemite line (142), which is a dynasty that originated in the Hejaz (now part of Saudi Arabia) and in 1921 was established via the British as the ruling dynasty of Jordan. This strengthens the association between the novel's al-Wali and Hassan II, who is part of the Alaouite Dynasty, a branch of the Hashemites.

37. Although Judas is not mentioned in the Quran, according to that text Jesus ascended to heaven and someone else was crucified in his place. One theory believed by many Muslims is that Judas Iscariot was crucified in place of Jesus.

38. In contrast with Fatima's status as the last Idrisid princess, though in many Spanish texts Wallada is presented as "the last Umayyad princess," here Wallada is

not referred to as being the last and is apparently immortal. She is the embodiment of the textual version of Wallada that can live forever.

39. The rest of Nafzāwī's text is not so favorable toward women. However, the fact that Yūnus selected this particular passage for inclusion supports the idea that the novel upholds women's right to sexual fulfillment.

Chapter 6

1. The story was written in 1964, first published in the Beirut literary magazine *al-Ādāb* in 1965, and published in al-Amīr's second collection of short stories in 1969. My citations in English are from the translation by Cassimy and Frazier, who rendered the title "An Andalusian Tale" and the author's name as Daisy Ellameere.

2. Al-Amīr spent two years studying at Cambridge University, so that has generally been taken to be the setting of the story.

3. I cite from the individual edition of *Gharnāṭa* and the joint edition of the last two parts of the trilogy, but the trilogy was also published in 1998 in a single volume as *Thulāthīyat Gharnāṭa*. My English citations of *Gharnāṭa* are from the translation by Granara. Part I of the trilogy, *Gharnāṭa*, won the 1994 Book of the Year Award of the Cairo International Book Fair (organized by the General Egyptian Book Organization), and the trilogy won the 1995 First Prize of the First Arab Women's Book Fair in Cairo. *Gharnāṭa* was also selected by the Arab Writers Union as one of the best 100 Arabic novels of the twentieth century.

4. Khalīl notes that this book-burning scene is similar to that of another novel set during the decline of Muslim Spain, *Shadows of the Pomegranate Tree* (1992) by the Pakistani British writer Tariq Ali. See 144–54 in Khalīl for a comparison between these works.

5. Most of this quotation is from Granara's translation (223); however, the first sentence is my translation of the multilayered Arabic:

والانسان، أليس الإنسان كالورقة مكتوباً... سلسلة من الكلمات كل
منها دال على مدلول ومجملها أيضاً ألا يشي به المخطوط من الكلام ؟

Granara renders this sentence as "Weren't human beings inscribed sheets, strings of words having meaning that, when put together, connote the whole that a person signifies?"

6. Interestingly, ʿAli takes on something of a Scheherazade role in part II of the trilogy when, on returning to Granada, he runs into a figure from his youth: Fidda, the black Muslim domestic slave of an Old Christian family. ʿAli had been good friends with the Christian boy whose family Fidda served and also Fidda's son. When Fidda and ʿAli run into each other years later, she asks for ʿAli's help with reading a letter in Arabic that was delivered to her, which she believes is from her son, reporting that he is alive and well. ʿAli, who was taught Arabic by Hasan, is ready to decode the letter when he realizes that it is actually from an acquaintance of Fidda's son and bears the news of the son's death. Rather than destroy the hopes that Fidda has been harboring since receiving the letter two years prior, ʿAli creates a fictional version of the letter in which the son says that he is well. Surprised by his feelings for Fidda, who connects him to his childhood

and is also grieving absent loved ones, and hearing of her subjection to her master, ʿAli proposes marriage to her. Although she doesn't respond to his proposal, as a sort of parting gift for her, before leaving Granada ʿAli creates a fake letter from Fidda's son, in which the son details how well he is doing in Alexandria, and has the letter delivered to Fidda. Throughout this reencounter with Fidda, ʿAli uses storytelling to assuage Fidda's emotional pain.

7. See Thomas de Antonio, "La inquisición y los moriscos en la novela *Granada*" 217 and Menocal's foreword to Granara's translation x.

8. The bibliography of critical works on the reclaiming of Scheherazade, let alone her role in the *One Thousand and One Nights*, is extensive. See for instance, chapter 2, "Writing Scheherazade Now," in al-Musawi (71–115), Suyoufie, Gauch, Morsy, and Andary.

Conclusion

1. Calderwood, basing himself on *Box office des films marocaines année 2006*, notes that in Morocco this film was number one in ticket sales and number two in profits for the year of its release ("Proyectando al-Andalus" 220). See Calderwood for an in-depth analysis of this film, including its intertextual references to Chahine's *al-Maṣīr*.

2. On the journal *Bayt al-Ḥikma* see Kamal. The Al Mutamid Program in particular resulted in a two-volume bilingual anthology of texts in Arabic and Spanish and their translations, titled *Cuentos de las dos orillas* (Regàs and Monleón, Monleón and Copete). On the project of cultural dialogue in this anthology, see Dotson-Renta 19–29. On the *Cuentos de las dos orillas* anthology, the film *Cuento de las dos orillas* (Jesús Armesto, 2008), which fuses documentary and narrative elements to meditate on historical connections between Spain and Morocco, and similar initiatives, see Vega-Durán. On translation between Europe and the Maghreb, see Fernández Parrilla and Montoro Murillo and specifically from Arabic into Spanish, see Fernández Parrilla, "Translating Modern Arabic Literature into Spanish" and Fernández Parrilla, Pérez Cañada, and Montoro Murillo. On Moroccans who regularly translate from Spanish into Arabic, see de Agreda Burillo.

3. On critical literacy, see Graff 333–37, Freire, and Freire and Macedo.

4. On this distinction, see Scheffler 314–17, Walzer xi and 8–13, and Bernard Williams 18–27.

5. See also Žižek's discussion of Brown in "Tolerance as an Ideological Category."

6. Tønder questions the privileging of reason over sensorial experience and argues that by returning to the root meaning of tolerance—withstanding pain—and considering the corporeal dimensions of the process, we can enter a new practice of tolerance. For more on debates surrounding tolerance and toleration, see McKinnon and Castiglione; Fiala; Creppell, Hardin, and Macedo; M. Cruz; and Brown and Forst. On the role of tolerance in modern Arab and Muslim thought, see Asad, chapter 7: "Reconfigurations of Law and Ethics in Colonial Egypt"; Hamad; and Abu-ʿUksa.

7. In addition to the found manuscript that is reworked through translation in

Gala's *El manuscrito carmesí*, there is a manuscript (and a building) threatened with destruction in the novel *al-Bayt al-Andalusī* (*The Andalusi House*, 2011) by Algerian Wāsīnī al-Aʿraj [Waciny Laredj]. In a similar vein, in *Riḥlat al-Gharnāṭī* (*The Journey of the Granadan*, 2005) by Rabīʿ Jābir [Rabee Jaber], the protagonist's search for his brother lost in al-Andalus generates a dream tale about the search. Both of these works can be understood as commentaries on the fictionality and/or fragility of the fantasy of an Andalusi paradise and on sources of resilience in the face of loss.

Bibliography

ʿAbd al-ʿAẓīm, ʿAlī. *Wallāda*. Cairo: Lajnat al-Bayān al-ʿArabī, 1948.

ʿAbd al-Ḥalim, Salwa. "Raḍwa ʿĀshūr: Thaqāfatnā Tarfuḍu al-Ān Mā Kānat Taqbalahu qabla Alf Sana." *al-Ḥayat* 17420 (December 14, 2010): 18. http://daharchives.alhayat.com/.

ʿAbd al-Nāṣir, Taḥiyya [Tahia Abdel Nasser]. "al-Arshīf al-ʿArabī fī al-Waqiʿiyya al-Siḥriyya." *Alif: Journal of Comparative Poetics* 31 (2011): 185–214.

Abdo, Geneive. *Mecca and Main Street: Muslim life in America after 9/11*. New York: Oxford University Press, 2006.

ʿAbdū fī ʿAhd al-Muwaḥḥidīn. Dir. and perf. Saʿīd al-Nāṣirī [Saïd Naciri]. Mprod, 2006. Film.

Abend, Lisa. "Spain's New Muslims: A Historical Romance." *In the Light of Medieval Spain: Islam, the West, and the Relevance of the Past*. Simon R. Doubleday and David Coleman, eds. New York: Palgrave Macmillan, 2008, 133–56.

Abend, Lisa, and Geoff Pingree. "Morocco's Biggest European Export: People." *Christian Science Monitor*, September 29, 2005. http://www.csmonitor.com/2005/0929/p07s01-woeu.html.

Aboul-Ela, Hosam. *Other South: Faulkner, Coloniality, and the Mariátegui Tradition*. Pittsburgh: University of Pittsburgh Press, 2007.

Abū Bakr, Walīd. *al-Awwal wa-l-Akhīr: Masraḥiyyatān*. Safa, Kuwait: Sharikat al-Rubayʿān lil-Nashr wa-l-Tawzīʿ, 1981.

Abu-Jaber, Diana. *Crescent*. New York: Norton, 2003.

AbuKhalil, Asʿad. "A Note on the Study of Homosexuality in the Arab/Islamic Civilization." *Arab Studies Journal* 1:2 (Fall 1993): 32–34, 48.

Abu-Rabiʿ, Ibrahim M. *Contemporary Arab Thought: Studies in Post-1967 Arab Intellectual History*. London: Pluto Press, 2003.

Abu-ʿUksa, Wael. "Liberal Tolerance in Arab Political Thought: Translating Farah Antun (1874–1922)." *Journal of Levantine Studies* 3:2 (Winter 2013): 151–57.

Abū Zayd, Naṣr Ḥāmid. "Khiṭāb Ibn Rushd bayna Ḥaqq al-Maʿrifa wa-Ḍughūṭ al-Khiṭāb al-Naqīḍ." *Alif: Journal of Comparative Poetics* 16 (1996): 6–35.

Acosta Sánchez, José. *Andalucía: reconstrucción de una identidad y la lucha contra el centralismo*. Barcelona: Anagrama, 1978.

Adams, Susan M., Elena Bosch, Patricia L. Balaresque, Stéphane J. Ballereau, Andrew C. Lee, Eduardo Arroyo, et al. "The Genetic Legacy of Religious Diversity and Intolerance: Paternal Lineages of Christians, Jews, and Muslims in the Iberian Peninsula." *American Journal of Human Genetics* 83:6 (2008): 725–36.

Afsaruddin, Asma. "Poetry and Love: The Feminine Contribution in Muslim Spain." *Islamic Studies* 30:1/2 (Spring/Summer 1991): 157–69.

Agosto, Efraín. "Reading the Word in America: US Latino/a Religious Communities and Their Scriptures." *Misreading America: Scriptures and Difference*. Vincent L. Wimbush and Melissa Renee Reid, eds. New York: Oxford University Press, 2013, 117–64.

de Agreda Burillo, Fernando. "El hispanismo marroquí y la traducción de la literatura española e iberoamericana." http://hispanistasdetanger.blogspot.com/2008/04/el-hispanismo-marroqui-y-la-traduccion.html.

Aḥdab, Ibrāhīm. *Riwāyat al-Wazīr Abī al-Walīd ibn Zaydūn maʿa Wallāda bint al-Mustakfī [...]*. Cairo: al-Maktaba al-Azhariyya, Maṭbaʿat al-Maḥrūsa, 1899.

"Aḥmad ʿAbd al-Ḥalīm [. . .] fī Musalsal al-Ṭāriq." *al-Sharq al-Awṣat*. http://www.aawsat.com/details.asp?issueno=8800&article=186370#.UfVhuo3VCSo.

Ahmed, Sara. *Strange Encounters: Embodied Others in Post-Coloniality*. London: Routledge, 2000.

Aidi, Hishaam D. "The Interference of al-Andalus: Spain, Islam, and the West." *Social Text* 87, 24:2 (Summer 2006): 67–88.

———. "Jihadis in the Hood: Race, Urban Islam and the War on Terror." *Middle East Report* 32:224 (Fall 2002). http://www.merip.org/mer/mer224/jihadis-hood.

———. "'Let Us Be Moors': Islam, Race, and 'Connected Histories.'" *Middle East Report* 33:229 (Winter 2003). http://www.merip.org/mer/mer229/let-us-be-moors.

———. "Olé to Allah: New York's Latino Muslims." http://planete-afrique.com/afro-latino/Ole%20to%20Allah-New%20Yorks%20Latino%20Muslims.htm.

Akasoy, Anna. "Convivencia and Its Discontents: Interfaith Life in al-Andalus." *International Journal of Middle East Studies* 42 (2010): 489–99.

Akasoy, Anna, and Guido Giglioni. *Renaissance Averroism and Its Aftermath: Arabic Philosophy in Early Modern Europe*. Dordrecht: Springer, 2013.

al-Allaq, Ali J. "Tradition as a Factor of Arabic Modernism: Darwīsh's Application of a Mask." *Tradition and Modernity in Arabic Language and Literature*. J. R. Smart, ed. Richmond, UK: Curzon, 1996, 18–26.

al-Amīr, Dayzī [Daisy Ellameere]. "An Andalusian Tale." *Modern Iraqi Short Stories*. Ali M. Cassimy and W. McClung Frazier, trans. Baghdad: Ministry of Information, 1971, 89–96.

———. "Qiṣṣa Andalusiyya" [1964]. *Thumma Taʿūd al-Mawja*. Beirut: Manshūrāt Dār al-Niḍāl, 1986, 97–107.

al-Anṣārī, Muḥammad Jābir. "Kharāʾiṭ al-Wāqiʿ al-Ijtimāʿī . . . am Bukāʾiyyāt al-Andalus?" *al-Ḥayat*, August 1, 2011.

Alazraki, Jaime. *Versiones, Inversiones, Reversiones. El espejo como modelo estructural del relato en los cuentos de Borges*. Madrid: Gredos, 1977.

Albert-Llorca, Marlène, and J. A. González Alcantud. *Moros y cristianos: representaciones del otro en las fiestas del Mediterráneo occidental*. Toulouse: Presses Universitaires du Mirail, 2003.

Allen, Roger, and D. S. Richards, eds. *Arabic Literature in the Post-Classical Period*. Cambridge: Cambridge University Press, 2006.

Almond, Ian. "Borges the Post-Orientalist: Images of Islam from the Edge of the West." *Modern Fiction Studies* 50:2 (Summer 2004): 435–59.

Altamirano, Carlos, and Beatriz Sarlo. *Ensayos argentinos, de Sarmiento a la vanguardia*. Buenos Aires: Centro Editor de América Latina, 1983, 109–11.

Altschul, Nadia. "Andrés Bello and the Poem of the Cid: Latin America, Occidentalism, and the Foundations of Spain's 'National Philology.'" *Medievalisms in the Postcolonial World: The Idea of the "Middle Ages" Outside Europe*. Kathleen Davis and Nadia Altschul, eds. Baltimore, MD: Johns Hopkins University Press, 2009, 217–36.

Alviz, Jesús. *Wallada*. Madrid: Comunidad de Madrid, Centro de Estudios y Actividades Culturales, 1990.

Amer, Sahar. "Medieval Arab Lesbians and Lesbian-Like Women." *Journal of the History of Sexuality* 18:2 (2009): 215–36.

Amjad, Zara, and Gulzar Haider. "Re-imagining the Cordoba Mosque." *Critical Muslim* 6 (April–June 2013): 153–70.

Andary, Nezar Ajaj. "A Consuming Fever of History: A Study of Five Urgent Flashbacks in Arabic Film and Literature." PhD thesis, UCLA, 2008.

Anidjar, Gil. "Postscript: Futures of al-Andalus." *In the Light of Medieval Spain: Islam, the West, and the Relevance of the Past*. Simon R. Doubleday and David Coleman, eds. New York: Palgrave Macmillan, 2008, 189–208.

"Antonio Gala publica sus guiones del programa de TVE 'Paisaje con figuras.'" *El País*, April 19, 1985. http://elpais.com/diario/1985/04/19/cultura/482709607_850215.html.

Aponte, Edwin David. *¡Santo!: Varieties of Latino/a Spirituality*. Maryknoll, NY: Orbis Books, 2012.

Apter, Emily. *Against World Literature: On the Politics of Untranslatability*. London: Verso, 2013.

———. *The Translation Zone*. Princeton, NJ: Princeton University Press, 2006.

Aragón Huerta, Mercedes. "La princesa omeya Wallada: poetisa, musa y mito en las fuentes árabes." *Revista Jábega* 97 (2008): 35–39. http://hdl.handle.net/10498/11113.

Armas Marcelo, Juan Jesús. "Mestizo ideológico." http://carloscano.es/2011/05/17/mestizo-ideologico-carlos-cano-j-j-armas-marcelo/), s.d.

Asad, Talal. *Formations of the Secular: Christianity, Islam, Modernity*. Stanford, CA: Stanford University Press, 2003.

Ashcroft, Bill, Gareth Griffiths, and Helen Tiffin, eds. *The Post-Colonial Studies Reader*. New York: Routledge, 1995.

Ashour, Radwa [Raḍwa ʿĀshūr]. *Gharnāṭa*. [Cairo]: Dār al-Hilāl, 1994.

———. *Granada*. William Granara, trans. Syracuse, NY: Syracuse University Press, 2003.

———. Interview with Youssef Rakha. *Al-Ahram Weekly* 34 (October 14, 2001): 22–23.

———. *Maryama wa-l-Raḥīl*. Cairo: Dār al-Hilāl, 1995.

Assadi, Jamal, and Mahmud Naʿamneh. *The Road to Self-Revival: Sufism, Heritage, Intertextuality and Meta-Poetry in Modern Arabic Poetry*. New York: Peter Lang, 2011.

Assmann, Jan. *Moses the Egyptian: The Memory of Egypt in Western Monotheism*. Cambridge, MA: Harvard University Press, 1997.

ʿAẓma, Nadhīr. *Sīzīf al-Andalusī*. Damascus: Wizārat al-Thaqāfa wa-l-Irshād al-Qawmī, 1981.

Bahrami, Beebe. "Al-Andalus and Memory: The Past and Being Present among Hispano-Moroccan Andalusians from Rabat." *Charting Memory: Recalling Medieval Spain*. Stacy N. Beckwith, ed. New York: Taylor & Francis, 2000, 111–43.

Bahrawi, Nazry. "The Andalusi Secular." *Critical Muslim* 6 (April–June 2013): 47–56.

Bahri, Hamid, and Francesca Canadé Sautman. "Crossing History, Dis-Orienting the Orient: Amin Maalouf's Uses of the 'Medieval.'" *Medievalisms in the Postcolonial World: The Idea of "the Middle Ages" Outside Europe*. Kathleen Davis and Nadia Altschul, eds. Baltimore, MD: Johns Hopkins University Press, 2009, 174–205.

Balderston, Daniel. "Borges, Averroes, Aristotle: The Poetics of Poetics." *Hispania* 79:2 (May 1996): 201–7.

Baldwin-Edwards, Martin. "Between a Rock and a Hard Place: North Africa as a Region of Emigration, Immigration and Transit Migration." *Review of African Political Economy* 33:108 (June 2006): 311–24.

Barbero, Abilio, and Pascual M. Vigil. *Sobre los orígenes sociales de la Reconquista*. Esplugues de Llobregat: Editorial Ariel, 1974.

Barletta, Vincent. *Covert Gestures: Crypto-Islamic Literature as Cultural Practice in Early Modern Spain*. Minneapolis: University of Minnesota Press, 2005.

Barrios Aguilera, Manuel, and Francisco Andújar Castillo. *Hombre y territorio en el reino de Granada, 1570–1630: estudios sobre repoblación*. Almería: Instituto de Estudios Almerienses, Universidad de Granada, 1995.

Bartra, Roger. *Cultura y melancolía: las enfermedades del alma en la España del Siglo de Oro*. Barcelona: Editorial Anagrama, 2001.

Bassnett, Susan. "The Translation Turn in Cultural Studies." *Translation, Translation*. Susan Petrelli, ed. Amsterdam: Rodopi, 2003, 433–49.

de la Batie, Bernadette Dejean. "La langue de Driss Chraïbi: langue déplacée d'un écrivain déplacé." *International Journal of Francophone Studies* 4:1 (2001): 14–23.

Baue, Arnold J. *Goods, Power, History: Latin America's Material Culture*. Cambridge: Cambridge University Press, 2001, 47–49.

Beebee, Thomas O. *Transmesis: Inside Translation's Black Box*. New York: Palgrave Macmillan, 2012.

Bellido, Juan Félix. "La mujer noble en el Al-Andalus mediterráneo. Wallada Bint Al-Mustakfi, un ejemplo de mujer intelectual." *Desde Andalucía: mujeres del Mediterraneo*. Mercedes Arriaga Flórez et al., eds. Almería: Arcibel Editores, 2006, 54–62.

Ben Hassen, Nadia Mohamed Aziza. "Le texte en mosaïque dans *L'Astrolabe de la mer* et *Les Portiques de la mer* de Chams Nadir." *Expressions Maghrébines* 5:1 (Summer 2006): 143–64.

Benhamamouche, Fatma. "Le mythe de Boabdil dans *El manuscrito carmesí* de Antonio Gala (1990)." *Héroes, mitos y monstruos en la literatura española contemporánea*. Fidel López Criado, ed. Santiago de Compostela: Andavira, 2009, 193–200.

Berg, Nancy E. "When Ibn Rushd Met Borges." *Journal of Arabic Literature* 41 (2010): 148–59.

Bloomberg. "Cambio de tendencia: los españoles emigran a Marruecos huyendo del desempleo." *El Economista*, August 28, 2013. http://www.eleconomista.es/economia/noticias/5097775/08/13/Cambio-de-tercio-los-espanoles-emigran-a-Marruecos-huyendo-del-desempleo.html#.Kku8gdcsf8AX0a7.

Boone, Elizabeth Hill, and Walter Mignolo, eds. *Writing without Words: Alternative Literacies in Mesoamerica and the Andes*. Durham, NC: Duke University Press, 1994.

Borges, Jorge Luis. "Alhambra." *Historia de la noche*. Buenos Aires: Emecé, 1977, 17.

———. "Averroes' Search." James E. Irby, trans. *Labyrinths, Selected Stories and Other Writings*. Donald A. Yates and James E. Irby, trans. New York: New Directions, 1962, 148–55.

——— [Kh. L. Būrkhīs]. "Baḥth ibn Rushd." *al-Mirāyā wa-l-Matāhāt*. Ibrāhīm al-Khatīb, trans. Casablanca: Dār Tūbqāl lil-Nashr, 1987, 20–27.

———. "La busca de Averroes." *El Aleph*. Madrid: Alianza/Emecé Editores, 1990, 93–104.

Boudjedra, Rachid [Rashīd Abū Jadra]. "La fascination de la forme." *Le Matin* Algiers (June 24, 2003). *Europas islamische Nachbarn: Studien zur Literatur und Geschichte* 1. Ernstpeter Ruhe, ed. Würzburg: Königshausen and Neumann, 1993, 34–35.

———. *Maʿrakat al-Zuqāq*. Algiers: al-Mu'assasa al-Waṭaniyya lil-Kitāb, 1986.

———. *La Prise de Gibraltar*. Antoine Moussali, trans. (in collaboration with author). Paris: Éditions Denoël, 1987.

Bourget, Carine. "L'Islam syncrétique de Driss Chraïbi." *Esprit Créateur* 38:1 (1998): 57–68.

Boym, Svetlana. *The Future of Nostalgia*. New York: Basic Books, 2001.

Brann, Ross. "The Moors?" *Medieval Encounters* 15 (2009): 307–18.

———. *Power in the Portrayal: Representations of Muslims and Jews in Islamic Spain*. Princeton, NJ: Princeton University Press, 2002.

Bravo Caro, Juan Jesús. *Felipe II y la repoblación del reino de Granada: la taha de Comares*. Granada: Universidad de Granada, Universidad de Málaga, 1995.

Brown, Wendy. *Regulating Aversion: Tolerance in the Age of Identity and Empire*. Princeton, NJ: Princeton University Press, 2006.

Brown, Wendy, and Rainer Forst. *The Power of Tolerance: A Debate*. Luca Di Blasi and Christoph F. E. Holzhey, eds. New York: Columbia University Press, 2014.

Bruquetas de Castro, Fernando. *Outing en España: los españoles salen del armario*. Madrid: Hijos de Muley-Rubio, 2000.

Burnett, Charles. *Arabic into Latin in the Middle Ages: The Translators and their Intellectual and Social Context.* Farnman, Surrey: Ashgate, 2009.

———. "Communities of Learning in Twelfth Century Toledo." *Communities of Learning: Networks and the Shaping of Intellectual Identity in Europe, 1100–1500.* Constant J. Mews and John N. Crossley, eds. Turnhout: Brepols, 2011, 9–18.

Cabello, Matilde. *Wallada, la última luna* (2000). Cordoba, Spain: Almuzara, 2005.

Calderwood, Eric. "'In Andalucía, There Are No Foreigners': Andalucismo from Transperipheral Critique to Colonial Apology." *Journal of Spanish Cultural Studies* 15:4 (2015): 399–417.

———. "The Invention of al-Andalus: Discovering the Past and Creating the Present in Granada's Islamic Tourism Sites." *Journal of North African Studies* 19:1 (2014): 27–55.

———. "Proyectando al-Andalus: alegorías andalusíes en el cine árabe moderno." *Andalusíes: antropología e historia cultural de una elite marroquí.* José Antonio González Alcantud and Sandra Rojo Flores, eds. Madrid: Abada, 2015, 213–40.

———. "The Reconquista of the Mosque of Cordoba." *Foreign Policy.* April 10, 2015. http://foreignpolicy.com/2015/04/10/the-reconquista-of-the-mosque-of-cordoba-spain-catholic-church-islam/.

Cáliz, Miguel. *Horas Para Wallada.* Alcalá de Guadaíra: Paréntesis, 2009.

Campoy-Cubillo, Adolfo. *Memories of the Maghreb: Transnational Identities in Spanish Cultural Production.* New York: Palgrave Macmillan, 2012.

Carr, David. *Time, Narrative and History.* Bloomington: Indiana University Press, 1986.

Carr, Matthew. *Blood and Faith: The Purging of Muslim Spain.* New York: New Press, 2009.

Carrasco Urgoiti, María Soledad. *El moro de Granada en la literatura (del siglo XV al XX).* Madrid, Revista de Occidente, 1956. http://www.cervantesvirtual.com/obra-visor/el-moro-de-granada-en-la-literatura-del-siglo-xv-al-xix/html/c9e7a9fa-35ff-11e1-b1fb-00163ebf5e63_57.html.

Castro-Gómez, Santiago. "The Missing Chapter of Empire: Postmodern Reorganization of Coloniality and Post-Fordist Capitalism." *Cultural Studies* 21:2–3 (March–May 2007): 428–48.

Ceccato, Rosella Dorigo. "Drama in the Post-Classical Period: A Survey." *Arabic Literature in the Post-Classical Period.* Roger Allen and D. S. Richards, eds. Cambridge, MA: Cambridge University Press, 2006, 347–68.

Chaddock, Gail R. "A Flotilla of Quincentenary Books." *Christian Science Monitor,* October 11, 1991, 10.

Chahine, Youssef (Yūsuf Shāhīn), dir. *al-Maṣīr* (*Destiny*). France 2 Cinéma, Misr International Films, and Ognon Pictures (1997). DVD.

Chakor, Mohammad, and Carmelo Pérez Beltrán. *Entre las dos orillas: literatura marroquí en lengua española.* Granada: Editorial Universidad de Granada, 2007.

Cheng, Anne Anlin. *The Melancholy of Race: Psychoanalysis, Assimilation, and Hidden Grief.* Oxford: Oxford University Press, 2001.

Chikhi, Beïda. "D'un rivage à l'autre, le sens d'une perte: L'Algérie pour Camus, l'Andalousie pour Chams Nadir et les Maghrébins." *Imaginaires francophones.* R.

Chemain and A. Chemain Degrange, eds. Nice: Université de Nice Sophia-Antipolis, 1996, 169–82.

Childers, William. "Disappearing Moriscos." *Cross-Cultural History and the Domestication of Otherness.* Michal Rozbicki and George O. Ndege, eds. New York: Palgrave Macmillan, 2012, 51–64.

Chraïbi, Driss. *Birth at Dawn.* Ann Woollcombe, trans. Washington, DC: Three Continents Press, 1990.

———. *La Mère du printemps (l'Oum-er-Bia).* Paris: Éditions du Seuil, 1982.

———. *Naissance à l'aube.* Paris: Éditions du Seuil, 1986.

Civantos, Christina. *Between Argentines and Arabs: Argentine Orientalism, Arab Immigrants, and the Writing of Identity.* Albany: State University of New York Press, 2006.

Cohen, Jeffrey Jerome ed., *The Postcolonial Middle Ages.* New York: Palgrave, 2000.

Collins, Roger. *The Arab Conquest of Spain, 710–797.* Oxford : Blackwell, 1989.

Confino, Alon. "Collective Memory and Cultural History: Problems of Method." *American Historical Review* 105:2 (December 1997): 1386–403.

Connolly, W. E. "Pluralism, Multiculturalism and the Nation-State: Rethinking the Connections." *Journal of Political Ideologies* 1:1 (1996): 53–73.

Correa Ramón, Amelina. "Nicolás María López: cautivado en el país de los sueños." *Biblioteca Virtual Andalucía.* http://www.bibliotecavirtualdeandalucia.es/opencms/lecturas-pendientes/023-tristeza_andaluza.html.

Crapanzano, Vincent. *Imaginative Horizons: An Essay in Literary-Philosophical Anthropology.* Chicago: University of Chicago Press, 2003.

Creppell, Ingrid, Russell Hardin, and Stephen Macedo. *Toleration on Trial.* Lanham, MD: Lexington Books, 2008.

Cruz, Manuel. *Hacerse cargo: sobre responsabilidad e identidad personal.* Barcelona: Paidós, 1999.

Cruz, Victor Hernández. *In the Shadow of Al-Andalus: Poems.* Minneapolis: Coffee House Press, 2011.

D'Amico, Héctor. "Una visita a Borges." *La Nación,* November 20, 1993, 7, primera sección.

Dadson, Trevor J. "The Assimilation of Spain's Moriscos: Fiction or Reality?" *Journal of Levantine Studies* 1:2 (Winter 2011): 11–30.

Dakhlia, Jocelyne, ed. *Trames de langues. Usages et métissages linguistiques dans l'histoire du Maghreb.* Paris: Maisonneuve et Larose; Tunis: Institut de recherche sur le Maghreb contemporain, 2004.

Daly, Glyn, and Slavoj Žižek. *Conversations with Žižek.* Cambridge: Polity, 2004.

Danto, Arthur. *Narration and Knowledge.* New York: Columbia University Press, 1985.

Dapía, Silvia G. "The Myth of the Framework in Borges's 'Averroes's Search.'" *Variaciones Borges* 7 (1999): 147–65.

Darwish, Iman Said. "Courtly Culture and Gender Poetics: Wallada Bint Al-Mustakfī and Christine De Pizan." PhD thesis, American University in Cairo.

Davila, Carl. *The Andalusian Music of Morocco: Al-Āla: History, Society and Text.* Wiesbaden: Reichert, 2013.

Davis, Kathleen, and Nadia Altschul. "Introduction: The Idea of the 'Middle Ages'

Outside Europe." *Medievalisms in the Postcolonial World: The Idea of "the Middle Ages" Outside Europe*. Kathleen Davis and Nadia Altschul, eds. Baltimore, MD: Johns Hopkins University Press, 2009, 1–24.

Delgado Gómez-Escalonilla, Lorenzo. "La política latinoamericana de España en el siglo XX." *Ayer* 49 (2003): 121–60.

Delpech, François. "El hallazgo del escrito oculto en la literatura española del Siglo de Oro: elementos para una mitología del libro." *Revista de Dialectología y Tradiciones Populares* 53:1 (1998): 5–38.

Denny, J. Peter. "Rational Thought in Oral Culture and Literate Decontextualization." *Literacy and Orality*. David Olson and Nancy Torrance, eds. Cambridge: Cambridge University Press, 1991, 66–89.

Derrida, Jacques. *Of Grammatology*. Gayatri Chakravorty Spivak, trans. Baltimore: Johns Hopkins University Press, 1974.

———. *Margins of Philosophy*. Alan Bass, trans. Chicago: University of Chicago Press, 1982.

Di-Capua, Yoav. "*Nahda*: The Arab Project of Enlightenment." *The Cambridge Companion to Modern Arab Culture*. Dwight Reynolds, ed. Cambridge: Cambridge University Press, 2015, 54–74.

Domínguez García, Javier. *Memorias del futuro: ideología y ficción en el símbolo de Santiago Apóstol*. Madrid: Iberoamericana, 2008.

Donner, Fred. *Narratives of Islamic Origins: The Beginnings of Islamic Historical Writing*. Princeton, NJ: Darwin Press, 1998.

Dotson-Renta, Lara. *Immigration, Popular Culture, and the Re-routing of European Muslim Identity*. New York: Palgrave Macmillan, 2012.

Douki, Caroline, and Philippe Minard. "Histoire globale, histoires connectées: un changement d'échelle historiographique?" *Revue d'Histoire Moderne et Contemporaine* 5:54–4bis (2007): 7–21.

Drayson, Elizabeth. *The King and the Whore: King Roderick and La Cava*. New York: Palgrave Macmillan, 2007.

Duran, Khalid. "Andalusia's Nostalgia for Progress and Harmonious Heresy." *Middle East Report* 178:22 (September/October 1992). http://www.merip.org/mer/mer178/andalusias-nostalgia-progress-harmonious-heresy.

Durkheim, Émile. "The Cultural Logic of Collective Representations." *Social Theory: the Multicultural and Classic Readings*. C. Lemert, ed. Boulder, CO: Westview Press, 2004, 90–99.

———. *The Elementary Forms of the Religious Life*. J. W. Swain, trans. London: Allen and Unwin, [1915] 1968.

EFE. "El 89% de los españoles que emigran en busca de empleo cuenta con educación superior." *El País*, November 7, 2013. http://economia.elpais.com/economia/2013/11/07/empleo/1383838356_819951.html.

Egea Fernández-Montesinos, Alberto. *Garcia Lorca, Blas Infante y Antonio Gala: un nacionalismo alternativo en la literatura andaluza*. Seville: Fundación Blas Infante, 2001.

El Mountassir, Abdallah. *Amarg: chants et poésie amazighs, sud-ouest du Maroc*. Paris: L'Harmattan, 2004.

Elam, Keir. *The Semiotics of Theatre and Drama*. London: Routledge, 1980.

Elger, Ralf. "Adab and Historical Memory: The Andalusian Poet/Politician Ibn Al-Khaṭīb as Presented in Aḥmad al-Maqqarī. 986/1577–1041/1632), *Nafḥ aṭ-Ṭīb.*" *Welt Des Islams: International Journal for the Study of Modern Islam* 42:3 (2002): 289–306.

Elinson, Alexander. "*Dārija* and Changing Writing Practices in Morocco." *International Journal of Middle East Studies* 45.4 (2013): 715–30.

———. *Looking Back at al-Andalus: The Poetics of Loss and Nostalgia in Medieval Arabic and Hebrew Literature.* Leiden: Brill, 2009.

Epps, Brad. "Goytisolo, Juan." *Spanish Writers on Gay and Lesbian Themes: A Bio-critical Sourcebook.* David William Foster, ed. Westport, CT: Greenwood, 1999, 87–96.

———. "The Politics of Ventriloquism: Cava, Revolution and Sexual Discourse in *Conde Julián.*" *MLN* 107:2 (March 1992): 274–97.

———. *Significant Violence: Oppression and Resistance in the Narratives of Juan Goytisolo, 1970–1990.* Oxford: Clarendon Press, 1996.

España en cifras. Instituto Nacional de Estadística. http://www.ine.es/ss/Satellite?L=0&c=INEPublicacion_C&cid=1259924856416&p=1254735110672&pagename=ProductosYServicios%2FPYSLayout&param1=PYSDetalleGratuitas.

Fakhry, Majid. *Averroes (Ibn Rushd): His Life, Works and Influence.* Oxford: Oneworld Publications, 2001.

Fanjul, Serafín. *Al-Andalus contra España: La forja del mito.* Madrid: Siglo XXI, 2000.

———. "Divulgación y falsificación de la novela histórica: el caso 'árabe.'" *Reflexiones sobre la novela histórica.* José Jurado Morales, ed. Cádiz: Universidad de Cádiz, 2006, 299–318.

———. *La quimera de al-Andalus.* Madrid: Siglo XXI de España, 2004.

Fargeon, Michael. "Interview: Youssef Chahine." *UNESCO Courier* 50:9 (September 1997): 47–49.

Fernández Martínez, Fidel. *Boabdil.* [Tánger]: Editorial Tánger, 1939.

Fernández Parrilla, Gonzalo. "Breaking the Canon: Zafzaf, Laroui and the Moroccan Novel." https://www.academia.edu/5412586/Moroccan_Literature._Breaking_the_canon_Zafzaf_Laroui_and_the_Moroccan_Novel.

———. "Translating Modern Arabic Literature into Spanish." *Middle Eastern Literatures* 16:1 (2013): 88–101.

Fernández Parrilla, Gonzalo, and Rosario Montoro Murillo, eds., *El Magreb y Europa: literatura y traducción.* Cuenca: Universidad de Castilla-La Mancha, 1999.

Fernández Parrilla, Gonzalo, Luis Miguel Pérez Cañada, and Rosario Montoro Murillo. "Panorámica de los estudios y traducciones de la literatura del Magreb en español." *Cuadernos Escuela de Traductores de Toledo* 1 (1998). https://www.uclm.es/escueladetraductores/investigacion/pdf/cuadernos/01.pdf.

Fernández Prieto, Celia. "La historia en la novela histórica." *Reflexiones sobre la novela histórica.* José Jurado Morales ed. Cádiz: Universidad de Cádiz, 2006, 165–83.

Fiala, Andrew. *Tolerance and the Ethical Life.* London: Continuum, 2005.

Fidora, Alexander. "Religious Diversity and the Philosophical Translations of Twelfth-Century Toledo." *Communities of Learning: Networks and the Shaping of Intellectual Identity in Europe, 1100–1500*. Constant J. Mews and John N. Crossley, eds. Turnhout: Brepols, 2011, 19–35.

Fierro, Maribel. "Al-Andalus en el pensamiento fascista español." *Al-Andalus/España: historiografías en contraste: siglos XVII-XXI*. Manuela Marín, ed. Madrid: Casa de Velázquez, 2009, 325–49.

———. "Decapitation of Christians and Muslims in the Medieval Iberian Peninsula: Narratives, Images, Contemporary Perceptions." *Comparative Literature Studies* 45:2 (2008): 137–64.

Filios, Denise K. "Expulsion from Paradise: Exiled Intellectuals and Andalusian Tolerance." *In the Light of Medieval Spain: Islam, the West, and the Relevance of the Past*. Simon R. Doubleday and David Coleman, eds. New York: Palgrave Macmillan, 2008, 91–113.

Flesler, Daniela. *The Return of the Moor: Spanish Responses to Contemporary Moroccan Immigration*. West Lafayette, IN: Purdue University Press, 2008.

Fludernik, Monika. "Narrative and Drama." *Theorizing Narrativity*. John Pier and José Ángel García Landa, eds. Berlin: de Gruyter, 2008, 353–81.

Freire, Paulo. *Pedagogy of the Oppressed*. New York: Seabury Press, 1968.

Freire, Paulo, and Donaldo P. Macedo. *Literacy: Reading the Word & the World*. South Hadley, MA: Bergin & Garvey, 1987.

Freud, Sigmund. "Mourning and Melancholia" [1917]. *The Standard Edition of the Complete Psychological Works of Sigmund Freud*, Volume XIV. James Strachey, Anna Freud, and Angela Richards, eds. London: Hogarth Press, 1966–1974, 243–58.

Frohlich, Margaret Gates. "The Violent Narration of 'Pure' Spain: National Identity and Treason in *Reivindicación del Conde don Julián* by Juan Goytisolo." *Romance Review* 13 (2003): 55–68.

Fuchs, Barbara. *Exotic Nation: Maurophilia and the Construction of Early Modern Spain*. Philadelphia: University of Pennsylvania Press, 2011.

———. *Mimesis and Empire: The New World, Islam, and European Identities*. Cambridge: Cambridge University Press, 2001.

Fuchs, Dale. "Pope Asked to Let Muslims Pray in Cathedral." *Guardian* (London), December 28, 2006.

Fuss, Diana. *Essentially Speaking: Feminism, Nature and Difference*. New York: Routledge, 1989.

Gala, Antonio. "¿Los elegidos?" *El Mundo*, July 24, 2014. http://www.elmundo.es/opinion/2014/07/24/53d16623ca4741be538b4573.html.

———. *Charlas con Troylo*. Madrid: Escasa-Calpe, 1981.

———. *El manuscrito carmesí*. Barcelona: Planeta, 1990.

———. *Paisaje andaluz con figuras*. Granada: Biblioteca de la Cultura Andaluza, 1984.

———. *Paisaje con figuras*. Madrid: Espasa-Calpe, 1985.

———. *En propia mano*. Madrid: Escasa-Calpe, 1983.

Gana, Nouri. "In Search of Andalusia: Reconfiguring Arabness in Diana Abu-Jaber's *Crescent*." *Comparative Literature Studies* 45:2 (2008): 228–46.

García-Arenal, Mercedes. "The Converted Muslims of Spain: Morisco Cultural Resistance and Engagement with Islamic Knowledge (1502–1610)." *Routledge*

Handbook of Islam in the West. Roberto Tottoli, ed. London: Routledge, 2015, 38–54.

García Castañón, Luz. *Moros y cristianos en las narraciones infantiles árabes y españolas*. Madrid: Ediciones de la Torre, 1995.

García de Cortázar, José Ángel, and José Ángel Sesma Muñoz. *Manual de historia medieval*. Madrid: Alianza, 2008.

García Moreno, Beatriz. "al-Andalus en el poeta palestino Maḥmūd Darwīš." *El saber en Al-Andalus*, Vol. 4. Clara María Thomas de Antonio and Antonio Giménez Reíllo, eds. Seville: Universidad de Sevilla, 2006, 135–46.

Gardner, Steven M. "The Andalusia of Antonio Gala: Mythic Moors versus Modern-Day Immigration." *Reflections on Europe in Transition*. Ursula E. Beitter, ed. New York: Peter Lang, 2007, 29–40.

Garrison, Lynsea. "Changing Faiths: Hispanic Americans Leaving Catholicism for Islam." BBC, August 20, 2013. http://www.bbc.co.uk/news/world-us-canada-23774334.

Garulo Muñoz, Teresa. "La biografía de Wallada, toda problemas." *Anaquel de Estudios Árabes* 20 (2009): 97–116.

Gauch, Suzanne. *Liberating Shahrazad: Feminism, Postcolonialism, and Islam*. Minneapolis: University of Minnesota Press, 2007.

Gaunt, Simon. "Can the Middle Ages Be Postcolonial?" *Comparative Literature* 61:2 (2009): 160–76.

al-Gharūsī, al-Mubārak. *al-Qurṭās wa-l-Qalam: Hākadhā Takallama Rashīd Nīnī*. Rabat: Rabat Net, 2011.

Gentzler, Edwin. "Translation, Poststructuralism, and Power." *Translation and Power*. Maria Tymoczko and Edwin Gentzler, eds.. Amherst: University of Massachusetts Press, 2002, 195–218.

Gil Sierra, Jacinto. *El retorno de Boabdil*. Madrid: Editorial Agrícola Española, 2009.

González Alcantud, José Antonio. "El canon andaluz y las fronteras imaginarias." *El orientalismo desde el sur*. José Antonio González Alcantud, ed. Sevilla: Junta de Andalucía, Consejería de Cultura, 2006, 368–80.

———, ed. *Marroquíes en la guerra civil española: campos equívocos*. Rubí [Barcelona]: Anthropos Editorial, 2003.

———. *Lo moro: las lógicas de la derrota y la formación del estereotipo islámico*. Rubí [Barcelona]: Anthropos, 2002.

———. "Social Memory of a World Heritage Site: The Alhambra of Granada." *International Journal of Social Science* 62 (2011): 179–97.

González Alcantud, José Antonio, and Antonio Malpica Cuello. *Pensar la Alhambra*. Granada: Diputación Provincial de Granada, Centro de Investigaciones Etnológicas Angel Ganivet, 2001.

González Alcantud, José Antonio, and Sandra Rojo Flores, eds. *Andalusíes: antropología e historia cultural de una elite marroquí*. Madrid: Abada, 2015.

González Ferrín, Emilio. "Al-Andalus: un estado de la cuestión." *Al-Andalus: paradigma y continuidad*. Emilio González Ferrín, ed. Sevilla: Fundación Tres Culturas, 2011, 11–20.

———. "Las tierras intermedias entre Oriente y Occidente." *Summa de voluntades* 4 (2004): 22–27.

González Jiménez, Manuel. "Sobre la ideología de la Reconquista: realidades y tópicos." *Memoria, mito y realidad en la historia medieval: XIII Semana de Estudios Medievales, Nájera*. José Ignacio de la Iglesia Duarte et al., eds. Logroño: Gobierno de La Rioja, Instituto de Estudios Riojanos, 2003, 151–70.

———. *En torno a los orígenes de Andalucía: la repoblación del siglo XIII*. Seville: Universidad de Sevilla, 1980.

González Troyano, Alberto. *La desventura de Carmen: una divagación sobre Andalucía*. Madrid: Espasa Calpe, 1990.

Goytisolo, Juan. *Coto vedado*. Barcelona: Seix Barral, 1988.

———. *Crónicas sarracinas* [1981]. Barcelona: Seix Barral, 1989.

———. *Reivindicación del Conde don Julián* [1970]. Madrid: Cátedra, 1985.

Graff, Harvey J. *The Labyrinths of Literacy: Reflections on Literacy Past and Present*. London: Falmer Press, 1987.

Granara, William. "*Extensio Animae*: The Artful Ways of Remembering 'Al-Andalus.'" *Journal of Social Affairs* [*Shu'ūn Ijtimā'iyya*] 19:75 (2002): 45–72.

———. "Nostalgia, Arab Nationalism, and the Andalusian Chronotope in the Evolution of the Modern Arabic Novel." *Journal of Arabic Literature* 36:1 (2005): 57–73.

Grieve, Patricia. *The Eve of Spain: Myths of Origins in the History of Christian, Muslim, and Jewish Conflict*. Baltimore, MD: Johns Hopkins University Press, 2009.

Gugler, J. "*Destiny*: Liberal and Fundamentalist Islam Clash amid the Splendor of 12th-Century Andalusia." *Film in the Middle East and North Africa: Creative Dissidence*. J. Gugler, ed. Austin: University of Texas Press, 2011, 253–60.

de Haas, Hein. "Morocco: From Emigration Country to Africa's Migration Passage to Europe." *Migration Information Source*, October 1, 2005. http://www.migrationpolicy.org/article/morocco-emigration-country-africas-migration-passage-europe.

Hadjadji, Houaria Kadra. *Contestation et révolte dans l'oeuvre de Driss Chraïbi*. Paris: Publisud, 1986.

Hafez, Sabry. *The Genesis of Arabic Narrative Discourse*. London: Saqi Books, 1993.

Halbwachs, Maurice. *The Collective Memory*. Mary Douglas, ed.; Francis J. Ditter Jr. and Vida Yazdi Ditter, trans. New York: Harper Colophon [1950] 1980.

———. *On Collective Memory*. Lewis A. Coser, ed. Chicago: University of Chicago Press, 1992.

Halevi-Wise, Yael, ed. *Sephardism: Spanish Jewish History and the Modern Literary Imagination*. Stanford, CA: Stanford University Press, 2012.

Ḥamad, 'Alī Khalīl. *al-Tasāmuḥ fī al-Fikr al-'Arabī*. Ramallah: Ramallah Center for Human Rights Studies, 2011.

Hammond, Marlé. "He Desires Her? Situating Nazhūn's *Muwashshaḥa* in an Androgynous Aesthetic of Courtly Love." *Muwashshah: Proceedings of the Conference on Arabic and Hebrew Strophic Poetry and Its Romance Parallels, School of Oriental and African Studies, London, 8–10 October 2004*. Ed Emery, ed. London: RN Books, 2006, 141–56.

———. "He Said 'She Said': Narrations of Women's Verse in Classical Arabic

Literature. A Case Study: Nazhūn's Hijā' of Abū Bakr al-Makhzūmī." *Middle Eastern Literatures* 6:1 (2003): 3–16.

Hanne, Michael. *The Power of the Story: Fiction and Political Change*. Oxford: Berghahn Books, 1994.

Harris, Max. *Aztecs, Moors, and Christians: Festivals of Reconquest in Mexico and Spain*. Austin: University of Texas Press, 2010.

———. "Muhammad and the Virgin: Folk Dramatizations of Battles between Moors and Christians in Modern Spain." *Drama Review* 38 (1994): 45–61.

Hartley, L. P. *The Go-Between*. London: H. Hamilton, 1953.

Harvey, Leonard Patrick. *Islamic Spain, 1250–1500*. Chicago: University of Chicago Press, 1990.

Hassan, Waïl S. "Postcolonial Theory and Modern Arabic Literature: Horizons of Application." *Journal of Arabic Literature* 33:1 (March 2002): 45–64.

Hawley, John C. "The Re-Racination of Driss Chraïbi: A Hajj in Search of a New Mecca." *The Marabout & the Muse: New Approaches to Islam in African Literature*. Kenneth W. Harrow, ed. Portsmouth, NH: Heinemann, 1996, 62–76.

Heath, Stephen. "Difference." *Screen* 19:3 (Autumn 1978): 50–112.

Hermes, Nizar F. "Nostalgia for al-Andalus in Early Modern Moroccan *Voyages en Espagne*: al-Ghassānī's *Riḥlat al-wazīr fī iftikāk al-asīr* (1690–91) as a Case Study." *Journal of North African Studies* 21:3 (2016): 433–52. doi: 10.1080/13629387.2015.1098541.

Hernández Juberías, Julia. *La peninsula imaginaria: mitos y leyendas sobre Al-Andalus*. Madrid: Consejo Superior de Investigaciones Científicas, 1996.

Himmich, Ben Salem [Bin Sālim Ḥimmīsh]. *Hādhā al-Andalusī*. Beirut: Dār al-Ādāb, 2007.

———. *A Muslim Suicide*. Roger Allen, trans. Syracuse: Syracuse University Press, 2011.

Hoenerbach, Wilheim. "Notas para una characterización de Wallada." *Al-Andalus* 36 (1971): 467–73.

Hoffman, Don. "Chahine's Destiny: Prophetic Nostalgia and the Other Middle Ages." *Race, Class, and Gender in "Medieval" Cinema*. Lynn T. Ramey and Tison Pugh, eds. New York: Palgrave Macmillan, 2007, 31–44.

Howe, Marvine. *Al-Andalus Rediscovered: Iberia's New Muslims*. London: Hurst, 2012.

Hühn, Peter, and Roy Sommer. "Narration in Poetry and Drama." *The Living Handbook of Narratology*. Peter Hühn et al., eds. Hamburg: Hamburg University Press. http://wikis.sub.uni-hamburg.de/lhn/index.php/Narration_in_Poetry_and_Drama

Hussin, Jabbar [Jabbār Yasīn/Jabbār Yasīn Ḥusayn]. "The Day in Buenos Aires." *Words without Borders: The World through the Eyes of Writers*. Randa Jarrar, trans.; Samantha Schnee, Alane Salierno Mason, and Dedi Felman, eds. New York: Anchor, 2007, 113–19.

———. *Le Lecteur de Bagdad: contes & nouvelles*. Mustapha Oulmane and Luc Barbulesco, trans. Villelongue d'Aude, France: Atelier du Gué, 2000.

———. *Memorias olvidadas*. Jocelyne Gacel Ávila and Dulce María Zúñiga, trans. Guadalajara: Universidad de Guadalajara, 2006.

———. "Yawm Bwaynus Ayris." *al-Qāriʾ al-Baghdādī*. Beirut: Dār al-Ādāb, 2003. 109–18.

Hustad, Karis. "'The World Upside Down': The Rise of Spanish Immigration to Morocco." *Christian Science Monitor*, March 21, 2013. http://www.csmonitor.com/World/Africa/2013/0321/The-world-upside-down-The-rise-of-Spanish-immigration-to-Morocco.

Hutcheon, Linda. *The Politics of Postmodernism*, London: Routledge, 2002 [1989]. West Lafayette, IN: Purdue University Press, 2008.

Ingham, Patricia Clare, and Michelle R. Warren, eds. *Postcolonial Moves: Medieval through Modern*. New York: Palgrave Macmillan, 2003.

Isabel. Dir. Jordi Frades. Diagonal TV and Televisión Española, September 10, 2012–December 1, 2014. Television.

Ismat, Riad [Riyāḍ ʿIṣmat]. "Columbus." 1989. Typescript. Collection of Pedro Martínez Montávez, Madrid.

Jādd, ʿIzzat. "Sīmiyūṭīqā al-Tārīkh fī Thulāthiyyat Gharnāṭa." *Fuṣūl* 66:14 (2005): 144–62.

Jameson, Fredric. *The Political Unconscious: Narrative as a Socially Symbolic Act*. Ithaca, NY: Cornell University Press, 1981.

al-Jārim, ʿAlī. *Hātif min al-Andalus*. Cairo: Dār al-Maʿārif, 1949.

Javitch, Daniel. "The Assimilation of Aristotle's *Poetics* in Sixteenth-Century Italy." *The Cambridge History of Literary Criticism*, Vol. III. Glyn P. Norton, ed. Cambridge: Cambridge University Press, 1999.

Johnson, Carroll B. "Phantom Pre-Texts and Fictional Authors: Sidi Hamid Benengeli, *Don Quijote*, and the Metafictional Conventions of Chivalric Romances." *Cervantes: Bulletin of the Cervantes Society of America* 27:1 (Spring 2007 [2008]): 179–99.

al-Juʿaydī, Muḥammad ʿAbd Allāh. *Aʿindakum Nabaʾ? Istidʿāʾ al-Andalus: al-Adab al-Filasṭīnī al-Ḥadīth*. Beirut: Dār al-Hādī, 2002.

Jullien, Dominique. "In Praise of Mistranslation: The Melancholy Cosmopolitanism of Jorge Luis Borges." *Romanic Review* 98:2–3 (March–May 2007): 205–23.

Juwayda, Fārūq. *al-Wazīr al-ʿĀshiq. al-Majmūʿa al-Kāmila*. Cairo: Markaz al-Ahrām lil-Tarjama wa-l-Nashr, 1987.

Kamal, Mustapha. "Averroes' Search Today: *Beit al-Hikmah* and Translation in Morocco." *Qui Parle* 7:2 (Spring/Summer 1994): 80–109.

Kāmil, Muṣṭafā. *Fatḥ al-Andalus: al-Naṣṣ al-Kāmil lil-Masraḥīyah al-Waḥīdah allatī Katabahā*. [Cairo]: [al-Hay'a al-ʿĀmma lil-Kitāb], 1973 [1893].

Kassab, Elizabeth Suzanne. *Contemporary Arab Thought: Cultural Critique in Comparative Perspective*. New York: Columbia University Press, 2010.

Kaveny, Cathleen. *A Culture of Engagement: Law, Religion and Morality*. Washington, DC: Georgetown University Press, 2016.

Kaye, Jacqueline, and Abdelhamid Zoubir. *The Ambiguous Compromise: Language, Literature, and National Identity in Algeria and Morocco*. London: Routledge, 1990.

Keeley, Graham. "Muslims Arrested for Trying to Pray in Cordoba's Former Great Mosque." *Times* (London), March 4, 2010.

Kellner, Douglas. "Globalization, Terrorism, and Democracy: 9/11 and Its Aftermath."

Confronting Globalization: Humanity, Justice and the Renewal of Politics. Patrick Hayden and Chamsy el-Ojeili, eds. London: Palgrave, 2005, 172–90.

Khalīl, Ibrāhīm. *Ẓilāl wa-Aṣdā' Andalusiyya fī al-Adab al-Muʿāṣir*. Damascus: Ittiḥād al-Kuttāb al-ʿArab, 2000.

al-Khiyārī, ʿAllāl al-Hāshimī. *Rabbat Shāʿir*. Casablanca: Maṭbaʿat al-Khabāḥ al-Jadīda, 1985.

Khouri, Malek. "Anxieties of Fundamentalism and the Dynamics of Modernist Resistance: Youssef Chahine's *Al Maseer* (*Destiny*)." *CineAction* 69 (May 2006): 12–23.

Kīlānī, Qamar. *Awrāq Musāfira: Dimashq, Isbāniyā, Tammūz-Āb 1984*. Damascus: Dār al-Jalīl, 1987.

Kilito, Abdelfattah [ʿAbd al-Fattāḥ Kīlīṭū]. "Du balcon d'Averroès." *Le cheval de Nietzsche*. Casablanca: Editions Fennec, 2007, 155–79.

———. "Borges et Averroès". *Horizons Maghrébins* 41 (1999): 13–16.

———. *Lisān Adam*. Casablanca: Dār Tūbqāl lil-Nashr, 1995.

———. "Le transfert d'Averroès." *Langue d'Adam et autres essais*. Casablanca: Editions Toubkal, 1995, 59–63.

———. "Yawm fī Ḥayāt Ibn Rushd." *al-Adab wa-l-Irtiyāb*. Casablanca: Dār Tūbqāl lil-Nashr, 2007.

King, Russell, ed. *The Mediterranean Passage: Migration and New Cultural Encounters in Southern Europe*. Liverpool: Liverpool University Press, 2001.

Kogan, Barry S. *Averroes and the Metaphysics of Causation*. Albany: State University of New York Press, 1985.

Kresdez, Juan. *El veneno del eunuco*. Madrid: Nowtilus, 2009.

von Kügelgen, A. "A Call for Rationalism: 'Arab Averroists' in the Twentieth Century." *Alif: Journal of Comparative Poetics* 16 (1996): 97–132.

Labanyi, Jo. "Love and Colonial Ambivalence in Spanish Africanist Cinema of the Early Franco Dictatorship." *Europe and Love in Cinema*. Lisa Passerini, Jo Labanyi, and Karen Diehl, eds. Bristol, UK: Intellect, 2012, 129–50.

———. "Love, Politics and the Making of the Modern European Subject: Spanish Romanticism and the Arab World." *Hispanic Research Journal: Iberian and Latin American Studies* 5:3 (2004): 229–43.

———. *Myth and History in the Contemporary Spanish Novel*. Cambridge: Cambridge University Press, 1989.

Lahoud, Nelly. *Political Thought in Islam: A Study in Intellectual Boundaries*. London: Routledge, Taylor & Francis Group, 2005.

Lalami, Laila. *Hope & Other Dangerous Pursuits*. Chapel Hill, NC: Algonquin Books, 2005.

Lantelme, Michel. "Rachid Boudjedra ou le 'phantasme' de Gibraltar." *French Review* 82:3 (2009): 518–28.

Laroui, Abdallah [ʿAbd Allāh al-ʿArawī]. *La crise des intellectuels arabes; traditionalisme ou historicisme?* Paris: Maspero, 1974.

———. *L'idéologie arabe contemporaine*. Paris: Maspero, 1967.

———. *Islam et histoire: essai d'épistémologie*. Paris: Albin Michel, 1999.

Larreta, Enrique. *Zogoibi*. Buenos Aires: Juan Roldán y Compañía, 1926.

Lasala, Magdalena. *Boabdil: tragedia del último rey de Granada*. Madrid: Ediciones Temas de Hoy, 2004.

———. *Wallāda la omeya: la vida apasionada y rebelde de la última princesa andalusí.* Madrid: Ediciones Martínez Roca, 2003.

Lévi-Strauss, Claude. *Myth and Meaning.* London: Routledge and Kegan Paul, 1978.

———. *Race et histoire.* Paris: UNESCO, 1952.

Lima, Robert. "Crisis and Response: The Dynamics of Spain's 'Generation of 1898.'" *Los hallazgos de la lectura: Estudio dedicado a Miguel Enguídanos.* John Crispin, Enrique Pupo-Walker, and Luís Lorenzo-Rivero, eds. Madrid: Porrúa Turanzas, 1989, 107–19.

Lionnet, Françoise, and Shu-mei Shih. "Introduction: Thinking through the Minor, Transnationally." *Minor Transnationalism.* Françoise Lionnet and Shu-mei Shih, eds. Durham, NC: Duke University Press, 2005, 1–23.

Lomax, Derek W. *The Reconquest of Spain.* London: Longman, 1978.

López García, Bernabé. "30 años de africanismo español: el fin de la almogaravía científica (1967–1997)." *Awraq* 18 (1997): 11–48.

———. "La sociedad civil y las relaciones con Marruecos: el Comité Averroes, ¿un instrumento para el acercamiento entre las sociedades o la retórica de la mediación civil?" *La política exterior española hacia el Magreb: actores e intereses.* Miguel Hernando de Larramendi and Aurelia Mañé Estrada, eds. Barcelona: Ariel-Real Instituto Elcano, 2009, 195–207.

Louayene, Atef. "Pathologies of Moorishness: Al-Andalus, Narrative, and 'Worldly Humanism.'" *Journal of East-West Thought* 1:3 (March 2013): 31–44.

Loya, Joe. "Criminal Justice; Rage Behind Bars." *Los Angeles Times,* June 23, 2002.

Lyotard, Jean-François. *The Postmodern Condition: A Report on Knowledge.* Geoff Bennington and Brian Massumi, trans. Minneapolis: University of Minnesota Press, 1984 [1979].

Maʿlūf, Fawzī. *Ibn Ḥāmid, aw, Suqūṭ Gharnāṭa.* São Paulo: Dār al-Ṭibāʿa wa-l-Nashr al-ʿArabiyya, 1952.

Maalouf, Amin. *In the Name of Identity: Violence and the Need to Belong.* Barbara Bray, trans. New York: Arcade, 2012.

———. *Léon l'Africain.* Paris: J. C. Lattès, 1986.

———. *Leo the African* [*Leo Africanus*]. Peter Sluglett, trans. London: Quartet Books, 1986.

Macfie, Alexander Lyon, ed. *Orientalism: A Reader.* New York, 2000.

al-Madanī, ʿIzz al-Dīn. *Shadharāt min al-Sīra al-Rushdiyya.* Tunis: al-Majmaʿ al-Tūnisī lil-ʿUlūm wa-al-Ādāb wa-al-Funūn, Bayt al-Ḥikma, 2001.

Maddy-Weitzman, Bruce. *The Berber Identity Movement and the Challenge to North African States.* Austin: University of Texas Press, 2011.

al-Madīnī, Aḥmad. "ʿAn al-Mīlūdī Shaghmūm: Dhāt Taḥkī Shajn al-Jamāʿa al-Maghmūra." *al Quds al-ʿArabi* 21:6402 (January 8, 2010): 10.

al-Maghrib-al-Mashriq: al-ʿAlāqāt wa-al-Ṣūra. Casablanca: Maṭbaʿat al-Najāḥ al-Jadīda and Jāmiʿat al-Qādī Ayyāḍ [Marrakech], 1999.

Majid, Anouar. *Freedom and Orthodoxy: Islam and Difference in the Post-Andalusian Age.* Stanford, CA: Stanford University Press, 2004.

Makkī, Maḥmūd ʿAlī. "Al-Andalus fī Shiʿr Aḥmad Shawqī wa-Nathrihi." *Fuṣūl* 3:2 (1983): 200–234. http://library.islamweb.net/hadith/display_hbook.php?bk_no=798&pid=379517&hid=12201.

Manzano Moreno, Eduardo. "Qurtuba: algunas reflexiones críticas sobre el Califato de Cordoba y el mito de la convivencia." *Awraq* 7 (2013): 225–46.

Maqdisī, Anīs. *Ilā al-Ḥamrā'*. Beirut: al-Maṭbaʿa al-Adabiyya, 1930.

al-Maqqarī, Aḥmad ibn Muḥammad. "Al Maqqari's 'Breath of Perfumes.'" *The Sacred Books and Early Literature of the East*, Vol. 6. Charles F. Horne, ed. New York: Parke, Austin, & Lipscomb, 1917. 241-42.

———. *Nafḥ al-Ṭīb min Ghuṣn al-Andalus al-Raṭīb*. Iḥsān 'Abbās, ed. Beirut: Dār Ṣādir, 1968.

Marín, Manuela, *Mujeres en al-Ándalus. estudios onomástico-biográficos de al-Andalus*. XI. Madrid: Consejo Superior de Investigaciones Científicas, 2000.

Marín, Manuela, and Joseph Pérez. "L'Espagne des trois religions: du mythe aux realités. Introduction." *Revue de Monde Musulman et de la Mediterranée* 63–64:1–2 (1992): 23–25.

Martín Muñoz, Gema. "A Thousand and One Histories." *Critical Muslim* 6 (April–June 2013): 57–68.

Martínez, María Elena. *Genealogical Fictions: Limpieza de Sangre, Religion, and Gender in Colonial Mexico.* Stanford, CA: Stanford University Press, 2008.

Martínez Montávez, Pedro. *Al-Andalus, España, en la literatura árabe contemporánea: la casa del pasado*. Madrid: MAPFRE, 1992.

———. "Al-Andalus y Nizar Qabbani: la tragedia." *Cuadernos 'Ilu: Revista de Ciencias de las Religiones* 1 (1998): 9–24.

———. *Significado y símbolo de al-Andalus*. Almería: Fundación Ibn Tufayl, 2011.

Martínez-Vázquez, Hjamil. *Latina/o y Musulman: The Construction of Latina/o Identity among Latina/o Muslims in the United States*. Eugene, OR: Pickwick, 2010.

Martin-Márquez, Susan. *Disorientations: Spanish Colonialism in Africa and the Performance of Identity*. New Haven, CT: Yale University Press, 2008.

Marx-Scouras, Danielle. "A Literature of Departure: The Cross-Cultural Writing of Driss Chraïbi." *Research in African Literatures* 23:2 (1992): 131–44.

McClintock, Anne. "The Angel of Progress: Pitfalls of the Term 'Post-Colonial.'" *Social Text* 31–32 (1992): 84–98.

———. *Imperial Leather: Race, Gender and Sexuality in the Colonial Contest*. New York: Routledge, 1995.

McKinnon, Catriona, and Dario Castiglione, eds. *Culture of Toleration in Diverse Societies: Reasonable Toleration*. Manchester: Manchester University Press, 2003.

Mejías-López, William. "Hernán Cortés y su intolerancia hacia la religión azteca en el contexto de la situación de los conversos y moriscos." *Bulletin hispanique* 95:2 (1993): 623–46.

Memmi, Albert. *Decolonization and the decolonized*. Robert Bononno, trans. Minneapolis: University of Minnesota Press, 2006.

———. *Portrait du décolonisé arabo-musulman et de quelques autres*. Paris: Gallimard, 2004.

Menéndez Alzamora, Manuel. *La Generación del 14: una aventura intelectual*. Madrid: Siglo XXI, 2006.

Menicucci, Garay. "Arab Film." *Encyclopedia of Religion and Film*. Eric Michael Mazur, ed. Santa Barbara, CA: ABC-CLIO, 2011, 32–39.

Menocal, María Rosa. "Foreword: Ways of Remembering Granada." Radwa Ashour

[ʿĀshūr], *Granada*. William Granara, trans. Syracuse, NY: Syracuse University Press, 2003, vii–xii.

———. *The Ornament of the World: How Muslims, Jews, and Christians Created a Culture of Tolerance in Medieval Spain*. Boston: Little, Brown, 2002.

Merino, Leonor. "Conquista de Al-Andalus en la novela magrebí y en los relatos árabes." *Mil Seiscientos Dieciséis* 12 (2006): 85–94.

———. "Coups de cœur en liberté: Interview avec Driss Chraïbi." *Expressions Maghrébines* 3:2 (Winter 2004): 29–33.

Merrell, Floyd. *Sensing Corporeally: Toward a Posthuman Understanding*. Toronto: University of Toronto Press, 2003.

Mignolo, Walter. *The Darker Side of Western Modernity: Global Futures, Decolonial Options*. Durham, NC: Duke University Press, 2011.

———. "The Geopolitics of Knowledge and the Colonial Difference." *South Atlantic Quarterly* 101:1 (Winter 2002): 57–96.

———. *Local Histories/Global Designs: Coloniality, Subaltern Knowledges, and Border Thinking*. Princeton, NJ: Princeton University Press, 2000.

Minder, Raphael, and Jim Yardley. "Desperation Fuels Trips of Migrants to Spain." *New York Times*, October 4, 2013. http://www.nytimes.com/2013/10/05/world/europe/as-desperation-mounts-more-migrants-cast-their-lot-on-a-troubled-sea.html accessed 11/21/13.

Mink, Louis. "Narrative Form as a Cognitive Instrument" [1978]. *The History and Narrative Reader*. Geoffrey Roberts, ed. London: Routledge, 2001, 211–20.

al-Misnāwī, Muṣṭafā [Mustapha El-Mesnaoui]. *Ṭāriq Alladhī Lam Yaftaḥ al-Andalus*. Beirut: al-Mu'assasa al-ʿArabiyya lil-Dirāsāt wa-al-Nashr, 1979.

———. "Ṭāriq Alladhī Lam Yaftaḥ al-Andalus." *Cuentos de las dos orillas*. Rosa Regàs and José Monleón, eds. Seville: Junta de Andalucía, Consejería de Cultura, 2001, 71–74.

———. "Tariq, the One Who Didn't Conquer al-Andalus." Christina Civantos, trans. *Middle Eastern Literatures* 18:3 (2015): 236–39.

al-Misri, Maram [Marām al-Miṣrī]. *El Retorno*. Rafael Ortega, trans. Granada: Universidad de Granada, 2007.

———. *Le Retour de Wallada: Poésie*. Alain Gorius, trans. Neuilly: Al Manar, SAIG, 2010.

Molina, Luis. Review of *La quimera de al-Andalus*, by Serafín Fanjul. *AQ* 25 (2004): 571–75.

Monleón, José, and Juan Copete, eds. *Cuentos de las dos orillas II*. Madrid: Agencia Española de Cooperación Internacional, 2002.

Monroe, James. *Islam and the Arabs in Spanish Scholarship, Sixteenth Century to the Present*. Leiden: Brill, 1970.

Morales, Harold. "Latina/o Muslim Religious Cultures." *Religion and American Cultures: An Encyclopedia of Traditions, Diversity, and Popular Expression*, Vol. 4. Gary Laderman and Luis D. León, eds. Santa Barbara, CA: ABC-CLIO, 2014, 977–1001.

Moreh, Shmuel. *Live Theatre and Dramatic Literature in the Medieval Arab World*. New York: New York University Press, 1992.

———. "Theater." *Medieval Islamic Civilization, An Encyclopedia*, Vol. 2. Josef W. Meri, ed. New York: Routledge, 2006, 805–8.

Moreno Torregrosa, Pasqual, and Mohamed El Gheryb. *Dormir al raso*. Madrid: VOSA, 1994.

Morsy, Faten. "Thus Spoke Shahrazad: Contemporary Arab Women's Recent Rewrit-ing's of *The Nights*." *Genre* 28 (2008): 231–48.

Moyano, Pilar. "Mujeres que se descubren: Wallada Bint al-Mustafki en la biografía novelada de Matilde Cabello." *Erie: a orillas del lago*. Erie, PA: Asociación de Licenciados y Doctores Españoles en Estados Unidos, 2008, 11–18.

Mulūk al-Ṭawā'if. Writ. Walīd Sayf. Dir. Hātim ʿAlī. Syrian Art Production International, 2005. Television.

al-Musawi, Muhsin Jassim. *The Postcolonial Arabic Novel: Debating Ambivalence.* Leiden: Brill, 2003.

Nadir, Chams. *Les Portiques de la mer*. Paris: Éditions Méridiens Klincksieck, 1990.

Nair, Parvati. *Rumbo al norte: inmigración y movimientos culturales entre el Magreb y España* Barcelona: Edicions Bellaterra, 2006.

Najjar, Fauzi M. "The Debate on Islam and Secularism in Egypt." *Arab Studies Quarterly* 18:2 (Spring 1996): 1–22.

Najjar, Ibrahim Y. "Ibn Rushd's Theory of Rationality." *Alif: Journal of Comparative Poetics* 16 (1996): 191–216.

al-Naqqāsh, Farīda. "Nahnu Lā Nabkī ʿalā al-Aṭlāl." *Adab wa-Naqd* 9:88 (December 1992): 9–12.

Nīnī, Rashīd. *Yawmīyāt Muhājir Sirrī*. [Rabat]: Wizārat al-Shuʾūn al-Thaqāfiyya, 1999.

Nirenberg, David. "What Can Medieval Spain Teach Us about Muslim-Jewish Relations?" *CCAR Journal* (Summer 2002): 17–36.

Noorani, Yaseen. "The Lost Garden of al-Andalus: Islamic Spain and the Poetic Inversion of Colonialism." *International Journal of Middle East Studies* 31:2 (1999): 237–54.

Nora, Pierre. "Between Memory and History: *Les Lieux de mémoire*," *Representations* 26 (1989): 7–24.

Nora, Pierre ed. *Les Lieux de mémoire*, Vols. I–III. Paris: Gallimard, 1984–1992.

Nünning, Ansgar, and Roy Sommer. "Diegetic and Mimetic Narrativity: Some Further Steps towards a Narratology of Drama." *Theorizing Narrativity*. John Pier and José Ángel García Landa, eds. Berlin: de Gruyter, 2008, 329–52.

Olick, Jeffrey K., Vered Vinitsky-Seroussi, and Daniel Levy, eds. *The Collective Memory Reader*. New York: Oxford University Press, 2011.

Ortega, José. "Cuatro crónicas noveladas de la destrucción de Granada." *La Palabra y el Hombre: Revista de la Universidad Veracruzana* 91 (1994): 85–107.

Otazu, Javier. "Un número creciente de españoles encuentra trabajo en Marruecos." ABC, June 19, 2013. http://www.abc.es/economia/20130617/abci-numero-creciente-espanoles- encuentra-201306170946.html.

Ouyang, Wen-Chin. *Politics of Nostalgia in the Arabic Novel: Nation-State, Modernity and Tradition*. Edinburgh: Edinburgh University Press, 2013.

Palma Ceballos, Miriam. *La huella de las ausencias: un relato sobre Walada*. Cordoba: Almendro, 2009.

Panier, Louis. "Fath al-Andalus: une lecture sémiotique." *Le Voyage et la langue*. Joseph Dichy and Hassan Hamzé, eds. Damascus: Institut Français du Proche-Orient, 2004, 125–35.

Paradela Alonso, Nieves. *El otro laberinto español: viajeros árabes a España entre el siglo XVII y 1936*. Madrid: Siglo XXI, 2005.

Pecellín, Manuel. "Muerte por inundación." *Libre con libros*, July 17, 2010. http://blogs.hoy.es/libreconlibros/2010/03/01/muerte-inundacion/.

de Pedro, Raquel. "The Translatability of Texts: A Historical Overview." *Meta: Journal des Traducteurs/Meta: Translators' Journal* 44:4 (1999): 546–59.

Pérez, J. J. "Los 'trenes de la esperanza' de los emigrantes andaluces a Cataluña hace 50 años." *Ideal*, October 19, 2014. http://www.ideal.es/granada/v/20100509/provincia/trenes-esperanza-emigrantes-andaluces-20100509.html.

Pérez Ornia, José Ramon. "'Averroes,' de Antonio Gala." *El País*, February 5, 1981. http://elpais.com/diario/1981/02/05/cultura/350175603_850215.html.

Pérez-Sánchez, Gema. *Queer Transitions in Contemporary Spanish Culture: From Franco to La Movida*. Albany: State University of New York Press, 2007.

Peri Rossi, Cristina. *Evohe: poemas eróticos*. Montevideo: Girón, 1971.

Perry, Mary Elizabeth. *The Handless Maiden: Moriscos and the Politics of Religion in Early Modern Spain*. Princeton, NJ: Princeton University Press, 2005.

Phillip, Thomas, Hilary Kilpatrick, Paul Starkey, and Jirjī Zaydān. *Jurji Zaidan and the Foundations of Arab Nationalism*. Syracuse, NY: Syracuse University Press, 2010.

Pouessel, Stéphanie. "Writing as Resistance: Berber Literature and the Challenges Surrounding the Emergence of a Berber Literary Field in Morocco." *Nationalities Papers: The Journal of Nationalism and Ethnicity* 40:3 (May 2012): 373–94.

Pym, A. *Negotiating the Frontier: Translators and Intercultures in Hispanic History*. Manchester: St. Jerome, 2000.

Qabbānī, Nizār. "al-Andalusī al-Akhīr." *Anā Rajul Wāḥid . . . wa-Anti Qabīla min al-Nisā'*. Beirut: Manshūrāt Qabbānī, 1993, 193–202.

Quijano, Aníbal. "Colonialidad y modernidad/racionalidad." *Perú Indígena* 13:29 (1991): 11–20.

———. "Colonialidad del poder, eurocentrismo y América Latina." *Colonialidad del saber, eurocentrismo y ciencias sociales*. Edgardo Lander, ed. Buenos Aires: CLACSO, 2000, 201–46.

Qunṣul, Ilyās. *Ma'sāt al-Harf al-ʿArabī fī al-Mahājir al-Amīrikiyya*. Damascus: Ittiḥād al-Kuttāb al-ʿArab, 1980.

Qunṣul, Zakī. *Taḥta Samā' al-Andalus*. Damascus: Wizārat al-Thaqāfa wa-al-Irshād al-Qawmī, Mudīrīyat al-Ta'līf wa-al-Tarjama, 1965.

Rahman, Najat. *Literary Disinheritance: The Writing of Home in the Work of Mahmoud Darwish and Assia Djebar*. Lanham, MD: Lexington, 2008.

Ratcliffe, Marjorie. *Mujeres épicas españolas: silencios, olvidos e ideologías*. Rochester NY: Tamesis, 2011.

Rawls, John. *Political Liberalism*. New York: Columbia University Press, 1993.

Recaño Valverde, Joaquín. "La emigración andaluza en España." http://www.juntadeandalucia.es/export/drupal/economia/TOMO_24/BEA24_119.pdf.

Regàs, Rosa, and José Monleón, eds. *Cuentos de las dos orillas*. Seville: Junta de Andalucía, Consejería de Cultura, 2001.

Reilly, Bernard F. *The Medieval Spains*. New York: Cambridge University Press, 2009.

Réquiem por Granada. Writ. and dir. Vicente Escrivá. Televisión Española, Radiotelevisione Italiana, ASPA, Midega Films, and Taurus. October 1991. Television.

Reynolds, Dwight F. "Musical 'Membrances of Medieval Muslim Spain." *Charting Memory: Recalling Medieval Spain*. Stacy N. Beckwith, ed. New York: Garland, 2000, 229–62.

Ribas-Mateos, Natalia. "Revising Mediterranean Contexts: The Mediterranean Caravanserai." *The Mediterranean Passage: Migration and New Cultural Encounters in Southern Europe*. Russell King, ed. Liverpool: Liverpool University Press, 2001, 22–40.

Ricci, Cristián. *¡Hay moros en la costa!: literatura marroquí fronteriza en castellano y catalán*. Madrid: Iberoamericana, 2014.

Richardson, Brian. "Drama and Narrative." *The Cambridge Companion to Narrative*. David Herman, ed. Cambridge: Cambridge University Press, 2007, 142–55.

Ricoeur, Paul. *Memory, History, Forgetting*. Kathleen Blamey and David Pellauer, trans. Chicago: University of Chicago Press, 2004.

Riding, Alan. "Madrid Journal; 500 Years Later, Latin America Can Forgive Spain." *New York Times*, February 13, 1992. http://www.nytimes.com/1992/02/13/world/madrid-journal-500-years-later-latin-america-can-forgive-spain.html.

Ríos Saloma, Martín F. "La Reconquista: génesis de un mito historiográfico." *Historia y Grafía* (2008): 191–216.

Riosalido, Jesús. *Wallada* [1986]. *Las damas de Santiago*. Madrid: J. García Verdugo, 1998, 9–71.

Rivière Gómez, Aurora. *Orientalismo y nacionalismo español: estudios árabes y hebreos en la Universidad de Madrid. 1843–1868*. Madrid: Universidad Carlos III, 2000.

Roberts, Geoffrey, ed. *The History and Narrative Reader*. London: Routledge, 2001.

Robinson, Alan. *Narrating the Past: Historiography, Memory and the Contemporary Novel*. New York: Palgrave Macmillan, 2011.

Robinson, Douglas. *Translation and Empire: Postcolonial Theories Explained*. New York: Routledge, 1997.

Rodríguez López, Ruth María. "Alándalus en la reflexión literaria de la experiencia migratoria en *Diario de un ilegal* de Rachid Nini." *Afroeuropa: Journal of Afroeuropean Studies* 1:1 (2007): 1–15.

Rodríguez Magda, Rosa María. *Inexistente Al Andalus: de cómo los intelectuales reinventan el Islam*. Oviedo: Nobel, 2008.

Rogers, Lynne. "*Reivindicación del Conde don Julián*: A Descent into Abjection," *Letras Peninsulares* 3.2–3 (1990): 279–91.

Rogozen-Soltar, Mikaela. "Al-Andalus in Andalusia: Negotiating Moorish History and Regional Identity in Southern Spain." *Anthropological Quarterly* 80:3 (Summer 2007): 863–86.

Rojo, Tito J., and M. Casares Porcel. *El jardín hispanomusulmán: los jardines de al-Andalus y su herencia*. Granada: Editorial Universidad de Granada, 2011.

Romero Valiente, Juan Manuel. "Migraciones." *Tendencias demográficas durante el siglo XX en España*. Andrés Arroyo Pérez, ed. Madrid: Instituto Nacional de Estadística, 2003, 209–53.

Rueda, Ana, and Sandra Martín, eds. *El retorno / el reencuentro: la inmigración en la literatura hispano-marroquí.* Madrid: Iberoamericana Editorial Vervuert, 2010.

Ruhe, Doris. "Transgression as Program: On the Novels of Rachid Boudjedra." *Arabic Literature: Postmodern Perspectives.* Angelika Neuwirth, Andreas Pflitsch, and Barbara Winckler, eds. London: Saqi, 2010, 397–409.

Sachs, Susan. "A Nation Challenged: The Videotape; Bin Laden Images Mesmerize Muslims." *New York Times,* October 9, 2001, B6.

Said, Edward W. *Orientalism.* New York: Vintage, 1978.

Ṣāliḥ, al-Ṭayyib [Tayeb Salih]. *Mawsim al-Hijra ilā al-Shamāl* [1966]. Dār al-ʿAwda, 1969.

———. *Season of Migration to the North.* Denys Johnson-Davies, trans. Portsmouth, NH: Heinemann, 1969.

Samīr, Iqbāl. "Ramziyyat Suqūṭ Gharnāṭa: Fī Thulāthiyyat Raḍwa ʿĀshūr *Gharnāṭa* wa-*Maryama* wa-*l-Raḥīl.*" *Fuṣūl* 66 (2005): 163–79.

Sánchez, Gabriela. "La emigración provoca que la población española descienda por primera vez desde 1971." *El Diario,* June 25, 2013. http://www.eldiario.es/sociedad/emigracion-extranjera-espanola-poblacion-descienda_0_146985530.html.

Sanmartín, Olga R. "El flujo de emigración de la población de nacionalidad española aumenta un 15,5%." *El Mundo,* December 10, 2014. http://www.elmundo.es/espana/2014/12/10/54882391ca47414a388b4579.html.

Santoyo, Julio-César. "Sobre la historia de la traducción en España: algunos errores recientes." *Hermeneus* 6 (2004): 169–82.

Sardar, Ziauddin. "Return to Al-Andalus." *Critical Muslim* 6 (April–June 2013): 3–23.

Sarlo, Beatriz. *Jorge Luis Borges: A Writer on the Edge.* New York and London: Verso, 1993.

Schaebler, Birgit, and Leif Stenberg, eds. *Globalization and the Muslim World: Culture, Religion, and Modernity.* Syracuse: Syracuse University Press, 2004.

Scheffler, Samuel. *Equality and Tradition: Questions of Value in Moral and Political Theory.* Oxford: Oxford University Press, 2010.

Schor, Naomi, and Elizabeth Weed, eds. *The Essential Difference.* Bloomington: Indiana University Press, 1994.

Schulz, Barbara. "Collective Memory in Miloudi Chaghmoum's 'La quema de los barcos.'" *International Journal of the Humanities* 6:8 (November 2008): 19–26.

Scott, David. *Conscripts of Modernity: The Tragedy of Colonial Enlightenment.* Durham, NC: Duke University Press, 2004.

Segura González, Wenceslao, ed. "*Inicio de la invasión árabe de España: fuentes documentales.*" *Al Qantir: Monografías y Documentos sobre la Historia de Tarifa* 10 (2010): 1–135.

Seymour-Jorn, Caroline. *Cultural Criticism in Egyptian Women's Writing.* Syracuse, NY: Syracuse University Press, 2011.

Shaghmūm, al-Mīlūdī [Miloudi Chaghmoum]. *Nisāʾ Āl al-Randī* [Rabat?]: Dar al-Manahil, 2000.

Shammarī, Hazzāʾ ibn ʿĪd. *Wallāda bint al-Mustakfī bayna al-ḥaqīqa wa-l-usṭūra.* Riyadh: Dār Ajā lil-Nashr wa-l-Tawzīʿ, 1997.

Shannon, Jonathan. *Performing al-Andalus: Music and Nostalgia across the Mediterranean*. Bloomington: Indiana University Press, 2015.

Shohat, Ella. "Notes on the 'Post-Colonial.'" *Social Text* 31–32 (1992): 99–113.

Shoup, John. "As It Was, and as It Should Be Now: Al Andalus in Contemporary Arab Television Dramas." *Transnational Broadcasting Studies* 15 (January–June 2006).

Shubert, Atika. "Muslims in Spain Campaign to Worship alongside Christians." CNN, July 9, 2010.

Silverstein, Paul, and David Crawford. "Amazigh Activism and the Moroccan State." *Middle East Report* 34:233 (Winter 2004). http://www.merip.org/mer/mer233/amazigh-activism-moroccan-state.

Sirāj, Ḥusayn ʿAbd Allāh. *Gharām Wallāda* [1952]. Jedda: Tihāma, 1982.

Snir, Reuven. "'Al-Andalus Arising from Damascus': al-Andalus in Modern Arabic Poetry." *Charting Memory: Recalling Medieval Spain*. Stacy N. Beckwith, ed. New York: Garland, 2000, 263–93.

Soler, Antonio. *Boabdil: un hombre contra el destino*. Barcelona: Espasa, 2012.

Somers, Margaret R. *Narrativity, Narrative Identity, and Social Action: Rethinking English Working-Class Formation*. Ann Arbor: University of Michigan Press, 1992.

Somers, Margaret R., and Gloria D. Gibson. "Reclaiming the Epistemological Other: Narrative and the Social Constitution of Identity." Comparative Study of Social Transformations Working Paper 94 (June 1993). http://hdl.handle.net.access.library.miami.edu/2027.42/51265.

Soria Mesa, Enrique. *Los últimos moriscos: pervivencias de la población de origen islámico en el Reino de Granada, siglos XVII–XVIII*. Valencia: Biblioteca de Estudios Moriscos, Universidades de Valencia, Zaragoza y Granada, 2014.

Spivak, Gayatri Chakravorty. "Can the Subaltern Speak?" *Marxism and the Interpretation of Culture*. Cary Nelson and Lawrence Grossberg, eds. Urbana: University of Illinois Press, 1988, 271–313.

———. "Subaltern Studies: Deconstructing Historiography." *The Spivak Reader: Selected Works of Gayatri Chakravorty Spivak*. Donna Landry and Gerald MacLean, eds. New York: Routledge, 1996, 203–35.

———. "Subaltern Talk: Interview with the Editors." *The Spivak Reader: Selected Works of Gayatri Chakravorty Spivak*. Donna Landry and Gerald MacLean, eds. New York: Routledge, 1996, 287–308.

Stallaert, Christiane. *Etnogénesis y etnicidad en España: una aproximación histórico-antropológica al casticismo*. Barcelona: Proyecto A, 1998.

Stavans, Ilan, ed. *The Schocken Book of Modern Sephardic Literature*. New York: Knopf Doubleday, 2010.

Stearns, Justin. "Representing and Remembering al-Andalus: Some Historical Considerations Regarding the End of Time and the Making of Nostalgia." *Medieval Encounters* 15:2–4 (2009): 355–74.

Stern, Steve J. "Paradigms of Conquest: History, Historiography, and Politics." *Journal of Latin American Studies* 24 (1992): 1–34.

Stewart, John. "Borges on Language and Translation." *Philosophy and Literature* 19:2 (1995): 320–29.

Subirats, Eduardo, ed. *Américo Castro y la revisión de la memoria: el Islam en España*. Madrid: Ediciones Libertarias, 2003.

Summerhill, Stephen J., and John Alexander Williams. *Sinking Columbus: Contested History, Cultural Politics, and Mythmaking during the Quincentenary*. Gainesville: University Press of Florida, 2000.

Suyoufie, Fadia. "The Appropriation of Tradition in Selected Works of Contemporary Arab Women Writers." *Journal of Arabic Literature* 39:2 (2008): 216–49.

Taboada, Hernán G. H. "'Reconquista' and the 'Three Religion Spain' in Latin American Thought." *Medievalisms in the Postcolonial World*. Kathleen Davis and Nadi Altschul, eds. Baltimore, MD: Johns Hopkins University Press, 2009, 123–40.

al-Ṭāriq. Writ. Yusrī al-Jundī. Dir. Aḥmad Ṣaqr. Ramadan 2004. Qiṭā' al-Intāj, Ittiḥād al-Idhā'a wa-l-Tilīfizyūn. Television.

Taussig, Michael. *Shamanism, Colonialism, and the Wild Man*. Chicago: University of Chicago Press, 1986.

Taylor, Richard C. "Ibn Rushd/Averroes and 'Islamic' Rationalism." *Medieval Encounters* 15:2–4 (2009): 225–35.

Taymūr, Maḥmūd. *Ṭāriq al-Andalus* [c. 1940]. [Cairo]: Maktabat al-Ādāb, 1973.

Thomas de Antonio, Clara María. "Granada en la literatura árabe contemporánea." *Revista del Instituto Egipcio de Estudios Islámicos* 28 (1996): 139–90.

———. "La inquisición y los moriscos en la novela *Granada*, de Radwà Asūr." *El saber en al-Andalus*, Vol. 3. Fátima Roldán Castro and Isabel Hervás Jávega, eds. Seville: Universidad de Sevilla, 2001, 205–33.

Tofiño-Quesada, Ignacio. "Spanish Orientalism: Uses of the Past in Spain's Colonization in Africa." *Comparative Studies of South Asia, Africa and the Middle East* 23:1–2 (2003): 141–48.

Tønder, Lars. *Tolerance: A Sensorial Orientation to Politics*. Oxford: Oxford University Press, 2013.

Tornielli, Pablo. "Algunos motivos árabes e islámicos en la obra de Borges." *Borges Studies Online*, 22:10 (October 2001): 1–5. http://borges.uiowa.edu/bsol/.

de Toro, Alfonso. *Épistémologies, le Maghreb: hybridité, transculturalité, transmédialité, transtextualité, corps, globalisation, diasporisation*. Paris: L'Harmattan, 2009.

Torremocha Silva, Antonio. *Tariq y Musa, conquistadores de al-Andalus*. Granada: Almed, 2011.

Torres-Pou, Joan. "La 'novela de los orígenes' como subtexto en *La gloria de don Ramiro* y *'Zogoibi' El dolor de la tierra* de Enrique Larreta." *Confluencia* 16:2 (2001): 92–98.

Toure, Thierno Dia. "Trois moments postmodernes dans le roman maghrébin francophone: l'exemple de La Prise de Gibraltar de Rachid Boudjedra." *Postmodernisme dans le roman africain*. Adama Coulibaly, Philip Amangoua Atcha, and Roger Tro Deho, eds. Paris: Harmattan, 2012, 13–25.

Townson, Duncan. *La España musulmana*. Torrejón de Ardoz (Madrid): Akal, 1990.

Tremlett, Giles. "Two Arrested after Fight in Cordoba's Former Mosque." *Guardian* (London), January 4, 2010.

'Uthmān, I'tidāl [Etidal Osman]. "al-Khiṭāb al-Adabī al-Nisā'ī: bayna Sulṭat al-Wāqi' wa-Sulṭat al-Takhayyul." *Ibdā'* (January 1993): 13–21.

Vega-Durán, Raquel. "Tales of Two Shores: The Re-Establishment of Dialogue across the Strait of Gibraltar." *African Immigrants in Contemporary Spanish Texts: Crossing the Strait.* Debra Faszer-McMahon and Victoria L. Ketz, eds. Burlington, VT: Ashgate, 2015.

Vegas González, Serafín. *La Escuela de Traductores de Toledo en la historia del pensamiento.* Toledo: Ayuntamiento de Toledo, 1998.

Venuti, Lawrence. *Translation Changes Everything: Theory and Practice.* New York: Routledge, 2013.

Veres, Luis. "La novela histórica y el cuestionamiento de la Historia." http://pendientedemigracion.ucm.es/info/especulo/numero36/novhist.html.

Vermeren, Pierre. "Morocco: Europe's Migrant Mexico." *Le Monde Diplomatique*, June 2002. http://mondediplo.com/2002/06/10morocco.

Viana, Mercé. *Las lágrimas de Boabdil: un paseo por Granada.* [Burriana, Castellón]: Dylar, 2010.

Viguera, María J. "Aṣluḥu li 'l-maʿālī: On the Social Status of Andalusī Women." *The Legacy of Muslim Spain.* Salma Khadra Jayyusi and Manuela Marín, eds. Leiden: Brill, 1992, 709–24

Viguera, María Jesús. "Al-Andalus y España: sobre el esencialismo de los Beni Codera." *Al-Andalus/España: historiografías en contraste, siglos XVII–XXI.* Manuela Marín, ed. Madrid: Casa de Velázquez, 2009, 67–81.

Villena, Leonardo. *El último suspiro del rey Boabdil.* Granada: Dulcinea, 2007.

Viscidi, Lisa. "Latino Muslims a Growing Presence in America." *Washington Report on Middle East Affairs* (June 2003): 56, 58. http://www.wrmea.org/2003-june/latino-muslims-a-growing-presence-in-america.html.

Waisman, Sergio. *Borges and Translation: The Irreverence of the Periphery.* Lewisburg, PA: Bucknell University Press, 2005.

Wakin, Daniel J. "Ranks of Latinos Turning to Islam Are Increasing; Many in City Were Catholics Seeking Old Muslim Roots." *New York Times*, January 2, 2002. http://www.nytimes.com/2002/01/02/nyregion/ranks-latinos-turning-islam-are-increasing-many-city-were-catholics-seeking-old.html.

Walker, Dennis. "Egypt's Arabism: Mustafa Kamil's 1893 Play (Fatḥ al-Andalus) on the Muslim Conquest of Spain." *Islamic Studies* 33:1 (Spring 1994): 49–76.

Walzer, Michael. *On Toleration.* New Haven, CT: Yale University Press, 1997.

Wertsch, James. *Voices of Collective Remembering.* Cambridge: Cambridge University Press, 2002.

Wey Gómez, Nicolás. *The Tropics of Empire: Why Columbus Sailed South to the Indies.* Cambridge, MA: MIT Press, 2008.

White, Hayden. *The Content of the Form: Narrative Discourse and Historical Representation.* Baltimore, MD: Johns Hopkins University Press, 1987.

———. *Figural Realism: Studies in the Mimesis Effect.* Baltimore, MD: Johns Hopkins University Press, 1999.

———. *Metahistory: The Historical Imagination in Nineteenth-Century Europe.* Baltimore, MD: Johns Hopkins University Press, 1973.

Williams, Bernard. "Toleration: An Impossible Virtue?" *Toleration: An Elusive Virtue.* David Heyd, ed. Princeton, NJ: Princeton University Press, 1996, 18–27.

Yiacoup, Sizen. *Frontier Memory: Cultural Conflict and Exchange in the* Romancero fronterizo. London: Modern Humanities Research Association, 2013.

Yūnus, ʿAbd al-Raḥmān Muḥammad. *Wallada bint al-Mustakfi fi Fās*. Beirut: Dār al-Kunūz al-Adabīya, 1997.

Zaydān, Jirjī [Jurji Zaidan]. *The Conquest of Andalusia*. Roger Allen, trans. Bethesda, MD: Zaidan Foundation, 2011.

———. *Fatḥ al-Andalus, aw, Ṭāriq ibn Ziyād*. [Cairo]: Dār al-Hilāl, 1965.

Žižek, Slavoj. "Tolerance as an Ideological Category." *Critical Inquiry* 34:4 (Summer 2008): 660–82.

Zohry, Ayman. "Migration without Borders: North Africa as a Reserve of Cheap Labour for Europe." UNESCO. http://unesdoc.unesco.org/images/0013/001391/139152e.pdf.

Index

Note: Page numbers with "n" indicate endnote.